VISIONS FOR AN
AFRICAN VALLEY

FUTURE RURAL AFRICA

Series Editors
Michael Bollig and Detlef Müller-Mahn

In recent years, there has been a social-ecological transformation in land use in Africa, brought about by climate change and the globalisation of natural resource management and rural landscapes, such that rural Africa has become a laboratory of global future making. This new series offers a rich and valuable perspective on the processes and practices that produce and critically reflect upon visions of the future on the continent. Volumes within the series will address social-ecological, cultural and economic development in sub-Saharan Africa, and their relation to climate change, sustainability and migration. Showcasing cutting-edge research into societal change and the reverberations of global dynamics playing out in sub-Saharan Africa, the series will provide an essential resource for an interdisciplinary scholarly audience in areas such as geography, anthropology, history, political science, natural science and African studies as well as political planners, governmental and non-governmental organisations.

Published in association with the University of Bonn and Cologne's Collaborative Research Centre 'Future Rural Africa', funded by the German Research Council (DFG), the series will be mainly monographs, but we also welcome occasional edited volumes that enable a continent-wide, multidisciplinary approach – see https://boydellandbrewer.com/future-rural-africa.

Please contact the Series Editors with an outline or download the proposal form at www.jamescurrey.com.

Prof. Dr. Michael Bollig, University of Cologne:
michael.bollig@uni-koeln.de

Prof. Dr. Detlef Müller-Mahn, University of Bonn:
mueller-mahn@uni-bonn.de

Previously published titles in the series are listed at the back of this volume.

Visions for an African Valley

Histories of Development in Kilombero,
Tanzania since 1877

Jonathan M. Jackson

© Jonathan M. Jackson 2025

All Rights Reserved. Except as permitted under current legislation no part of this work may be photocopied, stored in a retrieval system, published, performed in public, adapted, broadcast, transmitted, recorded or reproduced in any form or by any means, without the prior permission of the copyright owner

The right of Jonathan M. Jackson to be identified as the author of this work has been asserted in accordance with sections 77 and 78 of the Copyright, Designs and Patents Act 1988

First published 2025
James Currey

ISBN 978 1 84701 394 1

James Currey is an imprint of Boydell & Brewer Ltd
PO Box 9, Woodbridge, Suffolk IP12 3DF, UK
and of Boydell & Brewer Inc.
668 Mt. Hope Avenue, Rochester, NY 14620-2731 (US)
website: www.boydellandbrewer.com
A CIP catalogue record for this book is available from the British Library

The publisher has no responsibility for the continued existence or accuracy of URLs for external or third-party internet websites referred to in this book, and does not guarantee that any content on such websites is, or will remain, accurate or appropriate

Select material in Chapter 4 was first published in: Jackson, Jonathan M. 'Coercion and Dissent: Sleeping Sickness "Concentrations" and the Politics of Colonial Authority', *The Journal of African History* 63:1 (2022), 37–54.

Select material in Chapter 7 was first published in: Jackson, Jonathan M. '"Off to Sugar Valley": the Kilombero Settlement Scheme and "Nyerere's People", 1959–69', *Journal of Eastern African Studies* 15:3 (2021), 505–26.

Quotation on page 87 from *Going Solo* by Roald Dahl, published by Jonathan Cape Ltd & Penguin Books Ltd, © 1986, The Roald Dahl Story Company Limited; reproduced by permission of David Higham Associates.

for Ernest

CONTENTS

List of Illustrations   viii
Acknowledgements   ix
List of Abbreviations   xi
Maps   xiii
Timeline of Key Events   xvi

    Introduction: Past Futures and Histories of Development   1

1. Colonialism Comes to Kilombero: Skirting the Banks, 1877–1914   27
2. Visions under Mandate: Divergent Views, 1914–32   49
3. Between Rhetoric and Reality: The Strength of an Idea, 1931–45   78
4. Coercion and Dissent: Resettlement through Sleeping Sickness 'Concentrations', 1939–45   103
5. 'New Colonialism' Comes to Kilombero: Development and the State, 1939–61   125
6. New Nation, New Internationalism: *Maendeleo wa Jamhuri*, 1959–76   154
7. 'Off to Sugar Valley': The Kilombero Settlement Scheme, 1959–69   183

    Conclusion: Past Futures to the Present   210

Bibliography   225
Index   245

ILLUSTRATIONS

Maps

1: Provinces and Districts of Tanganyika, 1936–64.   xiii
2: Regions and Districts of Tanzania, 1970s.   xiv
3: The Kilombero Valley.   xv
4: Detail from 'Physiographical Map of Tanganyika Territory, 1932'.   xv

Plates

1: View from hills behind Kiberege to Kilombero River, May 1936.   59
2: Kiberege Bridge over Kiberege River in flood, 1932.   91
3: Car crossing on Kilombero Ferry, July 1933.   93
4: Flooded plains near Sakamaganga, May 1936.   102
5: Said Ramadhani Chamwenyewe and Athumani Ali Milulu converse at Sonjo, Kilombero Settlement Scheme, 1968.   203
6: 'Der Galeriewald, Flußszenerie am Ulanga' (trans. 'The Gallery Forest, River Scenery on the Ulanga') by Wilhelm Kuhnert, c. 1905.   212
7: 'Giraffen in bloeiende Ulanga-vlakte' (trans. 'Giraffes on the Ulanga Plain in bloom') by Wilhelm Kuhnert, c. 1905.   213
8: 'Magufuli Bridge' adjacent to the old Kilombero ferry site at Kivukoni, 2019.   223

ACKNOWLEDGEMENTS

This book could not have been written without research permission granted by the Commission for Science and Technology (COSTECH) in Tanzania, and funding awarded by the Deutsche Forschungsgemeinschaft (DFG) as part of the Collaborative Research Centre (CRC) 'Future Rural Africa' (Project ID: TRR-228; Grant number: 328966760). I wish to acknowledge the principal investigators and coordinating office of the CRC at the Universities of Cologne and Bonn, who together sustained the extended programme which bore this research. Special thanks to Ulrike Lindner, Carolin Neubert, Carolin Maevis, Matian van Soest, and Thomas Widlok.

This book began life as a research project at the Faculty of Arts and Humanities of the University of Cologne, and its publication would not be possible without the roles played by Michael Bollig and Detlef Müller-Mahn as editors of the Future Rural Africa series. Thank you also to commissioning editors Jaqueline Mitchell and Megan Milan at James Currey for Boydell & Brewer, and to Henry Lafferty. Further thanks to Ida Hadjivayanis for finessing the Kiswahili translation of the TANU songs; to Maria Lassak and Paula Nyarko for translations from German; and to master map-maker, Monika Feinen.

This moment marks a milestone on a road which itself began at SOAS, University of London, where I found a true home in the pursuit of learning. Thanks to those there who first inspired, challenged, and encouraged: Jim Brennan, Lindiwe Dovey, Margaret Kumbuka, Tom McCaskie, John Parker, Richard Reid, and Farouk Topan. That journey continued to Oxford, and there I am grateful to have found further inspiration and encouragement from David Anderson, Julie Archambault, William Beinart, Miles Larmer, Jonny Steinberg, and Jarad Zimbler.

Over the nineteen years since I first visited East Africa, I have been privileged to cross paths with many people who, in many ways, are the reasons I developed such an interest and love for the region. They are too legion to list, and not all will know the impressions they made. Their generosity of time and experience has shaped much of what I know and understand; both are deficient, but that is mine to own.

Acknowledgements

Special mention is reserved for several people who enriched my understanding of Kilombero's history, and generously shared their contacts, insights, materials, resources, stories, and time. There could never have been a book without them. Thank you to Simran Bindra, Paul Bolstad, Father Chahali, Geoff and Vicky Fox, Maulidi Kawala, Simon Kinyaga, Emmanuel Kiputa, Juma Juma Kiswanya, Lorne Larson, Thomas Likalagala, Father Mkude Luwanda, Mama Luwanda, Christoph Mahundi, Andrew Marshall, Sharon Moore, David Pletts, Hamisi Said Salum, Theo Theodory, and Bonnie Nicodamas Vyakuziwa.

I am forever indebted to Francis Ching'ota, whose guidance and friendship are woven into the bindings of this book. Thank you for sharing your valley with me, and for all we discovered together.

I would also like to acknowledge others who have – through their solidarity, kindnesses, and companionship – lessened the sense of precarity and frustration that periodically characterises contemporary academia, or at least my experience of it. Thanks to Abigail Branford, Lia Brazil, Peter Brooke, Simukai Chigudu, Jeremiah Garsha, Maia Green, Caro Hulke, Emma Hunter, Myfanwy Jones, Linus Kalvelage, Léa Lacan, Riley Linebaugh, Dr S. Mauskewitz, Jason Mosley, Séamus Nevin, Katy Phipps, Richard Reid (again), George Roberts, Biruk Terrefe, and Mads Yding.

And above all, to Bella, who has looked forward to seeing this on the shelf as much as I have. No one else has lived the years to this point – through fog, storm, and sun – more than you.

JMJ
Oxford

ABBREVIATIONS

BArch	*German Federal Archives – Bundesarchiv*
BnF	*Bibliothèque nationale de France* [National Library of France]
CDC	Colonial / Commonwealth Development Corporation
CS	Chief Secretary
DC	District Commissioner
DEG	*Deutsche Investitions- und Entwicklungsgesellschaft* [German Investment (and Development) Corporation]
DO	District Officer
DOA	*Deutsch-Ostafrika* [German East Africa]
DofA	Director of Agriculture
DOAG	*Deutsch-Ostafrikanische Gesellschaft* [German East Africa Company]
DM	*Deutsche Mark*
EAHC	East African High Commission
EARH	East African Railways and Harbours
FAO	Food and Agriculture Organisation [of the United Nations]
FRG	Federal Republic of Germany
GDR	German Democratic Republic
GfdK	*Gesellschaft für deutsche Kolonisation* [Society for German Colonisation]
GMTR	General Manager, Tanganyika Railways
HMSO	His / Her Majesty's Stationery Office
IBRD	International Bank for Reconstruction and Development
IDA	International Development Association
IFC	International Finance Corporation
ILACO	International Land Development Consultants, Ltd.
INT	Interview
KATRIN	Kilombero Agricultural Training and Research Institute
KOTACO	Korea and Tanzania Corporation
KPL	Kilombero Plantations, Ltd.

KSC	Kilombero Sugar Company
KSS	Kilombero Settlement Scheme
n.d.	No date
n.p.	No page number
NCM	Nigeria Consolidated Mines
OBL	The University of Oxford, Bodleian Library
OFC	Overseas Food Corporation
PC	Provincial Commissioner
PCEP	Provincial Commissioner, Eastern Province
PCSP	Provincial Commissioner, Southern Province
RBS	Rufiji Basin Survey
RGS	Royal Geographical Society
s.n.	[*sine nomino*] No publisher
SPS	Sudan Plantations Syndicate
STEP	Southern Tanzania Elephant Program
STIFL	Swiss Tropical Institute Field Laboratory
TAC	Tanganyika Agricultural Corporation
TAZARA	Tanzania-Zambia Railway Authority
TNA	Tanzania National Archives
TNAUK	The National Archives of the UK
TANU	Tanganyika / Tanzania African National Union
UN	The United Nations
UNESCO	The United Nations Educational, Scientific and Cultural Organisation
USAID	United States Agency for International Development
VKCM	Vereenigde Klattensche Cultuur Maatschappij

MAPS

Map 1 Provinces and Districts of Tanganyika, 1936–64.

Map 2 Regions and Districts of Tanzania, 1970s.

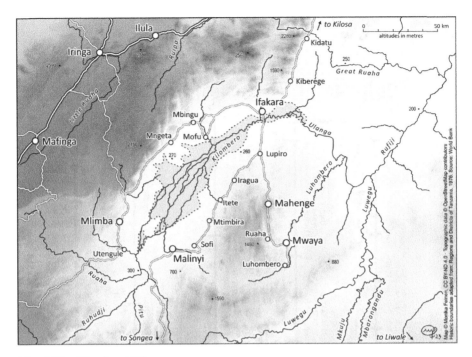

Map 3 The Kilombero Valley.

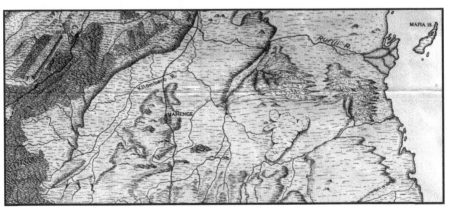

Map 4 Detail from 'Physiographical Map of Tanganyika Territory, 1932'. Source: Special Collections of the University of Cape Town Libraries.

Timeline of Key Events

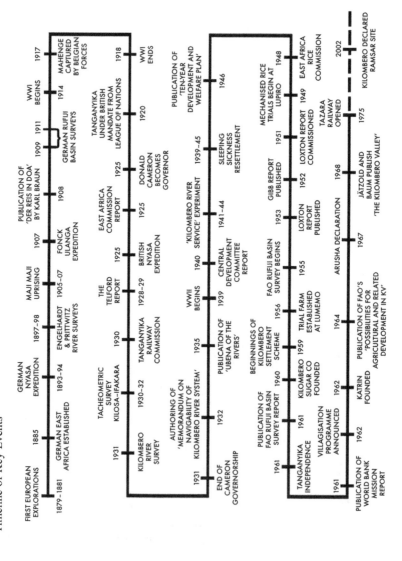

Introduction: Past Futures and Histories of Development

This book is full of ideas. It is a record of the ideas of those who believed this one valley in Tanzania held immense potential. What this potential was and how it might be realised varied across time and space. So, too, did the drivers of these ideas vary according to differing motives and the prevailing thinking of the day; thinking driven almost entirely by Western notions of development, progress, and modernity. Whatever the ideas themselves, they were all propelled by visions of the future and concerned with how these 'futures' might be made. This book applies this concept of 'future making' to development planning, and considers it among its principal and most potent forms in its designs for alternative futures within the many contexts such plans are made.

On one level, this book offers a micro-history of development visions for the Kilombero Valley in today's Morogoro Region, approximately 400 kilometres to the south-west of the coastal commercial capital, Dar es Salaam. In this way, it is region-specific. On another level, it is a survey of development ideas, practices, and their encountered 'problems' from the global to reveal their manifestations in the local. In *this* way, Kilombero became a vessel for blueprint development visions as much as it was a direct target for distilled designs and tailored schemes. The resulting chronicle therefore reveals much about the general, the specific, and the relationship between them. It is this interplay which generic histories of development often fail to capture.

The focus on one locale over more than a century of development visions enables a depth and richness through the collation and consolidation of archival and documentary material that only a study of this kind can achieve. Together with its use of oral histories, whose telling is both implicit and explicit, the book also promotes an emerging methodological approach in such a way as to decentre Kilombero and to speak to the broader historiography and promote novel approaches to development histories. By taking the notion of development planning as 'future making' and visions of development as 'imagined futures', this book considers the multiple futures envisaged for this region. It explores the idea of 'futures' from the past in relation to histories of development and the development episteme. Through these 'past futures' we can trace the potential and promise, the plans and possibilities projected onto Kilombero.

The histories presented are thus enshrouded by descriptions of past processes of 'future making' alongside analyses of the evolution and legacies of development plans and possibilities for Kilombero. Crucially, their relationships to national and international contexts are then illuminated. This is achieved through an examination of how these plans were conceived, an evaluation of their successes, and analyses of their shortcomings against changing political and economic landscapes. Each chapter that follows, therefore, addresses past visions of Kilombero's future. These forecasts and speculations – chiefly represented through forms of development planning – are prominent examples of 'future-making' processes. This is the central thread of the book, cutting a line through the long twentieth century and the multitude of ways that 'development' – through its many names and forms – has been taken, understood, and applied; as well as received, subverted, challenged, repurposed, or rejected.[1]

Since the early colonial period, outsiders consistently praised the apparent fertility of Kilombero, and envisaged scheme after scheme that not only sought to realise the verdant river valley's natural resources, but to shape its communities and effect radical rural transformations. Some suspected the valley's reputation of luxuriant fertility was deceptive, but Kilombero proved persuasive. Many attempts to develop the land from the late-nineteenth century to the present day often struggled to realise this alleged potential; but what, then, was the effect of these unsatisfied aspirations on the land and communities themselves, if any?

In the mind of the state and the developer, Kilombero was persistently viewed as 'undeveloped' and therefore fertile ground from which a myriad of development trajectories could spring. Through the writing of plans, recommendations, and reports that suggested different ways to shape the region, a pattern of 'anticipation' emerges from cycles of prediction and expectation. As Vincanne Adams, Michelle Murphy, and Adele Clarke have described: 'Anticipation is the palpable effect of the speculative future on the past.'[2] Their conceptualisation of 'anticipatory regimes [which] offer a future that may or may not arrive' can be readily applied to the phenomenon of development

---

[1] The placing of 'development' in quotation marks emphasises what is already presented as a problematic term. I do not follow James Ferguson, for example, who in *The Anti-Politics Machine*, consistently placed 'development' in quotation marks throughout the book to constantly remind the reader of his problematization of the concept. I do use quotation marks around 'development' periodically, however, when further emphasis is intended.

[2] Vincanne Adams, Michelle Murphy, and Adele E. Clarke, 'Anticipation: Technoscience, life, affect, temporality', *Subjectivity* 28 (2009), 247.

planning as such a regime; especially in light of their claim that, 'in their specificity [anticipatory regimes] can conjure many versions of the future'.[3]

One central question of this book is this: if visions of the future can be discerned from the present, how might they be viewed in the past? These 'past futures' may be evaluated for their potential in terms of possibility, probability, and preferability; but then, of course, whose future is preferenced? This kind of evaluation applies equally to moments of 'future making' in the present as for the past, except the key point is that outcomes of 'past futures' are largely known with the passage of time. This is most apparent when a particular vision is expected to materialise within a set period of time. For Tanzania, as elsewhere, this is best expressed within plans published in any one of the 'X-Year Plans' for state economic and social development that emerged during the colonial era and continue to be produced.[4] Such plans constitute a form of publicity for governments, and which is arguably largely rhetorical. Development plans serve to publicise government intent to other governments, to observing organisations such as the United Nations who ostensibly hold states to account, or to the people themselves. As a form of 'future making' this – to borrow from the art critic John Berger – is a form of publicity for which 'the present is by definition insufficient' and its rhetoric 'speaks in the future tense and yet the achievement of this future is endlessly deferred'.[5]

This point is particularly relevant to the 'past futures' of Kilombero, and a key tenet to understanding this approach is the linking of 'a chronological past, a lived present that was once an anticipated future, and expectations of the future – such that any given present is at the same time a "former future"'.[6] From this leads Ged Martin's assertion that 'the inconvenient problem that the future is unknowable does not excuse historians from exploring the influence of perceived or imagined past futures upon the shaping of the decisions that constitute the building blocks of history'.[7]

In this exploration of imagined past futures for Kilombero, then, visions of this valley cast by outsiders begin with those observations made by the

---

[3] Ibid., 249.

[4] Plans were mostly conceived as 1-, 5-, or 10-Year Plans. The most recent at the time of writing is Tanzania's 'National Five-Year Development Plan, 2021/22–2025/26: Realising Competitiveness and Industrialisation for Human Development', published June 2021. This was the first under President Samia Suluhu Hassan, and continued efforts to achieve goals set out from 2011 in the long-term perspective plan, 'National Development Vision 2025'.

[5] John Berger, *Ways of Seeing* (London, 1972), 144–6.

[6] Keith Tribe, 'Introduction', in Reinhart Koselleck, *Futures Past: On the Semantics of Historical Time*, trans. Keith Tribe (New York, 2004), x–xi.

[7] Ged Martin, *Past Futures: The Impossible Necessity of History* (Toronto, 2004), 5.

earliest European travellers and colonists from the late-nineteenth century, who thought the region possessed enormous agricultural potential. There were contrasting visions, too. This was also a pestilent place, wild and desolate; and yet lured by the perceived fertility, the scores of perennial streams, and apparent abundance of available land, these first attempts to map and survey the region would have far-reaching influence on the persistent idea that Kilombero held untapped potential. Successive visions would not conflict so much with each other – as despite some divergences they were largely similar – but they repeatedly came into conflict with the environmental challenges posed by an inaccessible, distant region whose capricious annual inundations, seasonal volatility, and variegated soil qualities consistently dashed hopes and broke dreams.

And yet this valley region was returned to again and again by developers. Kilombero proved a difficult place to develop, which to some extent only intensified the desire to do so. By 1955, this was 'the only large area in Tanganyika with good rainfall probability and fair to good soils, which remains largely unexploited'.[8] But was this notion – that while the region remained undeveloped, it also remained developable – a fallacy?

This book traces the emergence of this kernel of conviction in Kilombero's development potential as an idea, charting its trajectory through succeeding development initiatives and their impact, and shows how these histories have shaped the region, even though their implications are not always obvious to the valley visitor today.[9] This is a key point. The resulting multi-layered history is marked by different approaches to the reorganisation of rural life in Tanzania, providing an insight not only into a largely ignored aspect of African and colonial history, but also a methodologically rich and fresh approach to development history.

Running as strata through the book are four major themes that are no strangers to development histories: AGRICULTURAL INTENSIFICATION, ECOLOGY CONTROL, INFRASTRUCTURE, AND (RE)SETTLEMENT. Yet their co-constitutive influences and unique configuration in Kilombero render this history distinct. These central themes of this valley region's 'past futures' continue to shape its present and recent past, while the 'future' remains contested and contingent. By chronicling the results and consequences of human desires to shape and control the natural environment, then, this book tells a tale that is both fundamentally distinct and remarkably familiar.

---

[8] Great Britain. *East Africa Royal Commission 1953–1955 Report* (London, 1956), 6.
[9] For an exemplary examination of development as an idea in Africa, see Corrie Decker and Elisabeth McMahon, *The Idea of Development in Africa* (Cambridge, 2020).

This is a study that shines a light on Kilombero, but ultimately offers a new lens through which to view development and its discourses more widely. The historical development processes examined in this book reveal a rich nexus of economic, political, and social dynamics that intersect on local, regional, national, transnational, and international levels. In this way, it is argued that Kilombero is shown to be a prism that refracts broader phenomena across more than a century. Three further interconnected arguments are made. First, that notional beliefs in Kilombero as an area of high development possibility mythologised the region. The strength of the idea that Kilombero held unbounded agricultural potential did not always obscure the obstacles to development, but the persistence of the idea belied the likelihood of overcoming them. Second, that from the early colonial era, Kilombero has been – and continues to be – a site of ecological change and contestation. The specificities of this political ecology are explored through trajectories of evolution and transformation. Lastly, from this examination of past development visions and an analysis of their motives, features, and outcomes, it is argued that combinations of myopia, hubris, and ignorance characterised much of the development experience. Lessons were seldom learned, and a lack of historical awareness continues to reveal itself in the present.

British explorers Joseph Thomson and William Beardall were among the earliest to write of the region as 'one of the most fertile spots in Africa' and a 'land of plenty', circa 1880.[10] But it was the era of German East Africa, or *Deutsch-Ostafrika*, from 1885 that sewed notions of vast agricultural potential and future possibilities into the seams of imperial minds. Kilombero was known to German colonists as 'Ulanga' and the terms are synonymous in referring to the valley, its vast floodplain, and its eponymous, central river.[11] Following an expedition in 1908, Captain Heinrich Fonck declared that, 'One must see with one's eyes the astounding fertility and inexhaustible potential of this region, which has been favoured by its abundant water supply, in order to be able to say without exaggeration, "the Ulanga will become our Nile, if we wish it"'.[12] German East Africa's first Governor, Gustav von Götzen, believed

---

[10] Joseph Thomson, *To the Central African Lakes and Back: The Narrative of the Royal Geographical Society's East Central African Expedition, 1878–80, Vol. I* (London, 1881), 181; William Beardall, 'Exploration of the Rufiji River under the orders of the Sultan of Zanzibar', *Proceedings of the Royal Geographical Society and the Monthly Record* 3:11 (1881), 653.

[11] Use of 'Ulanga' is retained in direct quotes, but 'Kilombero' is used and reverted to consistently in narrative.

[12] Tanzania National Archives (TNA), Dar es Salaam, G7/100, Schiffbarkeit des Rufiji, Band I, H. Fonck, 'Bericht über die wirtschaftlichen Verhältnisse in der Ulangabene und ihren Nachbargebieten', 15 January 1908.

that rice yields of the 'fertile Ulanga Plain' were 'endlessly expandable' and was confident that the valley could provide rice for the entire colony.[13]

Following the First World War, comparable projections continued into the first decades of British administration under Mandate from the League of Nations. Emphasis remained on potential and promise, rather than its current state of development, with Kilombero 'recognised as agriculturally one of the most promising areas in Tanganyika' in official advisory reports.[14] During preliminary investigations into building a railway through to the south-west, Clement Gillman, Tanganyika Railways' Chief Engineer, declared:

> It is impossible to exaggerate the great and outstanding importance from the point of view of railway revenue, of this vast low-lying tropical plain, extremely well-watered from the slopes of high mountains which shut it in on three sides, with a fairly reliable rainfall, and very easily served by a comparatively cheap line.[15]

If this seems to be an overstatement, it is because it is. An appraisal of the valley in the 1960s considered its 'potential' and 'economic possibilities' to have been 'overrated in the past'.[16] Subsequent perceptions and attempted development initiatives have failed to recognise this history. Moreover, Kilombero has continued to present as a contentious region whose natural ecology and environmental challenges generate a certain set of problems, many of which remain unresolved.

Problems posed by this unpredictable environment are entwined with attempts to 'tame' or merely operate within it. Over the years this has resulted in scenes at times as comic as they are tragic. One incident that speaks to this took place on 1 November 1961. It reveals much, inferring more. From an article titled, 'Fall-out from a Wages Drop', this tale relates to the earliest industrial scheme to be established on a large scale in the valley, the Kilombero Sugar Company. It begins: 'Police yesterday were trying to recover a £3,000 "fall-out" resulting from an £8,000 wage-drop from a plane on Wednesday at Kilombero sugar estate, 200 miles inland from Dar es Salaam.'[17] It continues:

---

[13] Gustav Graf von Götzen, *Deutsch-Ostafrika im Aufstand, 1905–06* (Berlin: Dietrich Reimer, 1909), 104.

[14] The National Archives of the UK (TNAUK), London, CO 691/141/2, Memorandum by Secretary of State, 13 November 1934.

[15] Clement Gillman, *Report on the Preliminary Surveys for a Railway Line to Open Up the South-West of Tanganyika Territory, 1929* (London, 1929), 43.

[16] Ralph Jätzold and Eckhard Baum, *The Kilombero Valley* (Munich, 1968), 119.

[17] 'Fall-out from a Wages Drop', *Birmingham Post*, 3 November 1961.

So far, about £5,000 has been recovered. The money, wages for the estate workers, was flown out from Dar es Salaam when heavy rain made the road impassable. The crew of the chartered aircraft found they could not land and decided to drop the money. Some of the canvas money-bags burst in the air, and others on the ground, scattering notes and coins over the estate's football field and the waiting workers.[18]

It must have been a ridiculous scene to witness; and a farcical sight that tells us a great deal about both the challenges of ecology control and an inadequate infrastructure. Not only was Kilombero cut off at this time by road, but the ground was so sodden that the plane could not land. Then, someone thought it a good idea to throw the money on a low pass from above.

This tale could easily serve as a figurative encapsulation of a part of the development history; one that illustrates its futility, failures, misplaced motives, and false pretences. The illusion that there might be viable solutions to very real problems might well be symbolised by the very moment the first bag burst in mid-air. But there is also a great tragedy here. These were hard-earned wages, owed to local workers who had laboured for their pay, now likely lost or lay to be claimed by someone else. It could also be argued that the money figuratively rained down on Kilombero through development efforts has also failed to fulfil promises, realise underlying visions, and been spent wisely.

'Development' is a contentious thing. It is a mistake to presume its inherent goodness. It may be as destructive and disrupting as it is altruistic and advantageous. There is truth in the 'delusion of development' and continued questioning of whom the modern industry truly serves is equally valid.[19] This is inherent across the three constituent definitions of 'development' given by Decker and McMahon: first, 'the creation of knowledge about Africa's social, economic, political, environmental, intellectual, and physical conditions and how to improve them'; then, 'the specific policies and practices arising from this "knowledge" imposed onto African communities'; and lastly, as 'a discourse of power that "experts" have inflicted on Africans'.[20]

Taking their view, therefore, that 'development entails knowledge production, the power to implement this knowledge, and the impact this knowledge and power have on the experience of individuals caught in the system', it is within this context that Kilombero has stood for over a century among those areas of

---

[18] Ibid.
[19] See Toby Carroll, *Delusions of Development: The World Bank and the Post-Washington Consensus in Southeast Asia* (New York, 2010); and Allen and Barbara Isaacman, *Dams, Displacement and the Delusion of Development: Cahora Bassa and its Legacies in Mozambique, 1965–2007* (Athens, OH, 2013).
[20] Decker and McMahon, *Idea of Development*, 15.

Tanzania which have experienced high intensity development attention.[21] The levels of financial investment envisaged for the valley were consistently among the highest projected through the country, but the sheer scale of this forecasted expenditure was also part of the reason various visions never materialised. Indeed, had all initiatives been implemented as planned, the valley would be a very different place today. In order to better understand this history, this book establishes a chronology, sequence, and analysis of rural development in the Kilombero valley region from the early years of German East Africa, through the period of British administration as Tanganyika under League of Nations Mandate and subsequent United Nations Trusteeship, to an independent Tanganyika, and ultimately to the United Republic of Tanzania of today.[22] Emerging from this examination of development histories are many visions of rural transformation cast onto the landscape, but which did not materialise. There also emerges a multitude of initiatives that were attempted and trialled, but later abandoned. This is achieved through an episodic approach to offer windows into key moments in Kilombero's history, and insights into the obstacles – recurrent or singular – that have impeded development efforts through the decades.

Such an approach enables an in-depth assessment of the relationship between internal dynamics and external interventions. By researching the drivers of development, its primary agents, and the impact of past rural development initiatives, this book contributes to a better understanding of the likelihood of particular outcomes in the present and future. This historical perspective encourages more effective planning and implementation as lessons are learned from past experiences. This is particularly pertinent as rural development initiatives continue to play an important role in Tanzania's economy, in visions for its future, and for the livelihoods of its citizens. By charting the history of these rural development initiatives in the Kilombero valley region over such an extended period, this book deepens an understanding of how and why they came about, how they were shaped and constructed, and what impact they have – or have not – had on the landscape. From this timeline – constructed from archival, documentary, and oral sources – this book examines the aspirations, expectations, and visions embedded within such schemes. These were, of course, predominantly externally imposed, necessitating the reconstruction of the

---

[21] Ibid.

[22] Names used are contemporaneous with the period, i.e. German East Africa, 1885–1918; Former German East Africa, 1918–20; Tanganyika [Territory], 1920–46; Tanganyika, 1946–64; [The United Republic of] Tanzania, 1964–present. Where a period begins before 1964, but continues after, then 'Tanzania' is used for continuity.

'Mind-of-the-State' in its promotion of such interventions.[23] This is reflected in Bill Adams' assertion that, the 'development of Africa has always been driven by outsiders' and that 'rural Africans without formal education lie furthest away from the centre of such power'.[24] Moreover, Adams was convinced that it is important to be honest about the failure of past schemes, in order to imagine what action might be needed to support a sustainable future for floodplain development. This leads to several further questions, such as: How might we examine these past schemes and to what extent may they be said to be failures? What visions, therefore, were held by successive national governments? What role did future planning play in past development? What was intended for the region, and to what extent were these plans realised? What, therefore, were the forces and motivations driving these approaches to development? How did successive themes relate to one another and what were the broader historical, economic, social, and political contexts in which they can each be viewed? By seeking to address these questions and analyse the answers, this book not merely documents but traces both divergences and continuities.

What is 'development'?

The complex history of development in Kilombero involves a large cast of actors including successive states, prominent individuals, commercial companies, non-governmental agencies, and – most importantly – its local inhabitants, who often resisted so-called 'development' programmes imposed without consultation. This last act is central to the truth that outsiders' perceptions of the developmental potential of Kilombero persistently contained misapprehensions and falsehoods, raised expectations, and misplaced confidence. Ralph Jätzold once wrote of 'the great difficulties with which man has to contend in exploiting the area', but it is important to delineate common difficulties as they might relate to an individual resident of the valley, against those faced by those who sought to effect rural transformation from above.[25] Kilombero's difficulties are many, but they are not shared by all.

Any history of development anywhere must reiterate that definitions and understandings of 'development' in theory and praxis travel multifariously through time and space, through conflicting interpretations and applications. This fluidity is key to conceptualising and understanding 'histories of

---

[23] See James Scott, *Seeing Like a State: How Certain Schemes to Improve the Human Condition Have Failed* (New Haven, CT, 1998).

[24] W.M. Adams, *Wasting the Rain: Rivers, People and Planning in Africa* (London, 1992), 35.

[25] Jätzold and Baum, *Kilombero Valley*, 32.

development' because 'development' may allude to processes and practices that are both exclusive and inclusive, exploitative and philanthropic. Building on the definitions of development offered by Decker and McMahon above, what may be presented as 'development' can be equally interpreted by its intended or supposed beneficiaries, or others, as something altogether very different. Indeed, as Michael Cowen and Robert Shenton have reflected: 'Development seems to defy definition, although not for want of definitions on offer.'[26] They argue that part of this defiance is due to the difficulty in reconciling 'the intent to develop' with 'immanent development' and suggest that a better question than, 'What is development?' is 'What is intended by development?'[27] The term, then, has been historically difficult to define, and therefore must be understood to carry multiple meanings, values, and moralities which oscillate throughout history and whose complexities are clarified through broader contexts and specific examples. This book offers such an elucidation and clarification in its presentation of visions for development across time and space, but through the prism of one valley.

James Ferguson began his influential 1994 work, *The Anti-Politics Machine*, by asking the very question: 'What is "development"?' Through his examination on the phenomenon, failures, and effects of international aid agencies, he remarked on the recency (in the early 1990s) of how the centralising concept of 'development' had become 'so natural, so self-evidently necessary', but 'would have made no sense even a century ago'.[28] Development is now equated with notions of 'progress' or 'improvement' in social and economic terms, and it is in this way that through-lines can be drawn between that which made 'sense' then, and that which makes 'sense' now. Notions of development are therefore applied in the absence of the word, or where synonymic or related terms are used. Fred Cooper and Randall Packard note a wide, but not universal, 'set of operating assumptions' that emerged from the 1940s and constitute a 'development orthodoxy' which rests on the belief that 'foreign aid and investment on favourable terms, the transfer of knowledge of production techniques, measures to promote health and education, and economic planning would lead impoverished countries to be able to become "normal" market economies'.[29] This 'orthodoxy' aligns with what Cowen and Shenton called 'doctrines of development', a phrase which became central to the work of

---

[26] Michael Cowen and Robert Shenton, *Doctrines of Development* (London, 1996), 3.

[27] Ibid., viii, 438.

[28] James Ferguson, *The Anti-Politics Machine: "Development," Depoliticization, and Bureaucratic Power in Lesotho* (Minneapolis, 1994), xiii.

[29] Frederick Cooper and Randall Packard, 'Introduction', in F. Cooper and R. Packard (eds), *International Development and the Social Sciences: Essays on the History and Politics of Knowledge* (Berkeley, 1997), 2.

Joseph Hodge in his treatment of colonial science as a particular paradigm of agrarian development; while both resonate with this 1982 contribution towards a definition from the United Nations, who stated that 'rural development has come to be viewed as a means to improve the living conditions of the rural poor by increasing their productive capacity and improving actual income levels, eliminating the sources of exploitation to establish social justice and sensitizing them to be self-reliant' while claiming, furthermore, that 'there cannot be any universal model for rural development'.[30] The statement moves from a definition that could easily pass for colonial, towards clear undertones of the postcolonial era in its reaction against exploitation.

A central tenet of this book, then, is the belief that development is a 'contingent, contextualised, and changing phenomenon' and this frames its examination of the role that such processes have played in shaping histories of development in Kilombero.[31] Perceptions of development are often polarised, and it is worth being reminded of Cooper's point, that: 'Assertions that development is a project of self-evident benefit and critiques of development as the imposition of an unwanted modernity are in fact mirror images of each other.'[32] For colonial governments, the so-called 'benefits' of development were invariably viewed in economic terms, promoted through agriculture and industry, and connected to global markets by improvements in transport networks. During the years (1920–46) in which Tanganyika was formally administered by Great Britain under Mandate from the League of Nations – before its conversion after the Second World War to a United Nations Trusteeship (1946–61) – an expression of 'development' was written into Article 3 of the Mandate, which stated that: 'The Mandatory shall [...] undertake to promote to the utmost the material and moral well-bring and the social progress of its inhabitants.'[33] Development is implied, if not specifically named, and so it remains 'a protean word, subject to conflicting interpretations'.[34]

The history of rural development in eastern Africa is, furthermore, a well-established sub-field with close associations to environmental and conservation

---

[30] Joseph M. Hodge, *Triumph of the Expert: Agrarian Doctrines of Development and the Legacies of British Colonialism* (Athens, OH, 2007); UNESCO, *A Study on Strategies for Tackling the Problems of Rural Development with Particular Reference to the Role of the Education System* (Paris, 1982), i.

[31] Cooper and Packard, 'Introduction', 6.

[32] Frederick Cooper, 'Writing the history of development', *Journal of Modern European History* 8:1 (2010), 6.

[33] League of Nations. 'British Mandate for East Africa.' C. 449 (1) a. M. 345 (a). 1922. VI., 1 October 1922 (Geneva, 1922), 4.

[34] Cooper, *Africa since 1940*, 127.

histories.[35] The connection between the evolution of state policy and the economic development of rural areas emerged as a key theme alongside a greater consciousness of the environment.[36] The idea of development as social improvement and 'rural betterment' for local communities was a major driver of agrarian policies devised for the region in the first half of the twentieth century, growing in importance during the final years of colonialism, and becoming dominant in Tanzania from the late 1960s onwards with the implementation of *Ujamaa* – or, 'familyhood' as a basis for African socialism – and its associated processes of villagisation as an expression of rural socialism under first President, Julius Nyerere.[37] Studies challenging the colonial (and Eurocentric) perception of African rural political economy first emerged in the 1970s, the path-breaking study being Helge Kjekshus' (1977) account of environmental control and the collapse of indigenous socio-ecological systems under the impact of colonialism.[38] These ideas were further developed in subsequent historical works, most notably James Giblin's (1992) regional study of environmental history in Handeni, north-eastern Tanzania; also Christopher Conte's (2004) similarly localised study of land use and land cover in the

---

[35] See, for example, James C. McCann, *People of the Plow: An Agricultural History of Ethiopia, 1800–1990* (Madison, 1995); Juhani Koponen, *People and Production in Late Precolonial Tanzania: History and Structures* (Helsinki, 1995); Gregory Maddox, James Giblin, and Isaria N. Kimambo (eds), *Custodians of the Land: Ecology and Culture in the History of Tanzania* (Dar es Salaam, 1996); Maia Green, *The Development State: Aid, Culture and Civil Society in Tanzania* (Woodbridge, 2014).

[36] M.A. Havinden and D. Meredith, *Colonialism and Development: Britain and its Tropical Colonies, 1850–1960* (London, 1995); Göran Hydén, *No Shortcuts to Progress: African Development Management in Perspective* (Nairobi, 1983); William Beinart, *The Rise of Conservation in Southern Africa: Settlers, Livestock and the Environment, 1770–1950* (Oxford, 2008); James C. McCann, *Green Land, Brown Land, Black Land: An Environmental History of Africa, 1800–1990* (Oxford, 1999).

[37] For insights into 'betterment' through 'scientific agriculture' under colonialism, see William Allan, *The African Husbandman* (Edinburgh, 1965). For the later years of colonialism after 1945, see John Iliffe, *A Modern History of Tanganyika* (Cambridge, 1979), 436–84; D.A. Low and John M. Lonsdale, 'Introduction: Towards the new order 1945–63', in D.A. Low and Alison Smith (eds), *Oxford History of East Africa*, Vol. III (Oxford, 1977), 1–64. Key texts within a vast literature on *ujamaa* and villagisation include Dean McHenry, *Tanzania's Ujamaa Villages: The Implementation of a Rural Development Strategy* (Berkeley, 1994); Scott, *Seeing Like a State*, 223–61; Y. Lawi, 'Tanzania's Operation *Vijiji* and local ecological consciousness: The case of eastern Iraqwland, 1974–1976', *The Journal of African History* 48 (2007), 69–93; Michael Jennings, *Surrogates of the State: NGOs, Development, and Ujamaa in Tanzania* (Bloomfield, 2008); Leander Schneider, *Government of Development* (Bloomington, 2014).

[38] Helge Kjekshus, *Ecology Control and Economic Development in East African History: The Case of Tanganyika, 1850–1950*, 2nd ed. (London, 1997).

Usambara Mountains.[39] Following Kjekshus, an important group of studies emerged that recognised the resilience and adaptability of African rural systems in situations of stress and transformation.[40] Alongside this body of literature that celebrated African resilience was a parallel set of studies that acknowledged the repeated failures of state-led rural development programmes.[41] Works within this subset which hold most relevance to this study are those focusing on large-scale schemes of intensification and resettlement.[42] From the 1960s onwards, all these studies combined archival and documentary research with the collection of oral histories among African rural communities.

A highly important correlation to theories of development is the discourse on concepts of underdevelopment. In the opening pages of his seminal analysis of underdevelopment, Walter Rodney asks first, 'What is development?' and second, 'What is underdevelopment?'[43] The latter is not the absence of development, Rodney explains, but a concept best understood through a comparison of different levels of development. He asserted that 'human social development has been uneven and from a strictly economic viewpoint some human groups have advanced further by producing more and becoming more wealthy'.[44] Close engagement with histories of colonial development bring this statement into stark relief. Fellow Marxist theoretician, George Novack, also spoke to the concept of uneven development in historical processes, specifically addressing 'disparities in technical and social development' and stated that one of 'the most important and paradoxical consequences of uneven and combined development is the solution of the problems of one class through the agency of another'.[45] This is fundamentally the basic premise upon which colonial development was founded.

---

[39] James L. Giblin, *The Politics of Environmental Control in Northeastern Tanzania, 1840–1940* (Philadelphia, 1992); Christopher Conte, *Highland Sanctuary: Environmental History in Tanzania's Usambara Mountains* (Athens, OH, 2004).

[40] Maddox, Giblin, and Kimambo, *Custodians of the Land*.

[41] David M. Anderson, *Eroding the Commons: Politics of Ecology in Baringo, Kenya, 1890–1963* (Oxford, 2002); Kjell J. Havnevik, *Tanzania: The Limits to Development from Above* (Uppsala, 1993); Andrew Coulson, *Tanzania: A Political Economy* (Oxford, 1982).

[42] A. Wood, *The Groundnut Affair* (London, 1950); Robert Chambers, *Settlement Schemes in Tropical Africa: A Study of Organization and Development* (London, 1969); P.E. Peters, 'Land appropriation, surplus people and a battle over visions of agrarian futures in Africa', *Journal of Peasant Studies* 40:3 (2013), 537–62.

[43] Walter Rodney, *How Europe Underdeveloped Africa* (Cape Town, 2012), 3–13.

[44] Ibid., 13.

[45] George Novack, *Understanding History* (New York, 1995), 82–129.

Brian Bowles, who taught alongside Rodney at the University of Dar es Salaam (UDSM) in the early 1970s, also advanced underdevelopment discourse. Bowles argued that 'crops produced entirely for export, as sisal, coffee, and cotton during the colonial period, were contributing to the process of underdevelopment' and maintained that 'their increased production should not be described as development'.[46] John Iliffe, whose lectureship at UDSM coincided with Rodney and Bowles, sheds further light. He contended that one major indication of Tanganyika's underdevelopment was its dependency on the colonial metropolis. Another was 'the development within the country itself of a pattern of regional inequality which became relatively fixed and rigid during the 1930s'.[47] Iliffe does not deny that 'there had been development and progress', but stresses that 'developments must be weighed against the forms of underdevelopment which had also taken shape within the economy'.[48] The two processes, therefore, are concurrent and connected.

As for development, the concept of underdevelopment may also be loosely defined. Iliffe offers at least three different meanings: 'absolute' for the overall impoverishment of a country; 'relative' for how a country's overall living standards may improve at a lower rate than another country; and 'structural' for 'the evolution of certain economic and social structures which are characteristic of underdeveloped areas and which tend to be self-perpetuating'.[49] For Tanganyika, the defining patterns of underdevelopment were its dependence and its internal inequality. That is to say, the 'control of its economy was not in the hands of its own inhabitants' and there existed 'inequality between different rural areas [that] resulted from the much more rapid development of certain favoured regions, such as Kilimanjaro'.[50] These factors help to contextualise the development histories of Kilombero as told through these pages. The visitor to Kilombero today would be forgiven for thinking that the valley had not been a favoured region, historically, due to the clear absence of the kind of rapid and sustained development experienced in Kilimanjaro, for instance; but that would belie the underlying truth that Kilombero was, notionally at least, a highly favoured region. One major aim of this book is to expose this notional history, to liberate these histories of ideas from the archives, and bring them to light for the sake of the valley and its people today.

The history of development processes that have focused on and favoured Kilombero are neither evident in the valley today, nor well known. This book

[46] Brian D. Bowles, 'Export crops and underdevelopment in Tanganyika, 1929–61', *UTAFITI* 1:1 (1976), 71.
[47] John Iliffe, *Agricultural Change in Modern Tanganyika* (Nairobi, 1971), 30.
[48] Ibid., 27.
[49] Ibid., 27–8.
[50] Ibid., 6, 28.

is an attempt to change that. But to understand how these processes have shaped the valley to the present, it must be recognised, as aptly expressed by Kjell Havnevik, that 'the nature and development of the post-colonial model cannot be understood apart from the political, social, regional, and economic structures of the colonial regime from which it emerged'.[51] Kilombero today, then, cannot be understood without reference to the earliest and subsequent histories of 'development premised on multifaceted interventionist policies' that were pushed by the colonial and postcolonial states, then by external donor agencies and nations, and also most notably by the International Monetary Fund and the World Bank.[52]

These policies begin with those driving agricultural and economic development during the period of German East Africa – which were considerable, if exploitative and extractive – with production centred on plantation and settler economies. After the First World War and Great Britain's receipt of the Mandate to administer the territory under the League of Nations, what then became Tanganyika was, for the most part, 'hegemony on a shoestring' and 'during the inter-war years very little money was available for development'.[53] Development was approached through ad hoc schemes, with an official ethos towards the 'betterment' of its people. Progress was closely watched from Geneva and then Washington, to whom the government was always quick to profess: 'We want to see a healthy, prosperous, industrious and self-reliant population resident.'[54] But there was a belief that this was not a true priority for Britain and that 'Tanganyika, due to the logic of circumstances, held the position of stepchild among the British East African territories'.[55] This view is echoed for the period after the Second World War by James Karioki, who opined that: 'The British, having only derivative powers from the United Nations over Tanganyika, had no special interest in promoting the country's economic growth or in maintaining their grasp on the country under those terms.'[56]

The years following the Second World War are customarily considered to have dawned 'development' as a pervasive set of ideas and practices. Prior to this, the colonial state did not have a clear mind as to what 'development'

---

[51] Havnevik, *Limits to Development*, 18.

[52] Ibid., 17.

[53] Sara Berry, 'Hegemony on a shoestring: Indirect rule and access to agricultural land', *Africa: Journal of the International African Institute* 62:3 (1992), 327–55; J.F.R. Hill and J.P. Moffett, *Tanganyika: A Review of its Resources and their Development* (Dar es Salaam, 1955), v.

[54] Tanganyika Territory, *Report of the Central Development Committee* (Dar es Salaam, 1940), 7.

[55] Hans Ruthenberg, *Agricultural Development in Tanganyika* (Berlin, 1964), 45.

[56] James N. Karioki, *Tanzania's Human Revolution* (University Park, PA, 1979), 3.

really looked like. This 'second colonial occupation' after 1945 saw 'the emergence of a new kind of colonial rule, the state reinforced by an army of officials and technicians keen to impose a new order' alongside 'new forms of African resistance to this invasion'.[57] Chief among this army of officials was Norris E. Dodd, Director-General of the Food and Agricultural Organisation (FAO) of the United Nations 1948–52, who wrote in 1955 that FAO experts 'speak the same language of science and technology and share the same dream of human advancement'.[58] This Bretton-Woods institution was motivated by high developmentalist philosophies of modernisation, pursuing a particular kind of state-led, centrally planned development that was high on technology and imposed from above, but not at all participatory or inclusive. This partly informs the established connection between the rise of nationalism in the 1950s and a 'general resentment against enforced [agricultural] improvements' in Tanganyika.[59] Active opposition to the colonial government by 1957 led its Director of Agriculture to concede that 'the era of the big stick was over'.[60] New approaches pivoted to demonstration, persuasion, and 'community development' as continued suspicion of government stymied efforts to the point of high crisis in colonial rule. Many endeavours continued to falter, but nor did they have to be wildly ambitious to fail. One pattern of the limited success of small agricultural schemes during the early 1950s was highlighted by Hans Ruthenberg, who wrote:

> It may almost be considered a rule [...] that in the beginning some successes are achieved, whereupon optimistic reports are written; then, however, obstacles arise and the project is abandoned. The personnel change. After a few years hardly anybody knows that there had been a scheme, which had failed.[61]

After Tanganyika gained Independence in December 1961, state-led approaches to development were rhetorically refreshed but often structurally unchanged. Significant changes followed the Arusha Declaration of 1967 and its formal pursuit of the African socialism that defined the nation. From this moment rural development policies in Tanzania began to draw global attention – and international involvement on a scale hitherto unseen – leading

---

[57] Low and Lonsdale, 'Introduction', 12.
[58] Quoted in Gove Hambidge, *Story of FAO* (New York, 1955), iii.
[59] L. Cliffe, 'Nationalism and the reaction to enforced agricultural change in Tanganyika during the Colonial Period', in L. Cliffe and J. Saul (eds), *Socialism in Tanzania: Volume I* (Dar es Salaam, 1972), 18.
[60] Quoted in ibid., 23.
[61] Ruthenberg, *Agricultural Development in Tanganyika*, 59.

to a plethora of contemporaneous and continually retrospective critiques, such as that levied against independent Africa 'as a whole' which argued that it continued to reproduce 'dependence that limits state autonomy in the strategic area of socio-economic development' and that, from the early years of the postcolonial era, 'modernisation and financial support of agriculture, the central economic area in African states, [were] left to foreign aid agencies or international companies'.[62] While superficially altruistic, their ulterior motives were usually self-serving to various degrees.

The first attempt by the independent government to comprehensively plan socio-economic development was presented in the 'First Five-Year Development Plan' (1964–69), based mainly on the expectation of foreign investments to transform the rural sector through capital-intensive village settlement schemes.[63] The 'Second Five-Year Plan' shifted from reliance on external resources to dependence on national resources as well as emphasising rural development.[64] Nyerere promoted 'self-reliance' as an ideology and came to view 'development' as something for which high capital was unnecessary, nor predicated on the accumulation of material wealth. 'Development is for the people, by the people, and of the people', he believed, and progress was measured in terms of human well-being, not in prestigious cars, or televisions.[65] In 1968, Nyerere declared: 'For the truth is that development means the development of *people*. Roads, buildings, the increases of crop output, and other things of this nature, are not development; they are only tools of development.'[66] Nyerere distinguished between material and ideological development, and argued: 'But people cannot be developed; they can only develop themselves. For while it is possible for an outsider to build a man's house, an outsider cannot give the man pride and self-confidence in himself as a human being.'[67]

It is widely acknowledged that Nyerere's *Ujamaa* and his interpretation of African socialism did not achieve its ideals. Moreover, the implicit use of

---

[62] Werner Biermann, 'Introduction: Contextualising poverty in Africa', in Werner Biermann and Humphrey Moshi (eds), *Contextualising Poverty in Tanzania: Historical Origins, Policy Failures and Recent Threads* (Dar es Salaam, 1997), 3.

[63] United Republic of Tanganyika and Zanzibar, *Tanganyika Five-Year Plan for Economic and Social Development: 1st July, 1964 – 30th June, 1969*. 3 vols (Dar es Salaam, 1964).

[64] United Republic of Tanzania, *Tanzania Second Five-Year Plan for Economic and Social Development, 1st July, 1969 – 30th June, 1974. Volume I: General Analysis* (Dar es Salaam, 1969).

[65] See Julius K. Nyerere, *Man and Development* (Dar es Salaam, 1974).

[66] Ibid., 26.

[67] Ibid., 27.

coercion to enforce villagisation in the name of development and rural transformation brought infamy to Nyerere and the state. This was not foreseen. As noted by Leander Schneider: 'That developmental governing took the authoritarian shape in postcolonial Tanzania was unexpected.'[68] Others have viewed Nyerere's promotion of ideology – through *Ujamaa* and the Arusha Declaration – as a diversionary tool used against political instability, when and where the citizens' material expectations could not be met.[69] As noted by John Nellis: 'Reliance on ideology as a substitute plot for material fulfilment merely prolongs the inevitable; material cravings are fundamental in man and cannot be assuaged indefinitely by intangibles such as ideology.'[70] The inference was that this applied to urban and rural populations alike, but the promotion of Tanzania's agricultural economy has always remained at the forefront of development efforts: efforts that, by most accounts, have fallen short of expectations.

Unfulfilled aspirations, unmet expectations, and unmaterialised visions are thus shown to be a feature of the colonial and postcolonial development landscape, set against a backdrop of oscillating understandings of 'rural development' in theory and praxis. Most of its underlying concerns today do, in fact, remain cognate to those of the colonial era: diversification of the rural economy, water control, land conservation, communications, land productivity, forestry, and animal husbandry, to name a few. One fundamental distinction, naturally, lies in the difference in political legitimacy between a colonial and democratically elected state, even if thematic continuities, policy positions, and practical approaches can be readily identified. Now that the broader contexts are established, the specific set of political, social, economic, and ecological circumstances that have shaped the development experience in Kilombero may be brought into finer focus.

Central themes

The Kilombero Valley may be divided into 'inner' and 'outer' valleys that are unequal in size and geophysically distinct, but connected through economic, social, and political ties, and are mutually dependent. The 'inner' valley is most widely acknowledged as the valley proper due its inclusion of the vast floodplain, a defining characteristic. The plain, its marginal hills, and surrounding alluvial fans are enclosed on two sides by the Udzungwa and Mahenge mountains. The 'inner' valley opens to its 'outer' counterpart to the north-east beyond Ifakara, the principal lowland town. 'Kilombero', therefore, must be understood as incorporating both 'inner' and 'outer' valleys

---

[68] Schneider, *Government of Development*, 3.
[69] Karioki, *Human Revolution*, 3.
[70] Précised in ibid. See also John R. Nellis, *A Theory of Ideology: The Tanzanian Example* (Nairobi, 1972).

as well as the broader, but immediate, sphere of regional interconnectivity: the Kilombero valley region. The surrounding highlands, for example, are mighty precipitation barriers that collect the heavy rainfall which feed the Kilombero River through its tributaries. In political terms, it was from the highland Mahenge town that the valley was first administered, and the movement of trade and people between lowlands and highlands ensured close economic and social interaction. One colonial official suggested the following visualisation:

> The Ulanga Valley might be likened to the meat dish of a dinner service, the raised rim representing the foot-hills between the valley floor and enclosing escarpments of Iringa, Njombe, Songea, and Mahenge. Across the length of the dish wanders the Kilombero River, fed by innumerable tributaries from the encircling escarpments: these tributaries pass through the foot-hills and wander across the floor of the valley until they reach the main stream.[71]

The 'five great streams' that combine to form the Kilombero – the Ruhuji, Mnyera, Mgeta, Ruipa, and Kihansi Rivers – were once described as a 'veritable East African "Punjab" [...] gnawing with their countless tributaries deep in the southern tableland'.[72] It is unsurprising that this undeniably wet valleyscape, surrounded by arid neighbouring regions, drew the colonial gaze. For the German administration, the perceived potential for rice production contributed to Mahenge's status as an important and strategic district, if a remote one. But depending on which way the light refracted, Kilombero was either full of promise or a colonial backwater. For many, it was concurrently both, and there lay the rub. It was a region whose reputation frequently preceded itself. Greatly discussed, but little known. Frequently cited, but rarely visited. Kilombero was not en route to anywhere in particular, nor an easily accessible place in the best of conditions. This was a district divided by countless rivers and when the rains broke, 'the whole country would become an impassable morass'.[73] It was a capricious environment and, through its annual inundation, the Kilombero River was 'both the fairy godmother and the ogre of the valley. It brings the water, which makes the valley ideal for rice: it (and its tributaries) also bring down the heavy floods which may completely drown the rice crop.'[74]

---

[71] TNA 61/782, Agriculture and Communications in the Ulanga Valley, 1943.

[72] Clement Gillman, 'South-West Tanganyika Territory', *The Geographical Journal* 69:2 (1927), 101.

[73] F.L. Puxley, *In African Game Tracks: Wanderings with A Rifle through Eastern Africa* (London, 1929), 212.

[74] TNA 61/782/21, Agricultural and Communications in the Ulanga Valley, 1943.

For colonial officers, the district was frequently maligned as a hardship posting, lonely and unhealthy.[75] Michael Longford, District Officer (1958–60), wrote how 'viewed from a distance, the valley looked very attractive, but the climate was hot and humid, especially just before the rains started'.[76] For Longford this was 'the back of beyond' and the 'main feature [...] was its remoteness and inaccessibility'.[77] Despite its trying environment and desolation, the region continued to be earmarked for significant development. In 1926, the Director of Agriculture described Kilombero as 'virtually going begging' due to its 'never-failing flood period' and 'continually adequate rainfall' over a rich, constantly renewed alluvial soil' on which two crops of rice were grown every year.[78] These disparities in opinion prevailed, becoming a recurring trope in valley discourse. This is but one motif that emerges from an examination of the development histories. Expressed in simple terms, the core themes that run as strata through this book are by no means unique to Kilombero, and it is rather their commonality and recurrence in wider historiography that situate this study firmly within development and historical literatures. The specificities and interplay of these themes within this distinct environment do, however, tell an individual story.

Agricultural intensification

This first theme emerges as one of the earliest aspirations cast. Since the German era, developers have been preoccupied with increasing agricultural production, and almost every scheme proposed is predicated on achieving this. For Fonck and many since, 'the Ulanga Plain promises more!'[79] Realisation of the region's 'latent potential' lay persistently on a horizon that could never quite be reached. But, after all, the *imagined* possibilities of a place are virtually limitless, and far easier to conjure in the mind than to actually embark on practical attempts to realise these visions. Future possibilities were passed on from one year, decade, or era to the next, inherited and bequeathed by individuals who often held neither the responsibility, the capital, nor the capacity to bring them to fruition.

---

[75] E.K. Lumley, *Forgotten Mandate: A British District Officer in Tanganyika* (London, 1976), 113.

[76] Michael Longford, *The Flags Changed at Midnight* (Leominster, 2001), 258.

[77] Ibid., 254, 257.

[78] TNA 11746, 'Memorandum on two fertile regions awaiting development' by A.H. Kirby, Director of Agriculture (DofA), 23 September 1926.

[79] BArch, R1001/278/66–84, Heinrich Fonck, 'Bericht uber die wirtschaftliche Verhältnisse in der Ulangaebene und ihre Nachbargebieten', Dar es Salaam, 15 January 1908.

Developers donned green-tinted glasses, failing to see beyond the immediate and apparent verdure. Many failed to appreciate that agricultural production rested on flexible – not fixed – cultivation patterns. The reality was that local agronomy was tuned to local rivers' characteristics and niche production areas, which allowed for compound cropping to avert risk and promote balance within available soil resources and water availability. This set a natural limit to intensification, which profoundly affects local decision-making. In certain areas, climate and fertility meant that subsistence requirements were met with minimum effort. This led developers to imagine what might be achieved through intensive effort, which fanned the idea of the valley as the 'potential granary of East Africa'.[80] Confrontation with this complex valley ecology was a frequent reason for scheme failure, especially those proposals for wholesale monoculture production over extensive areas; and such visions remain unlikely to succeed without dramatic and expensive hydrological engineering.

Ecology control

Hydrological engineering is one example from within the second theme of 'ecology control' which recurs throughout the history. This may be defined along similar lines to what Helge Kjekshus calls 'the struggle for mastery of nature by man' and might equally be called 'environment management.'[81] The annual flooding of valley rivers held primary importance for local ecology, while dam construction for flood control and water storage for irrigation came to be viewed as indispensable to realise potential. The FAO estimated that four-fifths of the valley was seasonally or perennially flooded and that, 'only with the provision of large storage reservoirs to reduce and ultimately prevent flooding can the Kilombero Valley be developed at all' and 'so long as flooding continues on its present scale, most of its main communications are cut off for about half the year; trade cannot move, nor administration function'.[82] Further obstacles to 'development' – or, rather, disincentives to grow crash crops – were considered to be health, 'the inadequacy of tools', and 'destruction of crops by wild game'.[83] Here, wildlife management is also a crucial aspect of ecology control. 'No picture of Ulanga would be complete', wrote one colonial officer, 'without mention of its wildlife, against which, indeed, unceasing war has of necessity to be waged in the interests

---

[80] Jätzold and Baum, *Kilombero Valley*, 109.
[81] Kjekshus, *Ecology Control*, 4.
[82] FAO, *Rufiji Basin*, 101.
[83] FAO, *Possibilities for Agriculture and Related Development in the Kilombero Valley: Report to the Government of Tanganyika* (Rome, 1964), 9.

of human enterprise and progress'.[84] This was unsurprising, as the valley is flanked by Nyerere National Park and contains the Kilombero Game Control Area. Another colonial official dismayed that the 'ravages of game [had] to be seen to be believed' and suggested that a 'save more crops' campaign was more appropriate than a 'plant more crops' campaign.[85] The issue of wildlife management as a form of ecology control has a circuitous route through valley history to the present, as recent efforts to protect and conserve wildlife populations sit at odds with colonial cries for their total destruction.

Infrastructure

Low-cost transport systems to, through, and within Kilombero were long held as prerequisites to development. This notion – that realising potential was contingent upon an efficient transport structure – prolonged belief in the latent possibilities of the valley as long as this had not materialised. In developers' minds, this was the key to 'unlocking' Kilombero, and it was once thought that 'with [the] opening up of communications needed for development, trade and travel will become easier. Health and education will improve'.[86] The relationship between development and infrastructure – while cognisant of the view of infrastructure *as* development – begs the question of cause and effect. This evaded resolution, spawning circular arguments over whether transport would bring development, or development would justify transport. Railway construction, in particular, is repeatedly recommended and opinions were divided over whether 'development' was even possible without this. This proved central to persistent debates over Kilombero's worth and arguments over its future. In the absence of a railway, transport to, from, and within the valley relied on notoriously bad roads, bridges that required rebuilding after every flood, and rivers that frequently claimed goods and lives.

(Re)settlement

The final major theme developed is 'settlement and resettlement' – both *to* and *within* Kilombero. Outsiders often commented on a relatively low population density, fuelling the idea that land was underpopulated, underutilised, and widely available. This belief accounted for supposedly low levels of agricultural production and promoted belief in exponential growth. The

---

[84] A.T. Culwick and G.M. Culwick, 'Ulanga: The valley of the Kilombero river', *East African Annual, 1935–36* (Nairobi, 1936), 66.

[85] TNA 61/141/H/Vol. I, Handing Over Notes [Lumley to Culwick], 16 September 1939. 'Plant More Crops' was a British colonial campaign begun in the 1930s to increase agricultural production.

[86] FAO, *Rufiji Basin,* 99.

alleged misproportion between high potential and low population was in itself perceived as a problem, but it also led developers to view Kilombero as the solution to 'surplus' population elsewhere. It was thought that only by increasing the population through resettlement could its full development potential be realised. Perceived underpopulation was central to its 'suitability' for development, yet also its barrier.

There is little evidence that a naturally low limit to population was ever considered, either due to the expanded and varied areas of cultivation required to overcome seasonal volatilities, or the inhospitableness of the environment. Rather, the success of numerous schemes hinged on population increase, from plans for a *métayage* system of tenant farming in the 1930s, the idea of one South African firm to 'import' thousands of Zulu men to solve the 'problem' of labour supply for a proposed sugar estate in the 1950s, to one of the earliest schemes for the resettlement of urban unemployed young men promoted by Nyerere and the Tanganyika African National Union (TANU) as part of their vison for an independent Tanganyika.[87]

Resettlement *within* the region – rather than *to* it – is also prominent. This is highlighted by the creation of sleeping sickness 'concentrations' in the 1930s and 1940s that ostensibly provided protection from this disease, but were underlaid by ulterior motives that interpreted and pushed broader colonial 'development' agendas of social engineering through a specious spatial reordering of communities. The legacy of forced resettlement extends to the postcolonial era, most notably 1973–76 through the infamous use of compulsion to enforce a state policy of villagisation. Resettlement had the unintended effect of disrupting old practices of cultivating the land and, as Jamie Monson has noted, there was 'never any real possibility of permanent settlement in Kilombero, because farmers had to change their fields every one to four years, depending on the agro-ecology of the area'.[88] Agricultural practices, therefore, best operated in harmony with a social system that accommodated flexibility to seasonality. Over time, development projects involving resettlement fundamentally changed access to and control of the land. This led to a rigidification of systems and a narrowing of local options, diminishing the capacity to deal with the capricious environment.

The movement of people through resettlement and the concentration of populations is seen to be as much the creation of communities as their disruption. These processes also connect tangential issues such as improving agricultural productivity, advancing infrastructure, improving administrative

---

[87] TANU signified the 'Tanzania African National Union' from 1964.

[88] Jamie Monson, 'Agricultural Transformation in the Inner Kilombero Valley of Tanzania, 1840–1940' (PhD thesis, University of California, Los Angeles, 1991), 306–7.

efficiency, urban clearances of the un- and underemployed, and schemes to combat tsetse fly and sleeping sickness. Settlement – and associated issues of land rights, access, and use – remains contentious, highlighted by the arrival of agro-pastoralists to Kilombero that have altered its political, social, and ecological landscapes, most notably within the last thirty years. Forced evictions in 2012–13 prove the continued prominence of this theme as a regional and national concern.

This last coda to the theme of (RE)SETTLEMENT represents the importance of recognising the present state of development and its recent past in relationship to its deeper history. Over the past ten, twenty, and thirty years, Kilombero has witnessed a series of interventions that have vastly affected its social and ecological environments through settlement processes, land-use changes, and rural transformations. These have not necessarily fulfilled the numerous past futures once envisaged for the valley, but they align closely with the four central themes traced throughout this book, thus emphasising the thematic continuity from Kilombero's past to its present. Below are four important examples from the recent history of development in the valley. Their contemporary relevance to each of the identified themes is clear, and they are foregrounded here to highlight current contexts as the earlier histories unfold. This book therefore reveals how these same thematic strata have not only shaped the region for decades, but remain crucial to understanding the valley today.

On recent development

It is shown how in-migration by agro-pastoralists, subsequent land pressures on existing communities, and further consequences speak to themes of (RE)SETTLEMENT. Highly publicised evictions brought controversy to Kilombero, carried out as they were in the name of conservation efforts. These efforts relate to the landmark designation in 2002 of 'The Kilombero Valley Floodplain' as a Ramsar Site and thus recognised as a rare and unique wetland whose ecosystem and biodiversity is of international importance. Seasonal wildlife migrations are also the focus of conservation efforts and concerted attempts to promote wildlife corridors through the valley. This is a particular form of ECOLOGY CONTROL that sits at odds with past hopes to rid Kilombero of its game to save and promote its agriculture. However, AGRICULTURAL INTENSIFICATION remains arguably the most important theme. This is ably illustrated through the rise and fall of Kilombero Plantations Limited (KPL), who sought from 2008 to establish a 5,469 hectare rice farm in the valley with a view to producing up to 15,000 tons of milled wet season rice and 30,000 tons of dry season maize, before its collapse in 2018. Lastly, the opening of the expansive 'Magufuli Bridge' over the Kilombero River above the old site of the ferry crossing in 2018 brings the long saga of INFRASTRUCTURE sharply into present focus.

Chapter overview

From this present and recent past to the very beginning: this book opens by exploring the historical foundation of imagined futures for Kilombero in Chapter 1 (1877–1914) through the initial impressions and observations made by European travellers and colonists to the region from the late-nineteenth century. These visions cast Kilombero in various and often contrasting ways: from a highly fertile region with enormous agricultural potential to a pestilent place, wild and desolate. Through the first attempts to navigate, map and survey, this period marks the genesis of understanding and misunderstanding that colour the history. This marks the beginnings of plans to bring AGRICULTURAL INTENSIFICATION to the valley. The earliest visions for grandiose irrigation schemes appear, but not before the Maji Maji Rebellion and its devastating effects wreck Kilombero societies and environment.

Development trajectories are further ruptured by the outbreak of war as Chapter 2 (1914–32) continues to the early years of British administration. Divergent interpretations of the League of Nations Mandate shaped discourse during this period, and the future of Kilombero was highly contested. Visions for a railway were tabled and the parameters of the relationship between development potential and transport infrastructure explored. Plans ultimately proved too ambitious for financial capacities, and what may have transpired instead dissipated as economic depression descended. Here the theme of INFRASTRUCTURE is a key issue.

The theme of ECOLOGY CONTROL is then elaborated through Chapter 3 (1931–45) through the dimensions of colonial agricultural policies, the impact and character of local administration, and the effect that increased wartime production had on the region. Ambition plateaued, but colonial knowledge production broadened. The volatility and complexity of the region is more acutely appreciated, but these years also saw extended market, trade, and economic systems develop as a cash-strapped government encouraged private enterprise to invest.

The darker side of colonial development is central to Chapter 4 (1939–45) through processes of RESETTLEMENT and a study of how perceived threats of sleeping sickness epidemics were used to 'justify' the extensive reorganisation of rural populations. This was a coercive and paternalistic form of 'future making' from above. The prominent role of leading colonial officers, notably A.T. Culwick, is emphasised here and re-examined. Local resistance challenged colonial hegemony and the self-fashioned form of 'benign autocracy' constructed by officials like Culwick, who relied on prestige for political authority in his district and among his peers as he attempted to implement his version of 'development' in Kilombero.

'Future making' on a large and centralised scale is evidenced in Chapter 5 (1939–61) throughout a period in which AGRICULTURAL INTENSIFICATION remains a central focus. Framed by the planning of post-war development plans and independence, this chapter explores a particular paradigm of colonial development in which central government played a significant and determining role in the acceleration of schemes, especially in rural areas. This dramatic change reframes the colonial approach to future development, and yet within a matter of years Tanganyika would be independent, marking the most 'future-making' moment in its history. Development then took on an increasingly international character, while lingering colonial characteristics complicated the changing political landscape.

These themes are then drawn together into a fuller discussion of 'futures' surrounding the first decade of independence in Chapter 6 (1959–75) and Chapter 7 (1959–69). Remnants of colonial continuities are enshrouded by new ideologies, new frontiers, and a new internationalism in development dynamics. These years see the establishment of the Kilombero Sugar Company, one of the most prominent industrial developments of the early independence era. Numerous nations stake their claim in the valley as Dutch, German, and Swiss actors begin to occupy the development landscape. A railway through the valley is constructed, fulfilling a vision existing for over half a century. This period also explores the Kilombero Settlement Scheme in depth, whose extended trajectory reveals its palimpsestic nature through a history layered by different approaches to the reorganisation of rural life in Tanzania. For its failures more than its successes, this scheme became an important model for the nation's programme of social development and how cognisance of 'past futures' helped to mitigate the ongoing challenges of rural transformation.

The book concludes with a summary of its key findings and a return to its central questions. Drawing from the genealogy of place that has been crafted, the layers of intervention that have been discovered, and the implications of a development trajectory that is far from linear, the way in which the core themes of Kilombero's 'past futures' continue to shape the valleyscape are then spotlighted by examples from the recent past. These show how the future remains contested and contingent, and that an understanding of past aspirations reveals just as much, if not more, than an understanding of hopes fulfilled. The result is the chronicle of a history that is not always self-evident or materially manifested. It is a history, rather, of ideas, of thoughts and schemes, surveys, plans and reports, a history of blueprints and sketches and projections, trials and errors, and visions for a valley long since blurred on the horizon.

1

Colonialism Comes to Kilombero: Skirting the Banks, 1877–1914

Every trajectory has an origin, and to trace the evolution of outsiders' views of Kilombero, therefore, is to discover when these views began. It was only from the late-nineteenth century that explorers and colonialists first came to know the valley, produce knowledge of it, and forge ideas about shaping its future. From these early observations, circuitous routes through decades of development histories may be traced, resulting in an assembly of external perspectives to chart the evolution of their impact on the valley, if only ideationally. These first observations were made through lenses devoid of the developmental agendas that were later advanced, but from which formed their very foundation.

The very first written mention of the Kilombero River is found in the posthumously published travel journals of the English explorer, J. Frederic Elton, who died in December 1877 en route from Lake Nyasa to Zanzibar. Elton did not reach its banks, but wrote of 'the Ranga river' which 'flows east of mountain slopes, beyond gorge of Ruaha, to the Rufiji'.[1] Kilombero's reputation preceded itself as explorers learned of the valley before any set foot within it. It was then the Scottish explorer, Joseph Thomson, who claimed to be the first European to sight the Kilombero River itself, in late 1879. Thomson was a young geologist and naturalist on an expedition led by Keith Johnston, commissioned by the Royal Geographical Society. Their destination was the region encompassing Lake Tanganyika and Lake Nyasa, whose perceived economic significance was piquing interests abroad.

Before embarking on the route, Johnston spent months collecting information from traders at the coast about the country through which he would pass. He wrote in May 1879 that 'the most important country between Uzaramo and Ubena, in the direction of the head of Lake Nyassa, is that of M'henge, which lies between the main tributaries of the Lufigi, viz. the Ruaha, and Ranga, not far above their confluence'.[2] This 'country' was the Kilombero Valley.

---

[1] J.F. Elton, *Travels and Researches among the Lakes and Mountains of Eastern and Central Africa, from the journals of the late J.F. Elton, edited and completed by H.B. Cotterill* (London, 1879), 338.

[2] Keith Johnston, 'Native routes in East Africa, from Dar-es-Salaam towards Lake Nyassa', *Proceedings of the Royal Geographical Society and the Monthly Record* 1:7 (1879), 418.

Like Elton before him, Johnston's journey proved fatal. He died in June 1879 at Behobeho, in what is now Nyerere National Park.[3] Thomson continued the route and later wrote of the Kilombero as 'a river which though long heard of, had never yet been seen by any white man'.[4] But the 'canoe-men' who ferried Thomson through its backwaters would not take him on the river itself on account of 'exceedingly dangerous' hippopotami, while they did skirt crocodiles along its side-streams, lagoons, and swamps, which teemed with fish and 'innumerable flocks of all sorts of aquatic birds'.[5]

For Thomson, this was a wild, difficult, but seemingly fertile place. 'Owing to the proximity of the country to the mountains', he wrote, 'and the flat nature of the ground between the two boundary rivers [Great Ruaha and Kilombero], it is kept constantly damp throughout the year, and the soil being a rich alluvium is one of the most fertile spots in Africa.'[6]

> All the cereals of the coast, such as rice (the favourite food), millet, and maize, are grown extensively. So also are such vegetables as sweet potatoes, yams, ground-nuts, melons, pumpkins, and cucumbers, and many other excellent articles of food. Tobacco is grown very abundantly. The sugar-cane, the castor-oil plant, and cotton, are also cultivated.[7]

At this time, the extent of rivers' navigability was coveted intelligence and its pursuit was central to expeditions of this kind. Despite not exploring the Kilombero River itself, Thomson nonetheless reported on its perceived navigability, even though he mostly failed to determine its true width due to obstructing islands and 'huge bordering sedges [which] cut off any possible view of it either up or down'.[8] Yet he still had little doubt that the river was at least navigable as far as Mkomokero from its junction with the Ruaha. Beyond that he could derive little information, other than it flowed through a region absent of roads, whose population was sparse, and about whom little was seemingly known. Thomson lamented that he had 'at one time thought of exploring the Uranga, but in the face of such a discouraging report thought it advisable to give up the idea'.[9]

Certain significant tropes already begin to emerge. From Thomson's account alone there are descriptions of a highly fertile land, juxtaposed by a wild,

---

[3] Formerly the Selous Game Reserve.
[4] Thomson, *Central African Lakes*, 180.
[5] Ibid.
[6] Ibid.
[7] Ibid.
[8] Ibid.
[9] Ibid.

dangerous, but potentially navigable waterscape. This was a terrain difficult to traverse, an environment oscillating between stifling and salubrious. Another significant trope discerned is the application of hasty generalisations to various valley features as authoritative statements are made following obviously limited knowledge. Taken together, these characteristics of the Kilombero valley region ripple through the decades to the present.

Following Thomson was William Beardall, a British engineer commissioned in 1880 by the Sultan of Zanzibar to 'collect information of the country and people in the neighbourhood off the Rufiji River and its southern tributary, the Uranga'.[10] Beardall was then managing the construction of a road from Dar es Salaam to Lake Nyasa, funded by Sir William Mackinnon and Sir Fowell Buxton and styled as a 'philanthropic undertaking' with a 'civilising influence', but ultimately a capitalist venture for financial return.[11] As such, Beardall's exploration of the Kilombero valley region was naturally supported for its possible future returns for commercial enterprise. Lucrative mineral riches in the Congo and interlacustrine region had become a primary focus of British imperial ambition, to which the establishment of secure routes was of utmost importance. Thomson's recent reports, however, were not considered 'very encouraging for the successful continuance of the Mackinnon-Buxton road'.[12]

Beardall left Zanzibar on 2 December 1880 and on 22 January 1881 reached the Shughuli Falls, where the Kilombero and Luwegu Rivers converge to become the Rufiji. His expedition did not explore the Kilombero for more than ten miles west of this confluence as a shortage of food, guides, and porters forced him to turn back. Furthermore, the threat of early rains and resulting flooding risked impassability at best, fatalities at worst. The power of the flood was clearly known and not underestimated. From this 'dead end' Beardall noted substantial villages built on rocks and islands in the river, seemingly for protection. He was told there were many more such rocks and islands, and at one place even canoes could not pass. Based on this account alone, Beardall considered that its rocks and rapids rendered the Kilombero 'quite useless as a fluvial route into the interior'.[13] But to a caravan of traders from Kilwa, who encountered Beardall en route to 'Mahengi' to buy ivory and 'india-rubber', this was 'the land of plenty'.[14]

---

[10] Beardall, 'Exploration', 641.
[11] 'Geographical notes', *Proceedings of the Royal Geographical Society and Monthly Record of Geography* 3:5 (1881), 309.
[12] Collections of the Royal Geographical Society (RGS), CB6/2290, Gerald Waller to Henry Bates, 2 February 1880.
[13] 'Geographical notes', 308.
[14] Beardall, 'Exploration', 653.

Abundance in the region and river navigability for sizeable vessels were not paradoxical states. The Kilombero valley region had long lain along long-distance caravan trading routes from the coastal ports of Kilwa and Lindi to Lake Nyasa. These routes were alighted on before the period of unabashed colonial conquest, when expeditions to the African continent were framed as 'exploration narratives' that pushed the limits of cartographic knowledge and traced lines through regions previously unmarked on European maps. Throughout this period, to explorers and early colonialists alike, rivers proved paramount as both the means of travel and as destinations themselves. River networks afforded the most readily accessible and hopefully realistic route from deltaic coastal mouths to lands unknown. Navigable rivers led to the possibilities of new markets, natural resources or mineral wealth, and fertile lands. Every novel tributary was miniaturised onto fresh maps, each holding latent potential for rich discoveries. But many of the resulting travelogues contained a geographic and scientific focus that belies the underlying role these expeditions served as harbingers of imperialism.

Commercial interests preceded formal empire as the impetus for arduous and expensive expeditions that sought to trace and control strategic trade routes. The most established of these in nineteenth-century Tanzania – the so-called 'central' route – ran from Ujiji on the shores of Lake Tanganyika, through Tabora (the heart of Unyamwezi and its trading capital), and to the coast at Bagamoyo.[15] The Nyamwezi were 'prime movers' on this route, heavily traversed by European explorers. Few Europeans, however, cut the south-westerly line from the coast opposite Zanzibar, then south of the great barrier of the Eastern Arc mountains and to the region of the Kilombero Valley. For many Europeans poised at the coast, they could only glean secondary knowledge from traders who knew the land well from their pursuit of ivory, slaves, rice, and wild rubber.

These earliest written accounts that reference the region provide evidence of the ways in which Kilombero intersected with the growing sphere of European commercial interests in East Africa and how its future potential for performing a critical role within them was perceived. Water indeed flowed to the coast through Kilombero, but this was no indication that the river system could serve as a navigable passage to buoy imperial interests. Thomson was optimistic, while Beardall thought it a useless route, and they were not the last to explore its navigability. By the early 1880s, there remained a certain mutual respect between European powers as they sought access to valuable resources and strategic alliances were formed. But aggressive imperialism and colonial expansion would soon irrevocably change the nature of European engagement with the region and, indeed, the fate of the continent.

[15] Stephen Rockel, 'Porters and Imperialists: A Study of African Labour in Tanzania, 1850–1917' (PhD thesis, University of Toronto, 1990), 6.

German intervention and imperial ambition

Theories abound as to the true motives behind the decision by Otto von Bismarck to form a German colony in East Africa, made on 23 February 1885. It was a sudden decision that took even Germany by surprise. The implications for the balance of British and French commerce and power were significant and complex. The policy was arguably rooted in European diplomacy, which informed so many of the political stratagems for which Africa was a stage.[16] One argument holds that German colonies were, among other suppositions, the 'accidental by-product of an abortive Franco-German entente'.[17] Commercial rivalries and colonial jealousies emerged as enduring themes in pursuit of expanding overseas markets and their contribution to economic growth and stability in Europe. Capitalist pressures for investment, particularly in mining and plantation industries, were behind much of British annexation in Africa. There was also an anxiety that formal colonies would be expensive to govern and defend, unlike the economical protection offered to chartered companies with trading interests. But could financial profit be pursued this way without inevitable colonial expansion by government? Moreover, in Germany there was a palpable rise in public enthusiasm *for* empire. Jean Stengers writes of a 'colonial mania' in 1884 that manifested as 'a real fever of occupying and hoisting the German flag in all regions of the world'.[18] Thus followed a multitude of European lines cut across the continent by varying motives, manners, and means. Missionaries embarked on proselytising endeavours alongside suppression efforts and anti-slavery movements, while continued 'discoveries' by geographical societies and scientific organisations led to new markets and routes for imperial enterprise.

Behind the emanating horrors of the Berlin Conference of 1884–5 lay an attempt to promote European co-operation between nations and their rising 'spheres of influence' through common or free trade, particularly in the burgeoning markets of the Great Lakes and Congo Basin. There was debate over the economic value of the region to become *Deutsch-Ostafrika* (DOA), but its relative position ensured geopolitical importance. Regions were mostly perceived to be replete with riches unless proved otherwise, as reported by the Berlin correspondent of *The Globe* in late 1884:

---

[16] For further insight see Richard Reid, 'Africa's revolutionary nineteenth century and the idea of the "Scramble"', *The American Historical Review* 126:4 (2021), 1424–47.

[17] Harmut Pogge von Strandmann and Alison Smith, 'The German Empire in Africa and British perspectives: A historiographical essay', in Prosser Gifford and Wm. Roger Louis (eds), *Britain and Germany in Africa; Imperial Rivalry and Colonial Rule* (New Haven, CT, 1967), 713.

[18] Jean Stengers, 'British and German Imperial rivalry: A conclusion', in Gifford and Louis, *Britain and Germany*, 340.

So deeply are the people imbued with a vague but none the less enticing vision of the wealth to be won in Africa, that thousands of young men are longing and waiting for an opportunity to seek their fortunes in the new El Dorado.[19]

One such man was Carl Peters, whose 'frenzied imagination' – inspired in part by the writings of H.M. Stanley – led to his founding the Society for German Colonisation (*Gesellschaft für deutsche Kolonisation*, or GfdK) in March 1884.[20] Seven months later – together with Karl Ludwig Jühlke and Joachim Graf von Pfeil – he journeyed to East Africa to acquire land on which to hoist the German flag. This was the beginning of German interventions into the hinterland, despite being neither commissioned nor endorsed by the Reichstag. That changed within a year, and between 1884–6 no less than eighteen expeditions were dispatched to make territory-extending treaties. These were notoriously dubious and underhanded. Bismarck later considered territory acquisition in East Africa to be 'very simple' and 'for a few muskets one can obtain a paper with some native crosses'.[21]

Political and economic domination were driving ambitions, but reports of these expeditions continued to be published for the reading public as travel narratives, partly to mask the desire to acquire agricultural and commercial colonies. When a false report spread that Peters, Jühlke, and Pfeil were a party of colonisers bound for the Congo, the party deflected attention as they 'quietly embarked for Zanzibar, under assumed names, and as steerage passengers'.[22] Conventional interests in geographical exploration aside, a primary objective of the GfdK and its successor – the German East Africa Company, or *Deutsche Ostafrikanische Gesellschaft* (DOAG) – was to find 'wide stretches in which German agriculturalists can progress'.[23] It was in this twin vein of scientific investigation and colonial ambition that Pfeil first sighted the Kilombero River on 8 December 1885.

Pfeil followed the course of 'this important river, hitherto unknown' for 150 miles.[24] Fertile river valleys such as Kilombero were prominent fixations of colonial desire. They represented the idea of a promised land, a veritable

---

[19] Quoted in Stengers, 'British', 340.

[20] John Iliffe, *Tanganyika under German Rule, 1905–1912* (Cambridge, 1969), 11.

[21] Iliffe, *Modern History*, 90.

[22] 'Recent changes in the map of East Africa', *Proceedings of the Royal Geographical Society and Monthly Record of Geography*, 9:8 (1887), 490–96.

[23] Matthew Unangst, 'Changes in German travel writing about East Africa, 1884–1891', *Colloquia Germanica* 46:3 (2013), 266–71.

[24] 'Geographical notes', *Proceedings of the Royal Geographical Society and Monthly Record of Geography* 9:1 (1887), 48.

El Dorado. Discovery of such seemingly ideal landscapes filled the colonial prospector with high hopes for future settlement, agricultural production, and economic development. On reaching the Kilombero he felt strong 'reason to hope [it] would prove a highway into healthy and inhabitable regions'.[25] As Pfeil had travelled further from the coast, he wrote of progressively more fertile lands and a belief that he was ever closer to claiming that new El Dorado for Germany.[26]

Pfeil approached the valley from the north-east, passing Kidatu and crossing the Msolwa River before reaching the village of Ngahoma, then the 'chief of Mahenge' whose village was an important centre and gateway to the region. Before sighting the Kilombero for the first time, Pfeil wrote that 'we only knew this mighty river by name, and nothing was known about its significance'.[27] He knew of Thomson and Beardall's mentions of the river, and that neither had explored it. One man in Pfeil's caravan had, in fact, previously accompanied Beardall on his expedition. That the insights of those who assisted on these journeys are lost, and only European accounts remain, is a tragic casualty of history.

Pfeil spent over one month on the river, the view from his canoe frequently impeded. 'The banks are so perfectly flat', he wrote, 'that from the canoe never anything is visible but the broad ever lengthening sheet of muddy shady gliding water fringed by a barrier of tall reeds closely interwoven with the creepers of a convolvulus that to anyone but a hippo they formed an impenetrable barrier.'[28] The river wound continually with few fixed points of reference, which frustrated his map-making efforts. 'Occasionally', he wrote, 'a solitary palm tree could be discerned' although 'just in front and then apparently through half the points of the compass.'[29] Pfeil viewed these palm trees as rearing 'their solitary heads [...] to the leaden sky' as they 'conveyed an impression of unbounded desolation which neither the Lybian desert nor the Kalahari nor the silent dank forests of New Guinea have been able to produce again'.[30]

This stands in contrast to the fertile and verdant landscape Pfeil hoped to find, and yet Kilombero is so often described precisely in these terms. The truth lies somewhere in between, as within this valley region exists stark contrasts

---

[25] RGS/LMS/P22, 'Account of travel in East Africa: journeys through Kutu and exploration of the Ulanga, 1888', by Joachim Graf von Pfeil.

[26] Joachim Graf von Pfeil, 'Die Erforschung des Ulanga-Gebietes', *Petermanns geographische Mitteilungen* 12 (1886), 353–63.

[27] Pfeil, 'Die Erforschung', 357.

[28] RGS/LMS/P22, 'Account of travel', by Pfeil.

[29] Ibid.

[30] Ibid.

in landscape and ecology, climate and topography. Desolation juxtaposes luxuriant fertility, but these are not necessarily mutually exclusive characteristics within a vast area. The state of being both and the implications of this are wedded to the ways in which Kilombero was increasingly perceived. While the truth may lie in variegated locales possessing diverse seasonality and ecologies, opposing perceptions are significant for they created ambiguity in German minds as to the *kind* of valley this was. Pfeil imagined the river would prove a highway to healthy regions, but did not consider Kilombero itself as such a region, despite noting densely inhabited riverbanks due to what he believed must be considerable soil fertility.

These co-constituent conditions of high fertility in a relatively inhospitable environment frustrated the quest for paradisiacal landscapes and hidden treasures at the heart of German colonial desire. This is best understood alongside the creeping realisation that tropical exuberance has the potential to conceal a 'desert, covered with verdure' and where riches are illusory.[31] Sharae Deckard writes of this duality as a figuring of Africa as 'an anti-paradise punishing desire with feverish reality' and is 'characteristic of the European notion of tropical decadence, which promotes a dualistic conception of Africa as simultaneously "pestilential" and "paradisiacal"'.[32] Nineteenth-century imperialist literature on Africa often fluctuated between the 'desire for paradisal riches and guilty dread of the infernal continent'.[33] This fluctuation is evident in representations of Kilombero, where lushness and misery meet.

At one point on his journey, around Christmas 1885, Pfeil became lost in an 'enormous' and 'dismal swamp', likened to a 'thick huge sponge'.[34] This could have been one of several locales, such as the permanent Kibasira swamp as known today. He described being able to see only mountain peaks in the distance, which appeared grey due to the 'oppressively hot, hazy atmosphere of the swamps'.[35] Endurance of an oppressive climate and survival of this dismal swamp made for a fitting adventure narrative, but this was no Eden. Pfeil was also doubtful of the value the river held as a transport route, foreseeing difficulties in surveying its navigability. It was difficult to locate the main channel of the Kilombero as he and his guides rowed through newly discovered channels when previously navigated branches were subsequently blocked. Pfeil incorrectly believed that the tributaries that fed this powerful river were

[31] David Arnold, '"Illusory riches": Representations of the tropical world, 1840–1950', *Singapore Journal of Tropical Geography* 21:2 (2002), 16.
[32] Sharae Deckard, *Paradise Discourse, Imperialism, and Globalization: Exploiting Eden* (London, 2010), 85.
[33] Ibid.
[34] RGS/LMS/P22, 'Account of travel', by Pfeil.
[35] Pfeil, 'Die Erforschung', 360.

small and few, but he rightly presumed that its innumerable secondary arms received inflows invisible to any traveller on its main channel.

Perennial water sources were highly regarded for their sustenance and agricultural potential, and Pfeil's belief that the Kilombero carried a significant volume of water even in the driest season fed positive perceptions of the region's fertility. This speaks to the fact that the topography of any region has played an instrumental role in the historical dynamics between the natural environment and its human inhabitants for as long as they interacted. In this vein, river systems have – at the very least – impacted societal structures, agricultural systems, development visions, market frameworks, and transport infrastructure.

Rivers are both the means of connectivity and its barrier. In Kilombero, its eponymous river runs as the central stream, bisecting the valley, and virtually impassable in flood. Its waters, above all else, have fundamentally shaped the social, economic, and political landscape of the Kilombero Valley. 'With its swamps, its many arms and broad waters,' wrote Pfeil, 'the Ulanga forms a barrier that cannot be crossed so easily and has therefore become a divide of nations.'[36] This observation on the valley's heterogeneity illustrates the influence of the river in shaping the region's demography. Rivers have the power to connect and divide communities, and this is no more pertinent than in Kilombero.

Further descriptions of the valley as perceived by Pfeil in the late-nineteenth century are significant insofar as they laid foundations upon which Europeans, primarily readerships in Germany and Britain, would base their knowledge of Kilombero. The majority did so only from afar, but subsequent visitors furthered the knowledge obtained from this initial exploration, casting new insights and fresh visions onto the landscape. Pfeil's picture, however, was far from complete. He passed through before the rains and did not see the river in full spate; but 'what a magnificent sight it must be', he wrote, expressing awe at the imagined vision of the river as it 'unites its many arms into a single stream, flooding the entire surface'.[37] Pfeil could only visualise the immense power of the flood, and estimated the width of the river in its middle course as averaging 300 metres. In a moment of comparative abstraction, Pfeil wrote that his travelling companion, 'who knew the Rhine well, claimed that it never reached the average size of the Ulanga'.[38]

Such observations marked the beginning of German knowledge of the valley, but the area was yet to play a significant role in the development of

[36] Ibid.
[37] Ibid., 358.
[38] Ibid., 359.

German activities. This was partly due to the limited capacity of the DOAG, minimal support from the Reichstag, and that focus was initially on the coast, where the implementation of formal administration was attempted in 1888 and violently resisted. The extent of this fighting led to a government-dispatched military force to quell the uprising and assume administrative responsibilities over the territory. This then marked the beginning of colonial conquest proper as authority began to extend into the interior, while resistance continued as German rule spread unevenly in a bloody and hostile fashion.

Particularly fierce opposition was met in the highland area of Uhehe, which became coveted by the DOAG and lay 'between the Great Ruaha and Kilombero rivers, in the Usungwa mountains and the plateaux which lie in the northern part of the area known as the Southern Highlands'.[39] Uhehe was earmarked for settlement and agricultural development for its cool, healthy air and fertile soils. This and other highland areas such as Usambara, Kilimanjaro, and Meru became valorised and formed part of the German imagination of an 'African Switzerland'.[40] Attempts to secure hegemony here were understandably met by force. The ensuing conflict with the Hehe – rallied under the leadership of Mkwawa – became a significant thorn in the side of German imperial expansion. It was written in 1897 that 'no piece of German East Africa has been fought for so long and so violently, no part of the colony has cost so much blood'.[41]

The proximity of Kilombero to Uhehe saw the valley play a crucial role in the conflict. The Mahenge district served as the German base of operations between 1894 and 1898, during which time the valley was heavily relied upon for food by German forces and their allies, but also by Mkwawa's forces, and by populations dislocated by the fighting.[42] This placed a strain on agricultural production as the valley became a resource to exploit, but not develop.

Military might and punitive acts marred this period. At the beginning of German military advancement into Mahenge, Mbunga villages in the lower Kilombero Valley were destroyed in retaliation for raiding activities along the Rufiji corridor to the coast. This stretch was subsequently 'plugged' by two military posts founded in 1894, the western post being the Ulanga Station – or *Boma ya*

---

[39] Alison Redmayne, 'Mkwawa and the Hehe wars', *The Journal of African History* 9:3 (1968), 409.

[40] See Christopher Conte, 'Imperial science, tropical ecology, and indigenous history: Tropical research stations in northeastern German East Africa, 1896 to the present', in Gregory Blue, Martin Bunton, and Ralph Croizier (eds), *Colonialism and the Modern World: Selected Studies* (Armonk, 2002), 246–61.

[41] 'Nachrichten aus den deutschen Schutzgebieten: Deutsch-Ostafrika', *Deutsches Kolonialblatt: Amtsblatt für die Schutzgebiete des Deutschen Reichs* 8:21 (1897), 653.

[42] See Lorne Larson, 'A History of the Mahenge (Ulanga) District, c. 1860–1957' (PhD thesis, University of Dar es Salaam, 1976), 56–9.

Ulanga – on the eastern reaches of the Kilombero River.[43] This positioning was also intended to forge strategic political and economic relationships.

At this time, references to Kilombero are *only* found embedded in material on Uhehe and the Hehe wars, subsuming the valley into Hehe narratives of the period. One issue of *Deutsches Kolonialblatt* from October 1897 delineated five zones in Uhehe, the first being the 'tropical lowlands' of the 'northern part of the Ulanga river basin [...] between the left Ulanga bank and the edge of the high plateau'.[44] The agricultural richness of this area is lamented due to its perceived unsuitability for European settlement. Its climate was 'hot and humid' and 'from these three factors: the water, the warmth and the soil, the whole zone is enormously fertile for tropical cultures, but it is also rich in malaria and therefore unhealthy for the European'.[45] This fertility saw 'sorghum, corn, sugar cane, sweet potatoes and especially rice flourish wonderfully and provide abundant harvests'.[46]

From this same account also emerges an early example of the disparaging trope of the 'lazy native' in Kilombero. This would persist well into the second half of the twentieth century. The population was said to be 'limp due to the climate, sluggish due to the fertile soil and the convenient water transport'.[47] This racist and derogatory suggestion that greater worth is earned through the hard work required in less fertile areas is clearly senseless, but it proved a persistent notion in colonial thinking.

Several other expeditions throughout the 1890s provide further sources on Kilombero history, such as that led by Hans von Ramsay to Lake Nyasa in 1893–4 conducted under Governor Freiherr von Schele. Ramsay cut a line south of the Kilombero River, parallel to its right bank and along the mountain ridges of the Mahenge massif, before passing through lowland Ubene. The resulting map of the route was drawn up by Dr Richard Kiepert, who included metadata such as wildlife and settlement. One place, for example, is annotated as being 'very rich in game: buffalo, zebra, different species of antelopes' while around Kiberege there are 'very extensive plantings and settlements'.[48] Kiepert's cartography took into account routes taken by previous British explorers such as Thomson and Elton, Richard Burton and John Speke, and the French explorer Victor Giraud. Descriptions of their journeys were cross-referenced and tested for their reliability. As German colonists retraced routes under their own flag and covered new ground, they calculated their own distances

---

[43] *Boma* in this context refers to a colonial government station or (sometimes fortified) administration building(s).

[44] 'Nachrichten', *Deutsches Kolonialblatt*, 653.

[45] Ibid., 654.

[46] Ibid.

[47] Ibid.

[48] Bibliothèque nationale de France (BnF), IFN-53029138, 'Karte der Nyasa-Expedition des Gouverneurs Oberstenn Freiherrn von Schele' (Berlin, 1894).

and altitudes, curving their own contour lines upon their own maps. Kiepert considered Thomson's mapping of the route he and Keith Johnston began from Dar es Salaam in 1897 to be 'extremely meagre [...] like all Thomson's map attempts'.[49] As this route was 'covered and recorded anew' by Ramsay, Kiepert wrote that 'this Thomson's route will soon disappear from the map'.[50] Knowledge overwrote knowledge through new lines drawn on fresh maps.

Georg Lieder also wrote an account of this Nyasa expedition, which he joined from November 1893 to March 1894. Lieder mentions the great 'alluvial formations' of the 'Rufiyi and Ulanga lowlands' that 'must naturally attract attention' and 'are characterised by great fertility; the cultivation of both is highly developable, both quantitatively and qualitatively. In both lowlands there are other stretches of land with the best soil and completely uncultivated'.[51] He noted that the 'Ulanga lowlands' were relatively densely populated, and in which the Mafiti population took great care in farming. Lieder saw that 'the cultivation of the fields [was] done with great skill' and with 'careful observation of the local conditions [...] every [local] grain is cultivated, but [...] special emphasis is placed on the cultivation of rice'.[52] There is also mention of wild rubber extraction in Mahenge and that each year a plenitude of people from the coast journey to the area to trade, but also to extract the valued product themselves. During 1900–5 there were said to be approximately 700 rubber traders in Mahenge district, mostly from Kilwa.[53] 'But to make these rich areas useful for the coast', Lieder speculated, 'the first requirement is to establish a good connection with the coast, so that the surplus agricultural production can reach the coast cheaply.'[54] Three years later two surveys attempted to do just that.

In late 1897, Chief Officer Philipp Engelhardt and Captain Georg von Prittwitz und Gaffron were commissioned by Governor Eduard von Liebert to explore the river system of the 'Ulanga Plain'. The primary objective of the survey was to firmly establish whether the rivers provided a navigable waterway for flat, stern-wheeled steamboats from the coast to the Uhehe (Southern) Highlands, now that the area had been 'won' and could be settled

---

[49] Richard Kiepert, 'Begleitworte zur Karte der Nyasa-Expedition', *Mittheilungen von Forschungsreisenden und Gelehrten aus den Deutschen Schutzgebieten: VII* (Berlin, 1894), 302.

[50] Ibid.

[51] Georg Lieder, 'Beobachtungen auf der Ubena-Nyasa Expedition vom 11 November 1893 bis 30 Marz 1894', *Mittheilungen von Forschungsreisenden und Gelehrten aus den Deutschen Schutzgebieten: VII* (Berlin, 1894), 271.

[52] Ibid., 272.

[53] BArch, R1001/278/66–84, Fonck, 'Bericht', 1908.

[54] Lieder, 'Beobachtungen', 272.

and developed. Liebert had travelled to Uhehe in the summer of 1897 and thought the plateau healthy, fertile, and suitable for European settlement *if* an adequate and inexpensive route to the coast could be established. Engelhardt was commissioned to investigate the western part of the river system of the Ulanga lowlands, while Prittwitz was instructed to survey the smaller, eastern part. These were not the first accounts of the area since Pfeil, but they were the first technical surveys to focus specifically on the Kilombero River and its tributaries.

It was already held that the Rufiji River could, for the most part, be utilised as a shipping route to and from the coast, but a route through to the Kilombero was deemed impossible due to obstructing cataracts. These were the Pangani Rapids (or Falls), approximately 140 kilometres from the coast, and the Shughuli Falls found on the Rufiji at the confluence of the Kilombero and Luwegu. Some 100 kilometres further inland at Ngahoma's village – considered 'the entrance to the Great Ulanga Lowlands' – the Kilombero was again navigable. This had been established before 1897, by German officers of the Ulanga Station: Captain von Kleist and Medical Officer Arning.[55] Prittwitz was thus directed to investigate the Kihansi River to its confluence with the Kilombero, and the Kilombero to Ngahoma's village. Low water levels on the Kihansi were desired to ease navigation, but these also caused hippopotami to group together at certain points. At best these beasts blocked the way, at worst they would attack and even overturn passing boats. But further reasons rendered the Kihansi impassable by the envisaged steamships, whether due to its narrow widths, strong currents, thick reed grass, or short and sharp bends.[56]

The Kilombero, on the contrary, was thought smooth. Prittwitz recorded comfortable widths ranging of 40–110 metres. The Royal Geographical Society reported that the survey had found that the Kihansi and Ruipa Rivers were 'useless as waterways, but that the Ulanga can, in the section surveyed, be everywhere navigable by a light-draught steamer, even at low water, and will afford an easy means of communication towards from Ngahoma, above the Pangani falls'.[57]

Prittwitz concluded that the shortest and least demanding route from the coast to the Uhehe Highlands was possible, albeit in four sections. First, Rufiji River navigation from its mouth to the Pangani Falls. Then overland for 100

---

[55] Philipp Engelhardt, 'Meine reise durch Uhehe, die Ulanganiederung und Ubena über das Livingstone-Gebirge zum Nyassa,' *Beiträge zur Kolonialpolitik und Kolonialwirtschaft, Dritter Jahrgang, 1901–1902* (Berlin, 1903), 70.

[56] Georg von Prittwitz und Gaffron, 'Untersuchung der Schiffbarkeit des Kihansi und eines Theiles des Ulangaflusses', *Mittheilungen von Forschungsreisenden und Gelehrten aus den Deutschen Schutzgebieten*, 11 (Berlin, 1898), 266.

[57] 'The Monthly Record', *The Geographical Journal* 14:6 (1899), 660–1.

kilometres to Ngahoma's village before transhipment to a second steamship placed on the Kilombero River. Finally, from a point below the confluence with the Ruipa, another overland journey over three days and assisted by ox or donkey carts would reach Uhehe via Dwangire Station.[58] Such a convoluted and prolonged journey was certainly possible, but highly impractical. Nevertheless, the valley was confirmed as a hypothetical connection with the coast and thus a 'waterway would be opened in the middle of the colony' to bring 'the landscapes of the upper Ulanga, [...] the mountainous areas south of Uhehe, and the German part of the Nyassa region much closer to the traffic with Dar-es-Salaam'.[59]

There is reason to assume that the detailed map showing Prittwitz's route and produced by Kiepert is largely accurate. Alongside the numerous named tributaries, the map marks villages, military posts, waterfalls, river islands, sandbanks, and even single Borassus palm trees. The presence of countless water birds is noted, including pelican flocks, ibis, and purple herons. Rice fields are recorded in large numbers close to the rivers. This was not the first map to show the valley, but it was the most detailed to date. Prittwitz took great pains to record his bearings with precision, retracing his river routes by foot from adjacent banks, and returning to specific places to be certain of accuracy. But despite noting expansive and numerous rice fields, he did not comment on the region's future potential for anything other than part of a transport network.

Engelhardt's expedition began one year later, in September 1898. In 1893, he had become an officer of the Imperial Protection Force for DOA, after which he was involved in suppressing resistance and rebellion to German colonial encroachments; first led by Bwana Heri on the coast in 1894, and subsequently Chief Mkwawa in Uhehe in 1898.[60] Engelhardt had also 'forced the recalcitrant Wagwangara to obedience and established the Songea station' in 1897, and 'thus opened up the fertile and populous south-western part of the protected area, which had been closed until then to trade and traffic'.[61] It was with the same imperious attitude and imperial objectives that Engelhardt sought to further Germany's knowledge of Ulanga. 'The exploitation of our large East African colony', he wrote, 'is made extremely difficult by the lack of transport routes.'[62]

[58] Prittwitz, 'Unterschung', 281–2.
[59] Ibid.
[60] For a concise history of German conquest and coastal resistance, see Iliffe, *Modern History*, 88–97. For the Hehe wars, see Alison Redmayne, 'Mkwawa and the Hehe Wars', *The Journal of African History* 9:3 (1968), 409–36.
[61] Engelhardt, 'Meine reise', 69.
[62] Ibid.

Engelhardt's caravan reached the *boma* of German ally, 'Sultan' Kiwanga, in the upper, south-western reaches of the valley on 17 October 1898. He then began to explore the 'Great Ulanga Plain' from the Mpanga River in the only vessel he could acquire: a dugout canoe measuring ten metres long yet barely forty centimetres wide. By his own account, the trip was torture. Exposed to the scorching Kilombero sun for up to ten hours each day, he dared not move from his uncomfortable position and risk capsizing. Hippopotami frequently blocked the way and twice attacked the canoe, each time deterred only by rifle shots. Engelhardt could only sit on a box, 'constantly observing, measuring, writing, and sweating'.[63]

One observation made may well serve as the original statement – indeed, *overstatement* – on the agricultural potential of the valley as penned by a European hand. Engelhardt wrote that the primary and secondary crops were rice and maize respectively, and that 'under full and proper exploitation of the fertile lowlands, it alone could supply the entire protected area with grain'.[64] This is a crucial comment for its role in forming the original story of Kilombero as a breadbasket. This image is then perpetuated, rightly or wrongly, for over a century.

For Engelhardt, the 'Ulanga Plain' itself was also 'not a pleasant place to stay for Europeans' with its 'flocks of mosquitos' and 'unnerving sultriness' of the 'annually flooded and [...] slowly drying lowland' which brought 'heavy malaria illnesses'.[65] Testament to this was the fact that the Ulanga Station, having been founded in 1894 in a favourable political and economic position, was abandoned after the successive deaths of every officer and non-commissioned officer stationed there. Moreover, at the turn of the twentieth century the Berliner Mission and Benedictines of the Southern Highlands had considered Kilombero too unhealthy for missionary work and neither cared to settle the question of under whose jurisdiction it lay.[66]

Mahenge and Maji Maji

By the early 1900s, German rule was but a bloody legacy stemmed from suppressed challenges to its violent hegemony. This rule was again vehemently challenged in 1905 with the beginning of the Maji Maji Rebellion, which saw the *Mahenge Militärbezirk* – incorporating the Kilombero Valley – as a significant area of conflict. The military station at Mahenge was one of the four most powerful in the colony alongside Kilosa, Iringa, and Songea. Several key moments in the conflict occurred in the region, the most notable of which was

---

[63] Ibid., 79.
[64] Ibid., 82.
[65] Ibid., 83.
[66] Larson, 'History', 169.

the attempt by Mbunga and Pogoro forces to capture the *boma* at Mahenge. This has been described as the greatest single action of the rebellion, and its failure on 30 August 1905 is also considered a turning point in its defeat. The ultimate suppression of this resistance would mark a significant shift in administrative approaches to the colony.[67]

The resistance to colonial rule in Kilombero was manifestly fierce. The rush on Mahenge was preceded by an attack on a DOAG caravan between Ifakara and Mahenge, while Ifakara itself was left burning after scenes of bloody fighting.[68] At one *askari*[69] post in Ifakara the severed head of a guard was placed atop the pole from which the German flag had flown; and at the Ruipa River the 'greatest pitched battle of the war' took place in November 1905.[70]

In the theatre of war, the natural geography of the landscape sets the stage. Depending on the circumstances, seasonal variations in the Kilombero Valley and the flood levels of its rivers can be used to the benefit and detriment of warring parties. In guerrilla warfare tactics, such as those used against German forces, the natural environment is weaponised. Local knowledge of landscapes can facilitate mobilisation, movement, and concealment. Forests become places of hiding and refuge. Familiarity with complex river systems can be utilised to evade capture or mount attacks. Boats used for ferry crossings at established points were often hidden, preventing appropriation by German forces to ensure continued control over their use; whereas ferry boats at the river crossing south of Ifakara were destroyed, which effectively frustrated troops under Captain Nigmann from reaching Mahenge.[71] The rushing Kilombero River, in spate at this point with a width exceeding 200 metres, posed a great natural barrier too dangerous to cross with hastily built rafts. The potential for loss of life or supplies was not worth the risk. Great detours were necessary if the river was to be crossed at all, while in the meantime each side was critically cut off from the other. These acts did not alter the outcome of the rebellion, but they do contribute examples of how the impassability of the river possesses a form of latent agency within an overarching narrative of its influence on human actions in the valley. By this very token the river itself is expressly non-partisan, as the riverscape restricted the movement of German forces so

---

[67] G.C.K. Gwassa and John Iliffe (eds), 'Records of the Maji Maji Rising: Part One', *Historical Association of Tanzania*, Paper No. 4 (Nairobi, 1967), 20.

[68] James L. Giblin and Jamie Monson, 'Introduction' in James L. Giblin and Jamie Monson (eds), *Maji Maji: Lifting the Fog of War* (Leiden, 2010), 6.

[69] *Askari* (often pluralised in anglicised usage as *askaris*) were African men recruited into European colonial forces as soldiers or guards in military and police units.

[70] Götzen, *Deutsch-Ostafrika*, 114; Iliffe, *Modern History*, 197.

[71] Götzen, *Deutsch-Ostafrika*, 114.

did flood damage contribute to famine suffered by rebels. The duality of the river therefore presents as a truly reckonable force.

The effects of the Maji Maji Rebellion on the developmental history of Kilombero can be distilled to three residual impacts. First, for the people of the Kilombero Valley the fighting scarred their communities and landscape. The 'scorched earth' policies of the Germans destroyed harvests, pushing submission through starvation, while this was further exacerbated by disrupted agricultural schedules and flood damage. Entire villages were abandoned or disappeared, their inhabitants either dispersed or killed. This was particularly true in the eastern reaches of the valley. The second impact was that the rebellion became a 'stimulus for change' that marked a turning point in occupation policy for the government and administration of DOA.[72] The future of the colony had to be urgently addressed and decisions on approaches to economic development had to be made. No matter how rhetorical this ultimately proved, the result was a reconstruction and reconfiguring towards an 'enlightened economic imperialism' that shifted the 'developmental' philosophy towards 'an economic policy which tangibly benefit[ed] the subject peoples'.[73] Lastly, military efforts in the Kilombero valley region catalysed a steep learning curve for German understandings of the landscape. The true nature and full extent of the difficulties the environment posed, the importance of controlling water transport, the immense power and influence of the river, and the effect of rainfall and flooding on sickness and health. Kilombero proved notoriously difficult terrain for military operations.[74] In 'peacetime', this same terrain would frustrate efforts to establish the efficient transport networks required to progress economic development.

Towards 'enlightened economic imperialism'

Economic policies before 1905 were generally trained towards exploitation by a skeleton administration. A defining tenet in the programme of reform envisaged from 1907 was that 'German East Africa should be a country whose economy was based on African agriculture.'[75] Iliffe asserts, however, that 'Germany's African empire did not last long enough for an administrative theory to gain acceptance' and that a 'coherent policy' was only formulated shortly before 1914 when the outbreak of the First World War effectively

---

[72] John Iliffe, 'The effects of the Maji Maji Rebellion of 1905–06 on German occupation policy in East Africa', in Gifford and Louis, *Britain and Germany in Africa*, 574.
[73] Iliffe, *Tanganyika*, 54.
[74] Iliffe, *Modern History*, 244.
[75] Iliffe, *Tanganyika*, 7.

guillotined the full realisation of visions, plans, and further development.[76] Trade and economic activity did not, of course, begin and end with German rule, nor was every transaction and exchange controlled by the administration. Nevertheless, no other force or factor had as much of an exerting influence on the overall economy and individuals' lives.

The significant imposition of taxation in 1898 marked a departure from the previous aims of the decades, which were ostensibly military security and political control. Iliffe calls this the 'second phase' of the administration. The value of local compromises established in the 1890s depreciated as military security strengthened and, as administrative costs threatened to exceed government revenue, tax was considered a necessary measure. The creation of '*sultanates*' and '*jumbeates*'[77] consolidated systems of order and tax collection. In Kilombero, the continued German alliance with the Bena reinforced the latter's authority and control.[78]

The *Mahenge Militärbezirk* was an important and strategic district, but a remote one. It did not fall along the central trade route along which many sisal plantations were established and the central railway would be constructed, later fortified as a military belt. Neither highland Mahenge nor lowland Ifakara were on par with Bagamoyo, Tabora, or Lindi; and nor was the wider region equivalent in value and importance to others such as Usambara, Kilimanjaro, or Meru. These areas – around which trade, German settlement, or plantation efforts were focused – were given precedence. The higher altitude of Mahenge certainly made for a more pleasant climate for those stationed there, but it fell very short of the 'African Switzerland' of the German colonial imagination. The adjacent Southern Highlands resembled this vision more closely, but their settlement continued to be stifled by a lack of supporting transport infrastructure. The possible utilisation of the Kilombero valley river system to reach these highlands from the coast was still too tantalising to discard, despite the far-fetched conclusions drawn by Prittwitz. For this and other possibilities, further detailed and technical reconnaissance expeditions were subsequently commissioned.

---

[76] Iliffe, 'Effects', 557.

[77] *Sultanates* and *jumbeates* were scaled administrative areas first created by the German colonial government to 'order' societies. They were perpetuated by the British within the structure of 'native authorities' for political expediency, judicial administration, and to facilitate tax collection. While *sultanates* became chieftancies (or chiefdoms) under the British, the *jumbeate* remained the smallest administrative unit, overseen by a *jumbe* and equivalent to a village headman.

[78] Jamie Monson, 'Memory, migration and the authority of history in southern Tanzania, 1860–1960' *The Journal of African History* 41:3 (2000), 353.

Trade and economic activity were not historically absent from the Kilombero valley region by any means. Before the imposition of German rule, caravans came to the region in droves for products aplenty. As these were namely ivory, slaves, and rice, the nature of trade had adapted first to the abolition of slavery, and then to changes brought by depleting elephant numbers and German game laws that restricted local hunting rights. Rice maintained its importance, but tax brought new pressures on economic activities whether through production or extraction. In the Kilombero valley region, tax payments were met primarily by three means: the sale of rice, wage labour migration, and rubber collection.[79]

The densely wooded highlands straddling the Kilombero were one of the main sources of rubber in DOA. Its prominence was historically short but impactful, rising in volume and value from 1890 to a boom in 1910–12, followed by a hard bust in 1913 that effectively 'destroyed the original economic plan of the territory'.[80] Rubber extraction thus continued to the 'second phase' of administration and co-existed alongside an emerging emphasis on the production and export of traditional crops such as rice, in contrast to the prior inducement to cultivate certain cash crops such as cotton. This reflects the complex process inherent in ever-transforming economic and political systems, and shows that while Maji Maji represented a significant rupture, continuities prevailed as long as there were profits to be made and administration to finance. Crucially, the resulting reconstruction scheme was borne from the belief held by Governor Albrecht von Rechenberg that the cotton scheme imposed by his predecessor, Gustav von Götzen, was the primary cause of the uprising.[81] Prevention of further rebellion was crucial, and to this end Rechenberg believed that improving the general standards of living played a vital role. Rubber extraction was not viewed as equivalent to cotton growing, even if coercion of one kind or another was still embroiled in the manner of its collection. The important point is that rubber kept the Kilombero valley region on the map, strengthening trade connections with the coast, merchant presence in the region, and furthering the region's development from outpost to asset.

After all, this was a region with real and perceived fertility, far-reaching if variegated cultivation, and ideas exploring potential for agricultural

---

[79] Jamie Monson, 'From commerce to colonization: A history of the rubber trade in the Kilombero Valley of Tanzania, 1890–1914', *African Economic History* 21 (1993), 120.

[80] Margaret L. Bates, 'Tanganyika: The development of a trust territory', *International Organization* 9:1 (1955), 33.

[81] For an overview of the history of cotton in DOA, see Thaddeus Sunseri, 'The *Baumwollfrage*: Cotton colonialism in German East Africa', *Central European History* 34:1 (2001), 31–51.

development were beginning to form. In his 1909 account of Maji Maji, Götzen echoed Pfeil in believing that Kilombero could provide rice for the entire colony and considered the rice yields of the 'fertile Ulanga Plain' to be 'endlessly expandable'.[82] This followed a focus on the region as providing food – and, to a lesser extent, labour – to emerging sisal and rubber plantations elsewhere. Moreover, suppression of the rebellion had led to widespread famine, and the stimulation of agriculture with a particular focus on areas with the potential for high yields and diverse productivity became vitally important. Construction of the central railway saw rice exports from the valley increase sharply, and the railhead at Kilosa brought markets somewhat closer, but this was still a remote area with a skeletal transport infrastructure of its own. The practical requirements of fulfilling the new developmental philosophies of this period were predicated on effective transport above perhaps anything else. On this there are two principal issues that preoccupied both the German and British periods of administration. First, the prevailing belief was that, to develop agricultural production, facilities must first be developed. The opposite was also thought, and this was as true for Kilombero as it was anywhere else. But the form and scale of transport infrastructure depended on perceived levels of production, and therefore it was important to ascertain expected levels of return on the capital investment required. Railways were generally accepted as being key to economic progress, but they were by no means cheap to build or run. The second and connected consideration is whether there was a level of natural production that warranted capital investment in an extensive transport infrastructure; or rather, was there a potential for future production that would only be realised if this were first provided?

In the years before the First World War, the question of the navigability of the Kilombero River and wider Kilombero–Rufiji network was revisited together with possible railway routes, and no less than four technical surveys were conducted during 1904–11. The colony's development was progressing at an ever-increasing pace due to those railways and roads that had been constructed. Rechenberg then commissioned the 'Rufiyi-Ulanga' expedition of 1907, and an account published in 1908 by Heinrich Fonck stressed the 'constant need to look again and again for ways of supporting and accelerating [...] development'.[83] Emphasis was placed on regions whose production could reduce imports of foodstuffs 'such as rice from India in particular, first for the indigenous population of the colony and later, if possible, for the homeland'.[84] At this time, DOA imported approximately 2 million rupees' worth of Indian

---

[82] Götzen, *Deutsch-Ostafrika*, 104.
[83] BArch, R1001/278/66–84, Fonck, 'Bericht', 1908.
[84] Ibid.

rice every year, while Germany itself imported rice from British India to the annual tune of 40 million marks. Perhaps the Rufiji and Kilombero valleys could solve this problem.

That the Kilombero Valley had not yet been developed along lines of intensive cultivation seemed primarily due to the Rufiji River not proving continuously navigable through to the Kilombero. Fonck cited Dr Arning – the former officer of Ulanga Station – who saw in the plain 'the future larder of the colony' and, to Fonck, 'the Ulanga Plain promises more!'[85] He calculated that it was possible to increase current rice production fifty-fold for a total of 25,000 tonnes.[86] This would be done by harnessing the water and controlling the flood. Planned water management involving reservoirs and artificial irrigatioin through river draining, pumping, and water lifting systems were envisaged. 'Such a system,' Fonck wrote, 'would hardly be able to find a more grateful field in the colony as here in Ulanga.'[87] But his technical expertise was highly limited and he had little idea how to design such a system. Fonck hoped experts would implement what he imagined would be a simple undertaking. He envisaged that steam ploughs – the pinnacle of technical modernity at the time – would cultivate the plain itself and form a part of this European-led large-scale enterprise. Beyond the plain, Fonck believed further areas of rice cultivation and additional crops such as cotton, maize, sugar cane, bananas, sorghum, sesame, and sweet potatoes would also be expanded. Steamship traffic on the Kilombero River would be as blood through an artery, bringing life and growth to dormant regions.

It was thought this proposed connection with the coast would also draw neighbouring areas into an emerging economic sphere. The role and position of Kilombero continued to be considered within broader interregional contexts, particularly in relation to the 'opening up' of the south-west of the colony, but no significant transport schemes had been implemented by the onset of war. Nevertheless, Ifakara and Mahenge had already been developing as significant entrepôts since the late-nineteenth century, assisted principally by Indian merchants who had trickled into the valley. Now that the nearest railhead – Kilosa on the Central Line – was a mere 185 kilometres from Ifakara, the economic possibilities of the valley began to attract European settlement, including retired German military officers set on establishing plantations. One Hamburg firm – the 'Ulanga

---

[85] Ibid.
[86] Fonck gives the figure of current production as 1,000,000 *centner* and potential production as 50 x 100,000 *centner*, or 5 million *centner*. One German *centner* is equivalent to 50 kilograms, thus 25 million kilograms or 25,000 metric tonnes.
[87] BArch, R1001/278/66–84, Fonck, 'Bericht', 1908.

Reis- und Handelsgesellschaft' – was established in Ifakara and whose aim was 'to buy, mill and sell large quantities of rice, later branching into retail trade, cotton ginning and rubber cultivation'.[88] This company anticipated extraordinary opportunities presented by the possible construction of a railway from Dar es Salaam to Lake Nyasa, and arguably not without reason. A survey of rice production in the valley area published in 1908 estimated a district yield of 3,750 metric tonnes for the main harvest with a second harvest of approximately half the main, and identified twenty-eight varieties of rice, each adapted to specific soils, sites, and seasons.[89] Fonck wryly stated that 'even if Ifakara, like the whole Ulanga Plain, cannot be considered a sanatorium, this will not be an obstacle for European enterprises and settlements, because if you want to earn money, you'll also go where it's unhealthy'.[90]

Figurative and literal inroads to Kilombero were being built as a result of the repositioning of German policy in this period of 'progress and prosperity' and 'enlightened economic imperialism' as the valley was beginning to be seen through different eyes. Possibilities for investment were envisaged. Fresh visions recast the valley within the ever-increasing levels of interconnectivity between different regions. The outbreak of war irretrievably halted this particular trajectory in German hands, disrupting whatever momentum was building, and this not long since Maji Maji had previously upset earlier German trajectories in the colony. By 1914 the valley had been reframed numerous times, and its positioning as a promising area for development had begun to take shape and take hold. Early murmurings of its agricultural potential were being converted into real enterprise and the framework for a growing economy was being laid down. But this chapter of history – for Germany, for German East Africa, and for Kilombero – ends in 1914 with the declaration of war as conflict begins to ravage the region once more.

---

[88] Larson, 'History', 140.

[89] K. Braun, 'Der Reis in Deutsch-Ostafrika', Berichte über land- und forstwirtschaft in Deutsch-Ostafrika 3:4 (1908), 204–206.

[90] BArch, R1001/278/66–84, Fonck, 'Bericht' 1908.

2
Visions under Mandate: Divergent Views, 1914–32

At the outbreak of war only Mahenge and Iringa districts remained under German military administration, and orders to mobilise were received by the 12th Field Company at Mahenge town on 7 August 1914.[1] Lorne Larson wrote how 'the people of the Mahenge district were to be deeply enmeshed into the machinery of war' from its early days, as intense exploitation of agricultural resources risked severe local famine.[2] Labour was also extracted by German forces from a 'defenceless and unregarded population'.[3] By October 1916, following a German retreat to Mahenge, General Smuts wrote that 'with the exception of the Mahenge plateau [the Germans] have lost every healthy or valuable part of their Colony'.[4] Moreover, as German forces later withdrew from Mahenge they further destroyed crops and storage depots in an attempt to stymie Belgian pursuit.[5] Ecological destruction was caused by the seizure of food and people and the abandonment of villages; moreover, the devastation wreaked over the landscape cannot be underestimated. The famine and depopulation caused by Maji Maji was repeated by further conflict, inflicted onto a region that was far from recovered.

Belgian forces occupied Mahenge on 9 October 1917. It was one of the last garrisons under German control, lost following the 'Mahenge Offensive' after 'an advance through difficult country and in the face of strong opposition from the Ulanga (or Kilombero) River'.[6] Rains then rendered the road to Kilosa impassable, momentarily isolating the area from allied support, and only those soldiers that could be sustained by existing supplies remained.[7] The 'Mahenge region had been stripped bare by the Germans, and consequently

---

[1] For the First World War in Mahenge, see Larson, 'History', 209–17; and Monson, 'Agricultural Transformation', 285–90. For a history of the conflict on the continent, see Edward Paice, *Tip and Run: The Untold Tragedy of the Great War in Africa* (London, 2007).
[2] Larson, 'History', 210–211.
[3] Iliffe, *Modern History*, 246.
[4] Quoted in TNA MF.17, Mahenge District Book: Vol. I, 'The War, 1914–18', n.d.
[5] Larson, 'History', 217.
[6] 'Mahenge Occupied by Belgians', *The Times*, 11 October 1917.
[7] Hew Strachan, *The First World War. Volume 1: To Arms* (Oxford, 2001), 634.

the Belgians could not live off the land' as they had done elsewhere.[8] But while Captain Theodor Tafel had retreated from Mahenge, war dragged on elsewhere. Lettow-Vorbeck's formal surrender two weeks *after* Armistice was signed meant that, ultimately, 'the German Forces were never overcome'.[9]

Discussions at the Paris Peace Conference of 1919 resolved that German colonies 'would not become the possession of the conquerors, but be administered under mandates associated with the League of Nations'.[10] The Peace Treaty with Germany was then ratified on 10 January 1920, and the official Mandate confirmed in July 1922.[11] The true meaning of the mandated status of the territory now known as Tanganyika was a source of great confusion and consequence. Its integration into the British Empire – if it would be at all – was questioned from the outset. If sovereignty lay under the League of Nations, then this, together with policy restrictions, meant Tanganyika was neither colony nor protectorate, at least not on paper. Autonomy would thus be channelled through an entirely new category, bringing novel complexities and concerns for British administration. Despite the articulation of the role and responsibilities of the Council of the League of Nations across twenty-six Articles, and a further thirteen Articles specific to the British Mandate for East Africa, these all remained open to interpretation. Moreover, doubts over the Mandate's permanence bred further insecurities. It was remarked that 'a mandated country might aptly be described as Nomansland' and that there was an 'atmosphere of uncertainty about the future' due to 'the widespread view that somehow the British Government was only a tenant of the League of Nations, liable to possible eviction'.[12] One of the principal responsibilities now granted to Britain was outlined in Article 3 of the Mandate, that:

> The Mandatory shall be responsible for the peace, order and good government of the territory, and shall undertake to promote to the utmost the material and moral well-being and the social progress of its inhabitants. The Mandatory shall have full powers of legislation and administration.[13]

---

[8] Ibid., 634–5.

[9] Zoë Marsh, *East Africa through Contemporary Records* (London, 1961), 193–6.

[10] Judith Listowel, *The Making of Tanganyika* (London, 1965), 66.

[11] Michael D. Callahan, 'NOMANSLAND: The British Colonial Office and the League of Nations Mandate for German East Africa, 1916–1920', *Albion: A Quarterly Journal Concerned with British Studies* 25:3 (1993), 461.

[12] Ibid., 454; L.S. Amery, *My Political Life. Volume One: War and Peace, 1914–1929* (London, 1955), 180.

[13] League of Nations, 'British Mandate for East Africa.'

Emphasis on promoting 'to the utmost the material and moral well-being and the social progress of its inhabitants' became a critical clause, not least for divergences in interpretation. This pledge brought fresh focus on the morality of established practices of colonial resource extraction, land appropriation, and labour exploitation. One crux of contention rested on the extent to which authority could impede on 'the liberty of the subject' in order to achieve this 'progress' in Tanganyika. Paternalism was also codified, expressed through Article 22 of the Covenant of the League of Nations, which decreed that mandated territories were 'inhabited by peoples not yet able to stand by themselves under the strenuous conditions of the modern world' and 'the well-being and development of such peoples [would] form a sacred trust of civilisation'.[14]

The road ahead was long. War had devastated land and societies, systems and structures. There were 'enormous difficulties to make do with the remnants of the German system' and Britain effectively 'had to start from scratch'.[15] This was not to be a 'typical' colony. The emphasis on 'well-being and development' was underscored by clauses to protect local land rights and customs, abolish slavery and forced labour, and limit the terms of land alienation and concessions. In some respects the Mandate made little difference to the governance and perception of Tanganyika, as if it *were* any other British colony. In other respects it made *all* the difference.

The need for structural reform and reconstruction first dictated policy. Future development schemes would not be realised without established political and economic systems. Development along German lines had been proceeding for over twenty years, but much of this now lay, 'so to speak, in mothballs' to borrow the description given to the state of the tropical research station at Amani.[16] Various departments necessary for any functioning governmental apparatus were created anew, staffed to the best of availability but still short, and the entire organisational framework of the administration had to be decided upon and implemented.

Tanganyika was urged to follow an economic policy based largely on local peasant production, rather than one dominated by white settlers.[17] Nigeria was the model for this approach, which followed the sentiment of the Mandate and was in contrast to policies in neighbouring Kenya and Rhodesia. Tanganyika would not become closed to white settlement entirely, but a delicate balance

---

[14] Charlotte Leubuscher, *Tanganyika Territory: A Study of Economic Policy under Mandate* (London, 1944), 195.
[15] Listowel, *Making*, 67–9.
[16] Ibid., 71.
[17] See Coulson, *Tanzania*, 45.

was sought between peasants, settlers, and plantations. Advocates for white settlement campaigned to tip this balance in their favour, but from as early as 1920 it was expressed that 'Tanganyika can never be a white man's country' and 'can never become an outlet for the surplus population of the mother country', while 'the work of the colony will always have to be done by natives, and, since the agricultural resources of the country are very great, its trade might be greatly developed if native labour were properly stimulated and organized by Europeans'.[18] There were therefore key roles envisaged for Europeans, but clear limitations on wholescale settlement.

The post-war reconstruction period concluded in 1925 with the inauguration of Sir Donald Cameron as the second Governor of Tanganyika. The period under the first Governor, Sir Horace Byatt, was a crucial but nervous time, during which the prime drive was towards equilibrium. Then, from a state of relative economic and political stability came renewed capacity for development of all kinds. Inroads towards lasting futures could be built as capital could confidently be directed and supported within an established system. Cameron's dominant legacies are arguably his introduction of 'indirect rule' and the system of 'native administration' in Tanganyika.[19] Broad principles for this were outlined in July 1925 and the creation of a new political geography was an attempt to recreate a system believed to have prevailed before the German period, then destroyed by it. Cameron sought a sense of administrative order as he grappled with the political ramifications of the Mandate and what it meant for policies on economic development, settlement, and the balance of sovereignty between Britain and the League of Nations.

Weeks into the job, Cameron recalls in his memoir a 'matter of importance' in the form of 'a small advance guard of European settlers' from Kenya, who were armed with applications for farming land.[20] They eyed the same Southern Highlands as early German colonialists wished to settle, and to which the Kilombero Valley was envisaged as its link to the coast. Cameron forwarded the applications to the District Officer to report on available land beyond present and future requirements. During a subsequent tour through Iringa he then met with Lord Delamere, who had purchased a farm locally and invested private capital in a venture that he hoped would encourage British settlement to the Southern Highlands.[21] Delamere ultimately received no return

---

[18] G.W. Prothero (ed.), *Tanganyika (German East Africa)* (London, 1920), 105.

[19] On 'indirect rule' in Tanganyika, see Margery Perham, 'Some problems of indirect rule in Africa', *Journal of the Royal Society of Arts* 82:4252 (1934), 689–710; Donald Cameron, 'Native Administration in Tanganyika and Nigeria', *Journal of the Royal African Society* 36:145 (1937), 3–29; Justin Willis, 'The administration of Bonde, 1920–60: A study of the implementation of indirect rule in Tanganyika', *African Affairs* 92:366 (1993), 53–67.

[20] Donald Cameron, *My Tanganyika Service and Some Nigeria* (London, 1939), 37.

[21] Hugh Cholmondeley, third Baron Delamere (1870–1931). Delamere was one of Kenya's earliest and most influential British settlers, farming 150,000 acres by

from these investments, which included a bacon-curing factory. The whole venture proved premature, but when Delamere met with Cameron, he hoped that the Kenyan settlers' applications would proceed. Cameron believed that 'the policy of admitting such settlers [...] would be acceptable in Downing Street, and [he] was therefore considerably disconcerted on arriving back in Dar-es-Salaam [...] to find communications awaiting [him] to the effect that applications for land in the area concerned "should be discouraged"'.[22] This bewildered Cameron, who saw no reason why land should be refused if it were definitely available 'after due consideration of the interests of the African population' and he petitioned for the decision to be reconsidered.[23]

Cameron believed European settlement could be desired 'without depriving the native population of sufficient land for its own use'.[24] He believed that 'the interests of the native should be paramount' and this privileging of paramountcy distinguished Tanganyika from its neighbours, much to the consternation of supporters of European settlement.[25] Stewart Symes – who succeeded Cameron as Governor of Tanganyika (1931–4) – wrote that 'many protagonists of white settlement reacted to the word *paramountcy* like a bull to a red flag and conceived [Cameron] as a toreador behind the flag'.[26] Future visions for land alienation for European settlement and enterprise thus remained greatly debated and hotly contested.

Before the war there were almost 5,000 European settlers in Tanganyika and, while not all were German, one of the first tasks of the Byatt administration was to address prior German settlement and remaining settlers themselves. Policies were adopted to repatriate 'ex-enemy subjects' from Tanganyika and take custody of their property and estates. During the war, while prisoners of war were sent to concentration camps in India and Egypt, 'non-combatants' were allowed to remain on their farms or in towns under supervision until repatriation was possible.[27] The 'Former Enemy Aliens (Repatriation) Proclamation 1920' decreed that any 'former enemy alien' who wished to remain must apply for a permit.[28] Those who did not apply or whose applications were unsuccessful were deported.

1906. See Elspeth Huxley, *White Man's Country: Lord Delamere and the Making of Kenya* (London, 1935), alongside Edward Paice, *Lost Lion of Empire* (London, 2011). In Tanganyika, Delamere's farm was ex-German, acquired from its initial owner at auction from the Custodian of Enemy Property.

[22] Cameron, *Tanganyika Service*, 38.
[23] Ibid., 39.
[24] Harry Gailey, *Sir Donald Cameron: Colonial Governor* (Stanford, 1974), 52.
[25] TNAUK CO 691/83, Cameron to Amery, Confidential dispatch, 25 February 1926 (quoted in Gailey, *Sir Donald*, 52).
[26] Stewart Symes, *Tour of Duty* (London, 1946), 162.
[27] Gerald Sayers (ed.), *The Handbook of Tanganyika* (London, 1930), 96.
[28] 'Proclamation No. 1 of 1920', *Official Gazette of the Occupied Territory of German East Africa* 1:8 (1920), 1.

The first auction of German property was held in May 1921, beginning the process by which over half a million acres of land came under new ownership. Germans granted a permit to remain were not permitted to bid. In 1925, however, restrictions on immigration and land rights were lifted. By the late 1930s there were more German settlers in Tanganyika than British, and Lord Chesham campaigned to redress this imbalance.[29] Chesham had rights of occupancy to 200,000 acres and invited applications from 'suitable' British tenant farmers, producing a 1936 pamphlet that claimed 'the Southern Highlands of Tanganyika offer a decent life coupled with a decent income. No fever. No locusts. No drought and a good market.'[30] Fears that Tanganyika might be ceded to appease Hitler were also addressed in the section, 'The Mandate Question', in which prospective settlers were assured this was 'a scare manufactured by scaremongers, who know nothing of the country, its history, or the origin of the mandate', that it simply would not be allowed and, furthermore, that 'Herr Hitler himself has declared that Tanganyika is not worth to Germany the life of one single German'.[31]

Promotion of white settlement in a mandated territory was contentious, but because of the policy of 'native paramountcy' it was thought that 'the controversy which has elsewhere attended white settlement in South Africa need never be lit here'.[32] A paper written by Clement Gillman in 1938 – titled 'White Colonisation in East Africa with special regard to Tanganyika' – would have supported the scheme. Gillman was commissioned by the Directorate of the International Geographical Congress to submit such an 'unavoidably controversial' paper, which on reflection Gillman did not publish.[33] He did, however, write:

> Much has been argued whether the soil of East Africa can be economically employed by the native direct or by native manpower under European supervision and guidance. For Tanganyika, such argument is purely academic as the established policy safeguards the natives' self-determination.[34]

---

[29] John Compton Cavendish, 4th Baron Chesham (1894–1952).

[30] Tanganyika (Southern Highlands) Estates, Ltd. *Farming in the Southern Highlands* (Amersham, 1936), 1.

[31] Ibid., 5.

[32] 'White Settlement in Tanganyika: New Company's Plans', *The Times*, 15 December 1936.

[33] TNAUK CO 691/167/11, 'White Colonisation in East Africa with special regard to Tanganyika' by C. Gillman, 1938.

[34] Ibid.

This 'established policy' shaped the kind of development that could be envisioned for Tanganyika. This held high relevance to the potentialities of agricultural enterprise and production, and for European settlement. Agricultural development imagined for the pleasant climes of the Southern Highlands was thus centred on farms run by Europeans. This was a vision which contrasted with neighbouring Kilombero, where such a scheme was considered impractical in pestilent valley lowlands, despite supposed fertility and the persistent idea of its perceived potential.

The notion of potential is central to a 1920 text whose title neatly frames the period of transition from a German to British governance: *The Tanganyika Territory (formerly German East Africa: Characteristics and Potentialities)*. 'As a result of the World War this huge undeveloped land has come under our administration', wrote its author, and 'without a doubt its potentialities are marvellous'.[35] Published in the same year, one handbook neatly bridges earlier representations of Kilombero firmly to the British period through its stating that 'the low-lying alluvial plains of the River Ulanga are extremely fertile'.[36]

Publications such as these served as compendiums of the social, political, and economic conditions of Tanganyika, its agricultural products and productive regions, its commercial systems and material development. They recorded the history of German rule, what had been tried and tested, and what might have been attempted had war not intervened. Another publication that contributed to this baseline knowledge was Albert Calvert's *German East Africa*, published in 1917. Its purpose was 'to describe, for the benefit of future British settlers, traders and investors in Germany's East African colony, the nature and resources of the territory that General Smuts and his army are acquiring for the Empire, and the lines upon which the German authorities have developed them, in the past thirty years'.[37] Calvert sustained the impression that the Kilombero River was navigable almost throughout its whole course and wrote of 'isolated plantations' in the 'less accessible districts of Mahenge' and of mica found in the region, highly valued as electrical insulation.[38] But little industry developed from the mica in Mahenge. It was rather the 'extremely fertile' and 'low-lying alluvial plains of the River Ulanga' that piqued British interests as they had their predecessors. Most of the technical data, reports, and maps from German expeditions and surveys were available to the British, but there were gaps. For the material to hand, its usefulness was imperfect.

---

[35] F.S. Joelson, *The Tanganyika Territory (formerly German East Africa): Characteristics and Potentialities* (London, 1920), 7.
[36] Prothero, *Tanganyika*, 3.
[37] Alfred F. Calvert, *German East Africa* (London, 1917), 35, 40.
[38] Ibid., 80–5.

That it was almost entirely written in German was only a minor hindrance. Differences in technologies and technical approaches – coupled with diverging aims and objectives – ensured that the new administration created its own knowledge of Tanganyika from the outset. German material was tested on its own merit and either subsumed or dismissed.

'Shall the area serve a railway?'

In 1924 the East Africa Commission was appointed 'to consider and report on the measures to be taken to accelerate the general economic development of the British East Africa Dependencies' of Northern Rhodesia, Nyasaland, Tanganyika, Uganda, and Kenya.[39] The committee spent two weeks in Tanganyika, declaring that Britain held 'a special responsibility before the world for insuring [its] good government and development' but found 'grave misunderstandings regarding the nature and status of the country as a mandated territory'.[40] This was said to have 'undoubtedly had a prejudicial effect on the investment of capital and the undertaking of commercial enterprise', and other concerns were expressed over the extent to which the League of Nations could interfere, deprive Britain of the Mandate, hinder settlement, or indeed had the 'power of imposing German or other nationality upon British subjects resident in Tanganyika'.[41] The Commission considered the 'all-important question of railways and communications' and, noting prior German plans for routes from Lake Nyasa to a point on the Central Line, stated that 'the whole question of the development of the south-western highlands, as well as the basin of Lake Nyasa, depends on the construction of such a line'.[42] It was recommended this line branched from Ngerengere towards Kidatu on the Great Ruaha River and 'thence the railway should follow the left bank of the Kilombero River and thence by the Pitu Valley'.[43]

The committee did not visit Kilombero itself but drew from various memoranda prepared by heads of department and unofficial associations. They claimed that this proposed railway 'would do more to open up and develop a vast new area of Africa than any other line' and in which 'the Kilombero Valley may be described as a great alluvial plain which could be turned into one of the finest cotton, sugar, and rice producing areas in

---

[39] Great Britain and W.G.A. Ormsby-Gore, *Report of the East Africa Commission* (London, 1925), 3.
[40] Ibid., 113–5.
[41] Ibid., 115.
[42] Ibid., 120.
[43] Ibid., 121.

the world, and which by drainage and irrigation could eventually cover approximately 1,000 square miles'.[44]

Kilombero would connect by rail to Dar es Salaam along a line that also provided 'the cheapest and quickest route and outlet for the northern half of Nyasaland and the eastern parts of northeast Rhodesia'.[45] There was another possible route to Lake Nyasa that passed through the Southern Highlands, which appeared more direct, but was more expensive and more difficult to construct. The Southern Highlands, the Commission suggested, could still be served by a railway that passed through Kilombero as it could be connected 'by means of roads with [the] proposed line at different points in the Kilombero Valley'.[46] This was not viable due to the steepness of the dividing escarpment.

For state visions and imagined futures, the question of a railway through south-western Tanganyika, and its route, is absolutely central to Kilombero history. If the perceived production potential of Kilombero could be fulfilled, it was contingent on efficient transport to markets. In many respects, the history of development in Kilombero is the history of the development of a transport infrastructure, or ultimately its underdevelopment. Such an infrastructure and subsequent access to markets would, it was believed, bring social and economic development to the region. Proposals to build such a line 'led to a long and complex controversy, notable for a welter of conflicting ideas' – and over half a century would pass before a railway came to Kilombero.[47] In 1925, however, the Commission recommended an immediate survey and estimate of the line for its imminent construction.

A central figure on the reconnaissance survey to examine possible railway routes between the Central Line and the northern shore of Lake Nyasa was Clement Gillman, at the time Senior District Engineer of Tanganyika Railways. He was a pivotal figure for Tanganyika, and his work holds particular significance for Kilombero. Born in 1882 to a German mother and English father (but whose parents were Anglo-Swiss), he spent his childhood in Freiburg, Germany then Zurich, Switzerland. He arrived in German East Africa in 1905 as an Assistant Engineer contracted to construction of the Central Line.[48] His continued career in Tanganyika after the war was as an unquestionably unparalleled asset to the British administration. His knowledge and experience of the country and inner workings of the German period offered an 'unrivalled

[44] Ibid.
[45] Ibid.
[46] Ibid.
[47] M.F. Hill, *Permanent Way: The Story of the Tanganyika Railways, Volume II* (Nairobi, 1950), 213.
[48] The authoritative Gillman biography is Brian Hoyle, *Gillman of Tanganyika, 1882–1946: The Life and Work of a Pioneer Geographer* (Aldershot, 1987).

familiarity' and unique insights that no other could provide.[49] His fluency in German also made available any material requiring translation, and in the early years he represented a kind of counterintelligence. This dual status, of such benefit after the war had, in fact, led to his internment in Tabora during it.

In early 1922 Gillman submitted a memorandum on his views on railway extensions in Tanganyika which was 'based on intensive studies of all the accumulated material left by the Germans, as well as on such personal knowledge of the country as [he] possessed'.[50] It was his suggestion of the route of a southern railway via Kilombero that was reproduced in the report of the East Africa Commission. Reflecting on this memorandum in 1942, Gillman wrote that at the time he lacked 'an intimate appreciation of large parts of the Territory' and was also 'considerably misled by the optimism of our predecessors'.[51] But over the subsequent two decades, he would acquire a more intimate knowledge of Tanganyika than most, and no-one became better suited to reconfigure or repudiate previous optimism for large-scale development projects. The railway reconnaissance survey, which began on 15 July 1925 as Gillman turned south-westwards from Ngerengere on the Central Line, contributed vastly to this knowledge. Having reached Likwambi by 27 August, he wrote in his diary:

> From up there we also saw for the first time the mighty alluvial plain of the Kilombero, endless flat country, seamed by high mountains and beyond it in the south, the island-horst of the Mahenge hills. All new to me, as every step, every corner I turn on this wonderful 'safari', but all so full of problems, of unanswered, unanswerable questions![52]

Despite Gillman's tendency towards the portentous, this is an important encapsulation of a vision cast over Kilombero, and written from an elevated vantage point overlooking the valley itself. For Gillman, Kilombero was a problem, a seemingly unanswerable problem; but technical knowledge, gained through reconnaissance and from surveys, would solve its riddles.

Gillman reached Ifakara on 29 August and 'this old trading settlement in the middle of the Kilombero plain' was 'surrounded by vast permanent swamps' and 'reputed to be most unhealthy, but it is of course a necessary settlement as here the great trade route to Mahenge crosses the mighty [Kilombero] river and the water-routes from the fertile plain converge'.[53] He camped in the old

[49] Hoyle, *Gillman*, 108.
[50] Clement Gillman, 'A short history of the Tanganyika Railways', *Tanganyika Notes and Records* 13 June, 1942), 45.
[51] Ibid.
[52] University of Oxford, Bodleian Library (OBL), MSS.Afr.s.1175(9), Clement Gillman Diaries, Diary of the Nyasa Expedition, 1925–26.
[53] Ibid.

Plate 1 View from hills behind Kiberege to Kilombero River, May 1936 [Source: OBL MSS.Afr.s.2228].

German cemetery after a day in which he 'had all the Indians and crowds of native traders and peasants round [...] and thrashed out with them the potentialities of their great plain'.[54] Gillman was then sceptical, while those gathered were optimistic. He believed that 'they, as well as the German and British enthusiasts who have written so much on the untold wealth of the Kilombero, are much mistaken. However, we shall see more of it anon'.[55]

More of it he did see, and the resulting memorandum serves as one of the earliest formal reports written by a technical official during the British administration. Gillman had cast his scientific eye over a landscape whose potential he believed others had previously overestimated:

> The potential wealth of the great alluvial plain of the Kilombero River [...] has always figured prominently in the reports of all whose duty has taken them across it, and one finds the expression of many high hopes in the writings of German travellers and of German as well as British Officials.[56]

[54] Ibid.
[55] Ibid.
[56] TNA 13304, Report by Gillman, Senior Engineer, Tanganyika Railways, 30 September 1925.

Gillman spent five weeks on this survey, which he believed gave him 'a clear insight into the regime of its many great rivers' and offered 'considerably greater accuracy than can be reasonably expected from casual travellers or from enthusiastic officials who hurry from camp to camp and are apt to rush into well-meant but, as often as not, somewhat rash generalisations'.[57] This strikes on the important point that much of the basis of belief in the potential of Kilombero had indeed originated from the observations of casual travellers and enthusiastic officials, but that should not mean these beliefs had no inherent basis in truth. But five weeks was certainly not long enough to fully appreciate the regimes of the rivers. Any less than a full cycle of seasons over one year would offer an incomplete insight, and ideally far longer to consider volatility and variations in rainfall and flood over several years.

Gillman identified various morphological zones within the plain, one of which consisted of 'riverine or deltaic, relatively narrow strips and patches of ground' that 'form slightly raised areas, flooded annually for a few days at highest high water, by running water from which is deposited a much coarser, and chemically as well as physically, much more valuable silt than that from the stagnating flood water'.[58] It was 'this wide-spread network of extremely fertile ground' which Gillman believed had 'given rise to the ever repeated stories of fabulous agricultural wealth'.[59] Each survey, march, or expedition in Kilombero would begin and end at one of these areas and 'amidst the wealth of which one is liable to forget the many miles of intervening "desert" that one has crossed'.[60] Gillman believed that the extent of fertile areas had been overexaggerated as its numerous 'oases' struck the traveller's eye. He considered that between 80 and 90 per cent of the plain was not at all cultivatable. The true fertile land was naturally already well settled, but Gillman thought there was still room for increased population and cultivation. He saw potential for greater yields through improved methods of cultivation, and monetary inducement if a railway were built. However, the primary lens through which Gillman saw Kilombero was railway revenue, and he surmised that little profit would be derived if only this one zone would provide the traffic.

It was in fact a separate zone of the plain that Gillman considered possible for any future large-scale development, comprising alluvial fans of grey sandy loams and 'bush-steppe' vegetation. These were noted as being 'quite uninhabited' and 'quite unsuitable for rice' but Gillman believed that cotton,

[57] Ibid.
[58] Ibid.
[59] Ibid.
[60] Ibid.

by its comparatively high value, could be developed.[61] These areas of the plain, constituting approximately 60 per cent of the land area, were thought to hold real wealth in quantities attractive enough from the railway's point of view with or without irrigation. Gillman concluded with two caveats.

One was that his knowledge of soils was not adequate enough to make a 'more precise statement with regard to the future possibilities of this largest portion of the Kilombero area'; the second was the population, or rather its lack: 'If the great alluvial fans are to be thrown open to cultivation, whether by native peasants or native labourers working for large-scale European agricultural undertakings, it is through mass-immigration.'[62] Gillman noted signs 'everywhere' that before the Maji Maji Rebellion 'the plain and its bordering foothills were more densely populated than today' and that in addition to this depopulation – which had occurred barely twenty years earlier – low numbers could also be accounted for by labour migration to areas adjacent to the Central Line.[63]

Gillman presented his findings to an audience at the Royal Geographical Society in November 1926, and focused on the 'dormant possibilities' of 'South-West Tanganyika' and ways to increase agricultural production.[64] Attendees were introduced to the 'five great streams' that formed the Kilombero River – 'Kihanzi, Mpanga, Mnyera, Ruhuje, and Pitu' – which Gillman styled 'a veritable East African "Punjab."'[65] He advocated harnessing these waters, and the 'large-scale tapping of the vast stores of deep-seated ground water and, in suitable localities, e.g. the Kilombero plain, the storage of masses of water which not only run to waste annually, but by inundating vast tracts add very considerably to the uninhabitable area'.[66]

Gillman admitted that he could not speak with authority on the agronomy of Kilombero. His task had been to assess the feasibility of the proposed railway route from an engineering perspective, yet he was hardly unqualified to offer his opinion on the economic possibilities of the plain. The result was a kind of tempered optimism. But any action had to pass through the Department of Agriculture, which held the higher authority. At this time its Director was A.H. Kirby who, alongside Gillman, would highly influence British thinking on Kilombero and colonial visions for this valley.

[61] Ibid.
[62] Ibid.
[63] Ibid.
[64] Gillman, 'South-West Tanganyika', 98.
[65] Ibid., 101. The Kilombero River is thus compared to the Indus (Gillman), Nile (Fonck and Kirby), and Rhine (Pfeil).
[66] Ibid., 121.

'Is not a railway necessary to serve the area?'

Kirby followed Gillman's report with his own in January 1926, which described Kilombero as a 'region possessing a most fertile, deep soil, at least 1,000 square miles in area, which is thoroughly supplied with water and well drained every year'.[67] He began and ended his own survey at Sakamaganga – on the northern margin of the floodplain – and covered 300 miles. He wrote of the plain that 'the importance of this production and the possibility of its increase cannot be too vividly realised' and that the slopes of the valley, neighbouring foothills, and 'particularly their highly fertile flats where the streams of erosion have left rich alluvium' could surpass the plain in output and variety, being favourable – if not ideal – conditions for the production of all ordinary tropical crops.[68]

Most parts of Tanganyika had been 'in danger of serious dearth' during the previous season, whereas in Kilombero 'there was plenty of food everywhere'.[69] Kirby saw how rice was the most carefully cultivated and prized crop, and the ability of some parts to produce a crop at a time when no other district could do so – and at a time when it was most needed – led him to agree early German observations that the region could 'supply the whole Territory with grain' if only there were a railway to transport it.

On the prospect of direct European involvement in agricultural production, only cotton at times of high market prices and sugar cane on higher levels above the plain were thought suitable for a plantation model. Cotton was considered unsuitable in the floodlands. For most crops best suited to the valley, including rice, any European involvement was thought best applied 'to the provision of commercial encouragement of production, including means for the handling and marketing of produce'.[70] Kirby urged closer examination into the possibilities for sugar production and even proposed an outgrowers model.

Kirby concluded his report with the statement that a railway to southwestern Tanganyika 'could pass through no richer area than that of the Kilombero Valley; nor one which is more ready and quickly able to increase its production' and that should no longer be allowed to have for its 'gates of trade' no more than 'a precarious and uninsurable dhow traffic and a railway

---

[67] TNA 13304, 'Report on an Agricultural Survey of the Kilombero Region, 27 January 1926' by A.H. Kirby.
[68] Ibid.
[69] Ibid.
[70] Ibid.

approaching no nearer to it than 116 miles'.[71] The journey from Ifakara to Kilosa took fourteen days on foot, and thus a round trip almost one month's absence from home, but much longer for those farther from Ifakara. The costs and distance involved in reaching larger markets left producers with too little for their produce to encourage greater output. For Kirby it was unfathomable that this should be the case for a region whose agricultural production was fed by the third highest rainfall among similarly sized areas.

A subsequent memorandum in September 1926 further impressed the dormant potential of Kilombero. It was 'virtually going begging' through its 'never-failing flood-periods' and 'continually adequate rainfall' over a 'rich, constantly renewed alluvial soil' on which two crops of rice are grown every year.[72] To these two crops a 'great output of maize and beans, and more rice from the lower lands of the valley slopes' would be possible due to the valley's consistent rainfall and its irrigation possibilities from 'the abundant, perennial water supply'.[73] Crops thought worth trialling for 'direct European exploitation' under rain above the plain included oil palm, Liberian coffee, and cacao; and elsewhere: tobacco, Deccan and Sunn hemp, sesame for gingelly, Para rubber, wood oil and similar oils. Kirby believed that the agricultural suitability was 'fairly certain in every case, under the properly chosen conditions' but it was the economic suitability that required further investigation, especially regarding labour supply. Owing to the lack of local supply in sufficient numbers to make a success of any scheme of development by agricultural companies, it was considered imperative that labour must be derived from other districts.

For Kirby, if Kilombero remained 'undeveloped' then it would be a tremendous waste of one of Tanganyika's most promising resources. As the Director of Agriculture, his opinion carried substantial weight, which only served to inflate the air of importance historically attached to Kilombero. However, this vision – to bring the supposedly great economic and agricultural potential of the area to fruition – was matched in magnitude by the factors required to realise it. There was a need for further, detailed surveys. Kirby acknowledged: 'In the absence […] of information as to the extent of the different kinds of land and of population to cultivate it, all speculations as to total possible output of the area are futile.'[74] Kirby was not to know the veracity of this statement. It was not the absence of information or

---

[71] TNA 13304, 'Report on an Agricultural Survey of the Kilombero Region', by A.H. Kirby.

[72] TNA 11746, 'Memorandum on two fertile regions awaiting development, 23 September 1926' by A.H. Kirby, Director of Agriculture.

[73] Ibid.

[74] TNA 13304, 'Report on an Agricultural Survey of the Kilombero Region, 27 January 1926' by A.H. Kirby.

population *per se* that foreshadowed the futility of all speculations as to the total possible output of Kilombero, but that does not alter the fact that such speculations ultimately proved futile. This is all too plain to see in hindsight, but at the moment that these reports advanced British thinking on Kilombero, it seemed that the realisation of the region's development potential was on the near horizon. It was surely only a matter of time and technical expertise, an adequate transport infrastructure, and sufficient labour. The ultimate question for Kirby was not: 'Shall the area serve a railway?' but, 'Is not a railway necessary to serve the area?'[75]

'The scheme which I had in mind…'

The future of Kilombero was soon discussed far from the verdant valley, and in that engine of empire: London. While on leave in 1927, Cameron approached various individuals whom he thought might assist in developing the region. Confidential letters followed between the offices and private members' clubs of Whitehall and St James's. Correspondence was direct but informal, the paper trail revealing the centrality of the Governor in the drive to develop the valley. One letter to J.F.N. Green of the Colonial Office began with fond familiarity, 'My dear Green', and continued: 'As you are aware, I have been trying for some time to attract British capital to the development of the Kilombero and Rufiji areas.'[76] Cameron had returned to England with several copies of Kirby's report to support his efforts. He explained:

> The scheme which I had in mind was based on my conception of the activities of the Sudan Plantation Company, and that, in my judgment, it was essential that it should be a partnership scheme so as to be brought within the terms of the Mandate as a 'controlled agency'.[77]

Cameron was cautious of adhering to the terms of the Mandate, but confident they would be met. He envisioned that the private capital required to invest in purse-poor Tanganyika might be best provided by a syndicate comprised of private individuals or companies who shared a collective vision, and that would partner with the Tanganyika Government for legitimacy and accountability. Cameron had already asked Sir George Schuster (Economic and Financial Advisor to the Secretary of State for the Colonies) whether the Sudan Plantations Syndicate (SPS) would consider such a scheme. Cameron needed such a body to explore the proposition, as the Gillman and Kirby

---

[75] TNA 11746, 'Memorandum on two fertile regions awaiting development, 23 September 1926' by A.H. Kirby, Director of Agriculture.
[76] TNA 11746, Cameron to Green, 8 October 1927.
[77] Ibid.

reports did not hold sufficient authority to be laid before financiers and the British public. 'No report from a government officer would be of any value for this purpose', he reasoned.[78]

Cameron was also contacted by Ben Morgan, who was 'interested with some friends in finding some new areas for the production of sugar, rice and other products' and whose 'attention [had] been directed to the Rufigi [*sic.*] and Kilombero Districts as having great possibilities'.[79] Morgan had been given a copy of Kirby's report by Cameron, having previously sought to establish a power alcohol factory in Tanganyika.[80] Morgan assured Cameron that he had the necessary financial backing to form a syndicate to dispatch experts to investigate the area and its 'wonderful possibilities', and asked for an option during investigation and later a concession if permitted to form a syndicate.[81] Morgan held various positions – including Chairman of the Sugar Federation of the British Empire – and campaigned for developing a British imperial sugar industry to counter the 'criminal folly' that Britain was 'dependent on foreign sources of supply for nearly three-quarters of such an essential commodity'.[82] Kirby's mention of sugar possibilities in his report piqued interest, and Morgan saw an opportunity in Kilombero. For Cameron it was win-win. If the SPS were not interested, then Morgan was an alternative route to syndicated development. If the SPS *were* interested, then Cameron could still bring him in as an additional interest.

The SPS were interested, at least enough to part-finance a further survey. No promises were made. It was understood that the arrangement 'must necessarily be of a somewhat loose and indefinite nature, dependent for its interpretation on good faith on both sides'.[83] Neither side knew what form a potential partnership might take, while discussions remained tentative due to heightened sensitivities around the Mandate. This was standard practice. Mutual understanding over unspoken terms, informal conversations, and discretion were the very *lingua franca* of government, colonial firms, and private investors. Further participation depended entirely on the resulting report, and Cameron pinned his hopes on the findings of Alexander Telford, the 'suitably qualified expert with engineering and agricultural experience' sent from Sudan.[84]

---

[78] Ibid.
[79] TNA 11746, Morgan to Cameron, 29 September 1927.
[80] See B.H. Morgan, 'Power alcohol', *Royal United Services Institution. Journal* 71:482 (1926), 373–6.
[81] TNA 11746, Morgan to Cameron, 29 September 1927.
[82] 'Letter to the Editor of the Bermuda Colonist', *The Royal Gazette and Colonist Daily*, 2 December 1927. The Sugar Federation of the British Empire was founded April 1926. See also Leopold Amery papers for statements made while chairman of the Federation (1930–4), Churchill Archives Centre, University of Cambridge, GBR/0014/AMEL.
[83] Ibid.
[84] TNAUK CO 691/93/11, Green to F. Eckstein, 10 November 1927.

Hopes raised, hopes dashed

An extensive questionnaire was forwarded to Kirby ahead of Telford's arrival. Enquiries included: locality; ecology; rates for freight, imports, and exports; existing cultivation; land rights; government labour policies; prevalent diseases; and existing soil analyses. Kirby answered with 'some difficulty' as he possessed 'no knowledge of what is actually proposed' and thought it 'more satisfactory' if some questions were left open until after Telford examined the area.[85] Two questions on immigration and labour proved contentious: 'How many families can be obtained from other districts who would reside permanently on or near the area?' and 'What is government's policy with regard to labour obtained from other districts if there is not sufficient labour in the vicinity to populate the scheme?' Kirby could not say how many families 'if any' nor 'what labour is [...] and will be available' but that the policy must be 'rather persuasion not compulsion'.[86] Philip Mitchell (Secretary of Native Affairs) added that the policy on labour for private enterprise was that each man was 'free to go out and work where he pleases and as he desired'.[87] There was a suggestion that the success of the envisaged scheme relied on infringing the very freedoms this policy guaranteed. 'Special efforts', Mitchell reassured, 'would if necessary be made to induce labourers to settle in the [...] areas in the event of Government concluding an agreement with the Sudan Plantations Syndicate for the development of those areas.'[88] There was evidently a readiness to bend the rules, and for grey areas to be exploited.

Telford reached Tanganyika in April 1928. He was relatively young – his thirty-third birthday came days into the survey – but he was well qualified to survey the region. In 1923 he had become Chief Engineer to the Kassala Cotton Company in Sudan, where they aimed to develop 30,000 acres of the River Gash delta for cotton and food crops by canalisation. He subsequently developed a novel irrigation scheme covering 45,000 acres in Gezira 1927–8, and after his return to Sudan from Tanganyika he developed a one-million-acre irrigation scheme.[89] Telford planned to complete full investigations of the Rufiji and Kilombero regions during both wet and dry seasons. He left Dar es Salaam on 18 April for the wet season tour with Kirby, and reached Ifakara on 24 May 1928, before returning to Dar es Salaam a little over three weeks later. Telford was forced to expedite his dry season trip by Alexander MacIntyre

[85] TNA 11746, File Notes by Director of Agriculture, 22 March 1928.
[86] Ibid.
[87] TNA 11746, Replies by SNA to Questionnaire on Rufiji-Kilombero Scheme, n.d.
[88] Ibid.
[89] 'Obituary: Alexander McMenegal Telford, 1895–1963', *Proceedings of the Institution of Civil Engineers* 32:4 (1965), 697.

(Managing Director of SPS), who wished him back in Barakat. Returning in July and August rather than September and October was, Telford thought, a less than ideal period to examine the contrasts and dry season conditions. Kirby later took up this point to claim that the report was not authoritative. Telford's findings were not positive, and not the encouragement Cameron needed to pursue his idea for syndicated development. In a letter to MacIntyre, Telford felt that his report would be viewed as 'undoubtedly pessimistic' and that the 'general impression' received from most officials was that 'the Kilombero plains were marvellously fertile' but 'this view cannot be supported'.[90]

Telford not only doubted the extent of land that could be cultivated, but also whether production could be effected under the same conditions as Sudan. The prime issue was labour. Telford anticipated it necessary to 'import large numbers from other districts' and that if this proved difficult then it would seriously affect the company's decision.[91] Telford also closed his report with a 'warning note' that the 'most necessary element in the whole scheme is the control of the tenant in agricultural matters' and 'a considerable measure of authority will be necessary'.[92] This was a major limitation to the type of scheme that Telford thought would best suit the involvement of the SPS.

Telford also evaluated past German schemes and considered that 'the canalisation of the already excellently flooded alluvial fans by any such means as the Germans proposed is definitely wrong, and could only have been suggested with a very imperfect knowledge of the actual facts'.[93] The report thus combined fact, opinion, and conjecture. It nonetheless remains a substantial repository of information on all matters relating to past and present agricultural production, transport, and markets in the Rufiji and Kilombero regions as viewed in 1928. Telford also commented on what he perceived to be future production potential and considered possibilities for irrigation. His conclusion was that the expected increase of area gained by any scheme of protection banks or irrigation works would not justify the cost, nor would it advisable due to the annual rainfall in the area.[94] The Directors of the SPS drew three conclusions:

[90] TNA 13304, Telford to MacIntyre, 19 December 1928.
[91] TNA 13304, Chief Secretary (CS) to Orde-Browne, 19 June 1928.
[92] Alexander M. Telford, *Report on the Development of the Rufiji and Kilombero Valleys* (London, 1929), 74. The original typed manuscript is found in TNA 13304, Development of Kilombero Area, 1928.
[93] Telford, *Report*, 61.
[94] Ibid.

1   Parts of the regions are capable of producing largely increased quantities of rice, maize, cotton and other tropical crops.

2   In order to obtain such increased production, cheap transport facilities would have to be made available.

3   At the present stage the development of these regions can be carried out better under the authority and by the efforts of the Government than by private enterprise, and that the Syndicate cannot usefully co-operate in such development.[95]

This was a blow to Cameron. His future visions for Kilombero were blurred by a report that he hoped would inspire confidence in Government spending, attract external capital and technical investment, encourage further infrastructural development, and bring rapid economic returns. It confirmed 'the less sanguine opinion of Mr Gillman as to the area in the Kilombero Valley suitable for economic crops'.[96] Cameron doubted a second opinion from a more highly trained engineer could give 'any advice on which [Government] would be justified in embarking on any costly scheme'.[97]

The report also brought into clear focus the 'difficulty in applying to a mandated territory exactly the same *métayer* system operated by the Sudan Plantations Syndicate'.[98] In Tanganyika, 'the existing population had rights to their land' and thus 'a concessionaire company could not secure the full control that the [SPS] had' in Sudan.[99] In other words: 'here it rains, and you cannot bring a tenant to heel by turning off the water tap'.[100]

In Kilombero, that 'copious rainfall' made irrigation 'unnecessary' would 'render the cultivator independent of any syndicate for its water supply'.[101] Authority in the Gezira irrigation scheme in Sudan flowed through the water provided by Nile irrigation to otherwise arid regions. No such authority could be imposed over the well-watered Rufiji and Kilombero regions, and this undercurrent of requisite colonial conditions of control was the undoing of such a model in Tanganyika. Telford viewed any leverage that a developing agent might have over farmers as further reduced by the region's fertility:

[95] TNA 11746, Secretary [SPS] to USS [CO], 6 February 1929.
[96] TNA 11746, Secretariat Memorandum, 28 March 1929.
[97] TNA 13304, Extract from minute by H.E. the Governor [Cameron], 13 October 1929.
[98] TNA 26056, Notes of meeting held at Colonial Office, re: Kilombero Development Syndicate, 30 March 1931.
[99] TNA 11746/193, Development of Rufiji and Kilombero Areas: File Notes, 30 November 1932.
[100] Ibid.
[101] TNA 11746, Governor [Symes] to Secretary of State, 4 January 1933.

> It is evident that the customary prosperity of the inhabitants of this region, that accrues to them for no great labour on their part, prevents the existence of any permanent economic urgency due to poverty which would make them conscious that they require help for development which may be offered to them. Unlike most of the native inhabitants of the Sudan, for example, they do not require to be given a money-crop in order to be assured of their daily bread.[102]

The report, however, was far from useless; rather, it was held up as an authoritative resource, repurposed as a guide for all that might still be considered and achieved in Kilombero. Almost immediately, the Chief Secretary asked Kirby for his views on 'starting, if possible, some scheme of more intensive native production on the Kilombero, on the lines advocated by Mr Telford, in a comparatively small area to commence with'.[103] Kirby had disagreed with a number of Telford's points and felt compelled to defend not only his previously positive survey, but his position as Director of Agriculture. Kirby stood by his previous views save for two respects. First, he now believed 'the extent of the submersion of the Kilombero Plain by that river' was a myth originated by earlier investigators, misled by following the facile convention that limits travelling to the dry season'.[104] Kirby dispelled previous belief in a 'slow-moving flood, fifteen to twenty miles wide' and concluded that the Kilombero River overflowed its banks no more than two miles on either side'.[105] The second respect was that Kirby now believed the plain was not primarily flooded by the Kilombero, but its northern tributaries.

Kirby criticised the prematurity of the dry season tour, even though this was not the intention, and pressed that a later visit would have given a different impression. He also reckoned that Telford underestimated the agricultural ability of local farmers and erroneously omitted any prospects for sugar development.[106]

But the Telford Report had fulfilled its primary purpose: to report on an investigation of the Rufiji and Kilombero regions. It was commissioned in the hope it would encourage a particular kind of development in partnership with a particular company. It did not. It was, however, published, and it remains an important source that remains widely cited in literature on Kilombero. Less widely known are the circumstances that led to its writing as described here, and little understood is the type of development to which positive findings

---

[102] Telford, *Report*, 44.
[103] TNA 11746, Secretariat Memorandum, 28 March 1929.
[104] TNA 11746, DofA to CS, 14 June 1928.
[105] Ibid.
[106] TNA 13304, DofA to CS, 30 March 1929.

may have led. Other companies, in fact, viewed promise in the report. One firm was Nigerian Consolidated Mines (NCM), Ltd. who sought to expand into other regions and industries. Kirby assured its Chairman of Directors in 1929 that: 'There is no doubt of the fertility and promise under development of the lands of the Kilombero.'[107]

Stanley Bullock – a representative of NCM based in Bukoba – travelled to Mahenge in September 1929 and reported that 'there are great possibilities in the Ruaha and Kilombero valleys for [...] increased production [...] not only of rice, but also for maize, sugar, ground-nuts, and cotton'.[108] Bullock saw potential for one company to purchase and market all such products and 'thus ensuring against the failure of any one crop during any special period'.[109] This approach to diversification and risk aversion showed strong acumen for someone with only superficial knowledge of Kilombero. The character of this new proposal for company involvement was markedly different through its support for local production and development of a purchasing network and transport infrastructure. However, while Government sought the perceived advantages of outside companies to assist in Kilombero development, it neglected the prospects of incremental development on a smaller scale from the network of Indian merchants and traders who had long been part of the regional economy. This was admitted by one official as 'rather a vicious circle' and who expressed 'we do not want to permit the establishment of ginneries round Kilombero by Indians with perfectly small capital if the Nigerian Company is willing to enter the field' and yet, 'on the other hand, unless the seed is provided by February next [...] the whole cotton season will be wasted'.[110] Annual production was thus threatened by indecision and inaction. By hoping for development on a more substantial level, Government risked destroying smaller prospects for economic growth and therefore, arguably, all prospects.

By early December 1929, however, interest from NCM had waned, citing 'prevailing conditions in the metal market' for the reason why 'the Board [were] not prepared, at this juncture, to go further into the proposition'.[111] The delay in granting the applications of pioneer ginneries in Ifakara – one from Mr. Patel of Morogoro and another from Mr. Abulgani, a reputable merchant of Ifakara – and of distributing cotton seed via District Officers had been ultimately needless.

---

[107] TNA 13304/37, A.H. Kirby, Director of Agriculture to Chairman of Directors, Nigerian Consolidated Mines, Ltd. 11 October, 1929.
[108] TNA 13304, Bullock [NCM] to DofA, September 1928.
[109] Ibid.
[110] TNA 13304, CS to DCS, 25 October 1929. In the original file, the word 'perfectly' is struck through.
[111] TNA 13304, Secretary [NCM] to A.H. Kirby [DofA], 5 December 1929.

This sequence of events suggests that the pursuit of grand development resulted only in underdevelopment. The region's agricultural economy was being directly influenced by invisible and distant forces, but whose impact was only ever felt indirectly. Many visions and conjectures existed only on the pages of official reports and correspondence, and yet the sense of belief in their realisation is palpable. Most were not realised, but events may have sequenced completely differently. How, for example, would the social, political, economic, and ecological landscapes of the valley have been affected by investment and involvement from companies such as the SPS, or NCM? This question can be asked many times over at different times with different agencies, for these were not the last visions for Kilombero to rise and fall.

A permanent way?

Despite a reframing of colonial development possibilities, the valley continued to feature prominently in discussions on the most suitable route for a railway to south-western Tanganyika. Following the report of the East Africa Commission in 1925, Colonel Maxwell (General Manager of Tanganyika Railways) reviewed the Kilombero Valley and Iringa District in the context of future railway development south of the Central Line. He refuted the Commission's claim, and concluded that any line following the valley was 'useless' for serving the Southern Highlands as the steep escarpment was unpassable by mechanical or motor transport.[112] But nor did he recommend a railway to Iringa as a commercial proposition, only as a 'development railway' and one that 'cannot hope to pay for many years to come'.[113] Maxwell concluded that for *immediate* construction there were better commercial lines of shorter length. The question of a line to Lake Nyasa, however, remained open and all possibilities would be considered. This was the beginning of the 'long and complex controversy' and 'conflicting ideas' around which debates over the development potential of Kilombero and the Southern Highlands were centred.[114]

In 1929, Gillman (now Chief Engineer of Tanganyika Railways) published a report summarising accumulated findings for such a line. He closely considered the two potential routes proposed by the East Africa Commission. One – the 'Kilosa-Manda' line – branched from the Central Line at Kilosa and passed through the Kilombero and Pitu valleys to Manda Bay. The other – the

---

[112] TNAUK CO 691/79, Railway Development: General Report, Colonel Maxwell, 3 September 1925. Any gradient greater than 1:20 was thought impossible for heavy transport. Existing routes over the escarpment ranged from 1:4 to 1:2.
[113] Ibid.
[114] Hill, *Permanent Way*, 213.

'Dodoma-Fife' line – branched from Dodoma through Iringa and terminating near Fife on the Rhodesian border. Gillman strongly recommended the former, his once-pessimistic views of Kilombero now transformed:

> It is impossible to exaggerate the great and outstanding importance from the point of view of railway revenue, of this vast low-lying tropical plain, extremely well-watered from the slopes of high mountains which shut it in on three sides, with a fairly reliable rainfall, and very easily served by a comparatively cheap line. In addition to the large scale growing of rice, maize and cotton which will always form the staple produce, the possibilities of sugar cane and of an important export trade in dried fish from the tremendously rich Kilombero river must not be overlooked.[115]

Gillman was now an enthusiast! His initial scepticism and later high confidence indicate a volatility evident in outsiders' impressions of Kilombero and their visions for its development potential. Optimism ebbed and flowed. Opinions varied. This was largely due to the railway line being considered not only from the perspectives of engineering, but also agriculture and economy. Furthermore, Iringa and the Southern Highlands came to represent white settler farmers and 'non-native production' whereas lowland Kilombero represented 'native' production. This encapsulated something of the essence of broader debates on the entire future of agricultural production across Tanganyika, and along which line development would advance more quickly. A report by Brigadier-General F.D. Hammond in late 1929 supported Gillman's view, concluding that the Kilosa-Ifakara section of the proposed Kilosa-Manda line was 'one of the most promising in the country' and that 'opens up the fertile valley of the Kilombero, which is already well known for its rice' with 'excellent possibilities of development both in rice and cotton', and 'sugar production also holds out good hopes'.[116] As Tanganyika had no mineral wealth of its own to finance a railway network, he expected Central African mineral wealth and mineral traffic from the Rhodesian copper belt to fund the line, and agricultural production would then follow.

Gillman's report gravely disappointed settler farmers, but they did not yet represent a sizeable commercial proposition. Moreover, the route that would serve them also ran through 120 miles of unproductive land.[117] Gillman took a holistic view and saw the line as a 'geographical unit' that must 'fit into that

---

[115] Gillman, *Report on the Preliminary Surveys*, 43.

[116] Quoted in E.M. Jack, 'Railway development in Tanganyika Territory', *The Geographical Journal* 79:2 (1932), 120.

[117] TNAUK CO 691/79, Railway Development: General Report, Colonel Maxwell, 3 September 1925.

long series of cause and effect, or mutual determination and interdependence, which is indicated by the terms of geology, surface forms, draining, climate, soil, vegetation, population, commerce and industry'.[118] These factors were further explored by the Henn Railway Commission (after its chair, Sir Sydney Henn), appointed in July 1930 to consider the viability of each route and the prospects for all regions under consideration.[119] Whereas the Telford Report presented the opinion of essentially one man, the Henn Commission examined forty-two individual witnesses and deputations over twenty-six full sessions.

At the heart of the debate were the grounds to justify a railway: political and administrative, or economic. Strategic and imperial grounds were also considered. There was much conjecture, however, and few witnesses knew Kilombero at all. On being asked whether the valley could be developed if served by a system of water transport to a railhead at Ifakara, A.B. Chanter (Traffic Manager of Tanganyika Railways) replied: 'I think it is rather difficult for me to answer. I have not been there, not in any part of the country under discussion.'[120]

Other witnesses were more qualified, such as H.W.D. Pollock (Assistant District Officer, Kiberege) and Captain Eric Reid (District Officer, Mahenge). By the 19th Session, it was admitted that the Commission had 'received very little reliable information from verbal witnesses in regard to the Kilombero area, its population, production and prospects' and first asked Pollock to address this. He described a region where rice cultivation flourished for local consumption yet limited trade. Quantities cultivated were proportionate to market access, which was prohibited by distance, cost, and risk. Nevertheless, between 1918 – when Reid first arrived to Kilombero – and 1930, the number of rice gardens cultivated by each farmer quadrupled.[121] Surplus rice was often carried on foot over the escarpment to Iringa, Tossamaganga and as far as Malangali. However, the majority of market rice was purchased by local agents of the seventeen Indian merchants with shops in Ifakara. Pollock explained how each merchant contracted four or five local sub-agents throughout the valley who bought rice and sent it by canoe to Ifakara. This was precarious, but in most cases the risk was met by the trader, not the farmer. It was the trader who bought the rice at source, hired the canoe, and paid the wages of the three men required to transport up to 1.5 tonnes of rice (being the capacity of

---

[118] Gillman, *Report on the Preliminary Surveys*, 7.

[119] Tanganyika, *Report of the Tanganyika Railway Commission* (London, 1930).

[120] Tanganyika. Tanganyika Railway Division, *Appendices to the Report of the Tanganyika Railway Commission containing Oral Evidence and Memoranda.* (London, 1930), 13 [Second Session, 28 July 1930, Dar es Salaam].

[121] Tanganyika, *Appendices*, 66 [Seventh Session, 1 August 1930, Kilosa].

each canoe). This was obviously not a safe and stable system. Risk influenced price and therefore yield. Risks included water damage, leaking canoes, whole harvests lost to the riverbed by submerged trees, and life-threatening attacks by hippopotami. It was reported that in some areas there was simply 'no incentive to cultivate' whereas cotton areas had been 'killed for the future by transport' with necessarily low prices in Ifakara due to its distance from Kilosa.[122] Ifakara thus received valley produce by river, and from Mahenge by road. For the latter, contemporaneous figures held that between March and December, fourteen Indian traders cleared all produce by running twenty-eight trucks between Mahenge and Ifakara on one day, returning the next.[123]

There was a two-fold issue of transport: first to Ifakara, then to Kilosa. A functional transport network existed in Kilombero, but it was far from developed, efficient, and economic. The region was fertile but isolation had tempered growth, or so went the argument. Transport infrastructure was characterised by the poor state or even inexistence of roads, limited motor transport, damage to bridges in most floods, precarious canoe transport, and labour- and time-consuming head porterage. The crux of the matter still remained whether expenditure on a railway line was justified, so far as it rested on *potential* and not *current* production in a region whose population was frequently cited as being too low to effectively realise this potential. In this context the feasibility of the type of scheme explored by Telford continued to be discussed. Mitchell was asked during the Commission whether Government policy permitted the degree of control which Telford thought necessary. Mitchell did not think policy 'had anything to do with it' and in an administrative sense the Government had all the control which could be desired.[124] However, such control to 'cultivate to an extent, in a manner, and at a time [...] by a company could only be achieved in areas such as Gezira [in Sudan ...] where there was no rainfall and agriculture depended entirely on irrigation' so that 'if a tenant did not do what he was told he was brought to heel by the simple process of turning off his water supply'.[125] For Mitchell 'it was not a question of modifying the policy [...] but of eliminating the rainfall' and that 'if it never rained the tenant in the Kilombero Valley and Nile Valley would be in the same position'.[126] Reid also believed that 'such economic control' would conflict with current policy and, moreover, would 'create a class of helots in a

---

[122] Tanganyika, *Appendices*, 96 [Eleventh Session, 6 August 1930, Iringa]; Tanganyika, *Appendices*, 156 [Nineteenth Session, 23 August 1930, Dar es Salaam]. At this time the nearest ginnery was at Kilosa, 185km from Ifakara.
[123] Tanganyika, *Appendices*, 63 [Seventh Session, 1 August 1930, Kilosa].
[124] Tanganyika, *Appendices*, 17 [Second Session, 28 July 1930, Dar es Salaam].
[125] Ibid.
[126] Ibid.

mild form'.[127] These views were at odds with the Labour Commissioner, Major G. St. J. Orde-Browne, who replied 'yes' when asked if he could conceive of 'any sort of syndicate development [...] in view of the fact that we cannot have anything in the nature of a system of slavery introduced?'[128] Now that Mitchell had ruled out that such control could be given, many of Gillman's figures lay in doubt, for he had based his production estimates on syndicated development. The Commission had also heard repeatedly that a line through Kilombero was 'an impossible proposition owing to its being located in a swampy area and requiring too many bridges'.[129] On this point, Gillman was firm. Not only was it possible, but 'from a purely technical point of view', he assured, 'there is no person in this Territory at the present time who knows more about the Kilombero Valley than I do'.[130]

This was a bold statement and, while not exactly disputed, the committee called for 'a completely independent examination of the Kilombero route made by experts who [would] devote themselves entirely [to a technical survey]'.[131] That this route was considered at all was strongly criticised by 'the Iringa Business and Commercial Community' who disparaged the valley as a pestilent, practically submerged area that was 'unsuitable for cultivation except in patches of small areas, say one to five acres [and] useless for European settlement [thus,] in the absence of contact with Europeans, native production would not be increased by the advent of the railway'.[132] The argument against a line through Kilombero was summarised with remarkable brevity: 'No trade beyond Ifakara, no shops, no Europeans, no Asiatics, unhealthy, swamp, blackwater, line probably washed away annually, no roads, no telegraphs, no Boma, no aerodrome, no cattle.'[133] But the final word lay with the Commission. Its recommendation was the immediate construction of a branch railway from Kilosa to Ifakara. This would pass through 'fertile and well-watered country suitable for cotton, sisal, and maize' and it was believed rice production in Kilombero would increase if better prices were offered due to cheaper transport from Ifakara.[134] Beyond this, it was believed the district would be developed sufficiently by better roads and improved water transport, as canoe transport

---

[127] Tanganyika, *Appendices*, 68 [Seventh Session, 1 August 1930, Kilosa].
[128] Tanganyika, *Appendices*, 56 [Sixth Session, 1 August 1930, Morogoro].
[129] Tanganyika, *Appendices*, 149 [Eighteenth Session, 21 August 1930, Dar es Salaam].
[130] Ibid., 150.
[131] Ibid., 149.
[132] Tanganyika, *Appendices*, 212 [Telegram from J.S. Todd to Henn Commission, 28 July 1930].
[133] Tanganyika, *Appendices*, 221 [Memorandum by R.O. Thompson, PC Iringa].
[134] Tanganyika, *Report of the Tanganyika Railway Commission*, 11–12.

was 'costly, uncertain, and dangerous'.[135] The Commission also recommended a further expert investigation into improving river navigation. Surveys led to reports to commissions to reports and to more surveys, and all at a fraction of the cost of the development proposals themselves. It is almost conceivable that this cycle was designed to maintain a certain momentum, so that each annual report demonstrated enough activity to satisfy the League of Nations, but without actually implementing any major schemes at all. Development lay in the planning, not the doing. The imminent Great Depression, however, would soon shelve ambition.

The tacheometric survey for the railway had begun on 20 October 1930. Its final report was delivered on 25 February 1932 and noted that 'a very much altered world situation not only renders the whole complex question of additional development somewhat bewildering, at least for the present, but also makes one sceptical regarding the readiness with which the necessary capital might be forthcoming'.[136] The report reasoned that a branch line to Ifakara was not now an 'immediately paying proposition unless Syndicate Development on a large scale can be introduced', or so thought its author.[137] Alongside the tacheometric survey, a survey of the Kilombero River had also begun under Captain Gibson – recently retired from the Royal Navy – who arrived in Ifakara on 9 July 1931 to cover 110 miles of the river. This proved far too ambitious. Gibson and crew managed to survey a meagre half a mile a day. Progress was slowed by 'the unsurveyed nature of the surrounding country, the restriction of view by the long grass, the lack of natural marks along the banks of the river and the difficulty of fixing marks in floating reeds'.[138] These difficulties echoed those of the late-nineteenth-century explorers and German colonialists. Gibson concluded that 'no difficulty should be found in navigating a vessel 120 feet long and 30 feet broad that can draw as much as 2.5 feet' but that a full report was essential, one that explored the rest of the river and also while in flood.[139] The survey remained incomplete when Gibson left Tanganyika in early December 1931. He was anxious his assistants would continue the investigation, but they never did.

Almost exactly one year after Donald Cameron instigated the river survey, his successor shut it down on 13 January 1932. Stewart Symes later recalled Cameron's 'progressive schemes for the indigenous population of Tanganyika'

---

[135] Ibid., 14.

[136] TNAUK CO 691/125/17, Report on Tacheometric Survey from Kilosa to Ifakara, 1930–32.

[137] Ibid.

[138] TNAUK CO/691/115/7, 1st Report: Gibson to GM, Tanganyika Railways, 3 September 1931.

[139] TNAUK CO/691/115/7, Railway Commission: Survey of Kilombero River, 1931.

and it was clear that Kilombero been a significant part of his vision.[140] But at his succession, 'Tanganyika, a poor country, undeveloped and depending increasingly on export of raw materials, was caught, like so many other countries, in the trough of a world-wide financial depression'.[141] The global economic landscape had dramatically altered, which in turn altered colonial visions of Kilombero development. By 1932, then, and through no lack of effort, the landscape and economy of Kilombero since the advent of British administration had remained largely unchanged. There is a strong argument that the so-called 'failure' of wholescale intervention was, in fact, far from detrimental. Efforts to effect 'progress' and 'development' were, after all, colonial efforts imposed from above, and it is clear that much of what was envisaged for Kilombero and its people would have been just that: an imposition.

---

[140] Symes, *Tour of Duty*, 162.
[141] Ibid., 163.

3

Between Rhetoric and Reality: The Strength of an Idea, 1931–45

The years 1929–45 were 'the pivot of Tanganyika's modern history' as they mark 'the transition from the creation of a colonial society to the beginning of its dissolution'.[1] Moreover, this period reveals – more than most – that 'the concept and practice of "development" in colonial Africa was never static or monolithic in construction or implementation. Instead, "development" evolved and shifted, taking on multiple meanings and forms in different contexts'.[2] This chapter reveals the shifting concepts and practices that either orbited Kilombero or were fundamentally central to it. In these years, broadly framed by the beginning of the Great Depression and the end of the Second World War, the nature of colonial development in Kilombero is best understood through the lens of limitation: the limitations of a shoestring budget, a skeleton staff and an inadequate transport infrastructure, of nascent market systems dogged by shortcomings, and the limitations placed by the colonial administration on the lives of those most vulnerable to its impositions. The future was not bright.

Colonial demands on agricultural production, for example, were often paternalistic, exploitative, and frustrated by failures to provide the means to reach its own ends. Colonial authority prevailed despite this, and local lives came to be imposed upon and disrupted by state schemes. Britain's Colonial Development Act of 1929 clearly decreed how funding for colonial development must actively encourage 'commerce with and industry in the United Kingdom' and many schemes were driven towards these ends.[3] Due to the poor financial position of the 1930s, these schemes were modest successors to those once grandiose visions. But it is difficult to bury ideas; they tend to resurface.

---

[1] Iliffe, *Modern History*, 342.
[2] Joseph M. Hodge, 'Epilogue: Taking stock, looking ahead', in Joseph M. Hodge, Gerald Hödl, and Martina Kopf (eds), *Developing Africa: Concepts and Practices in Twentieth-Century Colonialism* (Manchester, 2014), 367.
[3] Great Britain. Colonial Office, *First Interim Report of the Colonial Development Advisory Committee Covering the Period 1st August 1929 – 28th February 1930* (London, 1930), 7.

On 30 March 1931 a meeting was held at the Colonial Office in London to again discuss the formation of a syndicate for Kilombero development. Donald Cameron was between governorships, and attended before sailing for Lagos.[4] Also present was Sydney Henn, who had taken a personal interest in the supposed potential of the valley since chairing the Tanganyika Railway Commission, and had been trying to advance 'this project' since September 1930.[5] Henn had held discussions with 'Mathesons' and Balfour, Beatty & Co., who 'proposed to take a share in [the] business' of 'granting a charter of concession to private enterprise for development of the Kilombero Valley'.[6] This kind of colonial capitalism had its sceptics at the time. In January 1931, the Power Securities Corporation executed an agreement with the Tanganyika Government to harness the hydropower of the Pangani Falls in Tanga region. When mentioned in the House of Commons, one member remarked: 'I hope this is not a case where the Government are handing any money over to some private company which is going to exploit the country.'[7] The same concern might have been raised for Kilombero.

Notes of the meeting were 'strictly confidential' and optimism was tempered due to hesitations over the Mandate. The meeting considered that the 'basic principal underlying the proposal to form the Kilombero Development Syndicate' was 'to promote the development of Native Agriculture in the Kilombero Valley' and the 'Articles of Association of the Syndicate will be drafted on lines calculated to comply strictly with the conditions laid down in Article 7 [of the Mandate]'.[8] For this purpose, the Government would partner with the Syndicate and participate in the trading and industrial operations of the scheme without interfering in its business operations. Its success rested on a branch line from Kilosa to Ifakara, funds for which would be raised by Government to 'avoid any criticism from Geneva' but the construction and operation of the line would be run by the Syndicate.[9] Despite outward appearances, this scheme would still put the most productive areas of Kilombero

---

4 Gailey, *Sir Donald*, 87–9.
5 TNA 26056, Henn to Jardine, 16 April 1931.
6 Ibid. Jardine Matheson & Co. was founded in 1832, growing to prominence in East Asia as a British foreign trading firm. In colonial Kenya it operated through a subsidiary, Jardine Matheson (East Africa) Ltd. It transmuted to the international conglomerate, Jardine Matheson Holdings. See the Jardine Matheson Archive (GBR/0012/MS JM) at the University of Cambridge. The British electrical engineering firm of Balfour, Beatty & Co. was founded in 1909 and acquired by the Power Securities Corporation in 1922.
7 'Tanganyika (Pangani Falls)', *Hansard* HC Deb, 23 February 1931, vol. 248 cc.1768–9.
8 TNA 26056, Draft Note: Kilombero Development Syndicate, 27 March 1931.
9 TNA 26056, Henn to Jardine, 16 April 1931.

under the stranglehold of private enterprise. It was revenue and not the welfare of people in Kilombero that drove the scheme, and there were clear attempts to enshroud the purely commercial motives of syndicated development in Kilombero to satisfy the League of Nations that this was not capitalist exploitation. As he was no longer Governor, Cameron's position was less compromised, and it is not clear whether he hoped to profit personally or was acting in an advisory capacity.

The scheme was endorsed by the utmost echelon of Tanganyikan Government: Cameron as ex-Governor; Douglas Jardine as Acting Governor wished the project 'every success'; and Stewart Symes as succeeding Governor 'expressed a friendly interest' and 'would most certainly lend it his sympathetic support'.[10]

Despite renewed discussion, syndicated development did not materialise for the second time. Kilombero farmers were not to discover the meaning of the *métayage* system of agriculture, or something close to it. During the Henn Commission, H.W.D. Pollock (Assistant District Officer, Kiberege) was asked whether farmers would respond to the scheme initially proposed by Telford. 'I think they would', he replied, 'but then they would be annoyed about it afterwards.'[11] Pollock was cautious not to sound unsympathetic to the scheme while also siding with its prospective tenants, who fortunately never experienced this 'annoyance' for themselves. If doubts of its viability did not deter investment, repercussions from the economic depression certainly did. Farmers were spared the loss of their best agricultural lands to a monopolistic company which sought to control the manner and means of crop production. The restrictions that this would have imposed were inimical to true local development, and a suppression of the general freedom that enabled farmers to practise agricultural methods and follow cycles in harmony with the specificities of their ecological environment.

Subsequent years, however, saw local government interventions, and enforced regulations proceeded insidiously. The period 1932–45 has been looked upon by nostalgic administrators and missionaries as a 'golden period', whereas for their subjects these were the years of their greatest 'humiliation, frustration, and diminution of their freedom'.[12] Orders were passed that prohibited the purchase, barter, or removal of foodstuffs without written permission from the District Officer (DO).[13] Barter was particularly discouraged as it did not generate cash for tax payments. Moreover, in 1934

[10] Ibid.
[11] Tanganyika, 'Appendices', 163 [Nineteenth Session, 23 August 1930, Dar es Salaam].
[12] Larson, 'History', 268.
[13] TNA 19454, The Native Foodstuffs (Rufiji) Order 1936, 11 May 1936.

between January and June alone, nine convictions were registered in Mahenge for 'failing to plant adequate crops'.[14] Between April and June in Kiberege, there were 149 convictions for the same offence.[15] Enforced planting was ostensibly an anti-famine measure, but this was a warped tactic employed by a colonial state who simultaneously exported greater volumes of food.

In the absence of a syndicate, then, it was left to Government alone to intervene in Kilombero affairs. This took various forms, such as the promotion of cash crop production, regulation of markets, and development of communications. This last shall be discussed first.

The lure of the map

After the abandonment of the river survey under Captain Gibson, in February 1932, Gillman wrote a memorandum on the navigability of its system, to consolidate colonial knowledge to that moment. It sought 'to sift this accumulated evidence in order to arrive, if possible, at a definite conclusion with regards to the navigability of the Kilombero River and to its usefulness towards the development of the plain'.[16] Gillman understood that here, hope seemed to spring eternal:

> The lure of the map and more particularly of the early inaccurate and of the small-scale map, has since the earliest days of European occupation ever and again stimulated hopes and projects for the utilisation of the Rufiji-Kilombero system, either as a whole or in parts, for the purposes of inland navigation.[17]

This 'lure of the map' is a compelling image. This enticement applies not only to the river system for transport, but to the wider valley as a fertile region, a granary, and an area of high development potential. The strength of the lure varied by context, as did the character of visions for the valley. By this time, however, ambitious German proposals for elaborate irrigation schemes, to train the river, improve its bends, and even lower its bed, had been disregarded. Gillman had long doubted German calculations and assumptions made regarding river behaviour, and whether economic gains could justify the required expenditure. Telford confirmed these doubts, but the prospect of greater utility of the river for produce transport prevailed. Gillman compared

---

[14] TNA 61/16/G, Annual Report on Food Supplies: Mahenge District, 16 July 1934.
[15] TNA 61/16/H, Annual Crop Report, Kiberege, 10 August 1934.
[16] TNAUK CO 691/125/17, Memorandum on the Navigability of the Kilombero River System, 1932.
[17] Ibid.

distances mapped by the 1897, 1909, and 1931 surveys and these correlated quite closely; yet other conditions were 'by no means static, but highly dynamic' over the years.[18] The Ruhuji River, for example, had changed its course in 1930 and now joined the Mnyera approximately ten miles above the former confluence. Other rivers were also far from static and, as typical fan rivers, the beds of many – such as the Mgeta, Ruipa, Itete, and Lumemo – were unstable. Gillman took German evidence to also show that the Kilombero was far from stable in 1909 and believed that then and since, the 'observed state of affairs' had been viewed erroneously as 'a static fact which has only got to be tackled in the right way to obey the wishes of Man'.[19] It was clearly more complicated than that. Gillman also believed that 'the great tectonic happenings of the very recent past have not yet come to rest' and 'a differential movement of very small dimensions' could readjust the equilibrium and destroy 'rashly designed training works'.[20] He may have been overly cautious to portend an earthquake in Kilombero, but he was right not to underestimate the variability and volatility of the river system. This assessment of available colonial knowledge further revealed the ecological complexities of Kilombero and the difficulties it posed to attempts to realise visions. The lure of the map did not align with the facts on the ground.

Despite limitations, it was concluded that an experimental river service on the Kilombero between Kotakota and Ifakara, and fed by canoes on the tributaries, could begin at any moment. Further surveys of all channels, lakes, and swamps were advised. Self-registering gauges were also recommended, and the accurate determining of levelling, cross-sections, depths, and velocities was vital. An aerial survey was also suggested to better understand the 'mosaic of the many water-courses' and eliminate unsuitable river channels that a ground survey could not detect. Periodic surveys would also provide important data on 'the tendencies of the various channels to shift their beds'.[21]

For the reconstruction of development histories in Kilombero, this is an important memorandum that blends objective facts with subjective perspectives. It reveals much about the valley, but even more about colonial thinking. For Gillman, comprehensive technical knowledge was paramount. His background as a geographer and engineer is evident in his approach to place and problem, avoiding rash generalisations or wild conjecture. He sought to base judgements on sound evidence. Conscious of the potential for wasted expenditure over grave mistakes, Gillman was wary of roseate optimism.

[18] Ibid.
[19] Ibid.
[20] Ibid.
[21] Ibid.

He later revealed his reason for writing the memorandum, which was that 'on a geographical basis, finally, it was hoped [it would] put a stop to all contemplation of such a scheme'.[22] This was never explicit, but it was heavily implied: this was a future that Gillman thought foolish to pursue.

There was a responsibility to writing memoranda such as this, but their recommendations (or discouragements) were not executive. Their nature was always advisory, never fully authoritative. This allowed for nuance in representation, as the burden of decision-making lay elsewhere. This elasticity allowed for both scepticism and optimism to be exaggerated, the extent of either varied between interpretations of differences between technical possibilities and colonial possibilities. Neither were fixed. Technical capabilities could mostly be abstracted and only improved towards the future, whereas colonial possibilities were contextually fixed, highly variable, and widely contingent. Solutions to problems could always be proposed, especially with unlimited finance and resources. These tended towards the kind of utopian thinking that Gillman, for one, regarded as pointless. It was technically possible to canalise the Kilombero, lower its bed, train its course, and contain its flood; but that was not the point. It was technically possible to run a steamship between two points on the river, but was it worthwhile and would it show a return on the investment?

The difference between technical and colonial possibilities is also illustrated by proposals to connect the valley to the Southern Highlands via escarpment roads. Colonel Maxwell described this route as 'impossible for motor transport' and clarified: 'I use this in the colonial term impossible.'[23] Construction of connecting roads was *technically* possible and even envisaged by blasting in the style of the Grand Corniche, but 'in colonial practice the cost would be prohibited' due to the necessity for large bridges, viaducts, and cuttings.[24] This determinant permeated many colonial visions for Kilombero, or at least their outcomes. Blurred lines often obscured what was possible in both technical *and* colonial terms. Ideals exist easily in the mind and on the page, but only wild alchemy can transform them.

Schemes in aspic

By the end of 1932 all capital expenditure throughout Tanganyika was suspended. The embargo was fortified by the 'Report of a Financial Mission to Tanganyika' by Sir Sydney Armitage-Smith, whose 'hand [fell] heavily upon the railway system' and asserted that 'schemes of construction must be

---

[22] Gillman, 'A short history', 53.
[23] TNAUK CO 691/79, Despatches: Tanganyika Territory, 1925.
[24] Ibid.

abandoned'.[25] He concluded, 'it should definitely be accepted that [...] the era of railway construction in this Territory is past'.[26] No case could be made for railway development without a major gold discovery and, while existing communications were 'obviously inadequate for economic development', Tanganyika could not 'afford to continue railway construction, and must rely for the future on motor transport to open up new areas'.[27] Hopes for a line from Kilosa to Ifakara had thus reached their terminus. At the government press, type was set, primed for ink, and poised to print a Command Paper on Gillman's memorandum; but this was recalled, the type returned to the printer's tray. The memorandum itself was thought 'likely to be the last word on this subject for some considerable time' and orders were given to 'close the print, on the ground that the suspension of development in Tanganyika has rendered the publication [...] unnecessary'.[28] The transformation of transport to, from, and within Kilombero by river and rail was now a scheme in aspic. These conclusions were 'the only sane ones which could be reached in present circumstances', whereas G.F. Seel thought a short statement ought to be written on how transport problems might be approached 'in the event of circumstances justifying the provision of capital funds for the purpose at any future time'.[29] This was overruled. 'In present circumstances,' wrote J.F.N. Green, 'we had better not ask even for as little as Mr. Seel suggests'.[30] In London, one comment on the file marked 'Development of the Kilombero Valley' poetically captured the mood: 'This reminds me of the dying words of Pitt: "Roll up that map of Europe, it will not be wanted these many years hence."'[31]

The valley would not be served by a railway, its closest railhead remained at Kilosa, 115 miles from Ifakara. This was just one of many shelved plans at this time, but it was a major one. Plans for this line had been repeatedly 'pigeon-holed' – to borrow a phrase used in one House of Commons debate for schemes that had been 'held up for months and years' despite being 'schemes that would give employment, schemes that were necessary, schemes that would

---

[25] 'Editorial notes', *Journal of the Royal African Society* 32:126 (1933), 98.

[26] Sydney Armitage-Smith, *Report on a Financial Mission to Tanganyika* (London, 1932), 85.

[27] Cyril Ehrlich, 'Some aspects of economic policy in Tanganyika, 1945–60', *The Journal of Modern African Studies* 2:2 (1964), 271; Armitage-Smith, *Financial Mission*, 85.

[28] TNAUK CO 691/125/15, G.F. Seel to J.F.N. Green, 22 September 1932.

[29] TNAUK CO 691/125/15, Note by G.F. Seel, 22 September 1932.

[30] TNAUK CO 691/125/15, Note by J.F.N. Green, 22 September 1932.

[31] TNAUK CO 691/125/15, Notes by G.F. Seel, 20 October 1932.

develop and benefit our Colonies'.[32] Now that plans were on indefinite hiatus, the improvement of the Kilosa-Ifakara road was recommended on the understanding that Government would take 'active measures immediately to increase agricultural production in the Kilombero Valley', but the Colonial Office were 'given no indication whether this [would] be possible' or even whether it was 'necessary for the Agricultural Department to be provided with additional funds for the purpose'.[33]

Any expenditure at this time was closely scrutinised, but the case was made that while 'the future outlook must remain uncertain [the scheme was] designed directly to promote development – especially native development' and for this reason it was encouraged.[34] As the 1930s progressed, in some circles there was renewed uncertainty as to whether Tanganyika could be returned to Germany. Governor Sir Harold MacMichael addressed these fears and the path out of retrenchment to an audience in June 1935:

> There is a great future for Tanganyika, but our work can only be done well if it is done with confidence in its durability. There are three essentials to success: first, vision to foresee the potentialities of the future and to realise opportunities when they present themselves; secondly, vigour to grasp the opportunities and press forward to prosperity; and thirdly, confidence in ourselves as a nation and in the future of Tanganyika.[35]

This was high rhetoric in the face of harsh realities. MacMichael detailed eleven road-building schemes to be financed from the Colonial Development Fund and through the balance of loan monies from the East African Guaranteed Loan Fund. The projected cost for all totalled GBP £250,000 and the most expensive – at £78,000 – was the Kilosa-Ifakara road.[36] 'The first idea was to develop the Kilombero Valley by [river] navigation', MacMichael explained, but 'the difficulties were so great that it was decided to tap the area by road'.[37] This was 'a potentially rich cotton, maize, and rice district' and – not for the first time – the words 'potentially rich' belied the difficulties in realising this 'potential'.[38] There were concerns the scheme was premature, but it

---

[32] 'Palestine and East Africa Loans Bill', 30 April 1931, *Hansard* HC Deb vol. 251, cols. 1876–1878.
[33] TNAUK CO 691/141/2, Note by M.A. Greenhill, 22 December 1934.
[34] TNAUK CO 691/141/2, Tanganyika Development Schemes: Road Construction and Telegraph Lines, allocations from E.A. Guaranteed Loans, 1934.
[35] TNAUK CO 691/141/2, Extract from *East Africa* magazine, 4 July 1935.
[36] £68,000 would be spent locally and £10,000 in Britain.
[37] TNAUK CO 691/141/2, Extract from *East Africa* magazine, 4 July 1935.
[38] Ibid.

was recommended that the road be built on the condition that definite steps to increase agricultural production were made.[39] Its proposed construction was 'based on the promise of future production' in a valley considered by the fund committee 'to be agriculturally one of the most promising areas in the Territory particularly as regards the production of cotton and rice'.[40] The nub was that its 'present productivity' could not justify the large sum required to bring a railway to Kilombero. Here, at least, certain realities were respected. Moreover, the committee deemed as unwise proposals for river transport between Kotakota and Ifakara due to the projected costs of shaping and maintaining the Kilombero River for navigation. Risks associated with water transport were also thought to negate any gain from economic efficiency.

Tax, trade, and transport

Grand visions of large-scale development projects had faded. Expected high capital expenditure proved a mirage. Subsequent years sustained a 'piecemeal' colonial administration characterised as 'hegemony on a shoestring' but whose control and authority were no less pervasive. The fabric of this power lay with the District Officers and Provincial Commissioners, considered at the time as the 'surest method and the best hope of implementing the obligations undertaken by the Mandatory Power, and of securing the progress and advancement of the mass of the people placed under its charge and authority'.[41] These officers were 'symbols of authority' and cardinal to colonial bureaucracy, for on their work hinged the whole mechanism of indirect rule, although the official authoritative reach and local influence of DOs relied heavily upon the manipulation and co-operation of local elites.[42] Each district presented its own distinct challenges to the pursuit of revenue and order. This period offers a window into these dynamics in Kilombero at this pivotal time, when the colonial administration was far from dissolution and determined to pursue tax, payable by revenue generated primarily through a trade in cash crop produce, and which relied on the development of transport infrastructures. It was the DO, then, who was the principal representative of this process by the 1930s and who had the greatest hand in promoting 'development' in 'his' district.

[39] TNAUK CO 691/141/2, Unknown to Smith [Colonial Office], 21 February 1935.
[40] TNAUK CO 691/141/2, Report of a Committee Appointed to Consider Schemes for the Development of the Territory, 15 September 1934.
[41] Armitage-Smith, *Financial Mission*, 95.
[42] See Anthony Kirk-Greene, *Symbol of Authority: The British District Officer in Africa* (London, 2006).

'District Officers in Tanganyika were a breed I admired,' wrote Roald Dahl, who docked at the 'tiny town of Dar es Salaam' in 1938 as one of three Shell Company employees in the country.[43] Dahl's description of the haughty DO accurately represents how most saw themselves, capturing the exaggerated sense of self-importance many held:

> In their lonely outposts they had to be all things to all men. They were the judges whose decisions settled both tribal and personal disputes. They were the advisers to tribal chiefs. They were often the givers of medicines and the saviours of the sick. They administered their own vast districts by keeping law and order under the most difficult circumstances.[44]

This is echoed by A.T. Culwick, who spent more years as an officer in Ulanga District during the 1930s and 1940s than any other. Culwick wrote of 'the colonial administrator' that 'his responsibilities were unlimited, for he was "In Charge". Though his district might be the size of England, everything which went on in it was up to him: finance, justice, police, medicine, education, public works, posts and telegraphs, etc.'[45] Crucially, '[s]o long as law and order were preserved, the taxes came in and the people were well fed, all was well at Headquarters'.[46]

This tax was an imposition, disruption, and unavoidable reality to local lives. District Officers were quick to report its collection. In 1932 tax was said to be 'coming in very satisfactorily', and especially in Kiberege.[47] This was unsurprising, as local authority was more easily exerted in the immediate vicinity of the district office; but in order to regularly inspect tax, court, and cash books in most other areas throughout the valley, the most efficient and 'most reliable all-the-year round communication' was by motorboat.[48]

Tax revenue in Kilombero was derived principally from sales of rice and/or cotton. Revenue was thus greatly affected, among other factors, by fluctuating prices, soil suitability, the 'success' of planting campaigns, and local zeal. Commodity prices in general had fallen due to the Depression, and the value of both exports and imports reduced. Between 1930 and 1935 the market price

---

[43] Roald Dahl, *Going Solo* (London, 1986), 40.
[44] Ibid., 40.
[45] A.T. Culwick, *Britannia Waives the Rules* (Cape Town, 1963), 16. At 15,000km² Ulanga was equivalent in area to the English county of Yorkshire.
[46] Ibid., 17.
[47] TNA 61/141/G, Handing Over Report: Mahenge and Kiberege Districts, 8 November 1932.
[48] TNA 61/141/H/Vol. I, Handing Over Notes – October 1940. From Ifakara, Utengule could be reached in four days by motorboat during the wet season, and Ngombo in three during the dry season.

for lint fell heavily. Price reductions tended to immediately reduce production acreage. A ginnery had been established at Kiberege in 1932, and attempts were made in 1932–3 to invest its proprietors with an interest in the condition and quantity of the crop grown in the area.[49] This was later said to be 'proving successful' and made 'a great difference to the material progress of the area'.[50] The alluvial lands of the valley were thought to be naturally suited to good quality cotton, but many areas lacked market access. It was hoped that potential growers could be brought within an expanding 'cotton economic orbit' through the establishment of buying posts.[51]

The success of cotton in rice-growing areas often depended 'on the prestige and enthusiasm of the individual officer' – thought 'hardly fair' to the officer – while the ginner also suffered the irregularities of production and remained 'in fear of a complete collapse in cotton production'.[52] Despite the great importance once shone on the agricultural potential of Kilombero, in 1935 a request to appoint a permanent agricultural officer to Kiberege was denied.[53] Alternatively, a mere Agricultural Assistant or 'temporary European' would have been an asset for 'propaganda' during the planting season, but no posting of any kind was made. Instead, the services of the District Agricultural Officer for Kilosa were offered when they could be spared.

Pressure was brought to bear on farmers to pay their taxes as soon as their produce could be sold. Markets for rice and cotton opened around 15 June and 1 September respectively, and farmers were harried after these dates. Where either rice or cotton could be grown, rice was preferred as one acre produced three times the weight of cotton under the same, but prices per kilo – at least in the mid-1930s – were almost the same.[54] Moreover, cotton was inedible and could not, like rice, also function as a food crop (as well as a cash crop). This dual status of edible crops mitigated the risk of price fluctuations insofar as labour was never wasted. If the price for rice was not right, then it could be stored for future use.

In Kilombero and beyond, the limit of production for any commodity may be measured by the amount that could be carried to market. It is a generally accepted rule that an increase in buying facilities spurs production increases.

[49] For an overview of the Tanganyika cotton industry 1930–5, see E. Harrison, 'Cotton in Tanganyika Territory', *The Empire Cotton Growing Review* 13:1 (1936), 1–11.
[50] TNA 61/141/G, Handing Over Report: Mahenge and Kiberege Districts, 8 November 1932.
[51] TNAUK CO 691/141/2, Memorandum on Kilosa-Ifakara-Kotakota Road Scheme, 15 September 1934.
[52] TNA 61/45/H, DofA [Wakefield] to PCEP, 18 October 1935.
[53] Ibid.
[54] Ibid.

The establishment of buying posts was therefore strongly encouraged by the administration; this would usually open either weekly or fortnightly during the appropriate months. 'With better transport facilities', one official believed, 'it is very probable that there would be an increase in the number of trading posts leading to increased competition for the rice crop, better prices and therefore increased production.'[55] In 1940, however, it was thought that the introduction of formal markets in Kilombero throughout the 1930s actually reduced rice production.[56] Rules and regulations served as a discouragement to farmers who preferred the informality and freedom from restriction of direct trade and exchange. Nevertheless, production remained contingent on market and transport infrastructures. In most cases, roads were built or improved as a response to higher production rates. The creation of efficient access to markets also incentivised greater yields, especially in fertile areas. It was largely for the DO to decide when, where, and how to improve Kilombero's roads. In 1939, for example, a ten-mile track between Kiberege and Ibiki was earmarked for conversion to a 'proper road' if cotton could be grown at a certain place within its locale; but there were also other interests to consider as 'incidentally', it was noted, 'there is excellent duck and game shooting at Ibiki'.[57]

Increases in cash crop production and broader transport infrastructure development certainly benefited the imperial economy, while positive impacts on African well-being were negligible. The binding of Kilombero farmers to the British colonial economy removed their capacity for innovation and ability to maximise opportunities.[58] Colonial efforts to produce cash crops thus came at 'the expense of economic activities that would have proved more useful to economic development'.[59] This mattered little to the Anglocentric industrialist, who perceived cotton production and its transportation as vital to *his* future and not that of the farmers far removed from the metropole. For example, the President of the Manchester Chamber of Commerce declared that 'Lancashire's future depends largely upon the amount of cotton which can be produced within the Empire. What could be more disastrous than that the development of the industry in one of our most promising colonies should

---

[55] TNAUK CO 691/141/2, Memorandum on Kilosa-Ifakara-Kotakota Road Scheme, 15 September 1934.

[56] TNA 61/141/H/Vol. I, Handing Over Report – October 1940. In 1940, produce markets were established at: Ifakara, Kiberege, Mofu, Mbingu, Mgeta, Kotakota, Ngombo, Malinyi, Utengule, Kilosa kwa Mpepo.

[57] TNA 61/141/H/Vol. I, Handing Over Notes [Lumley to Culwick], 16 September 1939.

[58] Mkeli Mbosa, 'Colonial Production and Underdevelopment in Ulanga District, 1894–1950' (MA thesis, University of Dar es Salaam, 1988), 135.

[59] David Sunderland (ed.), *Communications in Africa, 1880–1939: Volume I* (London, 2012), lii.

be prevented through the lack of transport facilities?'[60] This 'extraversion' of African economies by colonial interests is central to processes of so-called positive 'development' resulting ultimately in detrimental underdevelopment.[61]

The lack of local transport facilities in Kilombero was of far greater and immediate consequence to its inhabitants than to the looms of Lancashire. In a land divided by rivers, bridges were symbols of connection. They enabled movement across the flow of waters whose courses shaped the region. Canoe crossings would always serve the wider rivers and could bear heavier loads, but a network of bridges created interconnectivity between otherwise separated areas. Each year this layer of infrastructure was exposed to the mercy of the flood. Bridges washed away, restoring divisions. Each January, some of the larger bridges were often stripped of their decking and road bearers by hand to save a complete rebuild later, which was usually only possible in July once floods had subsided.[62] Therefore, from January to June (or mid-July) practically all roads in the district were impassable for motor traffic due to the flood and ruination of wooden bridges.[63] As nearly all roads crossed rivers and streams, the re-establishment of communications in Kilombero after the rains was not so much a road problem, but a bridge problem.

Mahenge was often isolated for up to eight months in particularly wet years, but motor transport to areas served by suitable roads was usually possible by mid-August. Until then, only head porterage could suffer the otherwise impassable roads. Even the 'all-weather' Kilosa-Ifakara road was defeated in 1940 after heavy rains in April–May. One official exasperated, 'I know no more difficult country to maintain roads in.'[64]

Each year the pendulum of change swung far in Kilombero. The forces of nature and humankind shared the valley, each taking turn to rule. Deluge brought refuge, and receding waters launched processes of restoration. Roads were repaired, bridges rebuilt, areas were brought out of isolation, the Kilombero River could be crossed, and the region fully reunited. But this was not a closely connected region at the best of times. Even during the dry season, DOs often reported an inability to travel as widely as their duties required. Any shortening of the expected dry season further reduced intra-district travel

---

[60] 'Development of Tropical Africa', *The Manchester Guardian*, 24 October 1925.

[61] See Gareth Austin, 'African economic development and colonial legacies', *International Development Policy* 1 (2010), 11–32.

[62] The scarcity of timber in some areas either stymied or prevented the rebuilding of damaged bridges.

[63] TNA 61/141/G, Handing Over Report: Mahenge District, July 1934.

[64] TNA 61/141/G, Handing Over Report: Mahenge and Kiberege Districts, 8 November 1932. Tax defaulters' debt often converted to free labour, frequently to restore roads after the rains.

Plate 2 Kiberege Bridge over Kiberege River in flood, 1932 [Source: OBL MSS.Afr.s.2228].

more generally. Broken wooden bush poles frequently interrupted telegraph communications; and in any case, there was no direct line between the administrative stations of Mahenge and Kiberege. The only mail runner service to Kilosa operated once a week, leaving Mahenge on a Wednesday and returning the following Tuesday. The telegraph line between Ifakara and Iringa (and then to Kilosa and Dar es Salaam) was often down due to heavy rain, further isolating the region. For Culwick, however, Kilombero's isolation brought respite from interference and 'ignorant intervention' from his superiors. 'In this way', he believed, 'poorness of communications contributed materially to efficient administration and progress.'[65]

River crossings were also monetised and ferries were a significant source of income for certain local treasuries. Crossings on frequent routes and through significant rice centres were particularly important, but canoes and pontoons were not always well maintained.[66] In late 1937, for example, ferries over the Mnyera and Ruhuji Rivers were 'a source of danger owing to their construction', and their rebuilding was urged.[67] The most important ferries

---

[65] Culwick, *Britannia Waives the Rules*, 19.
[66] TNA 61/134/G, District Office [Mkasu] to PC [Mahenge], 27 August 1929.
[67] TNA 61/134/H, APCEP to DO [Kiberege], 22 November 1937.

were those over the Kilombero and Ruaha rivers. These were maintained by the Mbunga Native Administration and operated solely from its treasury funds, but with this responsibility came great risk. To mitigate this, in 1932 it was proposed that the ferry service over the Kilombero be taken over by the Public Works Department. This would decrease Mbunga revenue by £325 (from £898) per annum and was successfully protested by the DO.[68] From 1939, however, formal rules governing the ferry were laid down, ostensibly for its safe operation. These regulations included: hours of operation from 6am to 6pm daily; closure to motor traffic during the wet season from March to July, the specific dates to be set by the DO; maximum permitted loads; and centralised control of the crossing point through the strict prohibition of any other conveyance of people or goods five miles up- or downstream of the pontoon.[69] These directives also ensured fares were duly captured. In 1941 it was again proposed that the Public Works Department took over its running due to a belief that 'the responsibility and risk taken is too great to be borne by a Native Treasury the size of Kiberege'.[70] Compensation to the Mbunga administration and the cost of replacing the ferry's five canoes was discussed, but its operation was not transferred.

Due to traffic increases during harvesting months, the ferry was, on occasion, permitted to run after dark at double the rate with a 50 per cent wage increase to ferrymen.[71] Any gains made towards transport efficiency could be swiftly lost to heightened risk of accident. In September 1941, the firm of Vithaldas Haridas and Company requested the ferry be kept open until 10pm during the cotton season.[72] This is indicative of the extent to which initiative, capital, and forward momentum behind crop marketing and transport relied on individual firms.[73] These were exclusively Indian-owned and run, and thus the Indian trading community played a crucial role in the development of economic and transport systems in Kilombero.[74] In 1930 there was no industry so to speak, and a lack of convenient markets discouraged increased agricultural production. Driven by opportunity and entrepreneurial capitalism, the 1930s saw a proliferation of Indian traders establish trading centres, ginneries, rice mills, and organised transport. The colonial government sought to keep this

[68] TNA 61/134/H, Ferries: Kiberege, Extract from letter from ADO [Kiberege] to PCEP, 18 January 1932.
[69] TNA 61/134/H/9, Draft Rules for Kilombero Ferry, 31 January 1939.
[70] TNA 61/134/H/16, PCEP to Director of Public Works, 29 April 1941.
[71] TNA 61/134/H/26, DO [Kiberege] to PCEP, 30 September 1941.
[72] Hereafter, 'Vithaldas' or VHC.
[73] TNA 61/134/H/26, PCEP to DO [Kiberege], 22 September 1941.
[74] Mbosa, 'Colonial Production', 87.

Plate 3 Car crossing on Kilombero Ferry, July 1933 [Source: OBL MSS.Afr.s.2228].

enterprise in check but, for an administration on a hamstrung budget, it was not only encouraged but virtually indispensable.

Vithaldas had established a considerable presence in Kilombero and increasingly sought greater control of the market. One representative – J.D. Patel – was lauded for having 'done a great deal to forward cotton production' through the opening up of buying centres in remote places, paying the same price in Kiberege as Morogoro, and for effective seed distribution.[75] Another was less exalting in private correspondence and described Patel as the 'type of business man who appears never to be satisfied and to expect miraculous development in the space of a year or so'.[76] Vithaldas were denied their request for exclusive rice buying rights, and a further request that pressure be borne on farmers to produce cotton was also rejected as 'the use of compulsion [...] is illegal and undesirable, and cannot be considered'.[77] Exclusive buying rights were later granted when circumstances suited Government.

Vithaldas played a crucial if complex role in the development of Kilombero. Its head office was in Jinja, Uganda near to the Kakira Sugar Works for which they were renowned. From cotton they expanded into sugar, and

---

[75] TNA 61/45/H, DofA [Wakefield] to PCEP, 18 October 1935.
[76] TNA 61/45/H/13, PCEP to CS, 23 October 1935.
[77] TNA 61/45/H, Acting Chief Secretary [G.J. Partridge] to Vithaldas, Haridas & Co. (VHC), 8 November 1935.

from Uganda into Kenya, then Tanganyika.[78] Operations in Kilombero were somewhat subsidiary yet supported by a strong base.[79] The company wrote to the Provincial Commissioner in 1936 regarding 'suggestions made by the Local Officers, time after time to us, to develop the district' and 'to co-operate with the market scheme even in the remote corner of the country'.[80] Encouragement had been given – to invest capital, to speculate and experiment – but with neither guarantee of profit nor safeguard against loss. Complaints were raised when expected protection – raised by DOs' suggestions – were unsubstantiated by officials from other departments. 'It will speak for itself', the manager wrote, 'how much government has gained due to our entry in this district directly and indirectly; while on the other hand how much we have suffered loss.'[81] Vithaldas was a commercial and enterprising firm, and risks would not have been taken in such a difficult and volatile region as Kilombero without strong inducement. In 1934, Culwick wrote to Vithaldas and recommended they entered the rice market as large buyers 'as I think it will pay you as well as re-acting to the general economic good of this area'.[82] In 1935, Culwick wrote to ask, 'Are you interested in the [Ngindo] bees-wax industry? We want someone to handle the trade there (exclusively). I think there is money to be made there.'[83] The mistake was to construe encouragement as protection. Local officials were not the highest authority.

But by 1937 Vithaldas had been granted various exclusive buying rights and held a virtual monopoly on cotton, which the administration thought was easier than managing a buying system with multiple competitors.[84] No system was particularly easy, however, and a calamity of errors ensued in 1943 after Vithaldas established a rice mill in Ifakara and agreed purchasing through an association of local traders responsible for buying and bagging paddy. Buying was held up through lack of cash and bags; there were no facilities for storage; paddy was lost to theft and white ants; and bags were adulterated by earth and stones. The shift to machine milling brought nearly the whole crop to market in 2.5 months and local traders did not have the means or organisation to handle it.[85] Previously, paddy was hand-hulled and sold over

[78] See Martha Honey, 'Asian industrial activities in Tanganyika', *Tanzania Notes and Records* 75 (1974), 55–70.

[79] From the company runs a direct line to the Madhvani Group, one of Uganda's largest conglomerates and its largest sugar producer, with assets (as of 2019) of over USD $750 million for its sugar business alone.

[80] TNA 61/45/H, Patel to PCEP, 16 April 1936.

[81] Ibid.

[82] TNA 61/141/H/Vol. I, Culwick to Manager [VHC], 3 October 1934.

[83] TNA 61/141/H/Vol. I, Culwick to Jethabhai, 5 December 1935.

[84] TNA 61/141/H/Vol. I, Handing Over Notes [Lumley to Culwick], 16 September 1939.

[85] TNA 61/574/13/47, A.H. Savile [Senior Agricultural Officer] PCEP, 20 November 1943.

a longer period of between eight and ten months. During this debacle, many farmers reverted to this process and carried their rice over the escarpment to Iringa.[86] Meanwhile, a dispute over transport rates led to a large accumulation of rice at the mill itself. The Produce Controller had little patience for it: 'The speedy evacuation of all rice produced at the Ifakara mill is a matter of the utmost importance' and 'under no circumstances must any of these trivial pursuits be allowed to interfere with the regular and prompt delivery of rice to railhead.'[87] The following year, the mill was considered uneconomic unless the price to the farmer was reduced, the price of milled rice was raised, or Vithaldas received a £2,000 annual government subsidy.[88]

Another prominent firm was the Ulanga Trading Company – 'Merchants, Planters, and Commission Agents' – who leased plots of land for crop experimentation.[89] All 'non-native' and commercial firms had to apply for such plots, which were granted if surplus to local requirements. In November 1938 the company leased 300 acres near Kiberege for cotton. When this failed, sugar and cashew nuts were trialled. Throughout the 1930s, Vithaldas repeatedly applied for an increase to their plot between the Kiberege and Kinyuku rivers, but this was never approved due to surrounding farmers and privileged local rights of occupancy.[90] In 1940, the three firms of Vithaldas, Ulanga Trading Company, and N. Gokhale and Company leased 1,300 acres collectively. A further 100 acres were leased by Hazara Singh.[91] Indian enterprise was structurally fundamental to the economy in Kilombero, but this was not unusual. By 1939, Indian economic stakes in Tanganyika equated to ownership of 17 per cent of non-African agricultural land, 80 per cent of cotton, sisal, and transport services, and 90 per cent of town property.[92] Armitage-Smith stated that 'the Indian trader, who is to be found all over the Territory wherever there is the chance of setting up the smallest trading settlement, performs it with success' and was 'indispensable'.[93] If they were not there, it was speculated, then no-one could take their place.[94]

---

[86] Approximately 100 tons was sold this way during 1943.
[87] TNA 61/574/13/33, Economic Control Board to DO [Kiberege], 27 September 1943.
[88] TNA 61/574/13/47, DC [Mahenge] to Economic Control Board, 28 July 1944.
[89] TNA 61/29/H/9, Ulanga Trading Company, 3 August 1938.
[90] TNA 61/141/H/Vol. I, Handing Over Notes [Lumley to Culwick], 16 September 1939.
[91] TNA 61/29/5, Agricultural and Pastoral Holdings – Eastern Province, 1942.
[92] R.G. Gregory, *India and East Africa: A History of Race Relations within the British Empire, 1890–1939* (Oxford, 1971), 485; see also Dharam P. Ghai (ed.), *Portrait of a Minority: Asians in East Africa* (Nairobi, 1965).
[93] Armitage-Smith, *Financial Mission*, 11.
[94] Gregory, *India and East Africa*, 482.

Towards centralised development

On 21 December 1938 a Central Development Committee was formed as an early effort to centralise planning. One plan included in its 1940s report was a revival of the idea to systematically transport produce on the Kilombero River. Gillman wrote that 'once more and after eight years of hibernating [this scheme] put out its hydra's head [...] proving again the old commonplace that the more hopeless, the more contrary to the dictates of nature a concept of the human mind is, the longer it takes to die'.[95] His head was in his hands. Once again the lure of the map brought Kilombero into focus. Published with war in full swing, the report also proposed the creation of smallholdings for 'African and Asian cultivators' as the committee regarded it 'as accepted policy that Tanganyika should produce as much as possible for export' while also wanting 'to see a healthy, prosperous, industrious and self-reliant population resident'.[96] It was envisaged this scheme would proceed in two stages. During the first two years an experienced agricultural officer would establish demonstration plots for improved methods of agricultural practice and also encourage increased production of rice and cotton. This officer would also 'accumulate data to indicate the area to be reserved for Asian settlement; the most suitable portion of the district for the controlled settlement of Africans; the type of African settlement to be encouraged, for example, individual homesteads with holdings or individual holdings with a communal village'.[97] The second stage would be consolidation and expansion. Permanent structures would replace temporary ones. Office and farm buildings, a school, and dispensary would be built. Farm machinery, a lorry, and tools would be bought. Costs were estimated to be £3,824 per annum for the first five years.

This scheme did not target general development in Kilombero at all, but was rather a single organised settlement scheme. The committee relied on the numerous reports and memoranda already produced, some of which were quoted verbatim. There are inherent flaws to the over-reliance on such sources to recommend development proposals. These are sharpened when a commission or committee does not even visit the areas in question. So it was during the East Africa Commission in 1925 and again by the Central Development Committee. This disconnection is highlighted by the latter's unusual suggestion for buildings for cattle and pigs' housing and dairying. The climate of lowland valleys then was not generally suited to livestock, and the widespread presence of tsetse fly further curbed pastoralism.

---

[95] Gillman, 'A short history', 53.
[96] Tanganyika, *Report of the Central Development Committee*, 7–9.
[97] Ibid., 49.

The Dar es Salaam Chamber of Commerce and Agriculture commented that 'neither [schemes for development in the Kilombero and Rufiji valleys] would make any particular direct contribution to the [Second World] war effort' but that, while no finance would be provided, 'if any preliminary steps in further developments can be taken, on the lines of the Committee's report, by existing staff, they should be taken'.[98] Consequently, most of the committee's recommendations were impossible to implement due to the war and were recycled into the Ten-Year Development Plan published in 1946.[99] In this vein, post-war planning directly incorporated pre-war visions. One recommendation was followed, however, and an experimental river service on the Kilombero was finally trialled. Against his better judgement, Gillman's 'hydra's head' was followed out of hibernation.

'Proving a failure' – the experimental river service

In 1941 the Provincial Commissioner approached the General Manager of Tanganyika Railways to reopen discussions on a river service. A memorandum followed that framed the proposal in its historical context, from early German suggestions for navigation and 'at various times grandiose schemes' for canalisation, to continued considerations by the British administration.[100] Following improvements to the Kilosa-Ifakara road, it was stated that 'too little attention has been devoted to the provision of transport facilities in the valley above Ifakara'.[101] Calculations were made. In 1941, production of seed cotton and rice was an estimated 350 tons apiece, and it was thought 100 tons of each could be marketed through centres set back from the Kilombero River, leaving the remainder as potential tonnage for a river transport service. At a rate of 30 Shs per ton, expected revenue from 500 tons was £750. Due to wartime conditions, however, it was thought quite impossible (and detrimental to the war effort) to obtain specially designed craft. In any case, it was undesirable to spend capital too lavishly on an experimental service.[102] But more pressing

---

[98] Chamber of Commerce and Agriculture, Dar es Salaam, *Memorandum on the Report of the Central Development Committee, Tanganyika* (Dar es Salaam, 1940), 6.

[99] Tanganyika. Development Commission, *A Ten-Year Development and Welfare Plan for Tanganyika Territory: Report by the Development Commission* (Dar es Salaam, 1946).

[100] TNA 61/635, 'Memorandum No. 58 by the General Manager to the railway advisory council regarding a transport service on the Kilombero River (Ref. No. 920), 19 May 1941; The main productive area of the valley was said to lie approximately 100 miles above Ifakara.

[101] Ibid.

[102] Ibid.

work led Tanganyika Railways to 'regret it will not be possible to undertake a service [...] during 1941' with assurances that preparations would be made for the 1942 season.[103]

In early 1941, Father Jerome of the Roman Catholic Mission at Ifakara had also agreed to build a suitably designed boat for produce in exchange for free timber. This vessel was to be made from local African mahogany, and a felling permit for three trees was issued.[104] For this alternative experiment, it was thought a craft with a very shallow draft similar to that used on the Zambezi River would also suit the Kilombero, and plans were sent to Kiberege by the Provincial Commissioner for Mongu in Northern Rhodesia.[105] Progress proved slow. 'How near completion is the boat of Northern Rhodesian design being built by the Ifakara mission?' asked the Provincial Commissioner twenty months later, in December 1942.[106] It was eventually launched over two years after its timber was felled.

Prior to this, however, in February 1942, one lighter in two pieces and one motorboat to tug it were sent by rail to Kilosa. One lorry then took three trips to complete the transport from Kilosa to Ifakara, each return trip unwasted by conveying either rice or cotton to the railhead.[107] In preparation for the vessels' use on the river, an overview of produce centres and their markets was prepared alongside a map showing the primary tributaries to be served by the main river service. This further revealed the volatility of Kilombero's rivers, as the DO remarked that 'the course of the river appears to have changed somewhat in recent years (c.f. Ruhuji, Mpanga, and Kihanji) and that accurate identification has therefore been somewhat difficult'.[108] Navigational limits also naturally varied at different times of year. Mofu on the Ruipa River, for example, could only be reached at the height of the wet season; and towards the end of the dry season after unusually light rains in 1941, Ngombo was shown to be unreachable whereas it could ordinarily be reached throughout the year.

Produce markets that might be served by the river service were divided into three zones according to their production tonnage, proximity and accessibility to the Kilombero River, and suitable transhipment sites. Ngombo fell within 'Zone A' alongside Utengule, Kilosa kwa Mpepo, Malinyi, and Kotakota.

---

[103] TNA 61/635, General Manager, Tanganyika Railways (GMTR) to PCEP, 4 September 1941.

[104] *Khaya anthotheca.*

[105] TNA 61/635, PCEP to Conservator of Forests, 22 March 1941; TNA 61/635, DO [Kiberege] to PCEP, 29 March 1941; TNA 61/635, PCEP to DO [Kiberege], 9 April 1941.

[106] TNA 61/635, PCEP to DO [Kiberege], 19 December 1942.

[107] TNA 61/635, Chief Mechanical Engineer [TR] to Loco. Foreman, Morogoro, 10 February 1942.

[108] TNA 61/635, DO [Kiberege] to PCEP, 10 February 1942.

These markets were prioritised due to their heavy tonnage of rice and cotton, and their location on either the river itself or near its headwaters. Produce from Mofu, Mbingu, and Mgeta was either transported to Ifakara by road, or brought down by canoe from the Ruipa, Mgeta, and Kihansi rivers. These markets were considered as 'Zone B' and their incorporation into a river service depended on either: a) whether the tug and lighter could navigate Kilombero's tributaries; or b) the ease of transhipping on the Kilombero itself. 'Zone C' included the markets of Majiji, Mtimbira, Itete, Rufiri, Madabadaba, and Iragua. These were to the south of the Kilombero River and produce mostly reached Ifakara by road. Their incorporation into the scheme was due to the cost of lengthy road haulage, but problematic due to their location relative to the river. It was also uneconomic to transport produce from 'Zone B' to Ngombo for transhipment, and canoe transport along existing tributaries was not established due to there being no perennial streams along the right bank of the Kilombero, unlike those that flowed to its left bank from the Udzungwa escarpment. One solution was to build a new road from Madabadaba to below Kotakota, but this could not be immediately considered.[109] Such was the *modus operandi* of colonial thinking, then, and arguably continued into the field of development planning; that is to say, visions were cast at leisure and ambitious proposals were made, while prospects for their implementation remained on distant horizons.

The tug and lighter were first trialled in April 1942 with the Kilombero in flood. A.J. Fernandes, the Goan helmsman, aimed to reach Ngombo but, after twenty-eight hours upstream turned back when just six hours away due to lack of petrol. It then took just eleven-and-a-half hours to return to Ifakara. Fernandes estimated the lighter would carry three tons of rice and consumed fifty-two gallons of fuel. This was 'appalling' as a lorry could achieve similar on twenty gallons.[110] Financial loss was inevitable, but the DO remained optimistic. Fernandes had seen the river at its worst. It remained to be seen how the service performed once markets opened and produce became available.

By October 1942 the service was 'proving a failure' and close to being withdrawn.[111] Low water levels limited its run to only three months when twice that was expected. After generating only £100 in revenue against an expenditure of £1,000 it was subsequently condemned as a 'complete failure' and it was thought that 'without proper arrangement of cotton buying posts, provision of storage accommodation at the river bank, and adequate roads to

---

[109] This paragraph is drawn from TNA 61/635, DO [Kiberege] to PCEP, 10 February 1942.
[110] TNA 61/635, DO [Kiberege] to PCEP, 23 April 1942.
[111] TNA 61/635, GMTR to CS, 6 October 1942.

feed into the river, the traffic would not pass that way'.[112] If the service could not run for six months then it would lose revenue from cotton transport and be limited only to paddy and maize. High costs and poor results were 'a waste of manpower and petrol' and canoes were reconsidered the best transport until 'a suitable higher capacity vessel can be obtained, designed for this class of work and running on cheaper fuel.[113] The Provincial Commissioner, however, thought that as an experiment it had been successful. 'Taking a long view', he explained, 'it would appear in reality to be a success in that the service has proved that a lighter and tug can move up and down the Kilombero.'[114] *This* was the object, not profit. 'It would appear that the present lack of success of this service,' he believed, 'is entirely due to the unsuitability of the craft.'[115] All this considered, the Chief Secretary thought the service was, in fact, 'most useful' and should be continued in 1943.[116] The General Manager of Tanganyika Railways promised: 'we will do our best to make a go of it'.[117]

In September 1943 the purpose-built 'Kilombero Barge' built by the Ifakara Mission was also trialled. This was towed to Ngombo behind the tug and lighter and returned to Ifakara by four men and its captain 'under paddles and poles' while loaded with 24 bags (1756kg) of paddy.[118] It was thought profit would be colossal by Kilombero Service standards and could be increased even further with two or three more such barges.[119] Further trials pushed capacity to 2.5 tons (33 sacks) and 3.5 (48 sacks) tons of paddy. It was found that 33 sacks comfortably filled the body of the boat, whereas 40 sacks (3 tons) took the level above the gunwale which was 'less satisfactory'.[120]

After 1943 the future of the Kilombero River Service was again in the 'melting pot' but continued into the 1944 season.[121] Two additional five-ton barges were trialled and overall operating costs confirmed 'the impossibility of making the service pay with the current type of boats'.[122] Increased rates would only be undercut by canoe transport; but more significantly, only 200 tons could be transported against a total regional production in 1944 of

[112] TNA 61/635, GMTR to PCEP, 22 December 1942.
[113] TNA 61/635, GMTR to PCEP, 10 February 1943.
[114] TNA 61/635, PCEP to CS, 16 February 1943.
[115] TNA 61/635, PCEP to GMTR, 19 January 1943.
[116] TNA 61/635, PC's Minutes on Secretariat File: Transport facilities on the Kilombero River, 2 November 1942; TNA 61/635, GMTR to PCEP, 22 December 1942.
[117] Ibid.
[118] TNA 61/635, DC [Kiberege] to PCEP, 6 October 1943.
[119] Ibid.
[120] Ibid.
[121] TNA 61/574/13/47/Vol. I, DO [Kiberege] to PCEP, 30 November 1943.
[122] TNA 61/635, DC [Kiberege] to PCEP, 13 October 1944.

1600 tons. This was an exceptionally high yield, but the prevailing feeling was that the service was 'clearly unnecessary' with capacity 'too small' and pace 'too slow'.[123]

Canoe transport also had its share of issues. In 1943 there was marked unwillingness to transport produce to Ifakara due to low rates and 'difficulties in [canoe men] getting their dues' from Vithaldas.[124] Fair rates were agreed for the following year, payments swiftly made, and a fleet of 100 canoes transported 250 tons of grain per month from Utengele and Ngombo to Ifakara.[125] The District Commissioner viewed canoe transport as 'quite satisfactory' and 'the only method practicable' while regarding 'further experiments in power transport as an unnecessary waste of money'.[126] Nevertheless, a suitable substitution for the canoe was 'a matter of the greatest importance for the future welfare' of Kilombero.[127] While uncertain and dangerous, it was no longer costly in comparison to the Kilombero River Service which – having existed hypothetically for years – proved to be an utter failure.

The service was formally suspended in December 1944 'as neither the traffic nor the other reasons advanced justify [its] continued subsidy'.[128] The argument remained that appropriate vessels could still transform and economise transport, but realities under colonial conditions and environmental limitations must be accepted. These were often harsh realities. Tragedy in 1944 prompted Vithaldas to urgently request procurement of a motorboat for their use on the river. The firm had contracted Mr. Vejabhai to assist the construction of their new ginnery at Malinyi. Vejabhai travelled from Uganda with his seven-year-old son, who sadly drowned following an accident while returning downstream to Ifakara.[129] The motorboat was for the 'safety of life' of their staff, but also 'for the smoother and better management of the river paddy centres' that were frequently visited.[130] The investments made in the ginnery would soon be followed by a rice mill, and they understandably did not wish to accept greater risks than necessary. Clearly the true costs of the canoe transport were not measured by its transport rates, nor by any produce lost to the river, but by the lives that could easily be claimed by its waters.

---

[123] Ibid.
[124] TNA 61/635, DC [Kiberege] to PCEP, 13 October 1944.
[125] In 1943 it was estimated canoes transported 1,000 tons.
[126] TNA 61/635, DO [Kiberege] to PCEP, 13 October 1944.
[127] Ibid.
[128] TNA 61/635, CS to GMTR, 23 December 1944.
[129] TNA 61/635, VHC to Economic Control Board, Dar es Salaam, 8 March 1944.
[130] Ibid.

Plate 4 Flooded plains near Sakamaganga, May 1936 [Source: OBL MSS.Afr.s.2228].

4

Coercion and Dissent: Resettlement through Sleeping Sickness 'Concentrations', 1939–45

This chapter provides a detailed example of how one aspect of colonial policy – the control of human trypanosomiasis, or 'sleeping sickness' – shaped approaches to development in the valley over a critical period. With funds available for sleeping sickness resettlement – and with the government prepared to invoke its full force of coercion and control if sleeping sickness was identified – colonial officials who wished to impose their own visions for development in the valley were briefly empowered. Yet the variant character of the colonial state, constrained as it were by the Mandate, acted as a brake on the ambitions of certain officials and frustrated their future visions. This chapter illustrates how aspects of both sleeping sickness control measures and broader tensions within the colonial administration reveal insights into the politics of colonial authority in the Kilombero valley region, but also throughout Tanganyika.

Measures to curtail and control both human and animal trypanosomiasis occupy a primary place in the histories of public health, agricultural and economic development, and social interventions in Africa. This was none more so than in Kilombero and throughout the Ulanga District, where we can examine the impact of the belief held by colonial states that sleeping sickness represented a 'threat to the occupation and potential productivity of African land and to the health of people and livestock' – and which fundamentally meant a threat to colonial economies.[1]

Sleeping sickness

In the twenty-first century, it is easy to view medical campaigns to eradicate looming epidemics as an altruistic and essential service to public health and welfare. However, as Mari Webel has argued, histories of anti-sleeping sickness

---

[1] K.A. Hoppe, *Lords of the Fly: Sleeping Sickness Control in British East Africa, 1900–1960* (Westport, 2003), 1. This chapter shifts local emphasis from the Kilombero Valley to the wider Ulanga District incorporating the valley.

campaigns in colonial Africa are among the most 'rigid and draconian manifestations of colonial power' as expressed by ultimately exploitative and self-serving states, and the long history of sleeping sickness in Africa attests to its sustained centrality as 'affected African populations have seen successive interventions by different regimes, states, and non-governmental organizations'.[2]

The historiography of sleeping sickness in East Africa is a developed but ever-broadening field.[3] The most comprehensive study remains Kirk Hoppe's *Lords of the Fly*, which provides a more generalised history of sleeping sickness in the areas around Lake Victoria over the colonial period.[4] Beyond East Africa, recent research on the history of sleeping sickness control measures in West Africa and in Portuguese Africa has highlighted the failure of past medical interventions and their profoundly detrimental effects upon populations, greatly diminishing their trust in professional medical interventions of all kinds as well as causing significant side effects and loss of life.[5] This chapter follows interventions that narrow the focus and foreground localised studies to offer further insights, such as Eileen Fisher's study of sleeping sickness control measures and coercive resettlement programmes on the Ugalla River in Tanzania, and adjacent social histories of sleeping sickness that move beyond the pathology to document the colonial utilisation of oppressive isolation camps as a means of controlling infection.[6] More recently, Mari Webel has expanded 'our histories of sleeping sickness [1890–1920] by orienting around affected communities and how they responded to and made sense of illness

---

[2] M.K. Webel, *The Politics of Disease Control: Sleeping Sickness in Eastern Africa, 1890–1920* (Athens, OH, 2019), 15, 18.

[3] For useful overviews, see D.R. Headrick, 'Sleeping sickness epidemics and colonial responses in East and Central Africa, 1900–1940', *PLoS Neglected Tropical Diseases* 8:4 (2014), 1–8; and G. Hide, 'History of sleeping sickness in East Africa', *Clinical Microbiology Review* 12:1 (1999), 112–25. See also the fundamental work by John Ford, *The Role of Trypanosomiasis in African History* (Oxford, 1971) alongside James L. Giblin, 'Trypanosomiasis control in African history: An evaded issue?', *The Journal of African History* 31:1 (1990), 59–80.

[4] Hoppe, *Lords*.

[5] See G. Lachenal, *The Lomidine Files: The Untold Story of a Medical Disaster* (Baltimore, 2014); S. Coghe, 'Sleeping sickness control and the transnational politics of mass chemoprophylaxis in Portuguese colonial Africa', *Portuguese Studies Review* 25:1 (2017), 57–89.

[6] E. Fisher, 'Forced resettlement, rural livelihoods and wildlife conservation along the Ugalla River in Tanzania', in D. Chatty and M. Colchester (eds), *Conservation and Mobile Indigenous Peoples: Displacement Forced Settlement, and Sustainable Development* (Oxford, 2002), 119–41. See also M. Lyons, 'From "death camps" to *cordon sanitaire*: The development of sleeping sickness policy in the Uele district of the Belgian Congo, 1903–14', *The Journal of African History* 26 (1985), 69–91; *The Colonial Disease: A Social History of Sleeping Sickness in Northern Zaire, 1900–1940* (Cambridge, 1992).

amid colonial control measures' while considering the fundamental importance of historical local contexts in trajectories of colonial public health. Webel provides 'productive new insights for an admittedly well-studied phenomenon' that only highlights how novel case studies, drawing from rich and unexhausted archival material, continue to uncover new findings that reassess and augment the limits of our knowledge.[7]

This chapter follows Webel by offering such a case study, linking sleeping sickness control to the politics of colonial development. In Kilombero, the threat of widespread epidemic – rather than a response to outbreak – drove measures that predominantly served as a vehicle to implement colonial visions of a spatial and political reorganisation of rural communities in Ulanga. Colonial approaches evolved, were never uniform, and often heavily 'depended on the interests and skills of local colonial officials' and 'relationships between local people, local elites, and colonial authorities'.[8] This chapter takes up this key point to illustrate how sleeping sickness control measures were approached and managed by colonial authorities in the distinct social and political landscape of the Ulanga District. The propriety of these measures and their coercion are examined alongside examples of local resistance to 'concentration' which reveal the darker side of colonialism, exposing tensions and contradictions in approaches to local governance. In Ulanga, the firmest advocate of sleeping sickness measures was A.T. Culwick, whose influence was central. This study presents Culwick as its protagonist and re-examines his character by illuminating certain ideologies that, while not uncommon among colonial officials, strike a discordant note in existing representations and understandings of this individual, highlighting the problematic interventions of self-styled amateur ethnographers in colonial Africa. Culwick subcribed to a paternalistic justification of authoritarian means to achieve 'progress' in 'his' district, resulting in interventions that were far more severe than mere inconveniences for Ulanga's communities. Moreover, this study offers a further example of the colonial tendency to exaggerate crises – in this case, epidemiological crisis – to achieve heightened control, and to pursue additional policy objectives. The Ulanga experience thus has its own distinctive elements that provide insight into the place of concentrated settlement in relation to wider colonial development policies, practices, and principles.[9]

---

[7] Webel, *Politics,* 6; also, 'Medical auxiliaries and the negotiation of public health in colonial north-western Tanzania', *The Journal of African History* 54 (2013), 393–416; 'Ziba politics and the German sleeping sickness camp at Kigarama, Tanzania, 1907–14', *The International Journal of African Historical Studies* 47:3 (2014), 399–423.

[8] Hoppe, *Lords*, 110.

[9] Critical texts on amateur ethnography in Africa include, G.I. Jones, 'Social anthropology in Nigeria during the colonial period', *Africa: Journal of the International African Institute* 44: 3 (1974), 280–9; P. Pels, 'The pidginization of Uluguru politics:

Sleeping sickness and 'concentration'

It is worth providing a brief history of sleeping sickness in East Africa to express how the gravity of the disease in certain places at certain times heightened fears of its spread. This contextualises how the looming shadow of sleeping sickness could then be utilised as 'justification' for colonial campaigns of closer settlement serving ulterior motives.

Colonial concerns about sleeping sickness in East Africa originated in the early twentieth century. The severity of initial experiences of the disease, amplified by the first struggles to understand the epidemiology, set the tone for subsequent engagement. First identified in Uganda in 1901, by 1905 the epidemic had killed at least 200,000 people in Busoga Province alone.[10] In this period, sleeping sickness was seen in colonial terms as the greatest barrier to Uganda's economic and social development. In 1907, during his tour of East Africa as Under Secretary of State for the Colonies, Winston Churchill wrote to King Edward VII of the 'many serious diseases' in Uganda, of which 'the worse of all is the sleeping sickness'.[11] Churchill barely understood the disease, but he grasped its potentially devastating impact. 'It is like an old time wizard's curse,' he told the King:

> In order that the spell may work, five separate conditions must all be present: Water, trees, bushes, the tsetse fly and one infected person. Remove any one of these and the charm is broken. But let them all be conjoined, and the absolute and certain extermination of every human being within the area is only a question of time.[12]

This thesis of 'ecological imbalance' due to 'quantitative changes in the relationships [between] man, his domestic livestock, and the wild fauna – and the effects of these changes upon [...] the trypanosomes and the tsetse' was the crucial framework upon which colonial thinking around sleeping sickness

---

Administrative ethnography and the paradoxes of indirect rule', *American Ethnologist* 23:4 (1996), 738–61; H. Tilley and R. Gordon (eds), *Ordering Africa: Anthropology, European Imperialism and the Politics of Knowledge* (Manchester, 2010). While this chapter focuses on the years 1939–45, its periodisation reflects developments within Ulanga and Tanganyika's sleeping sickness policy. The wartime context is coincidental, but did to some degree influence colonial responses to dissent.

[10] C.G. Knight, 'The ecology of sleeping sickness', *Annals of the Association of American Geographers* 61:1 (1971), 26–7.

[11] Chartwell Papers, University of Cambridge (CHAR) 10/27/66–69, Winston Churchill to King Edward VII, 27 November 1907.

[12] Ibid.

and its control developed.[13] As the tsetse fly is its only identified biological vector, its capacity for environmental devastation, specifically with regard to human settlement and husbandry, pivots on humankind's ability to control the fly, the disease, or both.

The first incidence in Tanganyika of a more virulent form of human sleeping sickness (Rhodesian, or *Trypanosoma rhodesiense*) was identified at Ruvuma River in 1911, followed by an extensive outbreak in Mwanza during 1922.[14] The response was institutionalised in 1926 by the establishment of a Sleeping Sickness Control division of the Department of Medical Services. In 1930, a research laboratory to investigate trypanosomiasis was established at Tinde, near Shinyanga.[15] Research was rooted in the Medical Department, yet its effects were a primary concern for other departments, particularly Agriculture and Game. The stratification of colonial administration was undermined by the tsetse fly as its pervading problems transcended the capacity for interdepartmental co-operation. A Sleeping Sickness Committee was established in 1933 in order to co-ordinate and manage government response but ultimately had limited effect.[16]

Prior to 1923 there had been no practical attempt to target tsetse directly and 'fight these flies' in Tanganyika, other than through game extermination.[17] Previously, wholesale depopulation of tsetse-infested areas was considered a swift but drastic measure to protect populations, and was a first response to curb rising epidemics and prevent the disease from 'devastating villages' and 'sweeping away entire populations'.[18] Elsewhere, tsetse presence did not unequivocally signify the existence of sleeping sickness, but this was increasingly assumed. Estimates of the extent of tsetse infestation in the 1920s suggested that two-thirds of Tanganyika's land was under threat.[19] Land clearances designed to 'reclaim' land from tsetse fly encroachments became a favoured approach to protect populations. 'Fly barriers' were maintained by grazing livestock and settlement. Ideas about the 'ideal' settlement density to prevent tsetse encroachment emerged by the 1930s: a population density of

---

[13] Kjekshus, *Ecology Control*, 166; Ford, *Role*, 494.

[14] Hill and Moffett, *Tanganyika: A Review of its Resources*, 94–5; TNAUK WO 287/18, Intelligence Notes on British and German East Africa, March 1916.

[15] K.C. Willet, 'Trypanosomiasis research at Tinde', *Tanganyika Notes and Records* 34 (1953), 33.

[16] A. Beck, *A History of the British Medical Administration of East Africa, 1900–1950* (Cambridge, 1970), 126.

[17] Tanganyika, *Tsetse Reclamation Annual Report for the year ended 31st March, 1929* (Dar es Salaam, 1930), 1.

[18] F. Oswald, *Alone in the Sleeping-Sickness Country* (London, 1923), 80–101.

[19] Hoppe, *Lords*, 81.

5–25 households to the square mile was deemed dangerous, while a density of 50–80 households allowed the maintenance of 'fly-free' land.[20] Some thought a higher ideal of 100 people to the square mile was required, spurring debates on the risks of soil erosion and diminished agricultural fertility.[21]

By the 1940s, then, colonial thinking in Tanganyika focused on two approaches to sleeping sickness control. The first was to eliminate animal reservoirs of the trypanosomes through the destruction or driving away of all game within the vicinity of settlements. The second required scattered communities living in fly-infested bush to be resettled in large, compact communities, maintained as 'fly-free areas' in a procedure known as 'concentration'. If no suitable area was available, then a resettlement site was created by large-scale bush clearing, relying on the 'concentrated' population to maintain the area fly-free through agriculture and reslashing. The practice of resettling 'scattered communities' into 'large, compact communities' had become well established in Tanganyika as the dominant and preferred response to tsetse infestation.

This method of 'concentration' had been evolving since the 1920s.[22] In 1926, government response to outbreaks already involved 'the treatment of infected cases and the concentration of the population in fly-free clearings'.[23] These arrangements resembled the creation of 'special camps' to isolate victims, akin to the *cordons sanitaires* that had been implemented in Belgian Congo.[24] In 1933 government formalised its own policies with the publication of a Sessional Paper arguing for 'the concentration of the people' wherever possible as large-scale treatment of patients in hospitals was not considered practicable.[25] The Sleeping Sickness Concentration Committee also highlighted the 'incidental advantages' of this process, as perceived by the colonial state, in 'the creation of economic self-supporting units, the greater

[20] G. Maclean, 'Sleeping sickness measures in Tanganyika Territory', *Kenya and East African Medical Journal* 7 (1930), 120–126.

[21] F. Apted, 'Sleeping sickness in Tanganyika: Past, present, and future', *Transactions of The Royal Society of Tropical Medicine and Hygiene*, 56:1 (1962), 23; P.A. Buxton, *Trypanosomiasis in Eastern Africa, 1947* (London, 1948), 35.

[22] The term 'concentration' was recognised as problematic by the mid-1940s, due to revelations of Nazi camps. In September 1943, the Director of Medical Services thought 'it advisable to drop the use of the word "concentration" in future and to substitute "resettlement"' as quoted from TNA 31731, Director of Medical Services (DMS) to CS, 27 September 1943.

[23] 'Sleeping sickness in Tanganyika Territory', *The Lancet* (3 July 1926), 29. The first 'settlements' were at Maswa (1922), and Tabora and Ufipa (1925), see Buxton, *Trypanosomiasis*, 25.

[24] Lyons, 'From "death camps"', 70.

[25] Tanganyika. Medical Department, *Sleeping Sickness Problem in the Western and Lake Provinces, and in relation to Uganda*. Sessional Paper No. 7 (Dar es Salaam, 1933).

practicability of affording medical and educational facilities, and, generally, the increased social amenities and advantages resulting from a denser local population'.[26] This 'policy of concentration' was ideologically extended so that 'the populations of all sleeping sickness areas should be collected in one great concentration'.[27] What had begun as 'wholesale evacuation' was transformed into 'beneficial development' and linked to wide-ranging socio-economic improvements. Advocates believed that not only would human lives be saved by stemming an epidemic, but here was a vehicle to drive development and improve livelihoods. It was concluded that 'by reason of the establishment of these concentrations, the area concerned, which was at the moment particularly backward, would become more highly developed than would have happened under the conditions of the people concerned as they are today'.[28]

This policy was considered by many to align with Article 3 of the Mandate for Tanganyika that legislated Britain's responsibility to 'promote to the utmost the material and moral well-being and the social progress of its inhabitants'.[29] Government rationale was such that it was not enough to save peoples' lives if those people did not then improve their economic standing through greater agricultural productivity, accentuating the impetus to promote a wider development agenda alongside sleeping sickness policies.[30] By August 1933, the Secretariat resolved to 'do everything possible to facilitate this execution of this project for concentration'[31] For the next decade, the creation of sleeping sickness 'concentrations' effectively became a keystone of British colonial development in Tanganyika.[32]

Culwick and 'concentration'

At this time the Ulanga District was divided between the highland and valley lowland administrative divisions of Mahenge and Kiberege respectively. Its topographical and social diversity posed various administrative challenges. Highland populations were less scattered than those in the valley, which were spread more thinly over a vast area consisting of 'long straggling swampy

---

[26] Ibid.

[27] Ibid.

[28] This was Uha, Kigoma Region. TNA 21709, Minutes of Meeting of Sleeping Sickness Concentration Committee, 17 July 1933.

[29] League of Nations, 'British Mandate', 4.

[30] TNA 21709, Minutes of the Sleeping Sickness Concentration Committee, 17 July 1933.

[31] TNA 21709, Secretariat Office note, 16 August 1933.

[32] TNA 31731, DMS to CS, 27 September 1943.

valleys stretching from the Songea and Njombe borders in the South to the Ruaha River in the North'.[33] The floodplain of the Kilombero River set the limits to settlement, the alluvial fans around its many tributaries offering rich but vulnerable farmlands. The social fabric of the valley comprised 'groups of people with diverse yet interconnected livelihood systems'.[34] The complexity of Ulanga's multi-ethnic settlement mirrored its ecological variance, the district being made up of a mosaic of distinct cultural entities.

An appreciation of the social and physical landscape of Ulanga and its complexities is important, not least as they served as the stimuli for numerous anthropological and ethnographic studies published by A.T. Culwick and his first wife, Geraldine Mary. Culwick was stationed in Ulanga for much of the 1930s and early 1940s. His prevailing reputation is that of 'administrator anthropologist' and, as described by Peter Pels, he was among the 'general practitioners' of colonial rule.[35] Born in 1905, he read Natural Sciences at Brasenose, Oxford, and hoped for a career in scientific research; but later took the Tropical African Services Course required for colonial service.[36] In 1928 he married Geraldine (née Sheppard), was elected an Ordinary Fellow of the Royal Anthropological Institute, and arrived in Tanganyika as a Cadet. Culwick later returned to Oxford to take its Diploma in Anthropology in 1930–1. Geraldine also took the course but, as a woman, she was discriminately prohibited from taking the examination. The Culwicks were then in Ulanga from 1931 and together wrote the ethnography for which they are well known – *Ubena of the Rivers* – as 'a permanent record of [Bena] tribal history and customs'.[37] Ubena was viewed as the most 'progressive' area of the district and occupied the paramount position in Culwick's racialised view of the social demography of Ulanga. The following year, aged 31, Culwick was awarded an MBE (Member of the British Empire).[38] He continued to publish on a variety of ethnographic, demographic, nutritional, and scientific topics – many of which in co-authorship with Geraldine – and most reported data

---

[33] Ibid.

[34] Monson, 'Agricultural transformation', 23.

[35] P. Pels, 'Global "experts" and "African" minds: Tanganyikan anthropology as public and secret service, 1925–61', *The Journal of the Royal Anthropological Institute* 17:4 (2011), 790.

[36] V. Berry (ed.), *The Culwick Papers, 1934–1944: Population, Food and Health in Colonial Tanganyika* (London, 1994), 15. An overview of the course and colonial 'Civil Service' is given in, Sayers, *Handbook of Tanganyika*, 150–66.

[37] A.T. Culwick and G.M. Culwick, *Ubena of the Rivers* (London, 1935), 5.

[38] TNAUK CO 448/45/10, Colonial Office Honours List, Birthday 1936.

gathered in Ulanga.[39] His writings present a strong-willed idealist, ostensibly promoting the social welfare of the Africans in 'his' district. Culwick was often critical of the shortcomings of government as he perceived them. He was a prominent 'non-medical academic researcher' whose voice was influential in shaping certain colonial ideas and policies, particularly around nutrition and demographics.[40] His pursuit of intellectual and scientific repute drew the ire of fellow officials, and one colleague thought him 'more interested in studying African diet than in handling the mundane tasks of administration'.[41] He frequently expressed opinions – many of which were published – as to what the 'job' of government was and how that 'job' ought to be done, often to the consternation of his superiors and fellow officers, who did not share his views or zeal. Culwick was described by one official as possessing 'wide administrative experience' – to which another added as marginalia: 'although a strong distaste for the ordinary work of an administrative officer'.[42] Nevertheless, Culwick was Ulanga's 'man on the spot' who exercised, in his own words, a 'system of benign autocracy' and 'benevolent authoritarianism'.[43] These two phrases are as paradoxical as they are delusional. The self-aggrandisement that perfused much of Culwick's colonial writings is echoed later in life by a staunch commitment to segregationist politics, revealing both an enduring inclination towards authoritarianism, and an understanding of goodwill that was profoundly hierarchical in nature.

Keenly aware of the activities of Tanganyika's Sleeping Sickness Committee from 1933, and watching the disease penetrate neighbouring districts, Culwick enthusiastically supported 'concentrated' settlement. Yet despite official policy allowing for the creation of tsetse barriers and planned resettlement by 1935, before cases of sleeping sickness were confirmed in the district Culwick could only *encourage* these policies and not *compel* them. Gentle 'persuasion' was

---

[39] For example, A.T. Culwick, 'The hoe in Ulanga,' *Man* 34 (1934), 9; A.T. Culwick and G.M. Culwick, 'What the Wabena think of indirect rule', *Journal of the Royal African Society* 36:143 (1937), 176–93; 'A study of population in Ulanga, Tanganyika Territory', *The Sociological Review* 30:4 (1938), 365–79, and 31:1 (1939), 25–43; 'A study of factors governing the food supply in Ulanga, Tanganyika Territory', *The East African Medical Journal* 16 (1939), 43–61.

[40] Shane Doyle, 'Social disease and social science: The intellectual influence of non-medical research on policy and practice in the Colonial Medical Service in Tanganyika and Uganda', in A. Greenwood (ed.), *Beyond the State: The Colonial Medical Service in British Africa* (Manchester, 2015), 126–52.

[41] Lumley, *Forgotten*, 114–5.

[42] TNA 31731, Resettlement of population as a preventative measure against sleeping sickness, n.d.

[43] Culwick, *Britannia Waives the Rules*, 13, 17.

applied in the valley, for example by refusing to shoot marauding game where the population was scattered. When sleeping sickness was reported in neighbouring Liwale in 1936, Culwick hoped to compel closer settlement as a preventative measure, but his superiors did not authorise 'concentration' of his district. Culwick officially closed the border with Liwale, but could take no further action.[44] Chief Secretary Phillip Mitchell was among those who worried about the implications of coercion and asked in 1934: 'Can inducement and persuasion legitimately pass into compulsion in certain circumstances, or can it not?'[45] This was a controversial and contentious issue, and opinion was divided from one Provincial Commissioner (PC) to the next.[46] A.E. Kitching was one PC who would not consider closer settlement for any reason during his tenure in order to protect African land rights.[47] For Culwick, however, it could unquestionably pass. But this was paternalism of the worst and most patronising kind.

Culwick's anthropological research in Ulanga provided data that convinced him of the need to 'concentrate' the district, and especially the Kilombero Valley 'with its low-lying, disease-ridden valleys'.[48] By 1939, the Culwicks had published findings that introduced the theory that there was a 'demographic crisis' in Ulanga as its population was not managing to reproduce itself.[49] In 1941 Culwick published 'The population trend' in *Tanganyika Notes and Records*, which reflected on a brief posting to Bukoba in north-west Tanganyika where there were 'no lack of educational and medical facilities' and 'a highly sophisticated people', in contrast to Ulanga where lived 'the more primitive inhabitants of the territory, people just beginning to reap the benefits of being drawn into the orbit of world economics'.[50] Culwick predicted a 'population landslide' without intervention.

Attitudes in favour of the urgent need for 'concentration' were shared by others. While Culwick was in Bukoba, Edward Lumley was DO in Ulanga and, on recalling a *safari* tour of the district in August 1939, wrote that his

---

[44] Larson, 'History', 301–2; TNA 61/141/H/Vol. 1/223, Handing Over Report, 13 March 1941.

[45] TNA 22494, Circular No. 40, 1934. Quoted in McHenry, *Tanzania's Ujamaa Villages*, 21.

[46] McHenry, *Tanzania's Ujamaa Villages*, 20–1.

[47] R. Neumann, 'Africa's "last wilderness": Reordering space for political and economic control in colonial Tanzania', *Africa: Journal of the International African Institute* 71:4 (2001), 656.

[48] Lumley, *Forgotten*, 115–116.

[49] Culwick and Culwick, 'Study'; see also, TNAUK CO 691/167/10, publication of 'A study of population in Ulanga, Tanganyika Territory, 1937–38'.

[50] A.T. Culwick, 'The population trend', *Tanganyika Notes and Records* 11 (1941), 13–17.

'purpose on this trip was to encourage and if necessary compel people who were living in isolated settlements to concentrate in large villages'.[51] Lumley observed crop destruction by marauding game and considered resettlement a solution, but that 'to persuade these people to change the habit of generations and live in organised settlements was never easy. Often compulsion was the only way.'[52] That only exceptional circumstances could singularly legitimise enforced resettlement frustrated Culwick and those that shared his views, as they presented 'betterment' arguments that 'justified' such dramatic and invasive social reorganisation. The prevalence of game was the easiest argument to make for the need for closer settlement. Maurading hippo, buffalo, elephant, and eland were a constant 'nuisance to agriculture' while 'the only solution seems to be closer settlement' was a message that colonial officials in Ulanga took 'every opportunity' to convey to both local communities and senior government.[53]

In March 1941, in his Handing Over Report after a brief period as DO for Ulanga, John Rooke-Johnston wrote:

> I have re-iterated frequently the necessity for concentration. Firstly, as a safeguard against Sleeping Sickness. Secondly, as a means for preventing at least half the crops being taken by marauding game. Thirdly, so that the social services may be developed.[54]

Rooke-Johnston was a colonial official in Buha 1933–40, during the most extensive sleeping sickness 'concentration' campaign in Tanganyika.[55] That he advocated for the same in Ulanga, despite the absence of an active epidemic, is not surprising. Rooke-Johnston was a staunch exponent of the strategy to be a part of general development policy, and prone to histrionics: 'I re-iterate again, and am firmly convinced that unless the inhabitants of the Ulanga valley are concentrated, they are doomed to extinction.'[56]

From the mid-1930s, Culwick advocated a scheme to gradually extend the larger settlements of Kilombero – namely Kiberege, Ifakara, and Utengule – and also to gather the *entire* scattered population living in the bush. He did not receive government support for these plans and, in 1941, retorted: 'I was informed that no powers of compulsion would be granted to me as His Excellency considered such

---

[51] Lumley, *Forgotten*, 135.
[52] Ibid.
[53] TNA 61/141/H/Vol. I, Handing Over Notes, October 1940.
[54] TNA 61/141/H/Vol. I, Handing Over Report, 13 March 1941.
[55] Julie Weiskopf, 'Resettling Buha: A Social History of Resettled Communities in Kigoma Region, Tanzania, 1933–1975' (PhD thesis, University of Minnesota, 2011), 77.
[56] TNA 61/141/H/Vol. I, Handing Over Report, 13 March 1941.

action would be an unwarranted interference with the liberty of the subject.'[57] Culwick could only 'implement the policy [...] so far as certain chiefs and headmen were willing to co-operate' as he could 'only stress again the desirability of continuing to concentrate the people of Ulanga in the larger settlements'.[58] Culwick was impatient, frustrated, and saw his being denied 'powers of compulsion' as antithetical to the self-imagined 'authoritarianism' he felt he exercised, or ought to exercise. He considered that sensitivities surrounding the Mandate were inflated, particularly Article 6, which stated: 'In the framing of laws relating to the holding or transfer of land, the Mandatory shall take into consideration native laws and customs, and shall respect the rights and safeguard the interests of the native population.'[59]

Colonial interpretations of the Mandate were divergent. The implementation of schemes under compulsion were contested. They were either a violation of rights, or a duty to the 'material and moral well-being and social progress' of the population. Officials such as Culwick saw conservative interpretations of the Mandate as an impediment to the means required to meet 'development' ends. He sought to exploit ambiguities, using intellectual clout and rhetoric to make the case, and was fully aware that 'in spite of the general principles laid down in Article 22 [of the League of Nations Covenant], very divergent policies, particularly in relation to native affairs, are possible within the system'.[60]

The first incidence of sleeping sickness in Ulanga, recorded in November 1939, came not from within the district, but as an 'outbreak' on the main labour migration route passing through it. This alarmed the Labour Department who feared its spread to major employment areas and ultimately as far as sisal estates in Tanga and Handeni. Cases had been identified to the south and east of Mahenge and measures to control movement through Ulanga, including an abandoned proposal for a quarantine camp, were mooted. For Culwick these confirmed cases in the district were all he needed to begin to resettle its entire population. The process of population 'concentration' in Ulanga was thus catalysed in 1939, by which point a certain colonial approach and paradigm had coalesced. For Culwick, this was overdue.

The initial centre of the 'outbreak' was Luhombero, to the south-east of Mahenge. During 1940 a further seventy-six cases were confirmed and 'concentration' measures focused on the Luhombero valley.[61] Elsewhere in

[57] TNA 61/104, Culwick to Provincial Office, Dar es Salaam, 3 April 1941.
[58] Ibid.
[59] League of Nations, *British Mandate*, 4.
[60] Leubuscher, *Tanganyika Territory*, 4.
[61] Larson, 'History', 302.

Ulanga, Culwick pushed ahead as quickly as permitted. In April 1941 he wrote of the risk to the Kilombero Valley from families migrating from Liwale, as conditions in Ulanga were deemed 'almost ideal for a sleeping sickness epidemic' and that 'an outbreak may occur at any time if infected natives from other areas are allowed to enter the "clean" areas', as had already happened in southern Mahenge.[62] Many of these families had in fact moved into the adjoining areas of the Eastern Province to avoid the creation of a sleeping sickness 'concentration' in Liwale.[63]

Each proposal for 'concentration' had to be planned in consultation with the relevant government departments, 'explained' to the local population, and then negotiated through *jumbes* to seek compliance with the resettlement orders. Compliance was never unanimous. At Mbingu, for example, the population was considered to be 'very scattered' and 'should be collected up at Mbingu itself where there are vast areas of fertile land and plenty of water'.[64] The resettlement site was originally surveyed in January 1942, but over the next three years it was 'found impossible to re-settle the area' because of resistance from the local population.[65] At this time the Mbingu 'chiefdom' was under *Wakili* Rashidi Mpumu, consisting of eight *jumbeates* comprising 466 people.[66] In the area also resided a Hehe 'chief' – Mzagila Ndapa – under whom were four *jumbeates* and 406 people.[67] For Culwick, 'Ndapa and his Wahehe' were 'difficult people' whom it was advised 'from the political and administrative point of view' were 'best kept together'.[68] Over half of those to be 'concentrated' at Mbingu were already living in the area around the proposed site nucleus, but they were unwilling to move. Culwick reported that 'the Native Authorities are in favour of the move, but the populace, who do not appreciate the need for it, naturally wish to remain where they are'.[69] Culwick was confident of over-ruling the will of the people, adding there was

---

[62] TNA 61/104/3/996, DO [Mahenge] to Provincial Commissioner, Eastern Province (PCEP), 3 April 1941.

[63] TNA 61/104/3/996, Provincial Commissioner, Southern Province (PCSP) to PCEP, 21 March 1941.

[64] TNA 61/141/H/Vol. I/223, Handing Over Report, 13 March 1941.

[65] TNA 61/104/H/5/2, Proposed Sleeping Sickness Settlement Report, n.d.

[66] TNA 61/104/H/5, Sleeping Sickness: Mbingu and Mgeta, Ulanga District; *Jumbes*: Ndunduwala, Mionga, Kasanduku, Towera, Ndenya, Kadunda, Mtolihela, and Kaganga.

[67] Ibid.; *Jumbes*: Kabandika, Makumba, Kasimili, Lucas.

[68] TNA 61/104/H/5, DO [Mahenge] to PCEP, 2 March 1945; TNA 61/104/H/5/2, Proposed Sleeping Sickness Settlement Report, 6 February 1945.

[69] TNA 61/104/H/5/12, DO [Mahenge] to PCEP, 29 March 1945.

'no great opposition to contend with'.[70] Processes elsewhere were disrupted and delayed. For Mgeta, he described the process of 'concentration' as a 'simple concertina' effect, as he sought to press the population from all sides towards a central point.[71] Of the 1,375 families bound to occupy the Mgeta settlement, 1,075 were already settled in the Mgeta area; but, as at Mbingu, people were reluctant to comply with government orders to move.

In early 1945, Culwick was determined to push ahead with resettlement at both Mbingu and Mgeta, but soon found himself in bureaucratic crisis. He was informed that, as the selected sites had not been inspected by the Agricultural Department, he could not proceed. This news passed down the hierarchy from the Chief Secretary to James Cheyne, the Provincial Commissioner for Eastern Province (PCEP), who wrote in July 1945 regretting 'that these settlements cannot be made until a survey by an Agricultural Officer has been made'.[72] Cheyne informed Culwick, acknowledging that 'cancellation may now cause embarrassment but under [the] circumstances [the] decision must be adhered to'.[73] Culwick was incensed by this 'most serious dilemma caused solely by failure [of the] Agricultural Department [to] inspect [the] area' and felt this would gravely undermine his authority in the district.[74] 'And what do I do now?' he challenged Cheyne. 'It is all very well for Government – whatever or whoever that may be? – to call a halt but the work has started, and I have thousands of people all ready to move.'[75] The Director of Medical Services intervened, stressing Culwick was competent, experienced, and his opinion should be considerable reliable. Moreover, those preparing to move had no reserve plantings and crop failure would risk famine. Delay would also defer tax payments. Politically, any deferment of the move was 'bound to cause discontent' and 'foment opposition to the move'.[76] Culwick was permitted to continue, and the agricultural survey carried out as soon as possible. This example of administrative inconsistency suggests a fundamental fragility to colonial schemes of social reorganisation under sleeping sickness regulations. Implementation attempts by the colonial state were easily undermined by the dysfunction of its own procedures and stymied by local resistance to the flagrant imposition of colonial authority.

---

[70] Ibid.

[71] TNA 61/104/H/3/11, District Commissioner (DC) [Mahenge] to PCEP, 21 January 1944.

[72] TNA 61/104/H/5/16, CS to PCEP, 21 July 1945.

[73] TNA 61/104/H/5/17, PCEP to DO [Mahenge], 23 July 1945.

[74] TNA 61/104/H/5/19, DC [Mahenge] to PCEP, 24 July 1945.

[75] TNA 61/104/H/5, DC [Ulanga] to PCEP, 25 July 1945.

[76] TNA 61/104/H/5, DMS to CS, 24 July 1945.

This case comes towards the end of a ragged history of 'concentration' in Ulanga that was characterised by the entanglements of administration and a rightful retraction of the 'willing cooperation' upon which Culwick relied to ensure 'successful' schemes. These circumstances are best illustrated by the experience of the first attempts to establish 'concentrations' in Ulanga – those imposed at Luhombero – after the initial sleeping sickness cases in 1939 and 1940. Plans to 'concentrate' the population into a settlement at Luhombero involved large numbers of Pogoro and Ngindo, many of whom had previously been living in an area that was evacuated on the enlargement of the Selous Game Reserve in 1940 and who had therefore already been recently displaced.[77] Ngindo households had been reluctant to move from areas in Liwale and were now repelled by government plans to compel them into condensed settlement. Culwick was aware of this recent history and that Ngindo preferred to live in isolated groups rather than larger settlements. 'The Ngindo dislike the settled life that agriculture entails', he wrote in 1938, preferring 'the lure of wild roaming existence'.[78] Thirty years later, Ralph Jätzold would reiterate that Ngindo 'preference for scattered settlements would seem to make them unsuitable to be gathered together in compact villages'.[79]

In October 1941, a 'considerable number' of Ngindo under 'Chief' Mponda were reported as having run away from the Luhombero sleeping sickness settlement.[80] They were pursued by *Jumbe* Kitolero and one *askari* who caught up with them but were fired at with poisoned arrows. The *askari* fired one rifle shot over their heads and they dispersed. Kitolero then sought help from two local *jumbes* – Abdulla Mshamu Mbama and Saidi Abdullah – who not only refused their assistance but 'snatched [the] *askari's* rifle and threw it against [a] wall' – splitting its wood – and 'unsuccessfully attempted [to] beat him up'.[81] This extraordinary account is a deeply troubling indictment of a colonial regime whose interference with local systems and authority resulted in intercommunity discord and violence.

Culwick considered those who had run away to be 'deserters' or 'fugitives' and were said to be hiding in the game reserve, or in open bush in neighbouring Liwale District, while others had 'fled' to Songea and Tunduru. Culwick's first response was to insist the 'deserters' be returned, to 'avoid wholesale desertions and consequent spread [of] sleeping sickness'.[82] Ngindo dissent

---

[77] Now Nyerere National Park. Larson, 'History', 302. See also, Neumann, 'Last wilderness'.
[78] A.T. Culwick, 'Ngindo honey-hunters', *Man* 36 (1936), 73–4.
[79] Jätzold and Baum, *Kilombero Valley*, 39.
[80] TNA 61/104/H/1, Deserters from Sleeping Sickness Concentrations, Mahenge, n.d.
[81] TNA 61/104/H/1/1, DO Mahenge to PCEP, 2 October 1941.
[82] Ibid.

was fuelled by the enforced creation of a settlement that brought Pogoro and Ngindo together. Culwick argued that the two groups were not mixed, as each community was placed under 'their own *jumbes*', but his distinction mattered little.[83]

Moreover, in the early months of the settlement, a spate of witchcraft accusations had been raised, which affected both Ngindo and Pogoro communities.[84] So intense were feelings that the witchcraft crisis threatened to disintegrate the entire Luhombero settlement, also adversely affecting the nearby Ruaha settlement, formed in 1942. To appease a situation caused by the stresses and social tensions of enforced resettlement, Culwick sent in a witchcraft eradicator in an attempt to 'cleanse and stabilise' the settlements.[85]

'These people do not like being concentrated,' Culwick admitted in his annual report, 'and we must not blind ourselves to this fact and also the fact they hate Europeans and loathe the Government and desire to be as far away from both as humanly possible.'[86] Culwick felt that to leave the 'runaways' unpunished would lead to the break-up of the settlements and that 'government prestige' would 'suffer severely' unless 'at least the very great majority' of those who had 'absconded' from Luhombero were returned.[87] He appealed to Liwale for those who had 'fled' there to be returned, but the District Commissioner (DC) for Liwale – P.H. Johnston – had a different view. Writing to the Provincial Commissioner for Southern Province (PCSP) he explained that those who had returned used to live in the Barikiwa, Njenje, and Liwale areas and were attempting to settle in the Njenje, Liwale, and Makata areas in order to avoid 'concentration' in Mahenge. A delegation had appealed for permission to 'settle again among their own tribesfolk' and stated that 'Mwenye Mponda of Mahenge had agreed to their evacuation without consulting them'.[88] Johnston 'view[ed] the application of these "runaways"

---

[83] TNA 61/104/H/1/16, PCEP to PCSP, 26 November 1941.

[84] Lorne Larson, 'Witchcraft Eradication Sequences among the People of the Ulanga (Mahenge) District, Tanzania' (unpublished working paper, 1975), 22.

[85] Larson, 'History', 303.

[86] TNA 61/141/H/1, Annual Report: Mahenge Division of Ulanga District, 1941, quoted in Larson, 'History', 303.

[87] TNA 61/104/H/1/18, DO [Mahenge] to PCEP, 14 November 1941. Several studies have highlighted colonial officials' sense that prestige was crucial for the retention of power, yet precarious. This was heightened by the Second World War. See, for example, F. Furedi, 'The demobilized African soldier and the blow to white prestige', in D. Killingray and D. Omissi (eds), *Guardians of Empire* (Manchester, 2017), 179–197.

[88] TNA 61/104/H/1/9, DC [Liwale] to PCSP, 30 October 1941.

with sympathy'.[89] Culwick was informed that an individual could only be returned to Mahenge if 'a Summons is issued against him or a Warrant issued for his arrest'.[90] This was not an encouragement to do so but a challenge, implying that Culwick could only have his way through litigation. Culwick baulked at this, as he did 'not wish [the] idea to get round that concentration is a gaol'.[91] But to all intents and purposes, it was. As Culwick had creatively interpreted the Mandate and pushed its limits to create 'concentrations' in Ulanga, so too did he seek to enforce his position by grounding the 'desertion' in legislation. Culwick asserted that the 'deserters' had acted contrary to Section 8(g) of the Native Authority Ordinance for the 'Prevention of Spread of Sleeping Sickness', which applied to the entire district and decreed that: 'All natives shall perform any legal work which the Native Authority deems necessary and orders to prevent the spread of sleeping sickness.'[92] Alongside the Mandate, this was also wide open to interpretation.

A political tug-of-war ensued as to whether the 'runaways' could – or should – be compelled to return. The PCEP, E.C. Baker, implored the PCSP to instruct the DC for Liwale 'that these runaways from Mahenge should not be given a sympathetic welcome'.[93] What was clear to Culwick was that without co-operation within the administration – by which he meant bending others to his will – imposing this legislation would prove practically impossible.[94] In terms of numbers, 113 were said to have gone to Songea between late 1941 and early 1943, while 127 were in Liwale. This left 1710 'taxpayers' remaining in the settlement, indicating that 14 per cent of the settlers had 'deserted'.[95] Culwick saw Liwale and Songea in affording 'sanctuary' for those he held as breaking legal orders and ruining 'discipline [...] and the efficacy of expensive sleeping sickness measurements'.[96] He felt that continued 'abscondment' was 'encouraged by the failure of the Liwale administration to return a single runaway who has escaped across the border' and that he 'cannot stop runaways if it appears [...] that the DC, Liwale does not intend to co-operate and his Native Authorities continue to welcome those absconding'.[97] He feared that unless the 'deserters' were returned to Luhombero, 'then the whole scheme of

---

[89] Ibid. Johnston's use of "runaways" in inverted commas demonstrates he did not consider they had run away at all.
[90] TNA 61/104/H/1/31, Note from PCSP, 9 March 1942.
[91] TNA 61/104/H/1/36, DO [Mahenge] to PCEP, 7 April 1942.
[92] TNAUK CO 1018/68, Notes on Eastern Province, n.d.
[93] TNA 61/104/H/1/16, PCEP to PCSP, 26 November 1941.
[94] TNA 61/104/H/1/6, DO [Kiberege] to PCEP, 17 June 1942.
[95] TNA 61/104/H/1/140, PCEP to CS, 8 June 1943.
[96] TNA 61/104/H/1/62, DO [Kiberege] to PCEP, 17 June 1942.
[97] TNA 61/104/H/1/28, Administrative Office Mahenge to PCEP, 6 December 1941.

concentration in this area is doomed to failure'.[98] Liwale was quick to place Culwick 'under a misapprehension' that there had been any such 'failure' or did not 'intend to co-operate', as Baker had since told Johnston that no-one should be returned by force and could be allowed to stay if all taxes owed to government were paid.[99] Culwick's arrogance and hubris is exposed as he wrote to the PCEP: 'It is not my custom to query my PC's instructions, but I feel bound to point out that important matters of principle have apparently been overlooked, and that serious consequences may follow unless the position is rectified.'[100] Culwick ends his polemic by referencing an 'enclosed permit from the Native Authority, Songea' that 'allows [his] people to break Government's orders' and 'will illustrate to what extent discipline and interprovincial cooperation has broken down'.[101] The permit, dated 10 December 1941 and signed by Nduna Mk. S. [Mkafu Saidi] Palango, lists the names of nine men followed by the statement: 'Therefore these people are not permitted to be arrested by anyone. They have paid all their tax to me. They are *my* people.'[102]

It is ironic that when Culwick perceived a threat of migrating families from Liwale to Ulanga he closed the border, whereas now that people had 'fled' from Ulanga to Liwale (and elsewhere) he insisted they be returned. This was a challenge to his autonomy and a matter more concerned with the politics of colonial authority than the health and welfare of people who ought to be afforded the freedom to manage their own societies. But this was not Culwick's view. He had woefully embodied Article 22 of the League of Nations Covenant that Tanganyika was 'inhabited by peoples not yet able to stand by themselves under the strenuous conditions of the modern world'.[103] Luhombero's 'deserters' offer a further example of considerable dissent against 'concentration' and the coercion required to establish and maintain the settlements. Throughout 1942–3 the situation at Luhombero remained difficult, and Culwick believed that the failure to return the 'deserters' to the settlement was the cause of his worsening struggle to foster local support for further resettlement in Ulanga, especially at Mofu, Mbingu, and Mgeta.[104] During 1942 some voluntarily returned, reportedly because food was 'plentiful' and a blind

[98] TNA 61/104/H/1/62, DO [Kiberege] to PCEP, 17 June 1942.
[99] TNA 61/104/H/1/29, PCSP to PCEP, 19 February 1942.
[100] TNA 61/104/H/1/63, DO [Mahenge] to PCEP, 9 June 1942.
[101] TNA 61/104/H/1/63, DO [Mahenge] to PCEP, 9 June 1942.
[102] This author's italics; TNA/61/104/H/1/63, 'Cheti ya ruksa': sgd. Nduna Mk. S. Palango, 10 December 1941; author's translation from Kiswahili: *Kwa hivi watu hawa hawana ruksa kukamatwa na mtu yeyote na kodi yao wamelipa kabisa kwangu ni watu wangu.*
[103] Leubuscher, *Tanganyika*, 195.
[104] TNA 61/104/H/1/133, DC [Ulanga] to PCEP, 23 May 1943.

Coercion and Dissent 121

eye was then turned. It was considered that the agricultural success of the settlement might be Culwick's 'best asset in stopping persons from leaving' in the future, rather than further acts of coercion.[105] For Culwick, discipline and authority had been diminished. 'Government has been weak', he wrote, and 'has been successfully defied, has made a laughing-stock of the *jumbes*, and has failed to keep its promises.'[106] Despite Culwick's complaints, it is important to note that, by 1945 when sleeping sickness resettlement concluded in Ulanga, estimates for the number of those resettled rank second highest by district throughout Tanganyika.[107] Between 1939 and 1945, at least 37,188 people – or 30 per cent of the entire population of Ulanga as recorded in 1948 – were resettled across ten settlements.[108]

Reflections and reappraisals

The use of coercion to implement sleeping sickness control measures in Tanganyika beyond Ulanga is well documented and hardly concealed. In a 1949 article for *Tanganyika Notes and Records*, G.W. Hatchell wrote that 'it was eventually necessary to employ the more forceful methods of threats of the anger of Government, with consequent punishment, if they refused to move'.[109] One memorandum detailed how, in enforcing removals, officials 'may have to "push" the people out and see that the old huts are burned'.[110] Coercion was thought of positively and even mythologised, while afflicted African populations were patronised. J.P. Moffett saw 'concentration' as a 'means of salvation' and that those who had been resettled were 'now happy and contented' as if stripped of all agency.[111] Sleeping sickness was certainly a real problem, tsetse were indeed widespread, and the presence of both in Ulanga was not fabricated. However, the way in which disproportionate threat served as grounds for the wholesale reordering of communities was subterfuge and a gross violation. Writing in 1948, Professor Patrick Buxton,

---

[105] TNA 61/104/H/1/55, PCEP to DO [Mahenge], 28 May 1942.
[106] TNA 61/104/H/1/68, DO [Mahenge] to PCEP, 22 June 1942.
[107] McHenry, *Tanzania's Ujamaa Villages*, 25.
[108] These were: Luhombero, Ruaha, Lupiro-Mchangani, Iragua, Itete, Mtimbira, Sofi-Majiji, Mofu, Mbingu, Mgeta.
[109] G.W. Hatchell, 'An early "sleeping-sickness settlement" in south-western Tanganyika', *Tanganyika Notes and Records* 27 (1949), 62.
[110] Wellcome Collection for Contemporary Archives, London (WCCA) WTI/TRY/C18/4, H.M.O. Lester, Memorandum on 'sleeping sickness concentration, Tanganyika Territory', 14 December 1938.
[111] J.P. Moffett, 'A strategic retreat from tsetse fly: Uyowa and Bugomba concentrations, 1937', *Tanganyika Notes and Records* 7 (1939), 35–7.

medical entomologist and author of the seminal 1948 text *Trypanosomiasis in Eastern Africa*, considered that 'because the Busoga epidemic was such an immense disaster, there is a tendency to exaggerate the importance of human sleeping sickness in Eastern Africa'.[112] Culwick was among the worst perpetrators of this hyperbole, evidenced through his tyrannical attempts to effect social engineering disguised as disease control.

This chapter also speaks to 'tensions of empire' as presented by Frederick Cooper and Ann Laura Stoler.[113] It is a contribution to the uncovering of 'conflicting conceptions of morality and progress, which shaped formal debates as well as subterranean discourses among high and low-level officials' while illustrating 'competing agendas for using power, competing strategies for maintaining control, and doubts about the legitimacy of the venture'.[114] In both cases presented here, Culwick is incandescent at his perception of how interdepartmental and interprovincial co-operation had broken down, providing further evidence of the 'anxiety of colonizers lest tensions among themselves [...] fracture the façade'.[115]

In 1943, H. Fairbairn as Sleeping Sickness Officer proposed that 'as post-war planning is discussed, it is urged that resettlement of all the people of Tanganyika, who are scattered in tsetse bush, should be adopted as part of the Government's policy'.[116] Fairbairn considered that grounds for resettlement should be undertaken 'as part of Government's deliberate policy to improve the social and economic welfare of the people for whom they are responsible' and noted that resettlement solely as an economic measure remained 'an interference with the liberty of the subject'.[117] Fairbairn proposed that the scheme for wholescale resettlement should be separated from the Medical Department and placed under the direction of a specially selected officer. Fairbairn suggested Culwick, outlining that:

> The Officer should be selected for his administrative ability and experience, his broad social outlook and scientific approach to social problems, his interest in nutrition and native welfare, his appreciation of the medical, agricultural, veterinary and educational problems with which he will have to deal, and his knowledge of native mentality and his ability to influence it.[118]

[112] Buxton, *Trypanosomiasis*, 43.

[113] Frederick Cooper and Ann Laura Stoler (eds), *Tensions of Empire: Colonial Cultures in a Bourgeois World* (Berkeley, 1997).

[114] Cooper and Stoler, 'Introduction', 609.

[115] Ibid.

[116] TNA 31731, Fairbairn to Governor, 17 September 1943.

[117] TNA 31731, Resettlement of population as preventative measure against sleeping sickness, n.d. Fairbairn considered the scheme had the same moral justification as compulsory slum clearance and rehousing in Britain.

[118] Ibid.

This description of the qualities the proposed 'Officer in Charge of Settlements' ought to possess is implicitly Fairbairn's description of Culwick. Moreover, it is not only how Culwick might have once described himself, but remains how Culwick might be broadly understood today. Culwick's published studies and articles are widely cited throughout scholarship, but many inadvertently reproduce his own representations of himself during the colonial era.[119] Few studies challenge these prevailing representations and approach a holistic analysis. He has therefore largely escaped far-reaching interrogation, critique, or criticism.[120] Scholarly engagement with Culwick is predominantly bound to the colonial era, and little connection has been made between the apparently genial, liberal, and progressive 'colonial ethnographer and administrator' who promoted the paramountcy of African welfare in the 1930s and 1940s, and the later Chairman of the Kenya United Party and supporter of racial segregation under *apartheid* in South Africa in the 1960s. But is it surprising?

It is clear that Culwick viewed the multi-ethnic population of Ulanga as a racial hierarchy. He counted Towegale Kiwanga – the 'Mtema of the Wabena' – as a 'close friend' and his ethnography placed the Bena at the utmost echelon of Ulanga's societies.[121] Further insights into Culwick's approach to colonial administration are found in his later writings of the 1960s.[122] He reflected that 'the prosperity of Towegale's people depended […] on what some would call his "unwarranted interference with the liberty of the subject"', recalling the phrase that Culwick and Fairbairn used in relation to the use of coercion in resettlement.[123] His vision of a 'benevolent authoritarianism' was modelled to some extent on his perception of 'tribal rule' and wrote that 'this tribal African [Kiwanga] realised what Democracy had missed – that 95% of people are only fit to obey orders and lack the mental equipment to form a balanced judgment on any matter other than their own very simple day-to-day affairs'.[124] While Kiwanga was but one local authority in Ulanga, Culwick considered himself omnipotent. 'One man, a white man,' he wrote, 'took the decision and he enforced it. *"La loi c'est moi"* – dictatorship? Very definitely, but nonetheless valuable for all that.'[125] This view was certainly not unique to Culwick, but rarely is it so brazenly expressed. His later writings speak directly to his colonial years, but reveal a racist and eugenic mindset that recasts Culwick and implies a distorted disillusionment after empire. In 1968 Culwick condemned the continent: 'Africa in the raw is returning,' he wrote.[126]

---

[119] For a typical representation of Culwick, see Monson, 'Memory'.
[120] One example that does achieve this is Doyle, 'Social disease'.
[121] Culwick and Culwick, *Bena*; see also, Monson, 'Memory'.
[122] Culwick, *Britannia*; also A.T. Culwick, *Don't Feed the Tiger* (Cape Town, 1968).
[123] Culwick, *Britannia*, 54.
[124] Ibid. 53–4.
[125] Ibid. 14.
[126] Culwick, *Don't Feed the Tiger*, 15.

Finally, a concluding note on the colonial legacy of coercive resettlement is particularly important in the Tanzanian context. A conflicting legacy of Julius Nyerere's premiership in postcolonial Tanzania remains the infamous use of compulsion to enforce a state policy of villagisation, largely between 1973 and 1976.[127] Force followed sufficient resistance or non-compliance to voluntarily participate in Nyerere's vision for the reorganisation of rural Tanzania into *Ujamaa* villages. This vision for rural reorganisation – or, 'transformation' – was a prominent policy of the national government from even before Independence.[128] The use of compulsion to effect this transformation was far from an initial intention of the independent state. I argue that in the first instance, the coercive character of colonial schemes influenced Nyerere's *Ujamaa* ideals and his emphasis on voluntary rural resettlement. Events such as those which transpired in Ulanga galvanised support for Nyerere and encouraged his 'hope to revive egalitarianism in *Ujamaa*'.[129] However, in the second instance, there developed a 'creeping breach of Nyerere's own injunction against forcing people [to resettle]'.[130] The ultimate resort to the use of force and compulsion by the state to achieve its ends reveals how villagisation in Tanzania came to resemble too closely the kind of colonial imposition it had never intended to repeat. As Michael Jennings has noted: 'Just as the colonial state had responded to resistance to its policies with increasing force, so too the independent state, when faced with similar problems of noncompliance, returned to that default position.'[131]

Despite the crucial distinction of legitimacy between contested colonial authority and a democratically elected government, no state can expect to intervene so dramatically without encountering dissent, and then expect to achieve its ends without coercion. This reveals the limitations of 'future making' from above and is a crucial part of the development history.

---

[127] For example, see McHenry, *Tanzania's Ujamaa Villages*, 116–52; Lawi, 'Tanzania's Operation *Vijiji*'; Jennings, *Surrogates of the State*; Weiskopf, 'Resettling', 267–309; Schneider, *Government of Development*.

[128] As discussed in Chapter 7.

[129] Lawi, 'Tanzania's Operation *Vijiji*', 73.

[130] Schneider, *Government of Development*, 76.

[131] Jennings, *Surrogates of the State*, 172.

5

'New Colonialism' Comes to Kilombero: Development and the State, 1939–61

When the Central Development Committee was appointed in December 1938, war in Europe was thought inevitable. Active fighting in Tanganyika was unlikely, but tensions mounted. Since the ban on alienating land to German nationals was lifted in 1925, settlers had increased to levels far higher than those during the years of *Deutsch-Ostafrika*. Fears persisted that the League of Nations would return the country to Germany. In 1938, over 45 per cent of over 2.1m acres of all alienated land was 'German'.[1] Moreover, in 1939 Germans outnumbered Britons, discounting government officials.[2] This contributed to fears over the economic, political, and social impacts of war held by the Colonial Office, Tanganyika Government, and British settlers. German business, industry, and estates accounted for a substantial part of the economy, while in some regions the provision of medical services and education was left entirely to German missions and schools. Plans to resist a coup were in place from September 1938 and building work for an internment camp in Dar es Salaam began in April 1939.[3] It was clear that war would severely alter, if not halt, any number of economic, political, and social factors. The extent to which the conflict would puncture development possibilities was severe. Shockwaves from the diversion of resources, shift in administrative focus, demographic shifts, and collapse of economic, medical, and educational systems, may not have reached Kilombero directly, but the indirect effects were unquestionable.

---

[1] Tanganyika, *Blue Book for the year ending 1938* (Dar es Salaam, 1939), 279.
[2] Likely figures were approximately 3,200 Germans to 2,100 Britons (excluding officials).
[3] Nicholas Westcott, 'The Impact of the Second World War on Tanganyika, 1939–1949' (PhD thesis, University of Cambridge, 1982), 32. There were concerns that Germans had considerable dumps of ammunition and arms. See, TNAUK CO 691/170/15, 'Permanency of Mandate: German aspirations and Nazi activities within the Territory, 1939.

The Committee's 1940 report is full of references to suspended schemes and uninitiated proposals. Circuitous colonial development thinking was first disrupted and then unequivocally changed by war. Most of whatever was thought possible in 1938 was in aspic by 1940, but with the hope that all would resume. The report suggests little thought that post-war development would be anything other than the implementation of pre-war plans. The future would simply be deferred.

The 'turning point' of political development is often viewed as 1945, but various moments during the war itself transformed the relationship between Britain and Tanganyika.[4] Some shifts were incremental, others substantial fulcra. Publication of 'An Outline of Post-War Development Proposals' in 1944 is proof that 1945 was neither the beginning nor the culmination of a process. This was part of a broader unfolding of post-war visions that began before its end. In June 1943 an opinion piece penned by A.T. Culwick was published in *Tanganyika Notes and Records*, to which the editors welcomed 'criticism and discussion' from 'readers who are interested in the future of Tanganyika from a social and scientific point of view'.[5]

'Speculation on the nature of the post-war world is widespread to-day', wrote Culwick, and 'many are wondering what the peace will bring.'[6] In other words, what the future would bring. Culwick's piece – 'New Beginning' – is a 'future-making' statement. It is also a dramatic and rhetorical polemic against 'the weaknesses in the organization' of the administration that 'the exigencies of war have made plain'.[7] His sense of self-importance is plain as he first problematises then singularly suggests solutions to government failings. Culwick thought himself progressive, and trumpeted his advocacy of change wherever he could. But his idea of 'change' was to restrict 'the liberty of the subject' to deliver 'a concerted advance against ill health, ignorance and poverty'.[8] He was the first to declare his unwavering commitment to 'the African's welfare' but had no qualms over the use of compulsion to achieve these ends. 'We must be prepared to teach, persuade, compel' he declared, 'adopting whichever line of attack is best suited to the people with which we have to deal'.[9] He was right that the world would become a very different place, but wrong to assume increased importance for individual officers such as himself. Another observation of his proved prescient:

[4] Iliffe, *Modern History*, 436.
[5] 'Editorial Note', *Tanganyika Notes and Records* 15 (1943), n.p.
[6] A.T. Culwick, 'New beginnings', *Tanganyika Notes and Records* 15 (1943), 1–6.
[7] Ibid.
[8] Ibid., 6.
[9] Ibid.

There is a growing body of opinion in Tanganyika which holds that our post-war life must be planned, planned as an oecological whole, that haphazard excursions along different lines of 'advance' must give way to a broadly conceived scheme based on the scientific utilization of our resources, human and material.[10]

This approach is traced to 'the New Order' as coined by D.A. Low and John Lonsdale for the period 1945–63, encompassing the notion of post-war colonial development as 'the second colonial occupation' – and for good reason.[11]

For Tanganyika, it was felt that 'a more detailed consideration of post-war planning' had become possible by the end of the 1943, when 'vitally needed energies' were no longer required to fulfil 'the more urgent demands of war'.[12] It was acknowledged that much had changed since 1940 and this led to 'changes in emphasis and priorities' in its recommendations.[13] A 'Development Branch' was established to collaborate closely with a nascent 'Planning Committee'.[14] Basic fields of development were devised: conservation and utilisation of natural resources; provision of adequate communications; and the extension of health and education services. The first was divided into sub-sections: agriculture, animal husbandry, forests, water development, soil conservation, and surveys. One settlement scheme under agriculture (reproduced from 1940) was for 'The Development of the Kilombero Valley' and its first stage was mooted to begin 'as soon as funds and staff can be made available'.[15] Here was possibility. This was anticipation. Colonial 'future making' is evidenced on a grand scale as a long-term development programme is tabled. Following the 1940 and 1943 reports, in 1946 'A Ten-Year Development and Welfare Plan for Tanganyika Territory' was published by the newly formed Development Commission, following the British Government's urging of colonial governments throughout the Empire to formulate such plans.[16] In this way, governments were invited to engage directly in 'future making' as development planning.

---

[10] Ibid.

[11] Low and Lonsdale, 'Introduction', 1–64.

[12] Tanganyika, *An Outline of Post-War Development Proposals* (Dar es Salaam, 1944), 1.

[13] Ibid.

[14] This committee was appointed in February 1944 and held its first meeting in April 1944.

[15] Tanganyika, *Outline of Post-War Development Proposals*, 4.

[16] E.R. Wicker, 'Colonial development and welfare, 1929–57: The evolution of a policy', *Social and Economic Studies* 7:4 (1958), 184.

Tanganyika was therefore not alone in publishing its first comprehensive development plan, and the new Governor of Tanganyika, Edward Twining (1946–58), considered it 'one of the best Colonial development plans which [he had] ever seen'.[17] This 'general and comprehensive plan of development and welfare' was not dissimilar in scope to the 'broadly conceived scheme' suggested by Culwick.[18] But it was felt that 'what is usually regarded as pioneer development [was] very far from complete' in Tanganyika, and it was 'well nigh impossible to draw a distinction between normal expansion of existing services and development'.[19]

> Luxuries and frills, whether in the nature of Government building programmes, housing schemes or other social services in advance of the present stage of development of the people [...] must come later and must be provided, in part at least, from the efforts of the people themselves and from the general increase in the country's productivity.[20]

It is a failure of the administration that certain schemes elemental elsewhere should be 'luxuries and frills' in Tanganyika. Optimism was certainly tempered. The Kilombero scheme was modest. Figures were recycled from 1940 with projected initial capital costs of £1,500 alongside total recurrent costs of £10,000 over the ten years. This amounted to a shade less than 1 per cent of the total estimated costs for all thirty-one of the 'Agricultural and Animal Husbandry' schemes proposed.[21] By comparison, schemes for Sukumaland and Mbulu District drew £213,000 (or 18 per cent) and £125,000 (or 10 per cent) respectively.[22] This is surprising due to the central position that Kilombero had held in European development visions for over half a century. However, if it had been widely acknowledged that vast sums of capital expenditure would be 'wasted' on Kilombero, then there was the rationale for more realistic visions at modest cost. The region seemed low priority in 1946, but not forgotten; and the days of grandiose schemes envisaged for Kilombero were not over.

---

[17] E.F. Twining, 'The last nine years in Tanganyika', *African Affairs* 58:230 (1959), 16.
[18] Tanganyika, *Ten-Year Development and Welfare Plan*, 1.
[19] Ibid., 6.
[20] Ibid., 8.
[21] In 1944, eleven such schemes were outlined. By 1946 this figure had almost trebled to 31.
[22] The scale and estimated costs for the Sukumaland and Mbulu schemes had risen significantly since 1944, whereas the scheme for Kilombero was unchanged.

Tapping the granary: the East Africa Rice Mission

Among the manifold outcomes of the war was a global cereals shortage. Reductions in the annual surplus of rice available from 'Burma, Siam and French Indo-China' led Britain to intensify focus on its colonial territories as exploitable resources. The East Africa Rice Mission was formed to report on rice production in East and Central Africa, following recommendations made by the Colonial Primary Products Committee in a report of January 1948.[23] This followed the Overseas Resources Development Bill of 1947 and the creation of the Colonial Development Corporation (CDC) and the Overseas Food Corporation (OFC), authorised to borrow up to £100m and £50m respectively. The years 1947–51 thus saw a 'colonial development offensive' designed to directly serve the British economy.[24]

The authors of the report – Gerald Lacey and Robert Watson – were retired colonial officers. Lacey had been Chief Engineer of the Irrigation Branch of the Public Works Department in India, and Watson had retired as the Director of Agriculture in Burma.[25] Their schedule put them in Tanganyika in May 1948, discounting ground inspections due to flooding in the Rufiji and Kilombero valleys. They took to the air instead and 'flew up the river Rufiji from its delta to its junction with the Great Ruaha, and over the very promising Kilombero River valley'.[26] They returned to Kilombero after the rains, concluding that this 'undeveloped area' was 'highly suited to small canals irrigating rice and other crops'.[27]

Lacey and Burton faced great difficulty in 'the almost complete absence of the essential information and data without which no agricultural or engineer consultant would venture to advise' and stressed the need for accurate survey plans and data on ground and water surface levels.[28] The detail of mapping in

---

[23] The survey visited Kenya, Uganda, Tanganyika, Nyasaland, and Northern Rhodesia, landing in Nairobi on 16 April 1948 and departing from Kisumu on 14 September 1948.

[24] Hodge, *Triumph of the Expert*, 208.

[25] Lacey (1887–1979) gained renown for his 'regime theory' in the design of major irrigation canals. See Asit K. Biswas, 'Irrigation in India: Past and Present', *Journal of the Irrigation and Drainage Division* 91:1 (1965), 179–89; and also Gerald Lacey, Claude Inglis, and A.M.R. Montague, 'Discussion of "Irrigation in India: Past and Present"', *Journal of the Irrigation and Drainage Division* 91:4 (1965), 123–130. A prestigious annual memorial lecture in his name continues to be held at the Institution of Civil Engineers, London.

[26] Great Britain. Colonial Office. Gerald Lacey and Robert Watson, *East Africa Rice Mission Report, 1948* (London, 1949), 9.

[27] Ibid.

[28] Ibid., 10.

India exposed corresponding African mapping as 'too small a scale and too inaccurate in detail to be really effective'.[29] They found that the distinction between mere proposals and viable projects was seldom made, and 'almost invariably the fewer the facts available the greater was the number of remedies put forward for the solution of a given local problem'.[30] Both of these assertions resonate for Kilombero. The strength of the 'lure of the map' relied on its small scale, a level of inaccuracy, and the omission of scientific data. Moreover, a paucity of data suggests unanswered questions, which breed speculation. In the absence of certainties, possibilities bloom.

The most detailed survey produced for Kilombero was the tacheometric survey for the Kilosa-Ifakara railway conducted in 1930–2, but this was the wrong kind of survey of few right places. Even the 'authoritative' Telford Report, produced a map of only 1:300,000 scale without altitudes, contour lines, or refined topographical markers. Further survey data is tabled throughout the report, but Telford warned this was 'liable to a certain amount of error'.[31] Telford's delineation of the valley into four categories of development suitability had some use to the planner or agricultural officer, but not the engineer. Yet two decades later, Lacey and Burton drew heavily from it. They recommended that it should be 'closely studied by those who may ultimately be responsible for large-scale rice development in these riverine tracts'.[32] They agreed that the unpredictability of rainfall and flood volatility bred uncertainty that offered little inducement to 'the cultivator to grow more paddy than will satisfy his own needs, and in any year which is climatically favourable he is inclined to store his surplus and crop less in the succeeding year'.[33] Telford's comments on the 'self-sufficiency of the peasant' were reproduced alongside the suggestion that 'material inducements' to the cultivator to expand acreages under rice were essential if the Kilombero and Rufiji valleys were to be 'efficiently developed'.[34] Estimates on potential acreages for production without irrigation were also replicated. This reflects the longevity and cachet of a report such as Telford's in the absence of revision. Authority is often fixed by publication, while opinions are fallible; estimates must be revised, and old data risks renewed misjudgements. There was agreement with Telford that the construction of a large irrigation canal on the unstable Kilombero

---

[29] Ibid. One example of inaccurate data was altitude. African maps often recorded barometric readings for heights above sea level, which could be inaccurate by six metres. Precise levelling for irrigation demanded accuracy to at least three centimetres.
[30] Ibid.
[31] Telford, *Report*, 63.
[32] Colonial Office, *East Africa Rice Mission Report*, 41.
[33] Ibid., 41–2.
[34] Ibid., 42.

River was folly, and that the small perennial tributaries that flowed into its left bank were more irrigable. The 'small canals' envisaged were likened to the 'canals from hill torrents in the foothills of the Himalayas' and would form a compact, controllable unit.[35]

Emphasis was placed on how differences between success and failure might rest on either 'the industry or lethargy of the cultivator' and an example given from an area of rice cultivation on the road between Ifakara and Mahenge whereby the crop was excellent on one side but poor on the other, while soil conditions were identical.[36] Lacey and Burton were informed that each side fell under the jurisdiction of different 'chiefs' and that discrepancies in local agricultural methods accounted for the difference.

Contrasts in method and crop quality are perhaps not surprising – even in such proximity – but this instance is a reminder of fragmentation throughout a valley so often viewed as a single entity. This was a region whose intersection by tangible boundaries – for example, by its rivers – were clear to the outside observer, while the same observers lacked the insight to fully appreciate the less visible societal boundaries that characterised Kilombero. These reflected the region's heterogeneity through its multi-ethnic population and their individual histories and practices. Broader debates on the imposition of colonial social reorganisation should not obfuscate cultural and social distinctions inherent in differentiated demographic development. For a region viewed predominantly through its natural environment, its inhabitants were often unduly homogenised. Moreover, the immigration or importation of families from outside the region was often cited as a solution to the perceived problem of underpopulation to fulfil production potential. This homogenisation limited both agency and humanity. In the case of the 'thousands of tenants' that Telford deemed necessary for the success of his scheme, there was 'no source' from which they might have come; and as one official contended, 'government does not dispose of populations it can move about like pieces on a chessboard'.[37] Local land and individual rights were not always acknowledged by consultants. Lacey and Burton also viewed agricultural potential as a kind of intrinsic absolute that could not be quantified but must be achieved. 'It is evident that time must elapse', they claimed, 'before the full rice potential of the Rufiji and Kilombero valleys can be realized.'[38]

Following the publication of the report, a conference was held in Tabora in October 1949 to consider its content and discuss the present and future of

---

[35] Ibid., 43.
[36] Ibid., 44.
[37] TNA 11746/192, Development of the Rufiji and Kilombero Areas, 1932.
[38] Colonial Office, *East Africa Rice Mission Report*, 44.

rice cultivation.[39] The conference brought together representatives of the East Africa High Commission, CDC, and OFC, with administrative and agricultural officers from Kenya, Northern Rhodesia, Nyasaland, Tanganyika, Uganda, and Zanzibar. A shift in tone, thinking, and practical action from pre-war approaches to development was evident. From the late 1940s, there was an intensification of activity throughout British Africa. The establishment of the East Africa High Commission (EAHC) on 1 January 1948 to co-ordinate interterritorial services was a significant moment, and this level of interdepartmental and interterritorial co-operation was a marked departure in colonial parameters.[40] The 'second colonial occupation' was underway.

Telford returns

Telford spent 1949–52 as Divisional Manager of Agriculture for the recently established CDC, and was involved throughout the empire from the West Indies to Borneo, West Africa to Malaya.[41] He also returned to Tanganyika, and in November 1950 discussed potential CDC involvement in an agricultural project in Kilombero. Government had declared its intention to alienate 100,000 acres of land in the valley for plantation projects that would utilise mechanised cultivation of rice, sugar, and other crops. This came after J.C. Muir – Member for Agricultural and Natural Resources – had flown over Kilombero and opined from 200 feet:

> We were greatly impressed by the immense area of apparently highly fertile land which was well watered to an extent that suggested that water control would be the dominant problem in developing the area. The population was extremely sparse. It appeared as if the area would be potentially one of the most rich in this country but that if [a] full plan [of] development was to take place considerable investigation by experts in water development would be required and capital expenditure of a very high order would be involved.[42]

Muir thought a survey team might be funded 'under the Truman Plan of assistance for underdeveloped areas' with an early gesture towards international involvement in development.[43] Telford thought the CDC might partner

[39] TNA 37511, Visit of Rice Mission, 1949.
[40] Low and Lonsdale, 'Introduction', 7; On the EAHC, see Jane Banfield Haynes, 'The British East Africa High Commission: An imperial experiment' in Harvey Dyck and H. Peter Krosby (eds), *Empire and Nations* (Toronto, 2017), 180–94.
[41] 'Obituary: Alexander McMenegal Telford', 697–8.
[42] TNA 40511/12, Note in CDC Projects: Kilombero Valley Agricultural Development, n.d.
[43] Ibid.

for a project covering 40,000 acres and promised to present the proposal on his return. He warned that 'if it were proposed to allocate adjacent areas to private European and Asian enterprise it did not appear likely that the CDC would be interested'.[44]

Muir looked forward to hearing of the Board's response to the proposal for a partnership, but he would be disappointed. The CDC could not envisage such a project as it would present 'certain difficulties which the Corporation in the light of experience gained elsewhere is not prepared at this stage to shoulder'.[45] It was thought 'the control of pests, production of crops, recruitment, importation and retention of labour' would be 'liable to cause serious friction between the other Estate owners and the Corporation and/or the Tanganyika Government'.[46] Hopes were raised, hopes were dashed. The proposal was abandoned and the CDC involved itself elsewhere in Tanganyika. But something approaching the full weight of scientific enquiry would yet descend on Kilombero in the 1950s.[47]

Survey. Report. Repeat.

Processes of knowledge production intensified, ranging from localised investigations with a skeleton crew to highly technical, expensive, and internationally co-ordinated regional surveys. Kilombero featured prominently in four major surveys and their subsequent reports. These, in chronological order, were: the Loxton Report; the Gibb Report; the East Africa Royal Commission Report; and the Rufiji Basin Survey.

The Loxton Report was the result of a government land-use survey commissioned in 1951 to assess an area of approximately 400 square miles north of the left bank of the Kilombero, between the Lumemo and Ruipa rivers. The area – 'Block A' – was chosen for its low population density, proximity to Ifakara, and that Telford's map had shown it to have the highest percentage of utilisable land. Lack of funds and staff shortages necessitated a detailed survey on one area only, but one with perceived high potential. The survey team comprised leader R.F. Loxton, his wife, and a field assistant. Initial reconnaissance spanned September to November 1951 while the survey proper ran from April 1952 to January 1953. Loxton encountered the usual challenges, noting that 'survey conditions [...] are difficult in the extreme' due to dense grass growth at least ten feet high, the few motorable roads

---

[44] TNA 40511/12, Notes of Meeting Held at the Secretariat, 27 November 1950.
[45] TNA 40511/12, Hood to Muir, 29 December 1950.
[46] Ibid.
[47] TNA 40511/12, Note in CDC Projects: Kilombero Valley Agricultural Development, 12 January 1951.

being unpassable for half the year due to flooding, following which bridge and road repairs further delayed progress.[48]

Loxton appreciated the volatility of the valley environment, noting unstable river channels and their tendency to change course. Intense storms on the escarpment could cause high fluctuations in water levels, often between six and ten feet. Such a spate occurred in November 1952, destroying bridges over the Lumemo and Ruipa rivers. Abnormally high rainfall in May that year also flattened much of a maturing rice crop. Paddy could ordinarily withstand floods up to three feet, but severe increases in volume and velocity could be devastating. Loxton thought any attempt to control the flood was 'a large and costly undertaking' and unwise.[49] Local bunding was feasible, but the cost of a scheme for complete control and drainage would be 'enormous' and 'not actually necessary, as flood water is required for the cultivation of rice'.[50] He did, however, consider the potential for irrigation to enable two rice crops from the same field. Up to 5,000 acres was thought irrigable by the Ruipa, and 200 by the Idete. Further irrigation was thought possible from boreholes or by pumping from the Kilombero itself, and a permanent experimental station near to the Ruipa was recommended.

The strength of the survey was its detailed focus on a limited area. The intimidating magnitude of the valley was partially overcome by this compartmentalisation and prioritisation. Its analyses of a specific area avoided the pitfall of conclusions made from broad averages or the assumption that what is true for one locale holds for another. Also notable is its application of laboratory analysis of soil types. Reports on fertility, alkalinity, and salinity were presented alongside commentary on present and potential land use, and the associated potential need for clearing, levelling, flood control, drainage, experimentation and crop trials, or timber extraction.

This was a typical example of a particular type of early post-war development initiative that, unlike those from district or departmental officers, sought to generate objective knowledge. Land-use surveys such as this emphasised scientific method and data generation and, as they were undertaken by non-government specialists, were more likely to be independent of the influence of policy or particular intent. In this way Loxton succeeded Telford, but with shades of difference. Loxton produced a somewhat depoliticised and holistic baseline study that presented a part of the valley not so much by what it could *be* or *do* but simply what it *was* in ecological terms. There was a sense that 'ecological land-use surveys in Africa [were] still in their infancy'

[48] TNAUK CO 892/12/5, Kilombero Valley Land Use Survey: Block A, April 1953.
[49] Ibid.
[50] Ibid.

in relation to development planning, and that 'the future will make insistent demand upon ecologists in land-use survey'; while the Loxton Report was cited as a valuable contribution in 'guiding policy and practice in the development of new country and in the planning of agricultural and reclamation in already farmed regions'.[51]

Alongside the relatively small scale of the Loxton Report, Kilombero featured in a far grander survey, dubbed the Gibb Report. The war led Britain to reconsider the usefulness of its empire with renewed appetite and, despite a political awakening that recast African understandings of the dynamics between government and governed, post-war development remained 'a specifically colonial kind' while emulsified with a burgeoning internationalism.[52] War also emphasised the strategic importance of railways and their role for imperial defence, and in 1946 the Colonial Office sought to reinvestigate prospects for a railway through south-west Tanganyika to Northern Rhodesia; but bureaucratic wrangling, interdepartmental differences of opinion, logistical obstacles, and a dearth of technical personnel delayed the project.[53] However, an investigative survey was eventually carried out in two phases. The findings of the 'Report on Central African Rail Link Development Survey' were published in June 1952 by the British firm of Sir Alexander Gibb & Partners together with Overseas Consultants, Inc. of New York.[54] This 'Gibb Report' had remarkably similar terms of reference to the Tanganyika Railway Commission of the 1930s. Michelle Boubonniere wrote of this precise reiteration as 'developmental amnesia' and at times this was practical and politically expedient. At other times it was pure ignorance. 'After 1947,' Bourbonniere observed, 'metropolitan officials thought of development after the war as something new. Local officials thought that it was something old.'[55] This caused confusion and friction, and led inevitably to a kind of *development déjà vu* that was also nothing new.

The Gibb Report hardly broke the mould by suggesting that 'the capital expenditure involved in this Rail Link would not be justified unless effective

---

[51] John Phillips, 'Ecology in the service of man in British Territories in Africa: Selected aspects and examples', *Vegetatio* 5/6:1 (1954), 76.

[52] Iliffe, *Modern History*, 470.

[53] See Michelle Elise Bourbonniere, 'Using the Past to Imagine the Future: The TAZARA Railway, 1925–1976' (PhD thesis, Stanford University, 2013), 119–91.

[54] Gibb provided the project manager, an economist and field engineer. Overseas Consultants provided an agronomist and soil specialist. An independent agricultural advisor completed the team.

[55] Bourbonniere, 'Using the Past', 122.

steps were taken to develop the areas traversed'.[56] Six 'development zones' were delineated and the historical importance attached to Kilombero greatly influenced the survey party, who spent as much time as possible there. Emphasis was placed on 'Future Possibilities', and past proposals for flood reduction were reconsidered. None of these were considered 'economic or practicable at least for many years to come' nor was a major irrigation project supported.[57] Proposals dismissed included those to lower the riverbed and increase velocity by canalisation, the construction of reservoirs to hold back flood water, and to retain the main river within narrow limit through flood levees. Alternatively, it was suggested that development should focus on the alluvial fan areas lying above the flood level along the slopes of the lower foothills. The control of local, secondary flooding from intersecting minor tributaries, alongside minor irrigation, was thought to provide the foundation for so-called primary development without the burden of excessive overhead expenditure. Characteristic of this kind of report, it suggested further examinations before work began.

The old view that population was insufficient for development was reiterated, and settlers from elsewhere were again encouraged. Even European settlement was endorsed 'to the overall benefit of the Valley and its inhabitants' as large areas of unoccupied land were thought to be alienable.[58] High importance was given to scientific and technical knowledge and, from their perspective, the whole valley – soil, vegetation, hydrography, topography – needed to be comprehensively surveyed. However, alongside calls for further studies, an agricultural experiment station, and a substantial extension service, was a tempered optimism; the 'rate of development' was viewed relative to capital and labour, and that for Kilombero 'it would not be realistic to budget for a high rate of development'.[59] Despite this, estimates for flood control and irrigation were still £3m, and up to £5m was expected for agricultural development. Investment on this scale was thought economically justifiable by either government or private enterprise. This was partially due to an emphasis on potential sugar production, which after ten or fifteen years could see production of 50–100,000 tons per annum alongside 30–40,000 tons of rice together with cotton, livestock, and other products. Hardwood was also highlighted for its commercial viability and a

[56] Sir Alexander Gibb & Partners and Overseas Consultants, Inc. *Report on Central African Rail Link Development Survey*, vol. 1 (London, 1952), 1.
[57] Gibb, *Report*, 16.
[58] Ibid., 17.
[59] Ibid.

conservative estimate of 10 million cubic feet of quality timber was given, resulting in 7–10,000 tons per annum, again after ten or fifteen years.[60]

The Gibb Report is notable for its bridging of inter-war and post-war development ideas, and for its duality of character as an international and external consultancy commissioned by and reporting to the Colonial Office. By this time, the failure of the Groundnut Scheme[61] could now be deplored 'not only for its financial losses but also for the unfortunate psychological and moral effects' which threw 'doubt on the wisdom of embarking on any large-scale agricultural project in Africa' and shook confidence in European enterprise.[62] This last point may be applied to emerging sentiments surrounding the right to sovereignty. The war exposed new generations to weaknesses in Western governments and, while independence may have seemed distant in 1952, gross governmental failures such as the Groundnut Scheme reduced confidence in the abilities of the administration. 'On the other hand' the report maintained, 'useful experience has been gained, new techniques learnt, and increased food production should result in due course'.[63] The independent consultants thus balanced the books and defaulted to the unwavering faith held by the colonial power to continue its forward momentum. In fact, momentum along lines of technical and scientific advances was only just gathering. The era of 'high modernism' in colonial development was barely underway.[64]

The East Africa Royal Commission Report

Formally appointed by Royal Warrant in 1953, this Commission (EARC) – the broadest of its kind to date – reported on present and future development in Kenya, Tanganyika, and Uganda. Such was its breadth that nearly three years passed between its being announced in October 1952 and the publication of its report in June 1955. Further significance is evidenced by the

---

[60] Ibid., 16–18.

[61] See Nicholas Westcott, *Imperialism and Development: The East African Groundnut Scheme and its Legacy* (Woodbridge, 2020)

[62] Ibid., 58. See Westcott, *Imperialism and Development*; Matteo Rizzo, 'The Groundnut Scheme Revisited: Colonial Disaster and African Accumulation in Nachingwea District, South-Eastern Tanzania, 1946–67' (PhD thesis, SOAS, 2005); Wood, *Groundnut Affair*.

[63] Ibid.

[64] Scott, *Seeing Like a State*, 4. Scott warns 'high modernism' should not be confused with 'scientific practice' as the former was an ideology and a 'faith that borrowed [...] the legitimacy of science and technology'. Scientific practice can, of course, exist without high modernism; but there is no high modernism without scientific practice.

inclusion of Chief David Kidaha Makwaia among its seven commissioners. As 'paramount chief' of the Sukuma Federation and a close ally of Twining, this reflected his recognition as an 'authoritative native voice' and a crucial bridge to independent Tanganyika.[65] Moreover, one review of the report, titled 'The Future of East Africa', reflected the surrounding air of portent.[66] Drawing from an English past to project an East African future, the commissioners claimed if certain recommendations were effected that the report may be 'as important for East Africa as was the compilation of the Domesday Book for England in the eleventh century'.[67]

Its terms of reference also resembled past commissions, but where previously foci were localised and narrow, the EARC was comprehensive and definitive. But on neither of the two tours of Tanganyika did the Commission visit Kilombero; rather, four members enjoyed what was certainly a delightful outing when they 'flew over the Rufiji and Kilombero river areas' before lunching at the Southern Highlands Club and returning to Dar es Salaam that same evening.[68] It was almost entirely from material evidence that conclusions were drawn and recommendations offered for developing the valley. Much of the emphasis on future visions and potentialities was therefore nothing new, just repackaged. The flood was volatile, peppered pockets of fertile land had led early observers to erroneously assume widespread fertility, and transport networks were poor. Indeed, this last point was the enduring paradox: that perceptions of great agricultural potential met with inadequate communications. This was a 'dilemma' in East Africa, but the potential for high agricultural productivity in many areas was largely unproven. This bred sufficient uncertainty to check spending on road and railway construction as the costs were disproportionate to the guaranteed, not merely potential, revenue from foreseeable traffic. It was an impasse, and by 1955 this had been a feature of colonial development approaches towards Kilombero for over half a century. 'Further development will not take place', the report declared, 'without the prior provisions of communications.'[69]

The report reiterated the idea of Kilombero as 'an area long considered as potentially productive' and that challenges posed by high costs in the process of development were beyond the limited resources of Government; but this was a common obstacle that stood in the way of 'winning from East Africa the greatest agricultural yields which it is capable of giving'.[70] Kilombero

---

[65] Awam Amkpa, 'Obituary of Chief David Kidaha Makwaia', *The Guardian*, 31 May 2007.

[66] R.W. Steel, 'The future of East Africa: Review of the report by the East Africa Royal Commission, 1953–1955' *The Geographical Journal* 122:3 (1956), 366–9.

[67] Quoted in Steel, 'The future of East Africa', 369.

[68] Great Britain, *East Africa Royal Commission*, 443.

[69] Ibid.

[70] Ibid., 266–7.

was described among those 'fertile areas of high potential or real productivity' which, in south-western Tanganyika, included 'a very extensive block of fertile country which remains virtually undeveloped in the face of the major difficulties of communications, [testse] fly, inaccessibility and lack of capital for irrigation and other projects'.[71] The interterritorial nature of the Commission informed how 'territorial development purely and simply would avail Kenya little, if at all, and the benefit would accrue entirely to Tanganyika', but that it seemed 'unlikely that [Tanganyika] will be able successfully to undertake development, in face of the manifold problems it presents, with the limited resources locally available'.[72] The Commission suggested a 'co-operative regional approach [...] in the interests of the whole of East Africa' and that '[i]t is perhaps only along these lines that it will be possible to use [Kilombero] at all'.[73] The report did not give concrete suggestions as to what form this could take, but reprised past emphases on the importance of investigations into irrigation possibilities.

Limited surveys and investigations in Kilombero continued. An incremental approach by necessity and design was sanctioned by new and overarching development frameworks, but in many respects this was no different to decades-long efforts of local officials. The crucial difference, of course, was one of centralisation and broader co-operation. The grandiose visions of the past had not disappeared, but had lost their fantastical tint. In a new era of technical and economic consciousness, large-scale development discourse was now imbued with a language of rationale and realism. In this vein, the following extract from the report is astute and shows a sound, if incomplete, understanding of the characteristics and limitations of Kilombero.

> Large scale development is not likely to be easy, inexpensive or quickly accomplished. The Kilombero is remote, and at present inaccessible. In this context the significance of the Central African rail-link is apparent. Moreover the present population of the area is small [...] and the environment not one which will naturally attract settlement. Malaria and bilharzia are real problems and [tsetse] fly exists in parts of the valley though not in the immediate riverain regions. If the ultimate development of the region depends upon the use of the main river, large technical and engineering problems will eventually have to be faced, because of the liability of the Kilombero to violent seasonal flooding. These difficulties will not have to be faced, however, until the present investigations are completed and the economics of agricultural development further established.[74]

---

[71] Ibid., 269–70.
[72] Ibid., 270.
[73] Ibid.
[74] Ibid. On its 'small population' the Commission observed: 'Only in the block of country along the Kilombero river and extending towards Lake Nyasa is there

'Present investigations' centred on alluvial fans and the use of the deltas of small perennial hill streams to irrigate modest areas of land through secondary flood waters. It was hoped this 'limited development' on 'sound and practical' lines would lead to several 'limited, but compact and controlled, local irrigation schemes' which might then be extended 'to play a greater part in the overall development of the Kilombero region'.[75] The Commission contended that 'sound agricultural development' would only be possible throughout East Africa by 'co-ordinated and systemic approach' and 'intimate liaison' at every stage of the process and at each level.[76] Further development would only be promoted if pilot schemes proved successful and it was expected that 'only gradually' would this 'reveal its productive possibilities'.[77]

The Colonial Office later published comments on the Commission's recommendations made by the Governors of Kenya, Uganda, and Tanganyika, and from the Administrator of the EAHC. Twining felt that the report was 'first-class' and would be constantly referenced for years, although he opposed certain points.[78] After his governorship in 1959, however, he wrote that he was 'a little diffident' about the Commission and believed its royal entrustment 'put it on rather a higher status than was needed'.[79] Twining considered himself a 'developer' and felt that this issue was most relevant for Tanganyika.[80] He commented: 'Communications must precede and not follow development: for without adequate connection between producer and market there can be no changeover from substance to economic farming.'[81]

The report maintained plans for a 200-mile branch railway line from Morogoro to Ifakara. Twining hoped the first half would be built 'in the near future' as it would 'serve an area open to immediate development', while the second would 'lead into the Kilombero Valley itself'.[82] Extension of the rail network had been postponed for lack of funds and, without substantial mineral traffic, an agricultural country such as Tanganyika struggled to raise capital.

---

a considerable expanse of green which does not, as yet, accommodate a heavy population.' They flew over in November, when the river was not in flood. It is true that population density was low; but the sight of the vast, uninhabitable floodplain may have led to false impressions of available land.

[75] Great Britain, *East Africa Royal Commission*, 276.
[76] Ibid., 419.
[77] Ibid., 344.
[78] Twining, 'The Last Nine Years', 20; Great Britain. Colonial Office, *Despatches from the Governors of Kenya, Uganda, and Tanganyika and the Administrator, East Africa High Commission, commenting on the East Africa Royal Commission 1953–1955 Report* (London, 1956), 157–80.
[79] Twining, 'The Last Nine Years', 20.
[80] Iliffe, *Modern History*, 442.
[81] Great Britain, *Despatches from the Governors*, 162.
[82] Ibid.

Twining was under no illusion that global conditions were unfavourable for an agricultural economy, as it relied on fluctuating world prices and 'the vagaries of rainfall'.[83] The future economic outlook was not promising and Twining was acutely aware that 'the trend of world agricultural prices' directly correlated to the viability of development schemes. He was certain that external financial assistance was required if Tanganyika were to follow an expanded programme of development and meet recurrent costs until the schemes became sustainable. The Government's own and necessarily modest programme for capital works development for the five years to 1960 would cost £26m. But £96m over ten years would be needed to meet the 'demands of the Commission's Report' and only half of this could be furnished from domestic finances. Twining was 'far from content at the sum of [his] conclusion' and regarded it as 'embarrassing [...] at a time when Her Majesty's Government are faced with the need to combat inflation in order to maintain and increase the strength of sterling'.[84]

The Colonial Office had been warning Twining against inflation from the early years of his governorship as he expanded development planning and expenditure. There were clear implications to Tanganyika's inability to raise sufficient capital itself to implement the recommended development plans to their full extent. Tanganyika was on the path towards independence and, while this was not considered immediately imminent, there was no desire on the part of the imperial government to inflate colonial sterling balances. From 1954 there was an 'unprecedented level of urgency' to achieve the very opposite, as accumulated colonial sterling balances – primarily those held by the Gold Coast, Malaya, and Nigeria – presented a danger to the international stability of the pound and to the British economy.[85] This negative correlation – between the funds required to implement the full development programme as proposed and the likelihood of the Treasury to cover Tanganyika's deficit of £48m – suggests that the Tanganyika Government had no choice but 'to resign [...] to half measures'.[86] For Twining, the 'one flaw in the exercise [of the Commission]' was that the terms of reference did not allow for suggestions on how recommendations could be financed. Andrew Cohen and Evelyn Baring – Governors of Uganda and Kenya respectively – also raised this point, and 'made it perfectly clear that unless some two hundred and fifty million pounds was made available during the next ten years, it would not be possible to implement the Royal Commission's Report effectively'.[87]

---

[83] Ibid., 170.
[84] Ibid., 171.
[85] Allister Hinds, 'Sterling and decolonization in the British Empire, 1945–1958', *Social and Economic Studies* 48:4 (1999), 111.
[86] Great Britain, *Despatches from the Governors*, 170–1.
[87] Twining, 'The Last Nine Years', 20.

The Rufiji Basin Survey

In July 1953 *The Times* newspaper reported: 'The first step in the long-term development of 68,500 square miles in the Rufiji basin area of Tanganyika is to begin in the near future when an irrigation expert arrives [...] to carry out a reconnaissance survey.'[88] The survey (RBS) was led by the Food and Agriculture Organization (FAO) of the United Nations, which submitted their final 'Report to the Government of Tanganyika on the Preliminary Reconnaissance of the Rufiji Basin' seven years later in seven volumes in June 1961, a shade over six months before Tanganyika achieved independence.[89] Twining first approached Norris E. Dodd, the second FAO Director-General, with proposals for the survey in 1952. After preliminary investigations in 1953, the survey began in earnest in 1955 and continued until 1960 before delivery of the final report the following year. The initial scope of the work was estimated to take only one year to complete, but after a short reconnaissance in 1953 it was apparent a more extensive survey was justified. By the time its findings were delivered by Binay Ranjan Sen, FAO's fifth Director-General, Twining had retired and his successor, Sir Richard Turnbull – having overseen Tanganyika gain responsible self-government in September 1960 – was preparing his own succession by Julius Nyerere. The survey began its investigations midway between the end of the Second World War and Tanganyika's independence, symbolising the transition from colonial to postcolonial forms of development.

By its long gestation, the RBS was not a surgical departure from past approaches to rural development, but part of an evolution, albeit a fairly rapid one. It was a major undertaking that represented, at the time, the high-water mark of technical, scientific, and international co-operation. For the oldest specialised organisation of the UN, this was also to be an important test for the FAO itself. The 'technical experts' who swept the Rufiji Basin aimed to gather more hydrographic and agronomic data than ever before. They were the new 'pioneers' assisting countries 'in the process of economic development to reach their goal of better living for their people', and who believed that 'without good statistics – and plenty of them – modern agriculture, industry, and commerce could not function as they do in the more technically advanced countries'.[90] The size of the core team varied throughout the period and ranged from two at its smallest, to forty-two at its largest. African assistants and additional employees took the full figure of personnel engaged on the

---

[88] 'Tanganyika Development', *The Times*, 20 July 1953.

[89] The volumes were: 1. General Report; 2. Hydrology and Water Resources; 3. Water Control; 4. Irrigation Department; 5. Mbarali Irrigation Scheme; 6. Geology; 7. Soils of the Main Irrigable Area.

[90] Hambidge, *Story of FAO*, 112.

survey into the many hundreds. This was a truly international endeavour, and was presented as such, as 'all members worked together in a friendly collaboration for the future benefit of Tanganyika and the development of its resources'.[91] The survey brought team members together from across Africa,[92] Australia, Austria, Great Britain, Canada, France, Holland, India, Italy, Lebanon, Norway, Poland, South Africa, and Switzerland. The Tanganyika Agricultural Corporation (TAC) co-ordinated the administration of the survey and led its experimental agricultural work. Employees engaged on the scheme were therefore either under the direct auspices of the FAO, the TAC, or the Tanganyika Government. The team leader was Nicholas Simansky who, like Telford before him, had experience as an irrigation engineer in Sudan.

The survey was essentially one of reconnaissance, with the following Terms of Reference:

1   To investigate and appraise the value and feasibility of possible development programmes for the conservation and utilisation of existing water resources in the Basin by such measures as flood control, reclamation, drainage, and gravity and pump irrigation systems.

2   To prepare proposals on possible methods and systems of water utilisation in the Basin.[93]

Three regions within the Rufiji Basin were earmarked for investigation: the Lower Rufiji, the Kilombero Valley, and the Usangu and Pawaga plains of the Great Ruaha River. The principal aims were to investigate water control for the benefit of local development, and its foci were flood control and irrigation for agricultural improvement. Hoag and Öhman have stated that the 'Rufiji Basin Survey marked the beginning of the formal planning of hydropower dams in the basin' but a close reading of the reports reveal this to not quite be the case.[94] The FAO explicitly stated that 'hydro-electric power' fell 'outside of the Terms of Reference of the Rufiji Basin Survey, and therefore not included above [in a list of recommended reservoirs]'.[95] The report mentions the potential for

---

[91] FAO, *The Rufiji Basin, Tanganyika: FAO Report to the Government of Tanganyika on the Preliminary Reconnaissance Survey of the Rufiji Basin, Vol. I, Part I – General Report* (Rome, 1961), 2.

[92] Individual African countries from which team members were drawn were not listed in the original FAO report.

[93] FAO, *Rufiji Basin: General Report*, 4.

[94] Heather J. Hoag and May-Britt Öhman. 'Turning water into power: Debates over the development of Tanzania's Rufiji River Basin', *Technology and Culture* 49:3 (2008), 641.

[95] FAO, *Rufiji Basin: General Report*, 18.

hydropower, however, and strongly suggests 'an investigation of the future requirements and means of provision of hydro-electric power, covering the whole of Tanganyika, but including the various possibilities of power from dams at Stiegler's Gorge, Mtera, and, if practicable, other sites in the Rufiji Basin'.[96] Hydropower was never the driving motivation for the survey and it was made clear that the 'generation of power should in no case prejudice the use of the works proposed, for flood control and irrigation'.[97] Flood control and irrigation possibilities were the primary aims of the survey and, moreover, it was reported that 'for most sites, control for the optimum generation of power would seriously affect the benefits for irrigation'.[98]

In Kilombero, survey teams sought to establish river gauges to measure discharge levels throughout the year. Catchment area maps were compiled, and from August 1956 one survey team commenced the 'very difficult search on foot of the tributaries of the Kilombero looking for water control sites'.[99] This began with the Ruhuji, Mnyera, and Mpanga systems. The hunt for dam sites continued, as did hydrometric work to determine water levels. Efforts to establish an automatic water recorder and ordinary gauge at the downstream limit of the flood area of the Kilombero at Swero River were often made under 'impossible conditions' and 'constituted a danger to staff working there' as they attempted to construct a 750ft cable-way and car across the river, which was claimed to be the first of its kind in East Africa. The Kilombero at Swero could reach 600 feet across 'with many crocodiles', but the first discharge measurements were successfully taken there in December 1959.[100] Heavy rains and flood conditions in the Basin often led to abandoned vehicles, and not all were recovered.[101] The dangers of wild game to survey members were very real. In 1959, the 'wild game hazards were the worst ever encountered in the history of the Rufiji Basin Survey' when 'one elephant, two rhino, and three hippopotami had to be shot in self-defence'.[102] Hazards from buffaloes and even lions were also reported, 'which sometimes attacked and disorganised the parties'.[103] When a hippopotamus charged and upset a boat carrying a hydrometrist, all records of measurements taken at several gauging stations were lost.[104] In April 1958 an African Survey Assistant employed on work in

[96] Ibid.
[97] Ibid., 56.
[98] FAO, *Rufiji Basin: Vol. I, Part II – Draft Summary of Conclusions and Recommendations*, 7.
[99] TNA 61/A3/9/A, TAC: Monthly Report for August 1956.
[100] Tanganyika, *TAC: Report and Accounts, 1958–59* (Dar es Salaam, 1960), 38.
[101] TNA 61/A3/9/A, TAC: Monthly Report for January 1958.
[102] Tanganyika: *TAC: Reports and Accounts, 1958–59*, 37.
[103] FAO, *Rufiji Basin: General Report*, 11.
[104] TNA 61/A3/9/A, TAC: Monthly Report for September 1957.

Kilombero was reported 'missing, believed drowned' but 'the accident [had] occurred in off duty hours' which makes it no less of a tragedy, but one that was not held against the RBS.[105] The survey also had difficulties recruiting local labour to assist with the work due to reluctance to work in such a 'wild and uninhabited area' and 'the unpopularity of another river safari'.[106]

When Simansky visited Rome and London in September 1957 he stressed the 'urgent necessity of expediting the hydrological investigations of some of the important river valleys, such as the Kilombero' and 'the factors at present handicapping the progress of hydrological work were discussed'.[107] These factors were given as primarily:

> The absence of all-weather bridges over the side rivers [...] which restricts and at times makes communications impossible – the extremely arduous task as a result of the limited staff available for the carrying out of reconnaissance over the large area involved – the difficulty of obtaining reliable local assistance to augment the FAO Team of Hydrometrists – the incidence of floods, the presence of big-game and dense bush.[108]

Environmental, human, and animal obstacles conspired to frustrate attempts to command Kilombero by technical and scientific mastery. Nevertheless, a detailed plan for flood control and irrigation in the valley was drawn up. Investigations incorporated aspects of meteorology, photography and mapping, water development and irrigation, river gauges, aerial surveys, and soil maps. It was concluded that 824,000 acres of land were irrigable in the valley, but that 'systematic irrigation is only possible if the flooding can be prevented'.[109] The emphasis on the importance of water control echoes a reflection that Gillman wrote in his diary in 1928:

> More than ever before – if, indeed, that were possible – have I been impressed during these last few days with the fact that *Water* is the fundamental problem if we wish to develop East Africa. Tsetse, population, economics, they will all solve more or less automatically if only we can provide water, water, water.[110]

---

[105] TNA 61/A3/9/A, TAC: Monthly Report for May 1958.
[106] Tanganyika: *TAC: Reports and Accounts, 1958–59*, 37; TNA 61/A3/9/A, TAC: Monthly Report for November 1956.
[107] TNA 61/A3/9/A, TAC: Monthly Report for September 1957.
[108] Ibid.
[109] FAO, *Rufiji Basin: General Report*, 14.
[110] Tanganyika. Clement Gillman, *Water Consultant's Report, No. 6 (1940): A Reconnaissance Survey of the Hydrology of Tanganyika Territory in its Geographical Settings* (Dar es Salaam, 1944), 1.

Gillman was not referring to arid regions only, but emphasising efficient water use in well-watered areas. The FAO report quoted Gillman's view that Tanganyika's rivers 'did not lend themselves to major schemes of irrigation or navigation which might justify the costs of gauging their flows' and deemed Gillman 'clearly mistaken' for his opinion that 'had the unfortunate effect of inhibiting for a considerable time the starting of systematic observations of river flows throughout Tanganyika as whole'.[111] But what kind of survey investigating the possibilities for water irrigation did not recommend schemes for water irrigation? Over a decade after Gillman's statement, and barely a few years before the RBS began, Loxton had also warned of the futility of large-scale flood control and irrigation schemes. But this is exactly what the report of the RBS proposed. The FAO expressed that flood reduction and control was the only means by which conditions conducive to general development could be achieved in Kilombero. 'It is not too much to say', stated the report, 'that the economic and administrative future of these large, fertile, and important regions will be transformed. In no other way will this be possible.'[112] In this imagined reality, however, mere flood control and irrigation could not transform the region. Transport and communications must also develop to export the vast quantities of produce available once Kilombero's waters were tamed. However, vastly improved roads were also required to carry construction materials for reservoir and irrigation works *into* the valley to begin with. The proposed 'Central African Link' railway was mentioned, but there were no assurances that this would be built or, if it did, that it would run through Kilombero.

Contingencies abound in the RBS report. A type of 'stepwise' or 'piecemeal' development was envisaged, which viewed the 'whole process spread over many years, beginning with pilot schemes of modest size, which can later be enlarged and increased in numbers in the light of experience gained'.[113] Despite this suggestion, the FAO appraised the potential area for irrigated agriculture in the Rufiji Basin as 1.5 million acres with a projected capital expenditure of £140 million.[114] In Kilombero, seven water storage reservoirs were proposed, although it was not suggested that all should be constructed, and various combinations were thought possible. The largest reservoir proposed, presented as having the greatest benefit, was the Mkasu Reservoir on the Ruhuji River in the upper reaches of the valley.[115] Its given capacity was 1,470,000 acre-feet,

[111] Ibid., 5.
[112] Ibid., 70.
[113] 'Letter from B.R. Sen, FAO Director-General, to Minister for Agriculture, Tanganyika, 5 June 1961', included in FAO, *General Report*, n.p.
[114] Ibid.
[115] Dams and reservoirs for flood control and irrigation were also proposed on the Mnyera, Mpanga, Kihansi, Ruipa, Kigogo-Ruaha, and Lumemo Rivers.

would cost £5,846,000 to build, and was expected to reduce flooding by 300,000 acres. This was far greater an area than could actually be developed. The population of the Kilombero Valley in 1961 was given by the FAO as approximately 56,000 people, but only one-fifth was thought would take up irrigated agriculture; therefore existing numbers were sufficient to cultivate an irrigable area of only 22,000 acres based on ten-acre holdings for a five-person family.[116] 'Ample numbers of cultivators could be found', it was claimed, 'from adjacent regions, possessing densely populated areas'.[117] This echoes past solutions to the perceived problem of underpopulation. The assumption that cultivators would move, or be compelled to move, was partly responsible for undoing the scheme for syndicated development investigated by Telford.

The 'First Stage' of development to 1965, however, comprised an area of 9,600 acres and requiring 1,000 families, for which minimal capital expenditure was required as irrigation would be provided from unregulated rivers. No storage dams were proposed, either for water supply or flood protection. The 'Second Stage' was intermediary, providing construction for larger works on a moderate scale. The 'Third Stage' conceived of 'full control of river flows for provision of irrigation water and prevention of flooding, and the extension of irrigated cultivation to the maximum ultimately possible'.[118]

The vision was monumental. Its scale surpassed all schemes proposed during the colonial era, when plenty were envisioned and repeatedly rendered unfeasible. This report had no such limitation. Anything was possible. It seemed that the bigger the dream, the better. The post-war and soon-to-be-postcolonial horizons were wider than ever before. The FAO forecast that the annual tonnage of crops from Kilombero would be 11,500 during the First Stage; 114,500 by the Second; and 850,000 after the Third.[119] By the application of scientific and technological expertise, enshrouding sheer conjecture, the possibilities were limitless. But the report was also cunningly noncommittal. Figures were 'conservative' and 'tentative' and only 'closer observation and investigation of conditions over several years [could provide] the basis for a more certain appraisal'.[120] In a letter to the Minister for Agriculture, the FAO Director-General advised that 'it will be wise not to take definite decisions about any particular project until such investigations have been completed and fully considered'.[121]

[116] FAO, *Rufiji Basin: General Report*, 92.
[117] Ibid., 96.
[118] Ibid., 50.
[119] Ibid., 74.
[120] Ibid., 52.
[121] 'Sen to Minister for Agriculture', included in FAO, *General Report*, n.p.

There is no doubt that the survey generated an unprecedented wealth of new data for Tanganyika, but it also encountered a multitude of old problems. This is none more evident than in the tribulations of one of the trial farms established as part of the survey in Kilombero at Lumemo, at which experimental work began in 1956. This joined an earlier tumultuous attempt at mechanised farming in the valley, at Lupiro.

A tale of two farms: Lupiro and Lumemo

Lupiro Farm comprised two sites – at Lupiro itself and Kivukoni – and was formally established as a rainfed experimental large-scale mechanised rice project in 1951. Earlier trials began at Lupiro in 1949 and Kivukoni the following year, situated fifteen and three miles south of Ifakara respectively. Kivukoni saw some flooding from the Kilombero, and 190 acres were protected by bunds; whereas Lupiro was proximal to the river but beyond the risk of flood damage. One European officer managed operations at first; a second and third were posted following expansion to 650 and 850 acres respectively. Periods of planting and harvesting brought 'a 10–12 hour day of hard physical labour over long periods without weekend breaks' and, as such, planned experimental work could not be carried out.[122]

In 1955 it was written that 'Lupiro might well be the embryo of mechanization in the Kilombero Valley and from which might grow other units to develop and utilise the vast area of uninhabited rich and fertile soil.'[123] It was hoped private enterprise might be enticed to Kilombero by proving that mechanisation was economic, and settlement and development could then expand into the valley. It was still thought company development was the most feasible route as 'it would be many years yet' before local farmers could employ mechanisation in their own fields.[124]

After three harvests – 1951/2, 1952/3, and 1953/4 – a rice variety 'really suitable for mechanization' had not yet been found, but it was thought that mechanised rice production was feasible.[125] Conditions for each year, however, were entirely variable and especially at the critical period of planting. Rain in 1953 following field preparation led to heavy and rapid weed growth, necessitating harrowing of the entire acreage again. In some areas this was

---

[122] TNA 461/28/6, Lupiro Farm: Annual Report, 1953–54.

[123] Great Britain. Colonial Office, *Notes on Some Agricultural Development Schemes in the British Colonial Territories.* 3rd ed., 2nd revise. (London, 1955), 68.

[124] Ibid.

[125] Ibid. The only variety grown to 1954 was *kahogo* from an indigenous variety, but its straw was too tall and weak to lodge well in the combine harvester.

done two or three times before drilling. Then heavy and consistent rain again during planting bogged down tractors and from January planting became a 'nightmare' until March.[126] At Kivukoni, 1.92 inches of rain fell in one hour on 13 March 1954, which 'turned the last planted land into a lake' for several days and ruined five acres of ungerminated seed.[127]

By the end of the 1956/7 season, Lupiro was declared commercially unviable. Continuous early rains and persistent flooding prevented planting over more than 240 acres and accounts from July 1955 to December 1957 showed a £58,000 loss.[128] The Director of Agriculture explained:

> Subsequent experience showed that the erratic behaviour of the uncontrolled Kilombero river makes planting and harvesting conditions completely unpredictable. Land may be prepared for planting, but early flooding may make it impossible to establish the crop. Late flooding may completely destroy what would otherwise have been an excellent crop.[129]

Furthermore, all rice varieties seemed to ripen practically simultaneously, regardless of time sown. This complicated harvesting. If harvested late, grain would shatter in the field or when combined. If harvested early, wet grain required drying by sun or artificial dryer. Either way, a high proportion of broken grain severely reduced gross returns.

There was no realisable value from the general development of the estate, and capital equipment sold at auction was below book value. This included everything from pipe wrenches to spirit levels, from a portable blacksmith's forge to a pair of hand shears. Two detonator buckets used as bird and game scarers were listed as fifty shillings each against a cost value two-and-a-half times that, and Tilley floodlights used in an attempt to keep game from destroying crops were half price. Marauding game had proved a 'grave danger' – especially trampling elephant and voracious hippopotami – and during the 1953/54 season caused the loss of thirty-six tons of paddy, which held the value of at least £1,000.[130] An area between the river and cultivated land was also ploughed and planted as a 'buffer zone' in the hope that this would satiate hippopotami appetite enough to prevent further intrusion. 'Buck' also caused considerable

---

[126] TNA 461/28/6, Lupiro Farm: Annual Report, 1953–54.
[127] Ibid.
[128] Great Britain. Colonial Office, *Tanganyika under United Kingdom Administration: Report to the United Nations for 1956* (London, 1957), 76.
[129] Tanganyika, *Lupiro Farm: Accounts, Reports of the Director of Audit and Report of the Director of Agriculture for period of operation as a commercial enterprise 1st July, 1955 to 31st December, 1957* (Dar es Salaam, 1959), 1.
[130] Great Britain, *Notes on Some Agricultural Development Schemes*, 68.

damage to young shoots after germination. The 'great menace to successful mechanised paddy production' was said to be 'game' and during this season alone, twenty elephants and seventy-eight 'buck' were killed within half a mile of the boundaries of cultivated land.[131] It was then suggested that *all* game should be destroyed within a radius of five miles.

The Director of Agriculture understated in 1959 that the experience of Lupiro Farm certainly 'brought to light some of the limitations and difficulties of mechanised rice production in the Kilombero Valley', but it was hoped that further investigations into rice varieties and flood control could 'make such an enterprise profitable in the future'.[132] This was expected as a result of the RBS. Otherwise, the site was abandoned with no interest shown in continuing the farm. But visions for a farm at Lumemo soon appeared on the horizon.

Trial farms were an early objective of the RBS, despite some believing that several years' worth of water control data was required. Development at Lumemo, however, began on 120 acres in 1956 and three seasons were trialled during the survey itself 1956–9, although FAO experts did not design the experiments or programme of crop trials. These were managed by the Agricultural Department and the TAC. At first, irrigation water was pumped from the Lumemo River and carried to the farm by canal. Early reports frequently cited slow progress due to the quality and availability of local labour. Shortages were thought due to local farmers' prioritisation of their own plots, but rising nationalism and imposed 'development' also bred resistance. Pay increases were agreed in November 1956, but still a labour strike followed the following year.[133]

The first season was 'marked by extremely difficult climatic conditions' after the Lumemo flooded following heavy rainfall in April 1957 of 17.64 inches. Various crops were trialled with varying levels of success. Early promise from good germination and steady growth was often overturned by heavy rain, flooding, insect and bird damage, fungus, or destruction by game. During the first year, thirty-seven varieties of rice were trialled, including cultivation of fifteen acres that 'withstood the flood but was destroyed by game in the course of a couple of nights'.[134] Dry season planting over ten acres followed and a wide variety of crops sown, including soya, groundnuts, beans, pulses, onions, hibiscus, rapeseed, simsim, sunflower, maize, Rhodes grass, glycine javanica, palm (for oil), and rice.[135]

[131] TNA 461/28/6, Lupiro Farm: Annual Report, 1953–54.
[132] Tanganyika, *Lupiro Farm*, 2.
[133] TNA 61/A3/9/A, TAC: Monthly Report for November 1957.
[134] FAO, *The Rufiji Basin, Tanganyika: Report on Agriculture and Trial Farms* (Rome, 1960), 11.
[135] TNA 61/A3/9/A, TAC: Monthly Report for August 1957.

Lumemo proved a concatenation of catastrophe. Tractor work was halted at various times due to waterlogged soils or very dry conditions. Dry conditions also caused leakages in several canals. Pumps occasionally failed, the pump battery charging plant was once damaged by fire, and a Land Rover was damaged after striking a buck.[136] Wild pigs were a constant nuisance. Buffalo favoured destruction of the maize crop, while rice crops were most often destroyed by elephant.

The following season was also marred by flooding after heavy rainfall, as 28.28 inches fell between March and April 1958.[137] Floods washed out quantities or entireties of rice, cotton, rape, soya, and hibiscus, and caused extensive damage to farm roads and earthworks.[138] On one day in March, two inches of rainfall was recorded in a little over half an hour. Later in the month floods 'carried away the Lumemo-Ifakara bridge, leaving a foot bridge the only link with the town' and 'water got into the store, damaging seeds and fertilizer, and also in the staff camp necessitating the evacuation of wives and children'.[139] The experience of Lumemo had once again shown that inexperience and insufficient local knowledge were punished by the vagaries of rainfall and power of the flood.

Despite clear failings and drawbacks, the final report suggested that irrigation trials at Lumemo should continue. It was an example of light shone on those 'single isolated instances' which were 'valuable as visible demonstrations of what can be done even with limited resources, but insignificant in proportion to the vast potentialities of the future'.[140]

Unmet expectations: Complaints against the state

For many, the Rufiji Basin Survey was yet another intervention and intrusion into the region and local lives. The growth of nationalism and anti-colonial sentiment throughout the 1950s, however, did not always manifest as a simple call for absolute freedom from the colonial yoke. In Kilombero, communities first took the state to task, revealing complex manifestations of rising nationalist sentiments. The influx of experts and officials was not interpreted as 'positive' development, but as indistinguishable from decades of colonial practices that had underdeveloped the region. More was expected from the state, and it would be held to account.

---

[136] TNA 61/A3/9/A, TAC: Monthly Report for September 1957.
[137] FAO, *Rufiji Basin: Report on Agriculture and Trial Farms*, 10.
[138] TNA 61/A3/9/A, TNA: Monthly Report for April 1958.
[139] TNA 61/A3/9/A, TNA: Monthly Report for March 1958.
[140] FAO, *Rufiji Basin: General Report*, 1.

At the height of the survey, in May 1957, a letter was sent from Ifakara by a Complaints Committee to the central government on behalf of valley residents. It is remarkable and significant, calling not for self-representation or independence from the current administration directly, but admonishes the Government and Ulanga's current DOs. 'Ulanga wants clever and genial DC and DO', its first subtitle declares, beginning: 'Since the end of 1955 Ulanga District has never had suitable officers to bring about developments of every kind as we expect.'[141] The district was 'in trouble in every way' and the committee was formed by those who 'opposed the cruel rule of DCs' and to which 'chiefs' were indifferent, 'callous' and could 'see nothing wrong' in the status quo. G.T.L. Scott, DC for Ulanga from early 1956, was named and initially thought of as 'a clever and genial man, but when we had learnt more about him', so unfolded the letter, 'we discovered that he was not a DC who could develop the country and that he did not like the people at all'. Scott was an 'indolent' and 'useless European' and when he left Ulanga 'nobody cared', whereas 'parties' had been held 'in the past' for outgoing DCs who had run the District 'in a constitutional manner'. One of these DCs, C.F. Beauclerk was described as a 'lover of the people' and since his departure, 'Ulanga has never had a DC who likes his people'. In contrast, of one DO under Scott, the Complaints Committee wrote that: 'Never since the Creation had we seen a lazier European.'

The letter reveals a rising mood in Kilombero and illuminates the reported grumblings concerning labour difficulties, wage disputes, and local strikes. Lumemo Farm itself was shown to be deeply resented. Its creation in 1956 was the 'unjust alienation of settled land' and a 'confiscation of traditional shambas',[142] for which 'the headmen concerned pleaded for their people but in vain'. The DC was shown 'shambas, coconut palms, mango trees, guava trees, sugarcanes, etc. in their effort to prove that the areas were settled' but, as 'the chief and sub-chief had agreed to the alienation' the protest fell on deaf ears. Scott then 'ordered all people who were living in the alienated land to leave it and abandon their shambas'.

There were also 'troubles' for those who lived 'near those Europeans' as they were 'not allowed to converse together in the evening, children cannot play about as they used to do and all must go to bed at 6pm'. The Complaints

---

[141] TNAUK FCO 141/17784, Complaints Committee, Ifakara to the Member for Local Government, Dar es Salaam, 29 May 1957. Subsequent quotations are drawn from this source.

[142] *Shamba* (plural *mashamba* in Kiswahili, and pluralised in the anglicised form as *shambas*) refers to a field or plot for cultivating crops. The term commonly refers to smaller, individual holdings, but magnitude varies and usage may apply to areas ranging in size from a small, private garden to a plantation or estate.

Committee asked: 'Have these Europeans come to farm or establish a new government?' Imposition into local lives was viewed as contrary to the perception of official government sentiment: 'While this is all going on, we people of Tanganyika continue hearing speeches and promises that the British Government ruled Tanganyika justly and develops it.' When this letter was written, Twining was Governor and cited as 'constantly' assuring that government policy was 'to bring about educational, agricultural, and economic development in the country' but the view of many in Ulanga was quite different. Political and nationalist feelings were clearly rising, 'because these are not the days when one can oppress and look down upon other people' as 'Tanganyika has now a new status and it would be better that justice is meted out to the people of Tanganyika.' The following year, Turnbull replaced Twining as Governor, who worked with Nyerere from the outset to ensure the people of Tanganyika received the justice they sought and the freedom to shape their own futures.

6

New Nation, New Internationalism: Maendeleo wa Jamhuri, 1959–76

One question drove Tanganyika through Independence from Britain on 9 December 1961 and prevailed: *What did the future hold for the new nation?*

Independence itself arguably remains the most significant 'future-making' event in Tanzania's history. In his 'Independence Message to TANU', Nyerere spoke of 'the moment we have all been working for' and which 'has come sooner than any of us dreamed possible in 1954 [...] because the people of Tanganyika have worked together [...] for this one purpose, the attainment of *Uhuru*'.[1] Turnbull declared 'the fulfilment of the aspirations of all the people of Tanganyika' and no single moment before or since has been bounded by the same scale of hope, promise, and optimism for the future.[2] Companies and industries heralded bright futures through development progress as they congratulated Nyerere and the nation through advertisements in print media, implicitly consolidating their status through the transition to realign themselves with the independent state. The CDC held 'development' as 'key to the future for Tanganyika', the Tanganyika Engineering and Contracting Co. (TECCO) declared it 'builds for the future', and the Tanganyika Electric Supply Company (TANESCO) captioned the illustration of an electricity meter: 'this gadget measures our country's progress'.[3] The tyre manufacturer, Dunlop, wished all 'a smooth trouble-free road into the future...'[4]

Nyerere was under no illusion that rapid development and exponential increases in living standards were crucial for Tanganyika, and wrote: 'We inherit a country which is poor economically although rich in potential and rich in the spirit of its people.'[5] He vowed to 'make independence work

---

[1] Julius K. Nyerere, 'Independence Message to TANU', in *Freedom and Unity: A Selection of Writings and Speeches, 1952–65* (Dar es Salaam, 1966), 138.

[2] TNAUK CO 822/2979, 'Address by His Excellency the Governor-General at the Independence Ceremony', Turnbull to Colonial Office, 20 November 1961.

[3] Tanganyika, *Souvenir Catalogue: Tanganyika 1961 Independence Exhibition* (Arusha, 1961), 20, 67, 69.

[4] *Tanganyika Standard*, 9 December 1961.

[5] 'A message from Mr. Julius K. Nyerere', *Tanganyika Standard*, 9 December 1961.

and thus remove poverty, ignorance, and disease from our land'.[6] There was, however, an uncomfortable recognition that transitory reliance on the experience and expertise of British administrative officers was inevitable. After Tanganyika gained full internal self-government in May 1961, Nyerere wrote a friendly and persuasive letter to all officers, imploring they work for the new Government:

> The first thing I want to make clear is that my Government, and therefore the great bulk of the people of Tanganyika whom we represent, are really in need of your help; and we will be for a long time to come. It is not only technical officers we wish to retain. We need our experienced administrators, our *'corps d'élite'* as the Governor called you the other day, because it is they who keep the whole machinery of Government working.[7]

Nyerere was critically aware that the first years would be crucial, testing years. The wealth of experience held by many officers was considered vitally important to ensure the new nation did not fall at its first hurdles. This was part of the difficult truth that 'political independence did not alter economic dependence' nor did Tanganyika possess 'sufficient trained manpower to replace all the expatriates [...] who held senior positions'.[8] The majority, however, chose to leave and 'all the liners going back to England [...] were fully booked' throughout the two months from late November 1961.[9] These were dubbed 'the *Uhuru* boats'.[10]

The first 'Three-Year Development Plan' for 1961–4 acknowledged its conception in a 'momentous [...] period of transition from the colonial type of administration to independence' but also how 'expatriate officers [formed] the backbone of all technical services [...] on which the fulfilment of the development plan depends' and 'any rapid decrease in their numbers could have a great effect on the plan itself'.[11] That may have been so, but that did not mean that Tanganyika could not look beyond its own borders for assistance. Indeed, the 'Proposals of the Tanganyika Government for a Republic' in 1962 described how:

---

[6] 'The Voice of the Commonwealth', *The Sphere*, 3 November 1962.
[7] Quoted in Richard F. Eberlie, *The Winds and Wounds of Change* (Bristol, 2016), 5.
[8] Isaria K. Kimambo, Gregory H. Maddox and Salvatory S. Nyanto. *A New History of Tanzania* (Dar es Salaam, 2017), 171.
[9] Eberlie, *Winds and Wounds*, 6.
[10] Ibid.
[11] Tanganyika, *Development Plan for Tanganyika, 1961–1964* (Dar es Salaam, 1961), 1.

Tanganyika is a young nation, faced with tremendous problems of nation-building and economic development. Our nationalism is a young nationalism, born of the desire to unite and free ourselves from the shackles of colonialism. While we must guard against a narrow, exclusive form of nationalism, which can lead to dangerous international rivalries, we need to foster our sense of nationhood within the large context of an African family of nations and the international community.[12]

Advanced ideological acrobatics celebrated political independence while necessarily and reluctantly accepting continued economic, technical, and financial dependence.[13] Nothing was more important than the idea that Tanganyika had freed itself from colonial shackles, but in reality its sense of nationhood had to sit within the context of an 'international community' comprised of current, and former colonial powers. These dynamics became a defining feature of 1960s Tanganyika and, crucially, its future.

New frontiers for a new internationalism

The first development plan penned for the independent era had all the trappings of colonial-era planning. This is perhaps unsurprising. One major departure, however, was that it was heavily influenced by Washington, and less by Whitehall. It was 'largely based on a plan worked out by the World Bank' after its report on 'The Economic Development of Tanganyika' had provided 'a comprehensive survey' as 'indispensable background to the work on the development plan'.[14] Emphasis was made on investment in development projects that offered swift returns for output and income. Long-term projects were suspended luxuries. In Kilombero, one project listed under consideration involved hibiscus fibre, and another year of trials was recommended before deciding whether it was an economic prospect.[15] Alongside five others, the project was approved for funding via a Colonial Development and Welfare

---

[12] Tanganyika, *Proposals of the Tanganyika Government for a Republic* (Dar es Salaam, 1962), 1–2.

[13] 'Economic dependence' through ties to trade patterns and world markets; 'Financial dependence' as reliance on capital credit or loans.

[14] 'Tanganyika Independence Bill', *Hansard* HL Deb, 16 November 1961, vol. 235 cols. 733–4; Tanganyika, *Development Plan, 1961–64*, 1. The 'World Bank' (WB) and the 'International Bank for Reconstruction and Development' (IBRD) are used virtually synonymously. On the creation of the 'International Development Association' (IDA) in 1960, the WB technically referred to the institution that comprised both the IBRD and the IDA, but in practice this distinction was never made.

[15] Tanganyika, *Development Plan, 1961–64*, 57.

grant to increase agricultural productivity.[16] Reflective of the new internationalism underlining development in Tanganyika, the project was not, in fact, initiated with British funding, but its undertaking resulted from a Dutch and West German collaboration.

Both the Governments of Tanganyika and Great Britain had requested the World Bank conduct its economic survey mission, its task was:

> to assess the resources available for future development, to consider how these might best contribute to a balanced program of social and economic development, to make recommendations for practical measures, to further such developments, and to indicate the financial implications of such recommendations.[17]

The inherent 'international character' of the mission reflected the gradual relinquishment of British hegemony over economic development in Tanganyika. Its reorientation of political status as a United Nations Trusteeship in 1946 represents a marked moment of this trajectory. Further reorientation followed Independence as new responsibilities and demands for socio-economic development preoccupied the new state. The early 1960s, therefore, saw Tanganyika position itself as globally outward-looking as it sought new and increasingly international sources of financial and technical assistance. Moreover, the years straddling Independence were rife with speculation as to how Tanganyika would emerge onto a global stage beset by Cold War politics. The US and USSR were acutely aware of the importance to geopolitical dynamics in securing African alliances as newly autonomous nations emerged. The superpowers presented different models in their offers for economic development, and there was no guarantee that Nyerere would look only to the West.

In 1962, Nyerere announced that Tanganyika would pursue a policy of 'African socialism' that defined and combined approaches to development thought most practical and ideologically resonant. Nyerere was aware of the need for the nation to maximise opportunity, and would not refuse offers of assistance because of broader political implications in an increasingly polarised world. He was among those pioneering African leaders within the 'Non-Aligned Movement' throughout the Cold War.[18] Nyerere believed he could prioritise Tanganyika's need for economic development while transcending the

---

[16] These were: cocoa, seed pea, tobacco production, tea in Lupembe, and a livestock-holding ground in Ilonga.

[17] International Bank for Reconstruction and Development, *The Economic Development of Tanganyika* (Baltimore, 1961), vii.

[18] See T.V. Sathyamurthy, 'Tanzania's non-aligned role in international relations', *India Quarterly* 37:1 (1981), 1–23; Julius K. Nyerere, 'Non-alignment and its future

politicisation of international financial and technical assistance with which he was reluctantly compelled to engage. Soon after the announcement that Tanganyika would have an African-majority Parliament in 1959 on the path to democracy, Nyerere was asked where he might source capital for public works. Implicit in the question was whether Soviet influence could be established through financial assistance. Nyerere's initial reply confirmed his leanings towards British and American sources of assistance and development models: 'We don't think in terms of roubles,' he said. 'We think in terms of pounds or dollars.'[19] He continued:

> But suppose we do not get the money – and this is not blackmail. If we want, for example, to dig a canal from Lake Victoria to irrigate our lands, do you think I am going to say 'No' to roubles if there is no other way we can get the money to irrigate our land?[20]

It was a fair point; and one that spurred, rather than dissuaded, Western engagement in Tanganyika's future. This was not a threat but a plea for the nation's predicament to be fully recognised at a time when Cold War and Tanzanian politics had not intersected to the extent they would in subsequent years.[21] Nevertheless, Nyerere respected association with Britain and the US, despite the former symbolising the colonial yoke. In 1961, he wrote to President John F. Kennedy with a 'blunt request' for economic aid so that the new nation's 'present political success' may be followed by 'reasonable economic hopes'.[22] In addition to the World Bank's economic survey, a study into possibilities for industrial development was also published. This was commissioned by the Ministry of Commerce and Industry under the aegis of the Agency for International Development of the US Government. Western fears of infiltrating roubles aside, here was evidence that, as far as Nyerere was concerned, there was no Iron Curtain drawn between Dar es Salaam and Washington.

---

prospects', *India Quarterly* 39:1 (1983), 1–5; and Robert B. Rakove, *Kennedy, Johnson, and the Nonaligned World* (New York, 2013).

[19] 'I'm no dictator, Africans told', *Daily Mirror*, 16 December 1959.

[20] Ibid.

[21] See Cranford Pratt, *The Critical Phase in Tanzania, 1945–68: Nyerere and the Emergence of a Socialist Strategy* (Cambridge, 1976); Maria Nzomo, 'The foreign policy of Tanzania: From Cold War to post-Cold War', in Stephen Wright (ed.), *African Foreign Policies* (New York, 1999), 182–98; George Roberts, *Revolutionary State-Making in Dar es Salaam: African Liberation and the Global Cold War, 1961–1974* (Cambridge, 2021).

[22] 'Letter from Julius Nyerere to President John F. Kennedy, undated, National Security Files, Box 388 of 'William H. Brubeck Series,' Folder 'Tanganyika, 7/61–12/62," JFKL', quoted in Philip E. Muehlenbeck, *Betting on the Africans: John F. Kennedy's Courting of African Nationalist Leaders* (Oxford, 2012), 99.

This study into industrial possibilities, published December 1961, was contracted to the Arthur D. Little Corporation. Founded in 1886 as 'the world's first management consultancy' its slogan, 'Other people's troubles are our business', was adopted in 1906.[23] The employment of such a consultancy firm was distinct, as was the scale of the international and collaborative character of the investigation. Minister for Commerce and Industry, C. George Kahama, wrote the report's foreword, asserting the 'importance of industrial development in furthering the economic progress of [Tanganyika] [...] and also the significance of the role of the private investor in this development, and [the Government] aims to encourage such investment'.[24] This was a new frontier for Tanganyika and for private investors now afforded greater opportunities for involvement in its economic and industrial growth. The report carried the liberating language of decolonisation as it recognised as desirable 'a rapid Africanization in the management of its own activities' of industrial development.[25] Implicit was the intent of American influence as a constitutive part of Tanganyika's future, while also promoting both the 'Africanization' of permanent positions and the temporary use of international consultants.

The 'Little Report' focused on industrial processing opportunities, separate from agriculture and animal husbandry. It emphasised training, skills, and technical assistance. Industrial engineering, marketing, accounting, finance, and problems associated with training schemes were also promoted. The report considered current and potential markets, but made recommendations without detailed regional analyses. Forest product industries were among those considered 'near-term opportunities' with a 'high profitability of being feasible'.[26] For Kilombero, the greatest potential for industrial development was considered the manufacture of plywood from mahogany and antiaris timber.[27] Mahogany was historically favoured for canoe building in the valley, while colonial forestry policies were often brought into contention with local practices of forest resources and timber felling.[28] Now, future prospects for

---

[23] Arthur D. Little Global, 'Our History', https://www.adlittle.com/en/about-us/history.

[24] Arthur D. Little, Inc. *Tanganyika Industrial Development: A Preliminary Study Of Bases for the Expansion of Industrial Processing Activities* (Dar es Salaam, 1961), vii.

[25] Ibid., 7.

[26] Ibid., 11.

[27] Ibid., 83. Antiaris *(Antiaris toxicaria)* belongs to the mulberry and fig family, known locally as: *mkunde* (Kiswahili); *msenda* (Hehe); *luwelu* (Pogoro); *mbukale* (Ngindo). It is described as a 'lightweight hardwood', but is relatively soft with little use as timber. In Kilombero today it often remains in open forest after surrounding trees have been felled. See Alexandra Boswell and Andrew Marshall, *Saving Our Forests: 1. Kilombero and the Udzungwa Lowlands* (Dar es Salaam, 2011), 20–6.

[28] See Jamie Monson, 'Canoe-building under colonialism: Forestry & food policies in the Inner Kilombero Valley, 1920–40' in Maddox et al., *Custodians of the Land*, 200–12. Monson cites one species of African mahogany used for canoe building as

current mahogany and antiaris stands included the manufacture of veneers and veneer-surfaced materials. It was recommended a plywood plant be installed to process the matured mahogany timber, estimated at three million cubic feet and at risk of being 'cut out' rapidly for the planting of a proposed commercial rubber tree plantation. Furthermore, large areas of natural forest on the escarpment were suggested as a source of pulp-wood and it was thought 'technically feasible' to establish other 'large-scale softwood plantations [...] in the uplands' surrounding the valley.[29] Other 'possible planting sites' were thought to exist 'in extensive areas of grassland within the Kilombero Forest Reserve running north-east from Mufindi' and its fifty inches of average annual rainfall would encourage 'high-yield timber growth'.[30] It was projected that national requirements for sawn timber would reach twelve million cubic feet by the year 2000, while in 1961 the Forest Department was 'already proceeding with the necessary planting of hardwoods and softwoods to meet this long-term requirement' which also correlated with FAO estimates on future demands of wood products.[31]

Kilombero was viewed as possessing developable resources for both swift and long-term returns. This was not the first recognition of its timber value as Kilombero had been earmarked within a wider colonial policy of forestry conservation to support timber concessions for private export enterprise, especially during the 1930s when an unrealised suggestion to construct a sawmill was made.[32] Previous colonial interest also cited African teak as a valued hardwood, but it did not historically exist in quantities sufficient for commercial exploitation. It was, however, another locally favoured timber for canoe building due to its size, durability, and resistance to rot.[33] Teak did not draw focus in the Little Report, but since the establishment of the Kilombero Valley Teak Company (KVTC) in 1992 with Commonwealth Development Corporation funding and support, a teak industry has enjoyed exponential growth. At the time of writing, teak is firmly associated with the valley,

---

Khaya nyasica (or *mwacwa* in Kiswahili), but it is possible that the mahogany referred to in the Little Report is *Khaya anthotheca*, one of several trees known as 'African mahogany' and popular for plantations, but now rare throughout Kilombero's forests due to logging. It remains common in the south-east corner of the Udzungwa National Park, and is known locally as: *mkangazi* (Kiswahili); *mwondo* (Hehe); *mbasamono* (Bena); *luhendo* (Pogoro); *mpilipili* (Ngindo).

[29] Ibid., 85–7.
[30] Ibid., 85.
[31] Ibid., 83.
[32] Monson, 'Canoe-building', 204.
[33] Ibid., 203. African teak *(Milicia excelsa)* is known locally as: *mvule* (Kiswahili, Pogoro, Ngindo); *miangi* (Hehe); *mkangazi* (Bena).

joining rice and sugar to form a trio of the highest profile commodities in Kilombero. The present industry and associated public awareness of the valley as a centre for commercial timber production, however, does not reflect a historic precedent. Rather, the suggestion to develop a plywood and related industry in Kilombero is emblematic of a different historical trend: that is to say, a development proposal and its subsequent *un*fulfillment, either within its expected timeframe or at all. While this trend is traced to the beginning of European visions for the valley from the late-nineteenth century, it is not the single model of development histories in Kilombero. Not all visions failed to materialise. Others originated as colonial ideas but manifested as postcolonial materialities. Development trajectories thus differed widely, subject as they were to widely varying contexts and project specificities. There are four development schemes that do well to illustrate this diversity within the Kilombero context during what might be called the 'short' 1960s, 1961–9; that is to say, from Independence to the first year of periodisation for the 'Second Five-Year Plan for Economic and Social Development, 1969–74'. This period is distinct for many reasons, not least for its representation of Tanganyika's transition from a new nation with a remnant Turnbull as Governor-General in 1961, to a period of nationalisation following the Arusha Declaration in 1967, which proclaimed TANU's policy of African socialism and self-reliance.

This period also serves as a comparative frame through which to view these schemes' trajectories, their divergent beginnings and ends beyond a momentary coexistence. Each scheme also represents a particular category within the development history that reflects broader trends in relation to the conception and (non-)implementation of visions. In short then described more fully, the four schemes that are integral to understanding the history of development in Kilombero, not only for the 1960s but beyond, are as follows.

1 **SUGAR.** The conception of a sugar scheme in Kilombero was colonial, and was very nearly implemented in the mid-1950s. Its revival became a symbol of nationalism as one of the first industrial projects to be inaugurated after Independence, and therefore most potently represents Tanganyika's transition from 1961 onwards.

2 **RAILWAY DEVELOPMENT.** Railway development to, for, and through Kilombero has a long history, and is interwoven into the earliest colonial visions of the valley. Some of the same proposals and reservations continued into the 1960s with varying outcomes.

3 **KATRIN** ('Kilombero Agricultural Training and Research Institute'). This is a project that could only have been possible in the postcolonial era. It is also wholly representative of a particular approach

to postcolonial development. This was an agricultural development project centred around a training institute and funded by an international government, which in this case was the Federal Republic of Germany (FRG). KATRIN is notable for being implemented within this period and not only continued beyond it, but remains active at the time of writing this volume.

4 **KENAF.**[34] This is an example of a project that emerged at the cusp of Independence, but did not ultimately come to full fruition. It originated through funding and support from the FRG in co-operation with the Dutch management firm which also oversaw operations at the Kilombero Sugar Company. Categorised as an ultimately unsuccessful (or discontinued) agricultural trial scheme, it was nothing new; but the international character and organisational structure of the scheme, with the co-operation of the Tanganyikan Government, renders it novel and noteworthy.

These schemes are all entwined to various degrees, but for clarity each is presented here separately – save for the grouping of KATRIN and kenaf – to better examine their contribution to the histories of development in the Kilombero valley region during this period.

The Kilombero sugar scheme

Sugar cane cultivation for jaggery began from the early 1920s, while cane itself has earlier origins in the valley.[35] Jaggery continued as 'the main concern of Asian-leased land' into the 1950s, the only mechanisation involved being the use of small engine-driven cane crushers.[36] Loxton noted in 1953 that 'management of the cane crop lacks system and planning'.[37] For areas of the inner valley suitable (in principle) for cane, large-scale cultivation was commonly perceived to be possible only through substantial and systematic irrigation, but there was 'little to recommend the design at this stage of a major draining and flood control plan, itself a vast and costly undertaking, in

---

[34] *Hibiscus cannabinus*, known variously as Deccan or Guinea hemp, and Java jute.

[35] Emmanuel Sulle, 'Social differentiation and the politics of land: Sugar cane outgrowing in Kilombero, Tanzania', *Journal of Southern African Studies* 43:3 (2017), 521. Earlier accounts include, 'Nachrichten aus den deutschen Schutzgebieten', 654; and BArch, R1001/278/66-84, Fonck, 'Bericht uber die wirtschaftliche'.

[36] TNAUK CO 892/12/5, 'Kilombero Valley Land Use Survey: Block A', April 1953. Prohibition on the importation into East Africa of sugar milling machinery was imposed in 1933 and revoked in 1952.

[37] Ibid.

order to provide for the cultivation of sugar'.[38] The potential for commercial sugar production was well recognised, but the considerable investment and capital outlay required had so far proved prohibitive.

In 1952, a report on the sugar industry in East Africa was produced by A.C. Barnes. He was invited by respective governments and the CDC, who was prepared to take a further financial stake in any future viable enterprise, 'preferably in conjunction with a commercial firm'.[39] But Kilombero was considered one of the 'areas regarded as suitable for large-scale sugar production which are too remote from rail or sea communication for immediate development'.[40] Barnes struck his visit to the valley from the itinerary after he read existing reports and deemed it 'clearly apparent that a short trip could add nothing of value to existing knowledge'.[41] Kilombero was not without considered potential, but Barnes believed that 'a sugar production project of economic size could not be successfully established in the absence of rail communication'.[42] A substantial transport infrastructure was again marked as a prerequisite for development.

Prior to the Barnes report in 1951, administrative officer A.G. Denton-Thompson had written to his uncle, Guy M. Hulett, chairman and managing director of South African firm Sir J.L. Hulett & Sons, to ask if there might be interest in developing the government's plans for sugar production in Tanganyika.[43] Hulett visited Twining in Dar es Salaam in 1954, and the following year saw more formal discussions on the establishment of a sugar processing factory somewhere in the Kilombero Valley.[44] By June 1956, Secretary of State for the Colonies, Alan Lennox-Boyd, announced in the House of Commons that the scheme would comprise over 60,000 acres and a 99-year lease.[45] The initial confidentiality of the project made it 'the subject

---

[38] TNAUK CO 892/12/5, 'Extract from Draft Memorandum, Kilombero Valley', n.d. No author or date for the memorandum is given, but likely penned by an Agricultural Officer or the Director of Agriculture in 1953–4.

[39] TNA 41189, Notes on Sugar Production, 30 October 1953.

[40] TNA 41189/1, 'The Present Position and Development of the Cane Sugar Industry in East Africa, A.C. Barnes', October 1952.

[41] TNA 41189, Director of Agriculture to Regional Assistant Director of Agriculture, 3 September 1952; TNA 41189/1, 'The Present Position and Development of the Cane Sugar Industry in East Africa, A.C. Barnes', October 1952.

[42] Ibid.

[43] 'Tanganyika Sugar Case Decision', *The Times*, 9 November 1959.

[44] James Liege Hulett (1838–1928) established the company in Natal, South Africa in 1892. For its history to the present company of Tongaat Hulett, Ltd., which continues to trade in sugar, see 'History Timeline', *Tongaat Hulett*, https://www.tongaat.com/overview/history .

[45] 'Tanganyika Sugar Scheme', *Tanganyika Standard*, 21 June 1956.

of a great deal of rumour', and especially regarding labour supply.⁴⁶ Hulett envisaged a labour force of 10,000 men drawn from throughout Tanganyika and beyond.⁴⁷ It was alleged that signing of an agreement between Government and Hulett was held up in February 1956 due to the Department of Labour's refusal to fix pay for three years, guarantee labour supplies, and allow the firm to bring Zulu men from South Africa for the scheme.⁴⁸

The *Tanganyika Standard* wrote that it 'hoped sincerely […] that the scheme will materialise, for it will add enormously to the industrial activities of the country and thus to its prosperity'.⁴⁹ It was thought employment brought by the scheme would provide 'social and other amenities at present denied to those living off the beaten track in one of Tanganyika's most promising agricultural areas'.⁵⁰ Therein lay the Kilombero paradox: promising yet remote.

Hulett withdrew and the scheme was dropped in 1957 citing government failure to raise £3.75m for a branch line to the factory as 'a road did not meet with Messrs. Hulett's requirements'.⁵¹ The Government announced its continued pursuit of the scheme in the *Tanganyika Gazette* in October 1957 with a call for tender, detailing how it was 'willing to consider development schemes for sugar production' in Kilombero.⁵² Hulett subsequently sued for over £800,000 of general damages for 'alleged breach of agreement' and costs lost to surveys, investigations, and planning.⁵³ The case was heard in Dar es Salaam over nine days in July 1959, during which Hulett claimed Twining gave assurances that a railway would be built. Ruling against Hulett, Chief Justice Sir Edward Davies concluded that no enforceable oral agreement had been made.⁵⁴

Interest in the scheme was then declared by Van Eeghen & Maclaine, Ltd.⁵⁵ E.H. van Eeghen established the Tanganyika Sugar Company, Ltd. and

---

⁴⁶ TNA 460/541/144/9, 'Extract from Monthly Report from Labour Officer, Kilosa for February 1956.'

⁴⁷ TNA 460/541/144, 'Note on the Kiberege Project', 1 July 1955.

⁴⁸ TNA 460/541/144/9, 'Extract from Monthly Report from Labour Officer, Kilosa for February 1956.'

⁴⁹ 'Agreement for Sugar Industry Drawn Up', *Tanganyika Standard*, 22 June 1956.

⁵⁰ Ibid.

⁵¹ 'Kilombero Railway', *Tanganyika Standard*, 10 April 1957.

⁵² 'General Notice No. 2375: Sugar Scheme – Kilombero Valley', *Tanganyika Gazette*, 4 October 1957.

⁵³ 'Tanganyika sugar plan is dropped', *Tanganyika Standard*, 8 April 1957; 'Tanganyika Claim Altered', *The Times*, 17 July 1959.

⁵⁴ 'Tanganyika Sugar Case Decision: Company Loses Against Government', *The Times*, 8 November 1959.

⁵⁵ Van Eeghen & Maclaine (VEM) established a presence in Tanganyika as an import-export subsidiary of its Amsterdam-based parent company, whose origins in marine mercantilism date to the seventeenth century. Based in Dar es Salaam, VEM

Tanganyika Agricultural Exploration Company, Ltd. to carry out investigations and encourage capital investment. The CDC and International Finance Corporation (IFC) were approached; so too were two Dutch companies with interests in agricultural development, one of which – N.V. Vereenigde Klattensche Cultuur Maatschappij (VKCM) – surveyed 6,000 acres in 1958–9 and produced plans for a factory and sugar estate.[56] In 1959 the first details of the revived project were publicised alongside 'staggering estimates of expenditure' exceeding £3m.[57] Of this, £700,000 would be raised through preference shares; the rest met by the CDC, the IFC, VKCM, the Dutch Overseas Financing Company (NOFC), and the Standard Bank of South Africa.[58] The *Tanganyika Standard* saw the project as proof of 'the confidence felt by the large overseas corporations who are backing [it] in the political and economic stability' of the country, and hoped that the project would provide 'a first-class example of the way in which local and overseas capital, technical skill, and labour can combine in the development of an enterprise which should prove of very real benefit to the whole of Tanganyika'.[59]

Land clearance began in July 1959, the Kilombero Sugar Company (KSC) was inaugurated in April 1960, and the factory was set for completion in early 1962 in time for the first milling season from June. 'Attempts to establish a sugar industry in Tanganyika have, in the past, petered out unhappily', began one article in the *Tanganyika Standard* from September 1960; 'Now, however, the picture is far rosier.'[60]

Ambitious designs for the sugar estate signalled expectations of scale and success. It was projected that 1,500 houses would be built for employees, and that a labour force of 3,700 would be required during full production, which was actually one-third of Hulett's peak estimates.[61] Plans also included an airstrip, swimming pool, tennis court, a club house, staff houses, a hospital and golf course. Most of this would more directly serve the expatriate management and core staff, providing all the 'essential' amenities required for a balanced life in the tropics. The estate constituted 'what is virtually a town […] complete

---

imported industrial products for East African markets such as agricultural machinery, building equipment, railway materials, fertilisers, electrical equipment and foodstuffs; and exported raw materials for the food industry, sisal, and mica.

[56] 'Kilombero Sugar Company', *Ngurumo*, 1 October 1960.
[57] 'It's a Big Step Up for Sugar', *Sunday News*, 23 July 1961. This is half the proposed expenditure that Hulett expected (£6m) excluding the cost of railway construction, TNA 460/541/144.
[58] '*Nederlanse Overzeese Financierings-Maatschappij*' (NOFC) in the original Dutch.
[59] 'New Sugar Industry', *Tanganyika Standard*, 30 September 1960.
[60] Ibid.
[61] TNA 460/541/149, LO [Kilosa] to LC [Dar es Salaam], 24 February 1960.

with roads and street lighting, seemingly surrounded by an ocean of waving cane stretching as far as the eye can see'.[62] According to one journalist writing in 1961, 'the pace with which the Kilombero Sugar Co. has progressed is a magnificent example to any enterprise and sets the necessary tone for future development in an emerging Tanganyika'.[63]

When the fanfare first sounded in the mid-1950s, the timbre was colonial, not nationalist; albeit during years in which TANU was in the ascendant. The tale of Hulett and the sugar factory came before the first elections in 1958–9, before self-government, and before a date for Independence. In 1956, TANU had openly declared its hostility to the grant of the land on long lease to the South African company, primarily as opposition to apartheid.[64] Moreover, hesitancy and scepticism towards a 'British' government-endorsed, foreign-financed scheme reflected uncertainties over who would ultimately benefit. Decades under colonial governments had conditioned Tanganyikans to suspect it would not be them. Nyerere was acutely conscious of this and sought to ensure the sugar project was not yet another extractive and exploitative scheme. He declared before the United Nations Fourth Committee in 1956, that: 'We are prepared to accept the proposed sugar scheme in the Kilombero Valley provided that the Africans shall participate in the scheme not as labourers providing cheap labour but as partners.'[65]

Great movements in political machinery over the subsequent five years laid the foundation for the reconfigured sugar scheme to be recast as a spearhead for industrial and economic development within the newly independent Tanganyika. Despite colonial undertones through CDC involvement, the factory was now silhouetted against a new horizon. From the registration of the company in 1960, Independence Day in 1961, and factory completion in 1962, this project was placed at the heart of the new nation. The Independence Day issue of the *Tanganyika Standard* cites how 'among the most important schemes involving the [Colonial Development] Corporation is the development of the Kilombero Sugar Estate'.[66] The scheme also aligned with the increasingly international approach to development through financial and technical assistance. The company's board of directors reflected 'an inter-racial and international outlook' as it comprised of 'two African, two Asian, two British and three Dutch directors', with estate management contracted to the

---

[62] 'It's a Big Step Up for Sugar', *Sunday News*, 23 July 1961.
[63] Ibid.
[64] 'Agreement for sugar industry drawn up', *Tanganyika Standard*, 22 June 1956.
[65] Nyerere, *Freedom and Unity*, 43.
[66] 'Prosperity through investment', *Tanganyika Standard*, 9 December 1961.

Dutch firm of VKCM.[67] Paul Bomani, prominent TANU politician and then Minister for Agriculture, was an early director.[68] Perhaps even Nyerere in 1956, when he hoped for Africans to participate in the scheme as partners and not mere labourers, did not imagine that participation would include company directorship quite so soon.

Broader histories of KSC can be told to the present day, particularly surrounding key moments of nationalisation, expansion, and privatisation. Following the IFC's initial investment in 1960, a further US $4.7m in March 1964 constituted 36 per cent of the company's capital and aided expanded production from 20,000 tons per annum to 31,500 tons. But the scheme faced several problems in its early years and turned a profit in only two of the first seven years in operation. Cane fields were stricken with an unidentified disease and two-thirds were replanted.[69] This proved to be the previously unknown 'yellow wilt' which severely reduced yields until mitigated by improved drainage and new varieties.[70] Early financial and mechanical issues found resolve after 1965 following new management with HVA International, another Dutch agency.[71] The company was then nationalised in 1969 following the Arusha Declaration of 1967 and its principal investors sold their interest to the Tanzanian Government, while HVA continued to manage the factory and estate. In 1974 the International Bank for Reconstruction and Development (IBRD) provided KSC with a $9m loan, matched with development credit by the IDA. This investment injection was to fund a first phase of expansion by way of a second estate and outgrowers' scheme. A second factory comprised the second phase, funded by Dutch-Danish bilateral assistance of $11m and $17.3 respectively. The company was then the first to be re-privatised in 1999 and remains majority-owned by Illovo Sugar, Ltd.[72] This moment catalysed the most recent phase in the company's history, and sugar – through its

[67] Ibid.
[68] In December 1960, the board of directors comprised: A.A. Lawrie [Chairman]; F.J. Mustill [Deputy Chairman]; Paul Bomani; E.H. van Eeghen; Willem van Leeuwen; Willem Lindner; N.M. Lyamuya; Abdul Nazerali; J.D. Shah.
[69] INT/TO/01, Tarquin Olivier, 10 March 2021.
[70] IBRD and IDA (World Bank), *Report and Recommendation of the President to the Executive Directors on a Proposed Loan and Credit to the United Republic of Tanzania for a Sugar Development Project*, Report No. P-1468-TA, 31 July 1974 (Washington, D.C., 1974), 12.
[71] '*Handelsvereniging Amsterdam*' (HVA).
[72] In June 2016, full ownership of Illovo Sugar Limited was obtained by Associated British Foods plc, headquartered in London, UK. See Associated British Foods, plc. 'Our History', https://www.abf.co.uk/about_us/our_history. Illovo hold a 75 per cent stake in KSC with the remainder held by the Tanzanian Government.

'Bwana Sukari' brand – is arguably the commodity most associated with Kilombero throughout Tanzania today. In May 2021, Illovo announced a $238.5m expansion project intended to increase production by 144,000 tons to 271,000 tons through a three-fold increase in cane supply from small-scale outgrowers' in Kilombero.[73] At the time of writing, completion of the project is on schedule and anticipated for June 2025. The newly-built factory at Kilombero at the centre of this expansion will crown the sugar production facility as the largest and most modern in East Africa.[74]

The KSC did not follow a linear trajectory of accumulative successes across the six decades from its establishment to the present. If it had done so, it would have been the exception, not the rule. Its fortunes ebbed and flowed, but recent plans for expansion may well secure at least another sixty years for the company.

Railway development

The question of whether to build a railway to and through the Kilombero Valley is the most contentious within its development histories. The dilemma was whether potential agriculture production would justify capital costs. If not, then would total traffic from a through-line stand a stronger chance of profit, or at least of breaking even? But shorter lines cost less, and visions veered from the grandiose to the pragmatic. A branch line to Ifakara only was a commonly cited compromise, yet even this proved impractical and was never built. Kilombero continued to be served by road only, albeit 'all-weather' and improved. This was the situation in the mid-1930s, and it would remain virtually unchanged for nearly forty years. By tracing the history of notional railway development, we find that a line was perpetually imminent, forever on the cusp of construction.

The perceived importance of railway transport to support general development and specific schemes is clear. It was considered essential for syndicated development, and without it the first significant opportunity for large-scale sugar production was lost. The earliest branch line that came close was

---

[73] Illovo Sugar Africa, 'Kilombero Announces Significant Sugar Expansion Project', 20 May 2021, https://www.illovosugarafrica.com/announcements/kilombero-announces-significant-sugar-expansion-project.

[74] See Illovo Sugar Africa, 'Engaging With Our Kilombero Growers – For Success!', 30 July 2024, available: https://www.illovosugarafrica.com/news/engaging-with-our-kilombero-growers-for-success; and ChiniMandi, 'Tanzania: Kilombero Sugar's Expansion Project to be Completed by June Next Year', 3 August 2024, available: https://www.chinimandi.com/tanzania-kilombero-sugars-expansion-project-to-be-completed-by-june-next-year.

completed in 1960 from Kilosa to Mikumi, the latter 45 kilometres north of the sugar estate.[75] This was considered to have 'greatly improved' the 'available facilities for the transport of goods and produce to and from the area'.[76] An 'all-weather' road from Mikumi to its crossing with the Great Ruaha River adjacent to the sugar factory was also reconstructed. In 1964, the 'Second Five-Year Plan for Social and Economic Development' listed 'another important road link planned in the [Morogoro] region' as 'the Msolwa-Ifakara road' which was set to be 'upgraded to engineered gravel standard to provide all-weather access to the Kilombero Valley'.[77] A branch line from Mikumi to the sugar factory was subsequently constructed with FRG assistance and completed in 1965.

Nyerere wrote of the 'very heavy responsibility' held by every employee of the East African Railways and Harbours (EARH) as 'the spearhead of the attack on poverty'.[78] 'Without good communications,' he continued, 'the efforts of our people to increase production in the villages and towns will be wasted.'[79] Railways were once the 'carrier of colonialism' but now, according to the self-branded maxim, EARH were 'developing the lifelines of independence'.[80] For Kilombero, however, its 'essential lifelines of communications' remained road and river, and not yet rail. Much of the post-war revival in the idea of a line through the valley can be attributed to the Gibb Report of 1952, but this was more of a rehashing of old ideas than anything new and reconsidered. Ideas are difficult to kill, and the fact that a railway had yet to be built possibly strengthened, rather than diminished, a sense of urgency. It was all too easy for planners to assume that the reasons behind the continued absence of a line were circumstantial, and not because the basic premise was fundamentally flawed.

In March 1961, a 'Report on the Kilombero Railway Project' was published by EARH which revisited proposals for a line from Mikumi to Makumbako via Ifakara. It held that construction could begin in January 1962, reach Kidatu by January 1964, Ifakara by June, and Makumbako by January 1968. It was thought most appropriate as an international aid project, and heavy financial

---

[75] Tanganyika, *Proposed Branch Railway from Kilosa to Mikumi* (Dar es Salaam, 1958).

[76] 'Kilombero Sugar Company', *Ngurumo*, 1 October 1960.

[77] United Republic of Tanzania, *Second Five-Year Plan for Economic and Social Development, 1st July, 1969 – 30th June, 1974. Volume III: Regional Perspectives* (Dar es Salaam, 1970), 191.

[78] Julius Nyerere, 'Message from the Prime Minister of Tanganyika', *SPEAR* 5:6 (1961), 123.

[79] Ibid.

[80] Werner Biermann, *Tanganyika Railways, Carrier of Colonialism: An Account of Economic Indicators and Social Fragments* (Münster, 1995).

losses were forecast until 1978, but it would then 'not only become viable but make an increasingly substantial contribution to general railway overheads' throughout the system.[81] So while it would not pay its way for ten to fifteen years, this was thought entirely usual.[82] There was 'no doubt' that 'a low cost transport system up the Kilombero Valley' would 'foster the development of the valley and the Highlands beyond' and yet the report admitted it was difficult to express this advantage in 'quantitative financial terms'.[83] Meanwhile, the results of the FAO Rufiji Basin Survey were imminent and its recommendations were expected to show that a railway through the valley was essential.

This was a project that projected into the future while repeating past opinions and reasoning. The report detailed potential outcomes from three types of development in the valley: so-called normal development; development through large-scale irrigation schemes; and industrial development from sugar, timber, and rubber. Past impressions of agricultural potential were reiterated, the juxtaposition of 'high potential' and 'low population' repeated. The perception perpetuated that Kilombero was 'ripe for development both for its own sake and to relieve the problem of surplus population in other parts of Tanganyika'.[84]

This proposal did not go so far into the south-west or indeed to Northern Rhodesia as previous visions had done, while notions of such a through-line re-emerged as the 1960s unfolded, and especially after Zambian Independence in October 1964. From both ends of the line, Nyerere and Kenneth Kaunda sought 'to persuade the international community to assist them in constructing a railway link' as part of a project for which Kilombero was but one part.[85] In September 1965, the governments of Japan, Canada, France, West Germany, and China were invited to consider financing some part of the project. Prospects of Chinese funding emerged most promisingly, strengthened by Nyerere's visit to Beijing in February 1965, and a reciprocal visit by the Chinese Premier Zhou Enlai four months later.[86] A feasibility study was also carried out by Maxwell Stamp Associates, co-funded by Britain and Canada, whose favourable forecast was published in 1966. The same year saw a negative report published by the

---

[81] EARH, *Report on the Kilombero Railway Project* (Nairobi, 1961), 3.

[82] For example, the Uganda Railway was not viable until 1922, twenty years after completion; and Tanganyika Railways was not viable until the 1940s, over thirty years after the Central Line was completed.

[83] Ibid., 3.

[84] Ibid., 6.

[85] Jamie Monson, *Africa's Freedom Railway: How a Chinese Development Project Changed Lives and Livelihoods in Tanzania* (Bloomington, 2009), 23.

[86] Ibid., 24.

Stanford Research Institute under the auspices of USAID, which advocated for a highway instead.[87]

Then, in 1967, an agreement was signed between China, Tanzania, and Zambia to construct the railway.[88] A Chinese ocean liner dropped anchor at Dar es Salaam harbour in August 1969 and over one thousand railway technicians disembarked. Construction was completed in 1975, concluding a project with a history far greater than merely its latest incarnation. What became the Tanzania-Zambia Railway Authority (TAZARA) railway was of course its own project, in its own image, for its own time.[89]

But a railway to and through the Kilombero Valley had been the subject of speculation for over five decades; and in simple terms this was the fulfilment of one of the earliest development visions for the region. The nature of the relationship between the concept of railway development and Kilombero was historically multifarious. The means, meanings, and methods by which a line was ultimately completed in 1975 differed significantly from 1925, when Gillman envisaged a railway to Lake Nyasa; and yet on a fundamental and functional level, it differs little. During the colonial and postcolonial eras, such a railway carried symbolic and practical value. As Monson observed, 'the same southern railway plans that had represented a grand "Imperial Link" in the colonial period were revived, this time as a post-colonial railway of liberation'.[90] This was an explicit act of positive appropriation that sought to peel away from the scheme its colonial undertones, to be transfigured as a nationalist and international project. Dubbed the 'Uhuru Railway' and symbolic of 'freedom' from the colonial yoke and economic dependency, this was an 'anti-hegemonic model of African development' supported by China.[91] The unfulfilled past vision of the colonial era was recast for a postcolonial

---

[87] Stanford Research Institute, *Tanzania-Zambia Highway Study* (Menlo Park, 1966). This echoed WB opinion. See Ngila Mwase, 'The Tanzania-Zambia Railway: The Chinese loan and the pre-investment analysis revisited', *The Journal of Modern African Studies* 21:3 (1983), 535.

[88] Mwase, 'Tanzania-Zambia Railway', 536.

[89] Beyond Monson's definitive *Freedom Railway*, see also James D. Graham, 'The Tanzam railway: Consolidating the people's development and building the internal economy', *Africa Today* 21:3 (1974), 27–42; Jacob K. Chitukuro, 'Impact of the Uhuru Railway on Agricultural Development in the Kilombero District' (MA thesis, University of Dar es Salaam, 1976); R. Hall and H. Peyman, *The Great Uhuru Railway* (London, 1976); Parbati K. Sircar, 'The Great Uhuru (Freedom) Railway: China's Link to Africa', *China Report* 14:2 (1978), 15–24; Zhichao Hu, 'The past, present and future of the Tanzania-Zambia railroad', *Economic Research of the Railroads* (2000), 46–7.

[90] Monson, *Freedom Railway*, 21.

[91] Ibid., 33–4; Coulson, *Political Economy*, 231–43. Also known as the 'Tanzam' railway.

future. The title of Kasuka Mutukwa's 1972 article perfectly encapsulate this transition as 'Imperial dream becomes pan-African reality'.[92]

The railway that was ultimately built must, however, be viewed as distinct from previous visions, while acknowledging nuanced continuities. There was also a converse significance, such as the fact that the 'Imperial Link would have connected white settler interests in the southeastern African region' while 'the post-colonial Freedom Railway sought to unravel them'.[93] This and other indicators clearly imbue the railway with an importance and symbolism far exceeding the local Kilombero context. The valley was not the focus. In this respect, TAZARA had more in common with the Tanganyika Railway Commission of 1930 than the EARH 'Report on the Kilombero Railway Project' of 1961. The line that was ultimately built had indeed had a significant social and economic impact, but this has been more incidental than might have been the case. Today it often appears to be little more than a very expensive footpath. This was ultimately a railway *through* and not *for* Kilombero, and with respect to associated schemes for agricultural development, that has made all the difference.

KATRIN, kenaf, and the competition for Kilombero

When founded with FRG funding and support in 1962, KATRIN shone as a beacon of international agency involvement in the agricultural development of an independent Tanzania. It was a development aid project that aimed 'to link practically oriented research closely with practice through intensified extension work'.[94] Its primary object was 'to promote smallholder farming and smallholder development' and research focused on aspects of 'rural economy, rural agronomy, and on the introduction of new agricultural techniques'.[95] The centre was initially divided into three sections: 1) a vegetables section for educating farmers on production techniques; 2) a nursery for citrus seedlings, for use and sale to farmers; and 3) an orchard of fruit trees that also served as a teaching area.[96] By 1971, facilities were underway for soil research, chemistry, entomology, pathology, and

---

[92] Kasuka Simwinji Mutukwa, 'Tanzania-Zambia railway: Imperial dream becomes pan-African reality', *Africa Report* 17:1 (1972), 10–15.

[93] Monson, *Freedom Railway*, 147.

[94] Eberhard Bohlen, *Crop Pests in Tanzania and their Control* (Berlin: Verlag Paul Parey, 1973), 2.

[95] Majda Žumer, 'Natural resources research in East Africa', *Bulletins from the Ecological Research Committee/NFR* 12 (1971), 64.

[96] Dudley Lameck, *My Autobiography: A Personal Journey in the Life of a Poor African Boy* (Bloomington, 2012), 36–41.

experimental work on fertiliser trials alongside cultivation and breeding programmes for rice, beans, coconuts, and other vegetables.[97] In 1975, the national rice research headquarters were moved to KATRIN, from which time – despite a momentary freeze on funding in the mid-1980s – the institute at Ifakara developed into a major centre for rice research.[98]

The early 1960s saw a blossoming of international involvement in Tanzania's social and economic development. Independence brought new frontiers for nations who had been previously excluded. Both by invitation and intervention, Tanzania soon found itself at the centre of a new form of territorialisation by international development agencies. The consensus from all sides was that Tanzania could not develop sufficiently and rapidly enough without this assistance, but it also exposed vulnerabilities during this 'Second Scramble for Africa' as dubbed by Nyerere in 1961.[99] He warned: 'Rich countries of the world – both Capitalist and Socialist – are using their Wealth to dominate poor countries. And they are trying to divide and weaken the poor countries for that purpose of domination.'[100] Nyerere was referring more explicitly to dangers posed to 'African Unity' as he advocated for pan-Africanism, but this is also cognate with the broadening ambit of international involvement in development through financial and technical assistance.

Similar to the way in which Nyerere sought to match sponsorship of a singular village settlement scheme to a particular donor country, so there emerged an apportionment of regions or projects throughout Tanzania with varying degrees of formality. This relied on a certain diplomatic harmony between nations, who occasionally vied for specific projects or entire regions. Kilombero was one such example where competing spheres of interest caused tension. In 1962, as the FRG began to invest in agricultural training and extension work in Kilombero through KATRIN, the Swiss government also began to discuss with Derek Bryceson the provision of £350,000 for development in the valley.[101] Swiss engineer Max Freimann was also involved following his role within

[97] Žumer, 'Natural Resources', 64.

[98] The first rice research station in Tanganyika was established in 1935 at Mwabagole, near Lake Victoria. There was a hiatus on rice research 1955–65 before its revival at the Ilonga Research Station, near to Kilosa in Morogoro Region. Relocation to Ifakara occurred in 1975.

[99] Julius K. Nyerere, *The Second Scramble* (Dar es Salaam, 1962).

[100] Ibid., para. 11.

[101] Lukas Meier, 'Striving for Excellence at the Margins: Science, Decolonization, and the History of the Swiss Tropical and Public Health Institute (Swiss TPH) in (post-)colonial Africa, 1943–2000' (PhD thesis, University of Basel, 2012), 134. Bryceson – as Minister for Agriculture – had travelled to Europe to garner financial support for development schemes throughout Tanganyika. See Tanganyika. Tanganyika Information

the FAO Rufiji Basin Survey team. Freimann envisaged a Swiss takeover and continuation of the Lumemo trial farm. No sooner had Swiss proposals begun to gather momentum than news emerged of FRG plans for technical assistance. Both nations had been drawn to Kilombero by the alluring potential described in the FAO reports. But FRG plans were more advanced and more generous. The proposed budget from Bonn of DM 10m (c. GBP £892,000 at the time) overshadowed the Swiss offering.[102] Matters were complicated by the long history of Swiss presence in Kilombero, since the Baldegg Sisters and Capuchin Roman Catholic orders established themselves from 1921 with a focus on health and mission work.[103] From the first dispensary in the 1920s to the establishment of the St. Francis Hospital in the 1950s, health services throughout the valley region seemed somewhat outsourced to the Swiss. This medical frontier was pushed further by the founding of the Swiss Tropical Institute Field Laboratory (STIFL) in Ifakara in 1957.[104] It was reasonable, but not inevitable, that Swiss-led epidemiological research efforts centring on malaria, trypanosomiasis, relapsing fever and more, might segue into broader research efforts at Lumemo, such as experimental agriculture, soil science, and crop trials. This diversification would also have been readily achieved were it not for competing interests, away from which founder Rudolf Geigy attempted to sway favour by arguing that 'the Lumemo river did not carry enough water for the running of two farms and that the local population would have difficulties in understanding the presence of two nations working at the very same location'.[105] Bryceson previously held that 'Ifakara and the Lumemo project are 100% Swiss and must remain so' and attempted to calm the competition by assuring Geigy that he would not let a German approach

---

Services, Press Release: 'Mr Bryceson Returns from Europe with Promises of Aid', 11 May 1962.

[102] Meier, 'Striving for Excellence', 135.

[103] See Marcel Dreier, 'Health, Welfare and Development in Rural Africa: Catholic Medical Mission and the Configuration of Development in Ulanga/Tanzania, 1920–1970' (PhD thesis, University of Basel, 2019).

[104] Founded by Rudolf Geigy (1902–95). See Meier, 'Striving for Excellence', 61–2. Geigy first visited Ifakara in 1949. For a history of the laboratory's evolution into 'the Ifakara Centre, a national but peripherally located research centre involved in applied, operational and health systems research, training, and direct health sector support activities', see Marcel Tanner et al., 'Developing health research capability in Tanzania: From a Swiss Tropical Institute field laboratory to the Ifakara Centre of the Tanzanian National Institute of Medical Research', *Acta Tropica* 57:2/3 (1994), 153–73. Today the centre is known as the Ifakara Health Institute, see https://www.ihi.or.tz/our-history.

[105] Meier, 'Striving for Excellence', 135.

'upset old friends like yourself simply because they have a lot of money to offer us'.[106] But the Bonn offer was difficult to refuse.

Initial ideas to co-ordinate or co-implement the projects withered. In July 1963, August Lindt, then official co-ordinator of Swiss aid, admitted that Switzerland simply had 'less leverage than other countries in the case of competition in the development sector'.[107] Rather than settle for involvement under FRG direction, Swiss aspirations rescinded. STIFL's activities in Ifakara remained firmly within medical research and intervention. The path was clear for West German interests to claim authority over the agricultural sector, showing that developmental territorialisation was not predicated on one nation per geographical area, but per sphere of interest. This was not always true; but proved so for Kilombero.

Similar themes emerged regarding a project to establish a kenaf plantation in the outer Kilombero Valley, adjacent to the sugar estate. This was a novel scheme borne from international assistance in a manner only possible post-Independence. Investigations, plans, and implementation of the project were driven by the German Development Corporation (GDC) of the FRG in collaboration with the Dutch firm, VKCM, who were managing operations at KSC. Ernst van Eeghen was also central to the scheme, which never proceeded beyond a trial phase. Depending on the perspective, it was ultimately unsuccessful, unfulfilled, or unimplemented: in other words, entirely typical for Kilombero. 'Since the early sixties', Baum wrote in 1968, 'a number of experiments have been carried out to test the conditions for new cash crops, but the results of all of them have proved unsatisfactory.'[108]

Van Eegen had approached the FRG in June 1961 via Minister-President (of Schleswig-Holstein) Kai-Uwe von Hassel with proposals for several projects to dovetail with the sugar scheme. Von Hassel's connections to then-Tanganyika were strong: it was his birthplace. His father was Major Theodor von Hassel, district official (*Bezirksamtmann*) for Mahenge from December 1904.[109] Returning in the 1920s, he attempted to grow coffee behind Mahenge, but by 1934 was in a poor financial state and died the following year from

---

[106] Schweizerisches Bundesarchiv (BAR), E 2200.83 (A), 1983/26/3, 'Rudolf Geigy, Lumemo River Irrigation Project, 9 July 1963', quoted in Meier, 'Striving for Excellence', 135.

[107] Quoted in Meier, 'Striving for Excellence', 136. For historical insights into Swiss official development assistance in Africa, see Marc Perrenoud, 'Switzerland's relationship with Africa during decolonisation and the beginnings of development cooperation', *International Development Policy* 1 (2010), 77–93.

[108] Jätzold and Baum, *Kilombero Valley*, 118.

[109] For an account of how Theodor von Hassel killed a ravaging elephant in Mahenge, and associated imperial symbolism and mythologisation, see Bernhard

cerebral malaria.[110] Kai-Uwe von Hassel had also returned in the 1930s as head of the plantations trading department of the former DOAG before he was interned on the outbreak of war.[111] He thus knew Kilombero well, the region part of a long familial legacy. After visiting East Africa in 1960, he spoke of his belief that 'rather than merely throwing money at the newly emerging African states, German experts should once again become actively involved in African development'.[112]

Van Eeghen hoped for German participation in satellite projects to the sugar estate, suggesting cassava (for tapioca), rubber, cocoa, and kenaf. Only kenaf (*Hibiscus cannabinus*) piqued interests, known by various names including Deccan or Guinea hemp, and Java jute. Cultivated for its fibre, the initial objective of planting trials was to ascertain whether large-scale cultivation had potential as a profitable crop. Then, if proved, the secondary objective was to ascertain whether the raw material of kenaf fibre could catalyse a viable bag, sack, and hessian cloth industry.[113] In July 1962 up to DM 300,000 (approximately £27,000) was approved by the GDC as 'technical assistance' with certain conditions attached to enable the funder to scrutinise the trials under Dutch supervision. Moreover, if a company was later founded then the funds would be repaid, but if the trials were unsuccessful then the credit would convert to a lost grant. The arrangement led to 'strong reservations' in some circles, expressed by Councillor Dr Roth of the Ministry of Finance:

1 That the FRG were providing funds for a project whose implementation was entrusted to non-Germans;

2 The enterprise was a private business to which the provision of funds was contrary to the guidelines for the use of funds for technical assistance to developing countries;

3 Funds made available would thus be beyond FRG control;

4 Neither cost estimates nor planning documents were available [in June 1962].[114]

Gissibl, *The Nature of German Imperialism: Conservation and the Politics of Wildlife in Colonial East Africa* (New York, 2019), 109–12.

[110] TNA, 61/141/G, Handing Over Report: Mahenge District, July 1934.

[111] See Britta Schilling, *Postcolonial Germany: Memories of Empire in a Decolonized Nation* (Oxford, 2014), 113–22.

[112] Ibid., 114.

[113] BArch, B 213/33060, Memorandum on the results of the kenaf trial (Kilombero Valley, Tanganyika) in 1962/63 and recommendations for further kenaf trials in 1963/64.

[114] BArch, B 213/33060, 'Technical Assistance: Establishment of Kenaf model farm in the Kilombero Valley', 14 June 1962.

Despite misgivings, trials began and discussions continued on how the project might develop. Van Eeghen calculated that £2.2m from multiple agencies would finance a 5,000 hectare plantation and processing factory. Further preparatory work included negotiations with a firm to install the fibre removal plant and another to supply spinning and weaving machines.[115] Questions continued to be raised over how multinational financing and involvement would work, or whether it were even feasible.

Dr von Natzmer, a FRG development advisor in Tanganyika, visited in March 1963 and found the trial fields 'expertly laid out and supervised' and added:

> I could not see why the German government should bear the costs, or at least bear them alone, especially since the project is regarded here as a Dutch one and the Government of Tanganyika, during the visit of the delegation led by Ambassador Schlitter, even expressly refused to include the project in the German Technical Assistance.[116]

Von Natzmer believed the Dutch government should bear at least half of the costs in the next phase of the project, not least as it was foreseen that, if a kenaf spinning mill were established, 'the Dutch will probably again look for outside capital and offer the management themselves'.[117] The introduction of Dutch finance would address the perceived imbalance as to who had 'rights' to the project and could therefore claim the all-important benefits for state relations that often motivated development assistance. Motives for granting such aid were varied, complex, and often underscored by political and economic factors. The negotiation of FRG capital aid to Tanganyika in 1962, for example, involved securing a commitment from Tanganyika to lobby the East African Common Services Organisation (EASCO) to grant Lufthansa traffic and landing rights in Nairobi.[118] Franz Heinrich Ulrich, board member of Deutsche Bank and chairman of the supervisory board of the German Development Finance Institution in Cologne, was quoted in 1964 as saying: 'Today's developing country is tomorrow's customer.'[119] The Federal Ministry of Economic Cooperation and Development in Bonn explained how German citizens might imagine development aid to Africa: 'Similar to the Marshall

---

[115] BArch, B 213/33060, Federal Office of Industrial Economics to the Federal Minister of Economics, 25 Oct 1963.

[116] BArch, B 213/33060, Note by Dr von Natzmer, Dar es Salaam, 26 November 1963.

[117] Ibid.

[118] BArch, B 213/33060, Meeting of the Committee of Advisers on Capital Aid to Tanganyika, 24 August 1962.

[119] 'Entwicklungshilfe/Afrika: Mit der Gießkanne', *Der Spiegel* 49 (1 December 1964), 51.

Plan Aid after the Second World War [...] today, development aid serves both sides, those who give and those who receive.'[120]

In 1964, *Der Spiegel* characterised and criticised the FRG's sweeping generosity across Africa as 'the watering can method' by which 'every developing country is given gifts' as 'the Bonn watering can trickles its windfall over the bush, steppe and tropical jungle, nobody is forgotten, little is achieved'.[121] The 'watering can' principle implied financial assistance was spread widely but thinly, often in the absence of central planning. On one hand, the kenaf project could be the centre of further development in the valley, while on the other it became clear that it could only be a strategic, somewhat charitable enterprise; with low returns for private finance, but potentially solid gains in other ways. The project was considered 'uninteresting from a private-sector point of view' due to its questionable rate of return, financing 'partly *à fonds perdu*', and in the absence of a private German partner who would provide the 'necessary technical know-how'.[122] But the Federal Ministry of Economic Co-operation and the Federal Foreign Office had 'always advocated concentrating German development aid measures in Tanzania on the Kilombero Valley as a regional focus', which cast pursuit of the kenaf project as not necessarily by its own merit, but as the 'best' of available options and as part of a broader strategy of claim-staking.[123] This showed returns, for in February 1965 it was noted that: 'English support is not envisaged for the Kilombero Valley, as it is considered to be an area of German interest.'[124]

By the end of July 1964, the initial phase of trials was complete and production on a small scale was successful. Questions of final costs and the viability of large-scale production and an industrial enterprise remained. The Government of Tanganyika thought the project worthy of continued support, but this was not straightforward. Due to various failings, the sugar estate was no longer under VKCM management. The firm had therefore 'lost its base in the Kilombero Valley' and it was suggested they should no longer be involved with the kenaf project.[125] Moreover, the director of KATRIN criticised the trials

[120] Ibid., 47–8.

[121] Ibid., 47.

[122] BArch, B 213/33060, Internal correspondence: Federal Ministry of Economics, 11 July 1964.

[123] BArch, B 213/33060, Development policy measures for the Kilombero Valley (Tanzania), 13 January 1965.

[124] BArch, B 213/33060, Report on an observation trip to Tanzania from 30 January to 22 February 1965, by Siegfried Graf von der Recke, 19 February 1965.

[125] BArch, B 213/33060, FRG Embassy, Dar es Salaam, to Federal Foreign Office, Bonn, 29 August 1964.

and made arrangements for further trials to be conducted in Ifakara. This was favoured by the FRG Embassy in Dar es Salaam, as 'the project would be recognisable to outsiders as German, which was not the case under previous management' and costs would be kept lower than those under a profit-seeking private company.[126] The involvement of VKCM was a 'unique case of a foreign company being commissioned within the framework of German Technical Assistance' and any Dutch expectation of their continued involvement was skirted by the logic of a German-funded project to be continued under the supervision of German-founded KATRIN.[127]

By late September 1964, a decision on whether to proceed with a full-scale operation was postponed pending further investigations. Doubts over the profitability of a 'sack factory' could not be allayed, and this ruled out possible involvement from the DEG, who had previously considered the scheme.[128] But broader German visions for Kilombero development had been simmering. In late January 1965, Dr Horst Geuting – who was based in Dar es Salaam as an economic and agricultural advisor from the FRG to the Government of Tanganyika – announced that 'after months of effort' he and his team had 'finally succeeded in drawing up a development plan for the Kilombero Valley' for the years 1965–9 that recommended 'integrated development on as many economic levels and sectors as possible at the same time'.[129] Tanzania had applied to the FRG for capital and technical aid, after which the plan was developed which specifically took into account 'German wishes' and was 'the first of its kind and scope in Tanzania, and most likely the only one of its type'.[130] One week before Geuting sent the plan to Principal Horst Dumke of the Federal Ministry of Economic Co-operation (FMEC), Federal Minister Walter Scheel (also of the FMEC) was in Tanzania and accompanied by Principal Böker of the Federal Foreign Office. Geuting informed Dumke that 'discussions with Nyerere were unfortunately overshadowed by some political difficulties related to the presence of the East Zonal representation in Zanzibar and our position on this issue, which has not always been clear so far'.[131] The kenaf project was a minor concern, but the transition beyond was complicated by worsening diplomatic relations between the FRG and Tanzania.

---

[126] Ibid.

[127] BArch, B 213/33060, Kenaf Project: Notes on meetings at Federal Office of Industrial Economics and Tanzanian Consulate, Frankfurt, 2 February 1965.

[128] The DEG was established in Cologne (where it remains headquartered) in 1962 as a FRG development policy initiative to finance private-sector companies and assist their move into developing countries. The first project was in Tanganyika.

[129] BArch, B 213/33060, Geuting to Dumke, 30 January 1965.

[130] Ibid.

[131] Ibid.

The treaty for economic co-operation signed between the FRG and Tanganyika in 1962 was threatened by political union with Zanzibar in 1964 due to the archipelago's relationship with the German Democratic Republic (GDR). The Hallstein Doctrine held that the FRG 'refused to maintain diplomatic relations with any state that recognised the GDR'.[132] In 1964, German news magazine *Der Spiegel* opined that the 'Hallstein Doctrine and East-West ideology are part of the standard inventory of Bonn's Africa missions' and quoted one West German ambassador, who 'sighed: "If the government here does not recognize the zone during my tenure, I have achieved my goal."'[133] The fact that political uncertainty threatened the continuation of KATRIN was fairly insignificant relative to the broader implications of an implosion in Tanzanian-FRG relations.[134] Geuting echoed the Federal Foreign Office belief that 'development policy pressure is not a suitable means to achieve our foreign policy goals in Tanzania'.[135] In this same vein, Godfrey Mwakikagile has claimed that 'Nyerere turned down foreign aid when there were heavy political strings attached' and cites an alleged refusal of 'the [West] German offer to build a sugar factory in the Kilombero Valley in exchange for a naval base on Zanzibar'.[136] Mwakikagile remarked that this was 'a principled stand, but one that hampered development' and yet the lack of periodisation and source references is suspect.[137]

Nevertheless, that Tanzania represented de facto recognition of both German states did not wash with the FRG. Its relationship with the mainland was gravely compromised by the GDR Embassy on Zanzibar.[138] The FRG first suspended military aid. Nyerere responded by refusing to accept any further

---

[132] Priya Lal, *African Socialism in Postcolonial Tanzania: Between the Village and the World* (Cambridge, 2015), 66.

[133] 'Entwicklungshilfe/Afrika: Mit der Gießkanne', *Der Spiegel* 49 (1 December 1964), 59 [47–65].

[134] Schilling, *Postcolonial Germany*, 117. See also, Roberts, *Revolutionary*, Chapter 3; Cranford Pratt, 'Foreign-policy issues and the emergence of socialism in Tanzania, 1961–8', *International Journal* 30:3 (1975), 445–70.

[135] BArch, B 213/33060, Geuting to Dumke, 30 January 1965.

[136] Godfrey Mwakikagile, *Nyerere and Africa: The End of an Era* (Dar es Salaam, 2010), 411.

[137] Ibid. I have found no other reference to such an offer or refusal. By the time Nyerere could refuse such an offer, the sugar factory had already been built. The political inference dates the moment years ahead of plans to build a second factory.

[138] A useful overview of 'the intrusion of the Cold War with the union of Tanganyika and Zanzibar' within 'The foreign policy crises of 1964–66' is found in Pratt, *Critical Phase*, 137–142. See also Winrich Kühne and Bernard von Plate, 'Two Germanys in Africa', *Africa Report* 25:4 (1980), 11–16.

economic aid from Bonn.[139] Diplomatic ties were cut, and resumed in 1966; but the break, compounded by a momentary severing of relations with Britain in late 1965, led Tanzania to further develop its relationship with China.[140]

The grand 'Kilombero Valley Project' envisaged by the FRG had been allotted DM 211m, or close to £19m. It was considered 'of great importance for the reputation of the Federal Republic of Germany in East Africa' and both complemented and dwarfed the DM 11m made available from late 1961 for KATRIN.[141] But the break in relations ensured the FRG never funded its large-scale development plan for Kilombero, and the kenaf project never grew beyond the trials stage. Diplomatic relations notwithstanding, success was far from inevitable. Expected yields for large-scale cultivation were never determined with sufficient reliability, and the supply of suitable kenaf seed in sufficient quantity was not guaranteed. The disassociation with KSC and the relocation of trials from Msolwa in the outer valley to the inner valley at Ifakara also reconfigured questions of land availability and suitability. It was suggested that fertile valley soils may be 'too valuable for kenaf cultivation' and kenaf should not supersede rice where either could be grown.[142] The whole purpose of growing kenaf was to provide the raw material for the industrial processing of sacks, but the viability of this 'bag factory' was threatened by proposals for a cellulose and paper factory in Kenya by the German firm of Parsons & Whittemore Aschaffenburg GmbH, with potential DEG investment. This project was 'more economical than the processing of kenaf fibres' and, as sales would be made to Tanzania, its proposal had direct consequences for the kenaf project.[143] The same fate did not befall KATRIN, which survived and continues its work in Ifakara and the valley today.

* * *

From 1960 to 1965, the FRG consciously and preferentially cultivated the Kilombero Valley as a regional beneficiary of financial and technical assistance, and perceived itself to hold informal proprietary rights over its agricultural and economic development, with the exception of the KSC. Revolution on

---

[139] Ibid., 12.

[140] Lal, *African Socialism*, 56–7;

[141] BArch, B 213/33060, Report on an observation trip to Tanzania, 30 January to 22 February 1965, by Siegfried Graf von der Rocke (Chief Inspector of Forests, retired), 19 February 1965.

[142] BArch, B 213/33060, Kenaf Project: Notes on meetings at Federal Office of Industrial Economics and Tanzanian Consulate, Frankfurt, 2 February 1965.

[143] BArch, BArch, B 213/33060, Kenya: Note on construction of a cellulose and paper factory by Dr Holzer, Bonn, 18 December 1963.

Zanzibar and political union with Tanganyika brought an unforeseen crisis with far-reaching ramifications; a fallout that inadvertently shaped the future of Kilombero. The rest of the decade took a different direction, mainly shaped by the beginnings of Chinese development assistance towards the construction of the Uhuru Railway.

The crucial point is that this period sees new futures on new horizons with more states, agents, and actors involved in 'future-making' processes than perhaps at any time in Tanzania's history. Both central and peripheral, Kilombero formed a prevalent role in the new apparatus of the new nation. This was *Maendeleo wa Jamhuri* – 'Development of the Republic' – in both process and practice. That is to say, the ways in which Tanzania developed as a new nation – economically, socially, and politically – and also the underlying forms that 'development' took during the first ten or so critical years of independence. For Nyerere, *Uhuru* finally brought freedom, and from freedom flowed development. 'Freedom and development are as completely linked together as are chicken and eggs!' he wrote in his signature style, allegorical and accessible.[144] Inherent in the very concept of development – and here Nyerere was not alone – was a belief in the importance of building for a better future. The root of the noun *maendeleo* is, after all, the verb stem *-endelea* meaning 'to move forward, continue, move on' and 'to develop, prosper, flourish, progress'.[145] These are all actions that fuel a 'capacity to aspire' and in so doing drive the present into the future.[146]

[144] Nyerere, *Man and Development*, 25.
[145] Taasisi ya Uchunguzi wa Kiswahili, *Kamusi ya Kiswahili-Kiingereza* (Dar es Salaam, 2001), 67.
[146] Phrase quoted from Arjun Appadurai, upon which he bases a chapter in *Future as Cultural Fact: Essays on the Global Condition* (London, 2013), 179–98.

7

'Off to Sugar Valley': The Kilombero Settlement Scheme, 1959–69

Peoples for a 'sparsely peopled' place

Outsiders to Kilombero frequently characterised the region as 'underpopulated' relative to perceived availability of land, and especially with reference to perceived fertile land and production potential. Established practices of shifting cultivation and the utilisation of a variety of areas for risk aversion in a volatile ecological environment – such as maintaining both highland and lowland cultivation areas – go some way to explain how far larger areas of land might be necessary to support fewer people than European observers might have deemed necessary. But evidence for greater population levels in the region prior to the Maji Maji Rebellion exists, and high fatalities inflicted by German troops during the conflict and subsequent repercussions, including scorched earth tactics that induced famine, also contribute to an explanation of 'underpopulation' in Kilombero.[1] Underappreciation of the hostility and volatility of the environment is also a factor. Despite pockets of fertile land that pepper the landscape, much of the valley is an oppressive and difficult place to live for large parts of each year. It is questionable, therefore, why Kilombero continued to be so 'underpopulated' despite such 'fertility' when this anomaly was not widely replicated elsewhere. If the more fertile and hospitable regions tend to carry the highest populations, then outside observers may have done well to wonder why Kilombero was not overrun.

Nevertheless, the trope of Kilombero as an 'empty' land persisted, or at least as a region that could carry far greater numbers of people than it did. This was both a problem and a solution. It was a problem for various visions of development whose schemes required far more farmers than inhabited

---

[1] TNA 13304, 'Memorandum of the Economic Possibilities of the Kilombero Plain, by Clement Gillman, 30 September 1925; also A.A. Kazimoto, 'Political Development of Mahenge' (Manuscript, University College, Dar es Salaam, 1967), 8. Kazimoto quotes the Eastern Province Annual Report for 1940: '[the] Mahenge area has never recovered from the brutal atrocities associated with the suppression of the Maji Maji rebellion'.

the valley region. From Telford to Hulett, the success of certain projects was predicated on bringing labour from elsewhere. This characterisation of land availability was also a solution, where the problem of overpopulation *elsewhere* demanded a suitable outlet to ease pressure and redistribute. This has historically taken several forms.

In the late 1930s, Tanganyika – as a League of Nations mandated territory – was viewed by the British Government as a potential solution to the settlement of Jewish refugees from Europe.[2] British Guiana, Kenya, Northern Rhodesia, and Nyasaland were also among those territories considered. Following a statement to this effect made by British Prime Minister Neville Chamberlain in November 1938, *The Times* reported that: 'In addition to the Southern Highlands and the Western Province, there is the fertile Kilombero Valley, a possible field for the small cultivator of the Palestinian type.'[3] This proposal was well received by those who feared Tanganyika might be ceded to Germany at this time, as Jewish settlement was thought to certainly prevent such a return.[4] But Chamberlain was also quoted as saying: 'As regards the Colonial Empire, it must be remembered that although covering a great extent of territory it is not necessarily capable of absorbing large numbers of refugees. Many of our colonies and protectorates and our mandated territories in East and West Africa contain native populations of millions for whom we are the trustees and whose interests must not be prejudiced.'[5] This same sentiment also prevented interference with land rights and freedom of movement where they might have been otherwise exploited by particular development schemes in the valley. Kilombero never did take up the cause, but during the Second World War several thousand Polish Jews did find refuge elsewhere in Tanganyika.[6]

Kilombero was again viewed in 1950 as a potential 'solution' to a distant problem. The broader context was Britain's obligation 'to promote European [post-war] recovery by cooperative action' and 'one of the most serious

---

[2] See TNA 26398, Settlement of German Jewish Refugees, 1934–39; TNA 26399, Settlement of Jewish Refugees in South-western Tanganyika, 1938; TNA 26340, Select Committee on the Settlement of Jewish Refugees; League of Nations, Permanent Mandates Commission. *Minutes of the Thirty-Seventh Session held at Geneva from December 12th to 21st, 1939* (Geneva, 1940), 24.

[3] 'Tanganyika and the Jews', *The Times*, 23 November 1938; also, 'Jewish Refugees (Settlement)', *Hansard* HC Deb, vol.341 col.1048, 17 November 1938.

[4] 'Tanganyika To Aid Jewish Colonization', *The Chicago Defender*, 24 December 1938.

[5] 'Refugees (Government Proposals)', *Hansard* HC Deb, vol.341 col.1313–7, 21 November 1938.

[6] Jochen Lingelbach, 'Refugee camps as forgotten portals of globalization: Polish World War II refugees in British Colonial East Africa', *Comparativ* 27: 3–4 (2017), 78–93.

problems in Europe preventing any return to viability [was] the burden of surplus manpower in countries such as Italy and Germany'.[7] A 'well-established local Italian resident' in Tanganyika proposed to Twining a 'small scale group settlement by Italian peasant agriculturalists' which the Governor found 'attractive' and supported 'as part of a scheme for settlement in the Kilombero Valley'.[8] This referred to the scheme featured in the Ten-Year Development and Welfare Plan for Tanganyika (1947–56), but whose origins lay in the 1940 report of the Central Development Committee.[9] Despite being 'sparsely peopled' the committee did not regard Kilombero as suitable for European settlement, and had envisaged the scheme would either incorporate Africans, Asians, or both. However, it was proposed by Twining that 'preliminary steps should be taken with a view to establish an Italian peasant colony in this area' along the same lines as the scheme.[10]

The proposal was heavily criticised and condemned by members of the British Government in Whitehall, who commented to 'strongly deprecate this proposal' and considered that 'the Governor should be discouraged from proceeding with this proposal' for various reasons, not least that it would have been 'quite a new departure for East Africa' involving 'the creation of a "poor white" working class', and 'European peasant farming on a low subsistence level' was 'a form of settlement which cannot be contemplated in a tropical country'.[11] Opinion differed on whether such a community would necessarily be 'poor', but confidential arguments against the proposal on political and economic grounds ultimately prevailed. A formal reply to Twining from Jim Griffiths, Secretary of State for the Colonies, stated that: 'The cost of medical, education and other social services for an Italian peasant colony living and multiplying in the territory would in my opinion be a formidable counterpoise to any economic benefit which their presence would bring'.[12]

Despite the imagined number of settlers eventually reaching a maximum of only fifty, 'African reaction to such a proposal' was expected to 'certainly be hostile' and it was thought 'unwise to pre-empt a vacant area in the territory which appears to be outstandingly suitable for Asian settlement without

[7] TNAUK CO 537/5875, European Settlement: Proposed Italian Settlement in Kilombero Valley, 1950.

[8] TNAUK CO 537/5875, Governor's Deputy to Secretary of State for the Colonies, 22 June 1950.

[9] Tanganyika, *Ten-Year Plan*, 30; Tanganyika, *Report of the Central Development Committee*, 48–9.

[10] TNAUK CO 537/5875, Note by E.L. Scott, 6 July 1950.

[11] TNAUK CO 537/5875, Notes in 'Proposed Italian Settlement', 1950.

[12] TNAUK CO 537/5875, Secretary of State for the Colonies to Governor of Tanganyika, 13 July 1950.

clashing in any way with European farming interests'.[13]. Twining later made it clear that 'he attached no importance to the proposal and was quite willing to let the matter drop' and ensured that 'care would be taken in replying to the Italian sponsor of the scheme not to suggest or to imply that the scheme was not being pursued because the immigrants would be Italian'.[14]

Less than one decade later, the valley would once again be viewed as a site for settlement to solve a distant demographic problem. In this instance, rather than British intervention in Italian dilemmas, it was a nationalist solution to a Tanganyikan problem, precipitated by unemployed young men in Dar es Salaam and Morogoro. In popular memory, settlement and resettlement processes in Tanzania are largely associated with Nyerere's villagisation drives under *Ujamaa* in the early 1970s, and the following case study of the Kilombero Settlement Scheme from 1959 is an important contribution to understanding the earlier and broader historical processes at work.

Introducing the Kilombero Settlement Scheme

'History is [...] an anvil of identity which is vulnerable to distortion', wrote John Lonsdale, and which 'is also open to interpretation'.[15] Historical enquiry therefore continually seeks greater cognisance of historical processes, and their layers of meaning, significance, and perception. This remains relevant, regardless of how vast the existing body of literature on any particular subject. For Tanzanian historiography, one subject that saturates discourse is Nyerere's policy of *Ujamaa* as an expression of 'African socialism' and the subsequent saga of *Ujamaa vijijini*, which saw the extensive reorganisation of rural society into '*Ujamaa* villages', initially mobilised on the expectation of voluntarism but eventually by 'coercive and occasionally violent "villagization" drives'.[16] The inception of this policy is customarily cited as the 1967 Arusha Declaration. Priya Lal writes that '[*Ujamaa*] began in 1967' but that the 'concept of *Ujamaa* first entered Tanzanian political discourse in 1962'.[17] These are moments of formalisation. True origins are often opaque and older still. By the same token that 9 December 1961 marked both the 'birth' of a nation

---

[13] TNAUK CO 537/5875, Note by E.L. Scott, 6 July 1950.

[14] TNAUK CO 537/5875, Note on Meeting held on 2 September 1950.

[15] John Lonsdale, 'African pasts in Africa's future', *Canadian Journal of African Studies* 23:1 (1989), 126–46.

[16] See McHenry, *Tanzania's Ujamaa Villages*; Michaela von Freyhold, *Ujamaa Villages in Tanzania: Analysis of a Social Experiment* (New York, 1979); Jennings, *Surrogates of the State*.

[17] Priya Lal, 'Self-reliance and the state: The multiple meanings of development in early post-colonial Tanzania', *Africa* 82:2 (2012), 212–34.

and arguably the 'death' of a liberation movement, inherent within the publication of the Arusha Declaration as a TANU party document on 5 February 1967 is everything that led to that moment.[18] If a historical event can be said to be the 'birth' of anything – and to extend the metaphor – then history must also consider its gestation. This chapter contributes to such an understanding of Tanzanian history through the examination of a settlement scheme that was conceived *before* Independence and played a crucial role *throughout* the 1960s in the development of Nyerere's notions of rural transformation and villagisation. This settlement scheme in the outer Kilombero Valley spans the years 1959–69, and this narrative reveals how the ideas and motivations that would shape *Ujamaa* were first given practical form. The scheme developed in sediments and is an illustration of historical layering as elements of colonial, postcolonial, and pre-socialist practices are evident at this one site. The history of the Kilombero Settlement Scheme (KSS) is multifaceted and entangled. Its liminal character reveals not one, but several trajectories of development thinking. This is best described as a palimpsest with complex entwinements, continuities, and contrasts. Settlement history constitutes a substantial aspect of Tanzania's history and this case study deepens awareness of an early scheme that is patently embryonic. Tracing this history through the archives and oral histories, this case is a prism through which a multitude of dimensions are refracted. The focus on one local scheme reveals the extent to which it was shaped by national and international dynamics during a monumental period in Tanzania's history, from the predawn of *Uhuru* through the first eight years as an independent state.

The KSS eventually comprised three villages along the 'Kiberege Strip' of the outer valley: Sonjo, Ichonde, and Kichangani. Each village was settled at different times, and they possessed both commonalities and differences, rendering the evolution of the scheme far from linear. The first village to be settled was Sonjo – from August 1959 – and, as this was a scheme that was first catalysed by the alleviation of urban unemployment, its true beginning is arguably found on the streets of Dar es Salaam.[19] From this vision, notions of a successful and economically viable co-operative farming settlement were seeded, onto which were also tacked ideologies of 'nation-building'.

Sonjo is remarkable in being established before Tanganyika achieved internal self-government. On the cusp of transition from British administration, this was the enaction of plans rather than their mere conception. The perceived political threat of urban unemployment was a driving factor, while

---

[18] 'Tanganyika: A nation is born', *Africa Today* 8:10 (1961): 6–9, 20.
[19] TNAUK CO 822/2962, Development Scheme for alleviation of urban unemployment in Tanganyika, 1960–62.

its resolution in a rural settlement scheme also served to promote agricultural development. The Rural Settlement Commission reported in 1965 that 'the main object of this scheme was to reduce the pressure of unemployment in the towns of Morogoro and Dar es Salaam'.[20] Nyerere felt he could kill two birds with one stone, especially if thrown with an imbued spirit of nationalism, 'self-help', and 'nation-building'. At its most potent, this spirit was transcendent; while the KSS itself, as it developed, required almost constant life support and experienced multiple attempts at its reorganisation.

This case study therefore intersects with a complex nexus of dynamics. Not least the well-developed sub-fields of youth and modernity that provide important contexts to this study.[21] Much focus has fallen on rural-urban migration and nationalism in the metropolis.[22] One contributing insight, therefore, is into the mechanisms by which attempts were made to reverse this migration, and in so doing it tells another part of the story.

The immediate rationale for selecting Sonjo as a site for settlers stemmed in part from a 1958–9 report by the District Agricultural Officer for Morogoro, who suggested that certain areas in Kilombero were suitable for agricultural settlement: specifically Sonjo and Ichonde.[23] At this time, the FAO-led Rufiji Basin Survey was well underway and investigating development potential throughout the region, and in 1959 the first details of a sugar factory and the KSC were announced. The idea that settlers would grow sugar as a cash crop to be sold to the nascent factory also served as the theoretical underpinning of the scheme. One of the leading principles behind Sonjo was the opportunity for rural development to promote new industrial growth in a country on the eve of Independence. This was a rare example of internal linkage as conscious connections between rural and industrial transformation at the time were few.

---

[20] United Republic of Tanzania. Ministry of Lands, Settlement and Water Development, *The Rural Settlement Commission: A Report on the Village Settlement Programme from the Inception of the Rural Settlement Commission to 31st December, 1965* (Dar es Salaam, 1966), 35.

[21] See Andrew Burton, 'Raw youth, school-leavers and the emergence of structural unemployment in late-colonial urban Tanganyika', *The Journal of African History* 47:3 (2006), 363–87; and James R. Brennan, 'Youth, the TANU Youth League, and managed vigilantism in Dar es Salaam, 1925–73' in Andrew Burton and Hélène Charton-Bigot (eds), *Generations Past: Youth in East African History* (Athens, OH, 2010), 196–220.

[22] See James R. Brennan, *Taifa: Making Nation and Race in Urban Tanzania* (Athens, OH, 2012); G. Thomas Burgess, 'Introduction to youth and citizenship in East Africa', *Africa Today* 51:3 (2005): vii–xxiv; and Michael Jennings, '"A very real war": Popular participation in development in Tanzania during the 1950s and 1960s', *The International Journal of African Historical Studies* 40:1 (2007), 71–95.

[23] Tanzania, *Rural Settlement Commission*, 2.

Land clearance for the creation of the sugar estate began on 11 July 1959, and Sonjo saw its first settlers arrive one month later.

In October 1960 a supplement to the newspaper *Ngurumo* presented an overview of the 'Kilombero Sugar Company Limited' alongside an invitation to purchase share capital.[24] The piece closes with the Directors 'looking ahead' and considered that:

> The establishment of a sugar industry in the Kilombero Valley might [...] ultimately open up a further field of co-operation between the Company and local inhabitants. It is hoped that smallholders might be encouraged, from seed cane supplied by the Company and under its supervision, to grow sugar cane for sale to the Company. The development of such a scheme will require careful examination when the present project has become fully productive, and in the light of the circumstances then existing.[25]

This 'field of co-operation' represents the very beginning of the sugar outgrowing industry in Kilombero. It was a leading principle in the establishment of 'the Sonjo scheme', as it was commonly referred to in its initial years. Crucially, however, Sonjo was not under the supervision of the KSC. Moreover, it is likely their speculative paragraph as to the future collaboration between the Company and local inhabitants was written in full consciousness of the emerging Sonjo and Ichonde initiatives. The veiled message embedded within this press release may infer that the Directors doubted the integrity of the Sonjo scheme and believed that co-operation was not a foregone conclusion. Nyerere's prior reservations over the previous incarnation of the sugar scheme under Hulett relate to this notional precursor to the establishment of an outgrowers' scheme that would see farmers earn profits and not simply wages. His wish for Tanganyikans to be partners in the scheme and not merely labourers reflects a changing character in both the project and its perception. The essential shift from colonial to postcolonial is echoed in the sentiment expressed in Nyerere's inaugural Presidential address in December 1962, in which he asserts that 'the Tanganyika we have inherited is a very different Tanganyika from the one we are setting out to build'.[26] The Hulett scheme had all the trappings of a colonial development project and Nyerere was right to feel the threat of marginalisation. Its successor had a very different and international character, and as a nationalist project for a new Tanganyika, the Sonjo scheme was intended to be a part of this vision.

---

[24] 'Nyongeza ya Ngurumo', *Ngurumo*, 1 October 1960.
[25] Ibid.
[26] Nyerere, *Freedom and Unity*, 43.

Sonjo and Ichonde: Origins

It is necessary to separate three fundamental aspects of the KSS to understand its emergence. The first is that the origin of the scheme stems in part from its being a perceived solution to a separate and distant problem: urban unemployment. Its inception was not entirely predicated on finding settlers to establish an outgrowers' farming settlement in Kilombero. Rather, one direction of impetus was to find a way to solve the rising numbers of unemployed, mainly young men, in Dar es Salaam and Morogoro. The second aspect is to acknowledge the basic premise of the scheme itself while assuming optimum conditions for its implementation. This might be summarised as the establishment of a farming settlement in a fertile valley region in which a variety of crops are grown within individual smallholdings for local consumption and exchange alongside increased earnings from the sale of sugar cane to a local factory. The third aspect is the resultant culmination of the first two and consideration of the various discrepancies and flaws that emerged.

There was a strong pragmatic justification for the scheme. Not least owing to the agricultural report suggesting that sites were suitable for settlement, the various development possibilities highlighted by the FAO survey as it progressed systematically through the region, and finally the sugar factory rising on the horizon. It seemed an ideal solution had been found to reverse the 'urban drift' and placate the political threat owing to public concern over growing joblessness. The perceived social threat posed by urban unemployment and the perception of a looming, malevolent shadow is captured in this headline published in the *Tanganyika Standard* in November 1960: 'Unemployed roam Iringa'.[27]

The Sonjo scheme, sponsored first by the Dar es Salaam branch of TANU, was considered 'the most prominent initiative targeting unemployment alleviation' and one that sought to effect both short and long-term measures to tackle joblessness.[28] 'Long-term measures' simply meant those settlers who it was envisaged would become resident farmers. 'Short-term measures' were rendered by the provision of temporary work in manual land clearance. Those that were engaged in temporary work at Sonjo outnumbered its expected settlers by ten-to-one. The 'propaganda value' that Sonjo represented in alleviating urban unemployment was heavily exploited. In January 1960, its political symbolism as a TANU scheme ascended as it was reported in the *Tanganyika Standard* that Bibi Titi Mohamed herself had planted the first rice at Sonjo.[29] The group at Sonjo was led by the 'progressive and energetic

---

[27] *Tanganyika Standard*, 24 November 1960.

[28] Burton, 'Raw youth', 383.

[29] *Tanganyika Standard*, 22 January 1960. Bibi Titi Mohamed was a prominent politician, freedom fighter, and TANU activist who was instrumental in the party's

leader', Frederick Njelima, who was an early member of TANU, President of the African Association in Dar es Salaam in 1940, and an ex-Government teacher said to have taught Nyerere at Tabora.[30]

Nyerere had personally fuelled the recruitment drive for the scheme, announcing on national broadcast radio: *Nataka vijana waje Kilombero* [trans. 'I want young men to come to Kilombero']. Thomas Likalagala, who was one of only three of the original surviving settlers when interviewed in 2019, remembered hearing Nyerere's summons on the radio and considered himself to have been *chosen* by Nyerere to go to Kilombero. He felt that Nyerere had taken the village into his personal custody, and truly cared for its future and its people. 'We were Nyerere's people', he proudly acclaimed.[31]

Hamisi Saidi Salum is another surviving settler. He was born in Kondoa and joined TANU in 1958 when he went to Dar es Salaam. He remembered Nyerere calling a meeting near his home in Manzese, and TANU Youth League members went to hear his message. Nyerere spoke of Kilombero and that he needed people to go there to begin farming, imploring them not to stay in the city or they would forfeit a better life. Mzee Salum remembered Nyerere's promise to find sponsors to fund the agricultural tools and inputs required.[32]

The first cohort of settlers to Sonjo did not arrive to cleared land and perfectly demarcated farm plots, as many expected. Furthermore, in addition to their not being farmers, before they could begin to farm the land had to be cleared of its forest, bush, and scrub. For many, compounded by a shortage of food, this was not what they signed up for and they simply left. Others arrived, and fifty-three settlers were cultivating land at Sonjo by 1960.[33] Yet the slow rate of land clearance led Government to step in and accelerate the process by enlisting hundreds of urban unemployed men to carry out the work. This process may have been accelerated even further by the use of machinery, but it was evidently more important to provide employment to scores of men as manual labourers than it was to clear the land as quickly as possible.

---

creation and early years. See Susan Geiger, *TANU Women: Gender and Culture in the Making of Tanganyikan Nationalism, 1955–1965* (Oxford, 1997).

[30] TNAUK FCO 141/17784, Director of Special Branch to Permanent Secretary, Ministry of Security and Immigration, Dar es Salaam, 18 March 1960. Njelima had also spent time in America from 1907 to 1916 and served with the British for two years in the First World War.

[31] INT/TL/01, Interview with Thomas Likalagala, Sonjo, 4 July 2019.

[32] INT/HS/02, Hamisi Saidi Salum interview, Mang'ula, 14 October 2019. Early supporters were the Rungwe Native Farmers' Co-operative who subscribed 100 sheets of corrugated iron and other building materials. African farmers from Mwanza and Arusha also helped with materials.

[33] An initial 100 settlers was originally intended.

The initial departure of the first forty men to leave Dar es Salaam was announced with great fanfare through media channels to maximise the scheme's 'propaganda value'. A prominent feature on the front page of the *Tanganyika Standard* from 24 November 1960 announced that the vanguard of approximately 500 men were 'Off to Sugar Valley' and 'happy to be off to work'.[34] Paul Bomani, Minister for Agricultural and Co-operative Development, gave recruits a 'heroic farewell' as they set off from Dar es Salaam railway station en route to the railhead at Kilosa, and from there by road to Kilombero, the branch line to Kidatu or even Mikumi having not yet been built.[35] This has been described as an attempt 'to harness political enthusiasm by shipping lorry loads off to open the bush, singing party songs'.[36] One of the first settlers to Ichonde from Morogoro in 1960 was Juma Juma Kiswanya, who became a prominent spokesperson for the Ichonde settlers. In 2019, he could recall two of these party songs of protest, liberation, and future promise to be delivered by TANU and rousingly evoked their spirit after nearly sixty years. Their transcription follows:

Enyi Waingereza

Enyi waingereza tupeni Uhuru
    You British, give us our Independence
Mungu hakuagiza kututawala sisi
    God never asked you to rule us
Kutawaliwa fedheha kwetu Tanganyika
    to be colonised brings shame upon Tanganyika.

Simba Waungurumao

Uchaguzi ulipowadia, wengi wao wamejiandikisha
    When the election came, the majority have registered
kugombea viti vyote vya LegiCo, kugombea viti vyote vya LegiCo
    to contest for all seats at the Legislative Council
kumbe TANU imefungua macho yake
    but TANU has opened up its eyes
kwa kumuweka mjumbe mmoja mmoja kila jimbo
    putting one candidate in each constituency
jimbo la Tanga aliwekwa Bwana John Keto
    Tanga constituency stood the Honourable John Keto.
jimbo la kaskazini Bwana Eliufoo
    the northern constituency stood the Honourable Eliofo,
jimbo la nyanda za juu Mwakangale
    the northern constituency was the Honourable Mwakangale

---

[34] 'Off to Sugar Valley', *Tanganyika Standard*, 24 November 1960.
[35] Ibid.
[36] Burton, 'Raw youth', 383.

> *jimbo la mashariki Bwana Nyerere*
> the eastern constituency was the Honourable Nyerere
> *Hao ndio simba waungurumao*
> Those are the roaring lions
> *kwao tumeweka nguvu mbele ya LegiCo*
> in them we trust to stand at the Legislative Council
> *wakaseme kura tatu hatutaki*
> to speak out against the three votes
> *Tunataka kura moja Tanganyika*
> We want a single vote in Tanganyika,
> *ambao hao ndio chanzo cha Uhuru*
> and they are the source of Independence [37]

These songs evoke a nostalgia of hope that speak to a potent moment of anticipation.[38] They do not mention the scheme, but they are imbued with the same spirit that urged Sonjo's settlers on. The strength of expectation for a different future is palpable, and Nyerere sought to harness this in the drive towards independence and to build a better Tanganyika. However, this nostalgia is also framed and intensified by the past and present.[39] All three of the surviving settlers spoke with great pride of their original grant of the land, perceived as from Nyerere's own hand. There was authority in this genesis that spoke to subsequent land pressures, a lamentable present, or the endurance of belonging. Mzee Salum remembers that after Nyerere's death in 1999 came a scramble and partition of farming land, 'since the one to defend our rights was no longer around'.[40] Mzee Juma Juma talked of President Magufuli's undelivered promise of a tarmac road and how he did not stop at Ichonde when Nyerere would always stop.[41] For Mzee Thomas, he never ceased to be one of 'Nyerere's People'.

TANU

While TANU could play a mobilising role within development initiatives such as this, as with other 'nation-building' endeavours, the party had a limited capacity to give technical advice or be effective in the realisation of the goals of development. As TANU grew as a national movement bound together by the drive for independence, its relevance as this approached during 1961 appeared

---

[37] INT/JJK/01, Interview with Juma Juma Kiswanya, Mgudeni, 8 July 2019.

[38] For songs as historical sources, see Frank Gunderson, *Sukuma Songs from Western Tanzania* (Leiden, 2010).

[39] See Robert M. Ahearne, 'Development and progress as historical phenomena in Tanzania: "Maendeleo? We had that in the past"', *African Studies Review* 59:1 (2016), 77–96.

[40] INT/HS/02, Hamisi Saidi Salum interview, Mang'ula, 14 October 2019.

[41] INT/JJK/01, Juma Juma Kiswanya interview, Mgudeni, 8 July 2019.

to many to be at an end.[42] This was addressed in 1959, the year that the first settlers went to Sonjo, when TANU's slogan was changed from *'Uhuru'* to *'Uhuru na Kazi'* – the emphasis shifting from 'Freedom' to also 'Work' as once freedom has been won, the real *work* in building the nation would begin.[43] The establishment of Sonjo coincided with this shift in emphasis and the renewed dictum was intended to imbue the scheme with this ethos of building the new nation. However, the politicisation of the scheme was also a concern for Government, to the extent that Special Branch evaluated whether it posed a threat. In a confidential report submitted to the Ministry of Security and Immigration on 18 March 1960, it was concluded that:

> Reports have indicated that relationships between the local people and the settlers at Kilombero are good, although the locals have shown little interest in joining the scheme. It is considered that the Kilombero scheme does not represent a security threat at the present time.[44]

The scheme continued, and several hundred men came to Kilombero in late 1960 to assist in land clearance. Their labour was registered by the TANU Provincial Office in Dar es Salaam, while the Ministry of Agriculture arranged their transport, accommodation, food, and pay. The press release expressed the hope that during the six-to-eight-week period estimated for the work, 'ways and means [would] be found [...] to provide continuing employment' and that 'it may be possible to select some [...] for permanent settlement'.[45] This was not published in the newspaper itself, possibly as it posed a promise too far and it was wiser to temper expectations.

These early years at Sonjo and Ichonde were unequivocally difficult, although differences between the two schemes and their utilisation of support was varied. At Sonjo, for example, the group was considered 'well organised, [...] aware of what it intends to achieve, and its leaders [were] most willing to accept help and advice from government officials'.[46] This differed from Ichonde, whose leader, as 'an ex-lorry driver and not well educated' was considered 'weak' and 'unwilling to accept advice or help from Government

---

[42] George Bennett, 'An outline history of TANU', *Makerere Journal* 7 (1963), 15–32.

[43] In the context of *Uhuru na Kazi*, '*kazi*' is often translated as 'toil'.

[44] TNAUK FCO 141/17784, Director of Special Branch to Permanent Secretary, Ministry of Security and Immigration, Dar es Salaam, 18 March 1960.

[45] TNAUK CO 822/2962, Development scheme for alleviation of urban unemployment in Tanganyika, 1960–62.

[46] TNAUK FCO 141/17784, Director of Special Branch to Permanent Secretary, Ministry of Security and Immigration, Dar es Salaam, 18 March 1960.

officers'.[47] Through a combination of factors, therefore, the lived reality of those who sought to sow the virgin soil did not follow in the slipstream of the great promise and expected success of the neighbouring sugar estate. A visit to Sonjo in late January 1961 by the Labour Officer for Kilosa reported land clearance workers complaining of poor rations and a lack of amenities and recreational facilities; nor had they acquired cleared land for personal use, as anticipated.[48] Some even complained they were treated like convicts.

In March 1961, Paul Bomani wrote to Roland Mwanjisi, the Secretary General of TANU, on the subject of the 'Co-operative Farming Settlement in the Kilombero Valley' and expressed how, 'while much has been written on the settlements, many people are not yet clear about the aims [...] nor about the progress made'.[49] Bomani described how the settlements were initiated in a 'modest way' as small areas cleared from forest, planted mainly with rice and maize and assisted by TANU with money and food.[50] The settlers *themselves*, it was reported, had requested the Agricultural Department visit the area to advise on the best crops and how to grow them. A survey followed, yet Bomani rightly noted that positive outcomes 'can only be done successfully by planning the work beforehand' and by 'drawing up contour maps of the land, dividing the land up into farms and building roads, drains and terraces, and setting aside suitable places for social centres, schools, etc'.[51] Bomani then struck upon a critical point: 'All this must normally be undertaken *before* the farmers start moving into a settlement area.'[52] He also considered the schemes at Sonjo and Ichonde to be 'experimental' only, and in a partial foreshadowing to *Ujamaa vijijini*, that 'Co-operative Farming Schemes have not yet proved successful in Tanganyika'.[53]

Moreover, while ardent anticipation of the building of the sugar factory was in the air from 1959 at the latest, the reality was that Sonjo settlers arriving from late 1959 could not grow cane for harvest in 1960 or 1961 as there was not yet an operational mill to process it. The observation that 'the project of settling town dwellers in the country is quite different from the

---

[47] Ibid.
[48] TNA 460/HL2/29/031, Makukita to Labour Commissioner, 3 February 1961. Quoted in Burton, 'Raw youth', 384.
[49] TNA 213/C2, Minister for Agriculture and Co-operative Development to Secretary General, TANU, 17 March 1961.
[50] TANU made two financial grants: 10,000 shillings in September 1959 and 5,000 shillings in March 1960.
[51] TNA 213/C2, Minister for Agriculture and Co-operative Development to Secretary General, TANU, 17 March 1961.
[52] Ibid. This author's italics.
[53] Ibid.

project of reorientating the lives of born country dwellers' is also valid as the latter 'would presumably have stocks of food' from the preceding year and 'sufficient [...] tools' whereas 'the town dwellers would have no stocks of food and probably few tools'.[54] In early 1960, the Ulanga Cotton & Rice Co. supplied food to the settlers on credit, and also assisted in clearance efforts by lending each settlement a tractor and plough. The initial seventeen settlers at Ichonde were also given a tractor by Fazel Kassam, a miller from Morogoro, but it was in a poor state and was never used. The settlers at Sonjo were also given a tractor and plough, by Stephen Emmanuel, a Greek sisal planter from Tanga, but despite it being reported there was 'little mechanically wrong with it', it had never been used up to March 1960.[55]

In 1963, F.A. Reynolds of the Commonwealth Relations Office, would recall and describe in his words 'the horrid example of Sonjo':

> This was a scheme started by TANU [who] took a lot of unemployed from Dar-es-Salaam and put them down at Sonjo and told them to farm. Somewhat naturally, this did not work. The so-called settlers expected to walk in and find farms laid out for them neatly without having anything to do except reap the crops. Eventually the [...] Government were obliged to move in and supply funds to get the land cleared, partly by hand and partly mechanically, and to second an Agricultural Officer to supervise the settlement. Even so, the settlers demanded free railway tickets to and from Dar-es-Salaam every weekend.[56]

Reynolds concluded that 'this was a misconceived scheme in the first place'.[57] Critically, however, the scheme was not abandoned, despite various flaws which had seemingly been baked into its foundation. Moreover, important lessons were already being learned and implemented in subsequent approaches to settlement planning.

It was written in 1960, in a report of the 'Working Party on Urban Unemployment', that a rural resettlement scheme to alleviate unemployment would necessarily have to involve a 'type of man' who 'would be unlikely to become a successful settler'.[58] A later advisory on the establishment of Pilot Settlement Schemes stressed that 'in the first instance, unemployed and

---

[54] TNAUK DO 166/61, Reynolds to Moore, 7 February 1963.
[55] TNAUK FCO 141/17784, Director of Special Branch to Permanent Secretary, Ministry of Security and Immigration, Dar es Salaam, 18 March 1960.
[56] TNAUK DO 166/61, Reynolds to Molyneaux, 28 January 1963.
[57] Ibid.
[58] TNAUK CO 822/2962/4, 'Development scheme', 1960–62.

partially employed urban dwellers should not be accepted'.[59] The KSS was noted in 1961 as having not been organised on a tenancy basis and 'being comprised of non-farmers' had 'faced a difficult struggle to become viable'.[60] As Cliffe and Cunningham observed:

> Attempts to use settlement to bring underemployed resources of labour and land into use have [...] had limited success, especially where they were used to resettle urban unemployed. Evidence [...] conclusively indicates that such urban elements have usually already rejected rural life and are the least likely material out of which to build pioneer rural settlements.[61]

Yet despite being fraught with initial failings and hardships, it seemed that new life was being breathed into the scheme as 'suitable' settlers gradually replaced those that had first come to Kilombero. As detailed in Tanganyika's 'Three-Year Development Plan' of 1961, work was said to be continuing on the TANU settlement farm at Sonjo, where a 'self-contained co-operative settlement was being planned'.[62] Recalling the Independence Day issue of the *Tanganyika Standard* and its citing that 'among the most important schemes involving the [Colonial Development] Corporation is the development of the Kilombero Sugar Estate', the article added that 'the company is also working with the Ministry of Agriculture to develop a scheme whereby smallholders can grow cane for sale to the Kilombero factory'.[63] Rhetoric and publicity was rife, but the promise of a 'bright future' was not so easily achieved.

The Tanganyika Agricultural Corporation

The TAC was asked by the Ministry of Agriculture to take over the management of Sonjo and Ichonde from 1 April 1962. Having risen from the ashes of the Overseas Food Corporation (OFC) – architect of the ill-fated 'Groundnut Scheme' – in 1954, the TAC was initially tasked to continue the OFC's 'experimental' work as Colonial and Development Welfare schemes. The TAC also undertook new projects and was responsible for the management

---

[59] TNAUK DO 166/61, Nyerere Plans for Village Development, 1962–63.
[60] Tanzania, *Rural Settlement Commission*, 2.
[61] L. Cliffe and G.L. Cunningham, 'Ideology, organization and the settlement experience in Tanzania', in L. Cliffe and J. Saul (eds), *Socialism in Tanzania: Volume 2* (Dar es Salaam, 1973), 135.
[62] Tanganyika, *Development Plan for Tanganyika, 1961–64*, 72.
[63] 'Prosperity through investment', *Tanganyika Standard*, 9 December 1961.

and administration of the Rufiji Basin Survey, including its associated trial farms such as that at Lumemo. The Corporation initially operated with no guarantee as to its future beyond Independence, until the World Bank Survey Mission recommended its establishment on a permanent basis. The dual role of the TAC was to undertake schemes which were likely to be commercially profitable, and also 'to undertake, on an agency basis, for and on behalf of Government, schemes which have no immediate prospect of self-sufficiency, but which were nevertheless justified as experiments because of their long-term or indirect benefits'.[64] It is unclear which category was conceived as belonging to the KSS: one with no immediate prospect of self-sufficiency, or likely to be commercially profitable.

The involvement of the TAC represents an enmeshment of colonial residue in the postcolony. The KSS had nationalism at its ideological heart, while the TAC was structurally and symbolically 'British' who, as was once sung, 'God had never asked to rule'. The development era after the Second World War – the 'second colonial occupation' – saw schemes such as the Groundnut Scheme designed to ultimately benefit Britain, in that case solve its imminent margarine famine.[65] This is what led Nyerere to accept Hulett's sugar project so long as Africans participated not as cheap labourers but partners. That the TAC with its OFC roots was now managing the KSS was surely problematic, but without support it faced ruin as did so many spontaneous settlements that mushroomed across Tanganyika around Independence. The KSS was designed as an experiment to allow TANU to determine the chances of success for such schemes. Subsequently, Nyerere had to incorporate the technical expertise, management personnel, and organisational structures from the late-colonial period because this was a transition and an amalgamation of approaches. It was convenient despite its compromise.

When the TAC took over management of Sonjo and Ichonde, of the 1,000 acres earmarked for each of the two schemes, just over one half had been cleared at Government expense. The rest was virgin bush. A local contractor was then employed to clear further land at Ichonde so that farmers could occupy their holdings in time for the upcoming season.

The TAC Annual Report for 1961/62 recorded that farmers at Sonjo had planted half an acre of sugar cane each, plus 200 acres of maize and 60 acres of rice. The crops were patchy and suffered damage from wild pig and baboon. Buffalo and elephant were also frequent marauders and regularly destroyed cane fields.[66] At Ichonde, a negligible amount of food crops were grown in a 'communal *shamba*' as most of the farmers had decided to wait until Government had cleared the land for them before attempting cultivation

---

[64] Tanganyika, *TAC: Report and Accounts 1960–61* (Dar es Salaam, 1961), ix.
[65] Low and Lonsdale, 'Introduction', 12.
[66] Tanganyika, *TAC: Report and Accounts for 1961–62* (Dar es Salaam, 1963), 42.

on any large and individual scale.[67] The TAC then introduced a scheme for the farmers themselves to clear two acres of forest land on contract for rubber planting. The area under cane was then planned to increase alongside a wide variety of crops grown, including rice, maize, groundnuts, cotton, and sesame. Early optimism (and patronisation) for the scheme was evident, one TAC report noting that 'provided the farmers are prepared to take advice and show willingness to work, there is no reason why they should fail to obtain above-average yields and good returns'.[68]

From February 1963, the TAC incorporated Kichangani into the scheme. This area covered approximately 4000 acres of open grassland and had first been settled spontaneously and without supervision by around forty people from Dar es Salaam and another sixty local farmers. The TAC doubted the agricultural suitability of the area and a survey revealed that 40 per cent of the land remained submerged beyond the long rains. A comprehensive study of the water-table and flood conditions was begun; but rather than wait for the data and lose a year's crop, the settlers chose to plant 100 acres of cane and take the risk.[69]

The inclusion of Kichangani alongside Sonjo and Ichonde under TAC management led to the full collectivisation of the KSS. Renewed organisation brought some order, but the schemes were far from exemplary. Nevertheless, 40 acres of cane planted at Sonjo in 1962 were cut the following August, yielding over 2,000 metric tons. There was dissatisfaction among the farmers with the average price obtained from the factory. TAC reports further reveal the scheme's structural weakness. Chief among these was the issue of cane haulage, considered 'a very knotty problem' as Sonjo was sited approximately 27 kilometres south of the factory, connected only by a public road in a poor state.[70] This had the potential to derail the economic viability of the scheme as it was necessary for the cane to be delivered as soon as possible after harvest to preserve its sucrose content, which begins to reduce as soon as the cane is cut.

Plans for reorganisation and post-TAC

During a meeting on 29 November 1963, Nyerere asked Horst Geuting whether he considered it 'reasonable and the right time to propose to the [West] German government that they support his idea of so-called villagisation'.[71]

---

[67] Ibid.
[68] Ibid.
[69] Tanganyika, *TAC: Report and Accounts, 1962–1963* (Dar es Salaam, 1964), 38.
[70] Ibid.
[71] BArch, B 213/33060, Geuting to Federal Ministry of Food, Agriculture and Forestry, 8 December 1963. Geuting was a West German Economic and Agricultural Advisor to the Government of Tanganyika, based in Dar es Salaam.

The following day, Geuting was also approached by Vice President Kawawa, after which Geuting reported as follows:

> He asked why the German government had not been able to decide to support some Village Settlement Schemes by sending experts and offering financial assistance. He specifically mentioned the United Kingdom, Ireland, Israel, and the Scandinavian countries, who have all taken up many of these settlement schemes in terms of staff and financing. It was also mentioned that Poland, Czechoslovakia, Bulgaria, East Germany, and the USSR had offered assistance, but the Tanganyikan cabinet had not yet determined what to do with it.[72]

Geuting cited the benefit to British industry by Britain's sponsoring such settlement schemes; for example, through the contracted use of British-constructed steel frames and metal roofs. There was an intention to utilise German technical and capital support to 'break Britain's import monopoly in agricultural tractors, machinery, crops, and general modes of transportation such as trucks and trailers in order to give German industry access to the Tanganyikan market'.[73] Geuting believed that 'spectacular economic and political success can be expected with the appropriate project selection' and advised that the FRG to 'concentrate its development aid efforts in Tanganyika as much as possible'.[74] 'The Kilombero Valley is a good place for this', he stressed, citing the FRG's financing of the Mikumi-Kidatu railway and KATRIN near Ifakara, to which he added: 'Consequently, the settlement projects to be supported should also be located in the Kilombero Valley.'[75] This exposes the motives through which Geuting internally proposed, in confidence, that the FRG 'took over' the settlement schemes at Sonjo and Ichonde. Kichangani was not mentioned.

On 9 May 1964 a meeting was held to prepare an application to the FRG for assistance towards the reorganisation of the KSS.[76] Three days later the Five-Year Plan for Economic and Social Development was announced, leading to a shift in the administration of the scheme from the TAC to the newly established Village Settlement Agency. While confirmation of further support was

---

[72] BArch, B 213/33060, Geuting to Federal Ministry of Food, Agriculture and Forestry, 8 December 1963.

[73] Ibid.

[74] Ibid.

[75] Ibid. It was considered desirable for German and African scientists at KATRIN to have 'direct access to the agricultural practices of African farmers' and therefore the two schemes were viewed holistically.

[76] OBL MSS.Afr.s.1295, Papers of M.J.W. English, 'Proposals for Reorganisation of the TAC Schemes, 28 July 1964.'

pending, proposals for reorganisation were drawn up. At this time there were seventy-eight farmers at Sonjo, 'all of whom seemed to have adapted well to form'.[77] There were seventy-two farmers at Ichonde, which was considered to have been rushed in its early stages and laid out poorly. Kichangani was felt to have a doubtful future, and it was later recommended it be abandoned completely. Expansion and consolidation was recommended for Sonjo and Ichonde and an entirely new layout proposed. This layout envisaged a central service nucleus around which would be sited three sub-villages. This design was in line with contemporary thinking around new village planning.[78]

The three-year plan for reorganisation assumed staffing would be paid by external sponsors and £93,000 per annum was estimated to provide for a vast staff. It is worth detailing the planned provision for three managers, thirty-five agricultural advisors, thirty-five counterpart staff, one veterinary surgeon, one community development officer, four teachers, five clerks, three storemen, three mechanics, ten drivers, three engine attendants, one medical aide, and a midwife. Further costs would cover vehicles, tractors, machinery, and tools; the additional clearing of dense forest; some 90 miles of secondary roads; and even compensation to farmers to be moved from their present plots to accommodate the new layout. Support until the first harvest was also considered as a food or cash allowance. In total, the costs of the proposal amounted to £230,000 a year for the three-year period of reorganisation, management, and maintenance. This far exceeded the recommended costs to establish one Pilot Settlement Scheme from scratch, which was estimated at £150,000.[79]

The proposed reorganisation was never funded. A report on the Village Settlement Programme wrote that 'until the break in relations it had been hoped that this would be achieved with advice and finance from the Federal Republic of Germany. Now ILACO [International Land Development Consultants, Ltd.] of the Netherlands are carrying out the survey from which it is hoped reorganisation will follow.'[80] Following a thorough survey, considerable cartography, and extensive report prepared by ILACO, further funding requisite for reorganisation did again not materialise.[81] This reveals the extent to which the future of a scheme such as this could hinge on the vicissitudes of foreign policy and relations, and the capricious nature of international development aid. It was relatively straightforward to commission international consultants to carry

---

[77] Ibid.
[78] See Tanzania, *Rural Settlement Commission*.
[79] Ibid., 6.
[80] Ibid., 35.
[81] See ILACO, *Interim Report Concerning the Results of the Field Study (1965) in the Kilombero Valley – Tanzania. Volumes I–II* (The Hague, 1966).

out surveys and bind their advice to a published report, but ongoing technical support and overall financial responsibility were more elusive.

Cane cultivation continued regardless and during the 1964/5 season all three schemes yielded over 12,000 tons of sugar cane from 500 acres resulting in revenue of £25,000. The farmers' income averaged £60 each, which was notable in that average per capita income in Tanganyika in 1963, including subsistence, was estimated at approximately £22 per year.[82] In fact, this only equated to 45 per cent of the gross crop sales after half was deducted for part repayment of old debt and recurrent costs, plus 5 per cent for savings accounts. An increase in both crop and revenue was anticipated for the following season.

In October 1966, Paul Bolstad was assigned to the scheme as a Peace Corps volunteer attached to the Rural Settlement Division. He arrived to find the scheme's accounts in a poor state and the farmers agitated and unhappy. They had recently demanded removal of the scheme manager, and his temporary replacement was working overtime to repair the government vehicles whose breakdown was threatening the delivery of sugar cane. Many farmers were impatient to harvest their cane; others who had harvested were impatient about being paid.[83] Recalling his two years on the scheme until October 1968, Bolstad remembers the farmers' great optimism that they would ultimately become prosperous, but also their underlying frustration with the scheme's management. As the project was run by Government and not an extension of the sugar company, accounts were entangled in bureaucratic convolutions that tested the farmers' patience. By the following season this had been rectified and relations improved between the farmers, the management, and the factory.

The problem of cane transportation during harvest remained a substantial issue and it was reckoned that 'the distance from Sonjo to the estate was in itself enough to defeat the scheme'.[84] Transporters from Dar es Salaam began to be recruited during the milling season to guarantee timely delivery and so avoid the lower rates of payment – or indeed outright rejection – should sucrose levels drop sufficiently if the cane was not delivered within two or three days of being cut. An innovative solution to the issue was sought and, together with the recently appointed Tanzanian manager – Felix Temu – a new road was sited along a shortcut to the factory. This provided a connection to the southern portion of the estate's road network; roads that were straight, level, and well maintained. This was partly due to their being covered with a mixture of molasses and water after grading, which then baked hard in the sun. They were literally paved with sugar.

[82] TNAUK DO/166/61, Reynolds to Buist, 23 September 1963.
[83] Paul Bolstad, 'Recollections and Observations: Kilombero Settlement Scheme, 1966–68' (Manuscript in author's possession), 3.
[84] INT/PB/03, Correspondence with Paul Bolstad, 12 May 2019.

Plate 5 Said Ramadhani Chamwenyewe and Athumani Ali Milulu converse at Sonjo, Kilombero Settlement Scheme, 1968 [Photo courtesy of Paul Bolstad].

But when Paul Bolstad returned to visit Sonjo in 1970 he found the mechanisms set in motion by the Arusha Declaration of 1967 had converted the scheme into a revised form of co-operative in the new era of rural socialism.[85] Government funding had been withdrawn and the Ulanga District administration had taken possession of the tools, vehicles and machinery.[86] Many farmers had chosen to leave; their empty plots primed for others to take over or for new farmers to acquire.

The scheme as a palimpsest

To trace the history of the scheme, from its origins to its subsumption under the eclipse of *Ujamaa vijijini*, reveals the contrails of entangled approaches to settlement, rural reorganisation, and the stimulation of agricultural economies across a critical decade in Tanzania's history. Some of these approaches possess clear colonial genealogies in their organisation, methods, and staffing. For

[85] See Monson, *Freedom Railway*, 71–92.
[86] INT/PB/02, Correspondence with Paul Bolstad, 8 March 2019; INT/HS/02, Interview with Hamisi Saidi Salum, Mang'ula, 14 October 2019.

Tanganyika, 'political independence did not alter economic dependence' nor did it possess 'sufficient trained manpower to replace all the expatriates (usually former colonial officials) who held senior positions'.[87] Referring to 'Nyerere's "pet" schemes' it was thought that 'little of what he proposed was actually new, with demonstration plots and farms already in existence all over Tanganyika'.[88] Yet for the sake of the 'new nation' the zeal that permeated nation-building rhetoric often sought to veneer any semblance of continuity. Deborah Bryceson draws from Benedict Anderson's phrase, 'imagining the nation', to present Nyerere's 'genius' in 'portraying the nationalist vision so vividly'.[89]

The KSS may therefore be viewed as a rural development palimpsest. Not only by the way it grew from one scheme at Sonjo, to Ichonde, and third to Kichangani – each with integral commonalities alongside particular differences – but then also by the way in which the scheme's collective lifespan underwent a layering of development interventions, changes in management, successes and struggles, and shifts in perception as to how the scheme should be structured and what it was supposed to achieve.

This is a notable example of a TANU initiative before Tanganyika obtained internal self-government, spearheaded by Nyerere in the first constituency (Morogoro) he represented in the Legislative Council, and to which he lent his prestige. This represents the embryonic stages of Tanzanian villagisation in ideology and praxis, while its failings informed the development of villagisation throughout the nation over the subsequent decade. Management of the scheme passed through various iterations, not because of local conditions, but due to changes in policy and ministerial structures on a national and governmental level. The fact that this scheme in its small scale had management at all reveals the disproportionality of expenditure characteristic of rural development initiatives during this period. 'We made a mistake in choosing money', Nyerere wrote in 1968, 'to be the big instrument of our development.'[90]

A further characteristic is the variegation of village settlement strategies that resulted in vision before pragmatism, and action before rationale. The initial settling of Sonjo predates Nyerere's official launch of the policy of 'villagisation' in Tanganyika – in December 1962 – by over three years. It was only after the inauguration of this policy that the Rural Settlement Commission and Village Settlement Agency were created, which *then* sought to define and enact 'villagisation' as the first attempt to establish a set of standards to guide

---

[87] Kimambo, Maddox, and Nyanto, *New History*, 171.

[88] TNAUK DO 166/61, J.A. Molyneux to Walsh-Atkins, 9 January 1963.

[89] D. Bryceson, 'Household, hoe and nation: Development policies of the Nyerere era' in Michael Hodd (ed.), *Tanzania after Nyerere* (London, 1988), 36–48; Benedict Anderson, *Imagined Communities: Reflections on the Origin and Spread of Nationalism* (London, 1985), 36.

[90] Julius K. Nyerere, *Ujamaa: Essays on Socialism* (Dar es Salaam, 1968), 25.

the development of settlements dates only to June 1963. This is still several years before the launch in earnest of *Ujamaa vijijini*.

In 1965 several categories of settlement were identified. These included Nyerere's so-called 'pet schemes' – five Pilot Settlement Schemes that became bound by such prestige that it was considered they could not be allowed to fail.[91] There were also Assisted Settlement Schemes, including World Food Programme schemes, some of which were partly financed by OXFAM while others were supported by the Regional Administration. Ex-TAC and Israeli Agricultural Development schemes constituted two further categories. A final category was listed as the voluntary and unplanned settlement schemes.[92] The KSS contains vestiges of at least three of these categories throughout its lifespan, which undoubtedly contributed to its shortcomings in that it was never entirely clear what kind of scheme it was, what its goals were, how they might be achieved, and what level of financial and technical support should be offered to it. The scheme found itself caught in the confusion of these categorisations, during a period when great emphasis was being placed on 'village settlement' but with little cohesion of policy.

Amid this confusion, Nyerere was compelled to clarify his policy of *Ujamaa* through the Arusha Declaration. The publication of the pamphlet 'Ujamaa – the Basis of African Socialism' in 1962, underlined TANU's official commitment to the building of a socialist society but, Nyerere admitted in 1968, 'for a long time the meaning of this philosophy in the conditions of Tanzania was left vague'; and while the pamphlet 'described the basic attitudes of socialism […] it was published in English and was never easily available to the people of Tanzania'.[93] This 'lack of an ideology' did not prevent the pursuit of socialist policies, but the Arusha Declaration 'supplied the need for a definition'.[94]

'A good idea, done in the wrong way'

The KSS remains an important episode in Tanzania's 'nation-building' history. The scheme was a 'pipe dream', but it was continually supported because it was both an integral part of a political project and an enduring part in the evolution of a national settlement experiment. Despite its critics and questionable viability, it was never abandoned or dissolved because of this political importance. It had failings as an agricultural scheme, and was even described as 'a good idea, done in the wrong way, in the wrong place, with the wrong people'.[95]

---

[91] TNAUK DO 166/61/17, Buist to Reynolds, 7 September 1963.
[92] Tanzania, *Rural Settlement Commission*, 6.
[93] Nyerere, *Ujamaa*, vii.
[94] Ibid.
[95] INT/PB/02, Correspondence with Paul Bolstad, 8 March 2019.

The latent power of the animating principles of such schemes were fuel for optimism. To withdraw support would have been antithetical to the spirit of promise Nyerere harnessed in propelling Tanzania forward. Sonjo was symbolic of Nyerere's commitment to the future *despite* the challenges ahead. Consequently, it was realised that schemes needed more than nationalist fervour to succeed: but generous financial and technical support could not guarantee success either. Nyerere was aware of the difficult balance between forging an original path in rural development that was distinctly 'Tanzanian' and 'independent', while also drawing from the models, wealth, and expertise of nations against whose hegemony Tanzania drew a unifying strength. Nyerere would pronounce in 1968 that 'gifts and loans will endanger our independence', but only after attempts to utilise both throughout settlement programmes over several years revealed the unfeasibility of this approach. In 1963, Nyerere had approached private British firms with interests in Tanganyika to make financial contributions to a village settlement scheme in his home district: United Africa Company, Shell, and the fibre merchants Wigglesworth were all propositioned.[96] Seeking funds for the northern Mara TANU Youth Farms, Maria Nyerere as patron requested financial support from the Ottoman, Barclays, National and Grindlays banks, and the Bank of India.[97] Even the Rural Settlement Commission acknowledged that 'settlement schemes are expensive ventures and there is no doubt that without aid from overseas it would have been impossible to launch Government's village settlement programme'.[98]

Guidance on settlement schemes was partly drawn from the Israeli 'moshav' settlement model in the early 1960s. In January 1961 an Israeli consultant, Benyamin Kaplan, was invited by Nyerere to suggest 'methods and means to plan and implement settlement [...] increase agricultural production [...] and develop and expand the agricultural co-operatives'.[99] Kaplan commented on settlement in general, and Sonjo specifically, starkly revealing what was both right and wrong in its beginnings. Kaplan believed that 'the considerable and impressive enthusiasm for freedom and progress so striking in all sections of the community, can find a practical outlet in [...] land settlement schemes'.[100] Notably, Kaplan's report was published before Independence in August 1961. Kaplan assumed that 'candidates chosen for settlement schemes [would] be

[96] TNAUK DO 166/61, W.G. Lamarque memorandum, 17 December 1963.
[97] TNA 589/BMC/12/01, Mara TANU Youth Settlement Farm, 1963–64.
[98] Tanzania, *Rural Settlement Commission*, 44.
[99] Benyamin Kaplan, *New Settlement and Agricultural Development in Tanganyika* (Be'er Sheva, 1961), Preface.
[100] Ibid., 4.

of average or above average ability'.[101] For Sonjo, he advised that 'great care should be taken in selecting candidates for the settlement'.[102] While there was great enthusiasm in Sonjo's beginnings, the practical work required to forge a successful settlement scheme proved to be beyond the reach of even the most fervent nationalists. Yet the idea prevailed, and despite the first candidates lacking experience they were progressively replaced by those more able. Sonjo was emblematic of a strong commitment to Tanzania's rural development and of the challenges it presented.

Nyerere was eager for Tanganyika to be granted its right to begin its own process of development and was under no illusion as to the practical challenges ahead. On 6 March 1960, Nyerere was at Brandeis University in Massachusetts recording a television programme for the series 'Prospects of Mankind with Eleanor Roosevelt'. Asked whether Tanganyika was 'ready' for independence, Nyerere replied:

> If you come into my house and steal my jacket, don't then ask me whether I am ready for my jacket. The jacket was mine. You had no right at all to take it from me. Well, it may take a long time to go to the High Courts and appeal and get all this done until I get my jacket back. But you have no right at all to ask me whether I was ready for my jacket. The mechanism of whether really I can look right in my jacket when I put it on: this is different. I may not look as smart in it as you look in it, but it's mine.[103]

These words amplify the spirit and sentiment upon which the early TANU settlement schemes were initiated. Nyerere felt strongly – and rightly – that it was for Tanganyika to rule itself, even if that meant making mistakes: it was important they were *Tanganyika's* mistakes. And in mapping out Tanzania's path to rural development, mistakes were made. From the haphazard circumstances of its origins, to its ragged development in fits and starts throughout the 1960s, the KSS illustrates the importance of 'villagisation' and 'settlement' on the national stage. The scheme numbered among its settlers the urban unemployed, selected able farmers, spontaneous settlers, and local Kilombero inhabitants. While it was imbued with ideologies of 'nation-building' and 'self-help' it was also assisted by an organisation with a colonial core. There

---

[101] Ibid., 13.
[102] Ibid., 63.
[103] 'Prospects for Mankind with Eleanor Roosevelt – Africa: Revolution in Haste', 6 March 1960. Great Blue Hill (GBH) Archives, available: https://youtu.be/MSmYoNmN40s?t=475.

were grandiose visions for its reorganisation at high capital cost, but these never materialised.

In December 1962, Nyerere used his inaugural address as President to announce that: 'For the next few years Government will be doing all it can do to enable the farmers of Tanganyika to come together in village communities.'[104] He later explained: 'Before we can bring any of the benefits of modern development to the farmers of Tanganyika, the very first step is [...] for them to start living in Village Communities.'[105] This was not a policy launch, but confirmation of a programme that was already underway. These statements were 'the basis on which the [...] Rural Settlement programme was started [in 1963]'.[106] Moreover, for many Tanzanians today, historical memory insists that villagisation began with the implementation of *Ujamaa* after the Arusha Declaration. Prominent dates inscribed in the stone casings of water pumps memorialise their installation, most dating from the early 1970s, and this is often misconstrued as the founding date of the villages themselves.[107] Remnants of this ruin of *Ujamaa* can be seen at Sonjo, engraved with 'MAJI 1973' and yet here the deeper history prior to *Ujamaa* is known and celebrated; a short local history notes its existence '*even* before the establishment of *Ujamaa* villages'.[108] Attempts to implement settlement strategies before the formal policy of *Ujamaa* are not to be dismissed as past failures with little relevance, but should be seen as an indispensable part of the process of its implementation. *Ujamaa* was formalised and implemented *because* of that which preceded it, and not merely *in spite* of it. In an address given on the implementation of *Ujamaa*, Nyerere explained:

> Ever since 1959 [...] TANU has encouraged people to go into groups to farm in the rural areas, and [...] initiated settlement schemes of many kinds. But we can now see that we have committed many mistakes, and it is important that we should learn the right lessons from them. [...] It is important therefore, to realize that the policy of *Ujamaa vijijini* is not intended to be merely a revival of the old settlement schemes under another name. The policy is, in fact, the result of learning from the failures which we have had, and from the successes which began and grew on a different basis.[109]

---

[104] Nyerere, *Freedom and Unity*, 183–4.
[105] Tanzania, *Rural Settlement*, 1.
[106] Ibid.
[107] INT/AM/01, Interview with Ally Mtemangani, Sonjo, 4 July 2019.
[108] United Republic of Tanzania. Halmashauri ya Wilaya ya Kilombero, *Rasimu ya Mpango wa Matumizi Bora ya Ardhi wa Kijiji cha Sonjo, 2012–2022* (Dar es Salaam: 2012), 4. This author's italics.
[109] Nyerere, *Man and Development*, 35–6.

This practice of learning from successes and failures is another way in which the history of the evolution of development in Tanzania reveals its palimpsestic nature. Nyerere was aware of this in his revisioning of settlement policies through the outset of *Ujamaa vijijini* as he interpreted past experience to inform and influence the present. Subsequently, *Ujamaa* became viewed as a 'past' event, its own 'successes and failures' drawing historical analysis. Its legacy, alongside that of Nyerere, continues to feature prominently in discourse and scholarship. This is unsurprising as, following Lonsdale, the reinterpretation of history is a *constant* process.

Conclusion: Past Futures to the Present

In 1951, an article – simply titled, 'Kilombero' – was published in *Tanganyika Notes and Records*. 'Let me take the reader in a dugout canoe for a day on the Kilombero', wrote the author.[1] It is a naturalistic piece, in which R.K.M. Battye – equipped with water bottle, .375 magnum rifle, pair of Zeiss binoculars, and food for the day – vividly describes the impressive birdlife seen from his canoe as he is 'propelled by two Wandamba paddlers in the stern and one with a bamboo pole in the prow'.[2] Aside from the 'constantly passing' hippopotami and a dozen crocodiles – 'in all their saurian ugliness' – Battye observes a 'striking' fish eagle, a pair of wattled plover, six spoonbill, three sacred ibis, a hadada ibis, and 'about a hundred brown and fawn Egyptian geese' together with thirty-nine crowned crane, several jacana, a pair of blacksmith plover, four pelicans, a goliath heron, and more.[3] Battye shoots one of the crocodile, of course, and also an elephant in alleged self-defence. From his camp 'crepuscular insects keep the air in constant vibration and bull-frogs maintain a croaking commentary from the swamps' while 'a bat flits across the moon as night descends on the Kilombero'.[4] The narrative is painfully poetic, embellished, and anecdotal, but it is an important historical representation of the valley as a wilderness. When Lorenzo and Mirella Ricardi wrote of the 'mysterious Kilombero' in an account of their travels 'across Africa by boat' in the 1980s, it was a 'surprising' river, 'which seems to wander like a raging free spirit over the land and the boulders, through the trees, sometimes soft and quiet, other times loud and violent, filling the air with spray that smelled of the wild'.[5] At the time the couple were writing their fantastical tale, Tanzania was in its third decade as an independent nation. Decades of past futures already layered; most existing on paper only. Forty years of British administration had come and gone. And over eighty years earlier – during the years of *Deutsch-Ostafrika* and before the First World War – the popular German wildlife painter Wilhem Kuhnert had also found himself in Kilombero.[6]

[1] R.K.M. Battye, 'Kilombero,' *Tanganyika Notes and Records* 30 (June 1951), 1.
[2] Ibid.
[3] Ibid., 1–3. Scientific names are noted, thus forming a useful historical record of valley ornithology.
[4] Ibid., 5.
[5] Lorenzo and Mirella Ricciardi, *African Rainbow: Across Africa by Boat* (London, 1989), 76.
[6] INT/01/AGW, Correspondence with Angelika Grettman-Werner, 20 January 2020. Dr Grettman-Werner is the global authority on Kuhnert (1865–1926) and custodian of his diaries, papers, and selected collection of his works.

Kuhnert was famed for eternalising the landscapes and wildlife of the German colonial imagination, promoting scenes of 'wild, undeveloped, and underused emptiness' alongside 'ideologically charged depictions of majestic African game'.[7] Two paintings remain from Kuhnert's visit to Kilombero. One is under private ownership in Bremen, Germany. The other hangs in the Rjiksmuseum Twenthe in the Dutch city of Enschede. Together they represent perhaps the only surviving examples of an artistic impression from this period. Both show a landscape resplendent, emptied of people. In one, hippopotami frolic in a mighty-yet-calm river, flanked by a gallery forest of deep greens. In the other, giraffe stand tall over a plain blanketed by violet flowers in bloom, against a background of richly foliaged baobab trees.

Over a century has passed since Kuhnert depicted these Edenic scenes, and in the intervening decades repeated attempts to control valley ecology and bring agricultural intensification to Kilombero have conflicted with both the vision and the reality of its multivalent landscape, both as a wilderness and a land of fertile promise. But which is it? Is it neither? Must it be either? Or can it be both? This book has demonstrated the duplicity of this environment and explored in depth 'the great difficulties with which man has to contend in exploiting the area'.[8] Visions of this valley and visions for its future have risen in hope and fallen to these difficulties; and no vision should be assumed as inherently 'good' or 'positive' development for Kilombero and its people. Nevertheless, this chronicle of these efforts has revealed the paradoxical nature of interpretations and understandings of this valley region. Kilombero was contradictorily viewed as both a wilderness and an agricultural wonderland. The archival and documentary evidence, therefore, is peppered with reports of crops lost to game depredation and the associated threat posed to human lives. Kilombero's rivers are indeed the mighty waterways through viridescent landscapes as rendered by Kuhnert and early travellers' accounts. But they are also volatile and capricious, both the provision and destroyer of infrastructure. The Kilombero River itself is 'both the fairy godmother and the ogre of the valley' – essential for cultivation, and its paramount threat.[9]

As this deep study has shown, Kilombero and its imagined futures have proved to be multifaceted in the past. This is strikingly evident through the historical record in both rhetoric and reality, through perceptions and place. But what of the valley today? The recent emergence of conservation efforts and narratives in the valley now form an integral part of this complex socio-ecological environment, but as this book has evidenced, wildlife and ecology control has long been a part of Kilombero history. The position that the valley holds in providing a dry season refuge for wildlife populations

---

[7] Gissibl, *Nature of German Imperialism*, 288–9, 311.
[8] Jätzold and Baum, *Kilombero Valley*, 32.
[9] TNA 61/782/21, Agricultural and Communications in the Ulanga Valley, 1943.

Plate 6 'Der Galeriewald, Flußszenerie am Ulanga' (trans. 'The Gallery Forest, River Scenery on the Ulanga') by Wilhelm Kuhnert, c. 1905 [Image courtesy of Angelika Grettman-Werner].

migrating between the Udzungwa Mountains and Nyerere National Park is a dominant concern for conservationists who wish to promote so-called 'wildlife corridors' through Kilombero. This role as an area of wildlife connectivity is now framed within conservation narratives as organisations such as STEP (the Southern Tanzania Elephant Program) seek to ensure positive long-term human-elephant coexistence. Elephants are terrified of bees, and one of the ways to achieve this coexistence is through the construction of beehive fences 'to safeguard and enhance livelihoods, reduce hostility towards elephants, and to eliminate the retaliatory killing of elephants by both farmers and game officers'.[10] Thus, concerted efforts to restore the so-called 'Ruipa Corridor' through Kilombero has highlighted the continued relevance of issues of human-wildlife conflict and the contestations between different approaches to land use and the environment.[11]

---

[10] STEP, 'Human-Elephant Coexistence', Information leaflet in author's possession (2019).

[11] See Andrew J. Bamford, Daniella Ferrol-Schulte, and Hillary Smith, *The Status of the Ruipa Corridor Between the Selous Game Reserve and the Udzungwa Mountains* (London, 2011); and Trevor Jones, Andrew J. Bamford, and Daniella Ferrol-Schulte,

Conclusion

Plate 7 'Giraffen in bloeiende Ulanga-vlakte' (trans. 'Giraffes on the Ulanga Plain in bloom') by Wilhelm Kuhnert, c. 1905 [Image courtesy of Rjiksmuseum Twenthe Collection].

The image of Kilombero as a wildlife haven was further underscored by the designation of 'The Kilombero Valley Floodplain' as a Ramsar Site on 2 May 2002, and therefore recognition of the valley as possessing a rare and unique wetland whose natural ecosystem and biodiversity is considered to be of 'global, national, regional and local importance'.[12] Qualifying criteria included its status as a rare and unique example of the largest seasonally freshwater lowland floodplain in East Africa, and its support of populations of wildlife, birds, and fish.[13] At the time of its designation, the wetland contained almost 75 per cent of the world's population of the wetland-dependent Puku Antelope (*Kobus vardonnii*) which is listed as near threatened on the IUCN Red List of Threatened Species.[14] Puku and the proliferation of birds have long been characteristic of the

---

'Vanishing wildlife corridors and options for restoration: A case study from Tanzania', *Tropical Conservation* 5:4 (2012), 463–74.

[12] Ramsar Convention, 'Information Sheet on Ramsar Wetlands: The Kilombero Valley Floodplain', Internal Ramsar document, 19 June 2002, available: https://rsis.ramsar.org/RISapp/files/RISrep/TZ1173RIS.pdf.

[13] See Ed Wilson, Robert McInnes, Damas Patrick Mbaga, and Paul Ouedraogo, 'Kilombero Valley, United Republic of Tanzania. Ramsar Site No. 1173', Ramsar Advisory Mission Report, April 2017.

[14] Ibid. IUCN is an initialism of the International Union for Conservation of Nature.

valley. In the 1920s, hunter and traveller F.L. Puxley wrote that this 'antelope, whose nature is essentially sweet, would make another very pleasant attraction in an English park'.[15] During Captain Prittwitz's survey of 1897–8 he noted the locations of '*zähllosen Wasservögeln*', or 'countless waterfowl'.[16]

Conservationist intervention is set against the backdrop of radical landscape change in Kilombero that is customarily cited as having been catalysed in the 1990s, and is characterised by sustained human immigration, significant expansion of rice cultivation, livestock grazing, deforestation, and infrastructure development.[17] After decades of attempts to increase agricultural productivity in Kilombero, it is increased rice cultivation and grazing, in particular, that are now considered to be degrading the environment and reducing the natural wetland habitat.[18] Numerous studies have highlighted how these transformations in land use and settlement size and spread are detrimental to wildlife connectivity.[19] There was once a call to destroy all game in the vicinity of settlements in order to preserve crops. Now the decimation of wildlife populations is a tragedy. In 2017 Kilombero was described as 'Tanzania's ghost safari' where 'western aid contributed to the decline of a wildlife haven'.[20] This counternarrative to what 'kind' of region Kilombero

[15] Puxley, *In African Game Tracks*, 227.

[16] BnF, 8-M-6250 (11), 'Aufnahme der Flüsse Kihansi, Ulanga, Ruipa und Routen in der Ulanga-Niederung, 1897–98', *Mittheilungen aus den deutschen Schutzgebieten* 11 (1898), Karte 10.

[17] See Constanze Leemhuis, Frank Thonfeld, Kristian Näschen, Stefanie Steinbach, et al., 'Sustainability in the food-water-ecosystem nexus: The role of land use and land cover change for water resources and ecosystems in the Kilombero Wetland, Tanzania', *Sustainability* 9:9 (2017), 1–18.

[18] See Subira Eva Munishi and Graham Hewitt, 'Degradation of Kilombero Valley Ramsar Wetlands in Tanzania', *Physics and Chemistry of the Earth* 112 (2019), 216–227.

[19] For example, Kennedy Sabas Haule, 'Wildlife Prospects in Kilombero Game Controlled Area' (MSc thesis, Centre for International Environment and Development Studies, Agricultural University of Norway, 1997); L. Dinesen, Thomas Lehmberg, Marcel C. Rahner, and J. Fjeldså, 'Conservation priorities for the forests of the Udzungwa Mountains, Tanzania, based on primates, duikers and birds', *Biological Conservation* 99 (2001), 223–36; M. Starkey, N. Birnie, A. Cameron. R.A. Daffa, et al., 'Kilombero Valley Wildlife Project: An Ecological and Social Survey in the Kilombero Valley, Tanzania', Final Report, Kilombero Valley Wildlife Project, Edinburgh (2002); and Hamidu A. Seki, Deo D. Shirima, and Colin J. Courtney Mustaphi, 'The impact of land use and land cover change on biodiversity within and adjacent to Kibasira Swamp in Kilombero Valley, Tanzania', *African Journal of Ecology* 56:3 (2018), 518–27.

[20] Bibi van der Zee and Sophie Tremblay, 'Tanzania's ghost safari: How western aid contributed to the decline of a wildlife haven', *The Guardian* [UK], published online 13 August 2017, https://www.theguardian.com/environment/2017/aug/13/tanzanias-ghost-safari-how-western-aid-contributed-to-the-decline-of-a-wildlife-haven.

ought to be seemed a dramatic shift, but it was part of a strong conservationist rhetoric that derogated environmental destruction wrought by human activities. 'Lions, elephants, and hippos have vanished from [the] Kilombero valley', it was reported in the British press, 'after UK- and US-funded projects helped turn a once-thriving habitat into farmland, teak, and sugar plantations.'[21] The insinuation here is that 'development' is to blame; the natural environment has been ruined by humankind's own 'progress'. By taking such a long view of 'development' visions in one locale, this book provides concrete evidence of how narratives can become paradoxical over time. But the notion that Kilombero is suddenly being destroyed by human activity forgets that, while Kilombero has long bordered game-controlled areas and a game reserve, the valley has always been a region where humans lived and farmed the land. As shown, it was wildlife that for decades was held responsible for environmental destruction through crop depredation, and so to the present. For the fate of Kilombero, this begs the question: whose valley for whose visions? In short, whose future?

In their presentation of the 'history of aid' in Kilombero in their portrayal of 'Tanzania's ghost safari' in the British press, journalists Bibi van der Zee and Sophie Tremblay conflate 'development aid' with 'colonial development'; but they do stumble on truth in their telling of how, 'For many years [the] Kilombero valley defied change' as 'enormous plans' made by Europeans drawn to the fertile soil 'kept falling through'.[22] Their retelling of valley history contains various minor inaccuracies – such as the assertion that Europeans arrived from 1800 and that Nyerere 'did not like western foreign investors' – but accurate is their claim that: 'Over and over again foreign dreams [...] withered and died in the valley.'[23] This book is a testament to these dreams, their withering and deaths demonstrated throughout these pages.

Recent contentions within contemporary conservation narratives lie in immigration, speaking directly to the central theme of settlement and resettlement. Kilombero was indeed sparsely populated for most of the twentieth century, with notable demographic change resulting from an 'influx' of pastoralists to the valley from the 1990s, after which further in-migration was encouraged by opportunities created by the newly founded Kilombero Valley Teak Company plantation and also the expanding outgrowers model promoted by the re-privatised Kilombero Sugar Company. In 2008, the British-based company, Agrica, acquired a 5,469 hectare farm in the valley with a view to producing up to 15,000 tons of milled wet season rice and 30,000 tons

---

[21] Ibid.
[22] Ibid.
[23] Ibid.

of dry season maize through its subsidiary, Kilombero Plantations Limited (KPL). This latter also represented future possibilities and suddenly Kilombero was in the ascendant with land in alleged abundance. British and Norwegian investment in KPL followed World Bank funds channelled through KVTC. Transport infrastructures in the valley were improved with USAID finance. For many, transformation of the valley through the intensification of agricultural production was arguably the elusive fulfilment of its long-held potential. This anthropocentric perspective was the dominant view for decades, but now an opposing conservationist view valued Kilombero as a fragile ecosystem that demanded protection. Trevor Jones of STEP has long since sought to establish wildlife corridors in Kilombero to preserve pachyderms' roaming rights. 'It has been very sad to see all the overgrazing and conversion to farmland of wildlife habitat in the Kilombero valley over the last decade', he has lamented.[24] There is a view, however, that it is not large-scale agricultural schemes that provide the greatest pressures on a balanced ecosystem and biodiversity, but small-scale farming – especially from recent arrivals to the valley – which is unregulated, unaccountable, and unforgiving to calls for sustainable practices. The tension that cuts to the centre of this debate is whether economic development is incompatible with environmental protection. This question is a relatively recent one in Kilombero, and emerged alongside discourse surrounding biodiversity degradation, fragmented natural ecosystems, and environmental sustainability. Where agricultural intensification and increased production were once the perfective end, they are now considered one of the most serious threats to global biodiversity.[25] Colonial 'conservation' concerns carried quite different applications in the past, as they sought to conserve soil fertility and promote long-term productivity by improving the carrying capacity of the land. It was the preservation of natural resources for their exploitation that led to a preoccupation with, for example, soil erosion between the 1930s and 1950s.[26] Environmental degradation was viewed as a threat to the future of colonial agriculture, and not to the environment itself for its own sake.

A recent example of how visions of agricultural intensification remain part of the Kilombero story is found in KPL, through its rise and fall. The lure of Kilombero remained strong into the twenty-first century as the valley continued

---

[24] Quoted in Van der Zee and Tremblay, 'Tanzania's ghost safari'.

[25] Sean L. Maxwell, R. Fuller, and T. Brooks, 'Biodiversity: The ravages of guns, nets and bulldozers', *Nature* 536 (2016), 143–5.

[26] For the origins of colonial conservationism, see William Beinart, 'Soil erosion, conservationism and ideas about development: A Southern African exploration, 1900–1960', *Journal of Southern African Studies* 11:1 (1984), 52–83; also David Anderson, 'Depression, dust bowl, demography, and drought: The colonial state and soil conservation in East Africa during the 1930s', *African Affairs* 83:332 (1984), 321–43.

to claim visions for ambitious development, with KPL as a recent example of a failed initiative which has proved highly contentious. This large-scale agricultural scheme at Mngeta was declared to be a socially responsible and sustainable agribusiness initiative. Several institutions invested heavily in the venture, including Norway's Norfund, the UK's Department for International Development (DfID), and the US-based Capricorn Investments. Additional bank loans of over $25m saw the project fund reach nearly twice that amount. It was, *The Sunday Times* reported, 'funded by a gaggle of deep-pocketed westerners, including the first president of eBay [and] feted by the World Economic Forum for doing industrial agriculture in Africa the "right way"'.[27]

But KPL proved a failure. The initiative generated global publicity, first due to the scale of investment, but subsequently through allegations of malpractice. Its critics deplored its development model as 'flawed' and claimed its practices devastated local communities through land dispossession and unfavourable farming contracts. These criticisms were refuted, but they damaged the company's reputation as financial damage was also experienced due to a suspension of import tariffs on rice in 2013, which led to a deluge of cheap imports that sunk prices dramatically. Moreover, low maize prices in 2017–18 contributed to losses reported across three consecutive years (2016–18).[28] The scheme was also marred by adverse weather, floods, and poor transport infrastructures – all obstacles that had blighted attempts to implement large-scale projects in Kilombero for decades. Despite the existence of the TAZARA railway and initial intent to utilise the line, costs far exceeded those of road transport. Local infrastructure inadequacies were exacerbated by the onus placed by the Tanzanian government onto the company itself to develop feeder roads from villages as a sign of goodwill.[29] This transfer of responsibility – from government to private enterprise – proved counterproductive. Heavy lies the burden of maintaining roads in an area that can see rainfall in the single month of March equivalent to the entire annual rainfall of the UK. Excessive rains in Kilombero are potentially devastating. At Mngeta, if the water table rises fifteen centimetres it can ruin an entire harvest.

---

[27] Danny Fortson, 'World grabs at Africa's land', *The Sunday Times*, 8 September 2013.

[28] The arrival of destructive army worm in 2017 also damaged the maize market, but a Tanzanian ban on maize exports in 2018 and the subsequent collapse of the maize price to an 11-year low saw the company spiral towards bankruptcy. For further insights, see Wilfred Makombe and Jaclyn Kropp, 'The Effects of Tanzanian Maize Export Bans on Producers' Welfare and Food Security', Paper presented at the Agricultural and Applied Economics Association's 2016 AAEA Annual Meeting, Boston, MA, 31 July – 2 August 2016.

[29] INT/GA/01, Interview with Graham Anderson, Dar es Salaam, 22 October 2019.

Kilombero was never the target, however, but the site was thought to be a 'fit' for a particular project mould.[30] The farm site had first been demarcated in 1986 following the establishment of a joint venture between the North Korean and Tanzanian governments (KOTACO).[31] But this too failed before it had truly begun, and the farm had lain virtually dormant since its abandonment in 1993.[32] Controversies surrounded the farm's reacquisition by KPL, as fifteen years of dormancy had seen its land settled, grazed, and cultivated by residents who were subsequently classed as 'squatters'.[33] The company was initially told there were 100–200 settlers on the land, but over 2,000 were recorded following an initial baseline survey.[34] A major resettlement campaign costing $1m did not appease universal rights activists, development aid 'watchers', and institutions that defended residents' rights; their reports marred the operation, embroiling KPL in a highly publicised dispute as it was accused of practices antithetical to its own commitment to social responsibility and its declaration to lift smallholders from subsistence to surplus.[35] The Oakland Institute was particularly involved in issuing communiqués that sought to expose, denounce, and challenge 'the devastating impacts that [KPL] has had on local communities'.[36] The investment venture and ensuing case drew the attention of numerous scholars due to its relevance to studies of land-use change, rice intensification, and large-scale agricultural development projects alongside their relationship

[30] Ibid.

[31] Mikael Bergius, Tor A. Benjaminsen, and Mats Widgren, 'Green economy, Scandinavian investments and agricultural modernization in Tanzania', *Journal of Peasant Studies* 45:4 (2018), 834.

[32] The collapse of the Soviet Union in 1991 severed North Korea from its primary source of economic aid, which soon led to widespread divestment such as the abandonment of the KOTACO project in Mngeta. One previous attempt to revive the farm by entrepreneur Eric Winson was shortlived, INT/01/RS, Interview with Ryan Skaife, 12 September 2021.

[33] Ibid. See also, 'Government orders 2000 people out of farm', *The Citizen*, 19 October 2009.

[34] INT/GA/01, Interview with Graham Anderson, Dar es Salaam, 22 October 2019.

[35] For example, Richard Smallteacher, 'Agrica's Tanzania Rice Scheme has devastated local farmers, say NGOs', *CorpWatch*, 7 July 2015, https://www.corpwatch.org/article/agricas-tanzania-rice-scheme-has-devastated-local-farmers-say-ngos.

[36] The Oakland Institute, 'Getting the Facts Right on Agrica/KPL Agricultural Investment in Tanzania', published 2 July 2015, https://www.oaklandinstitute.org/getting-facts-right-agrica. For the findings of an investigation carried out by the Oakland Institute 2011–15, see their report, 'Irresponsible Investment: Agrica's Broken Development Model in Tanzania' (Oakland, CA, 2015). For further press releases and public statements, see the Oakland Institute's collected material on Agrica at: https://www.oaklandinstitute.org/company/agrica.

to agribusiness, outgrowers' schemes, and contentions surrounding foreign aid in investment and accusations of 'land-grabbing'.[37]

In 2019 it was confirmed that KPL had ceased operations.[38] Its demise was by no means inevitable, but it does continue a pattern revealed by the preceding chapters. Seven years after operations began in Kilombero and four before they ended, Carter Coleman – founder and CEO of Agrica – emoted that 'farming in Africa is like farming on Mars' as 'all inputs such as fertilizers and machinery have to be procured externally' and further difficulties are faced 'from long investment horizons, limited infrastructure (e.g. electricity generation, drying and milling facilities) and insufficient financial support for small-scale farmers'.[39] Coleman was later maligned as the 'boss of a loss-making rice farm at the end of a dirt road in southern Tanzania'.[40] Graham Anderson, the General Manager of KPL, admitted: 'If I knew then, what I know now...' as he suggested that the catalogue of errors could have been avoided had they not chosen Kilombero as the site to fit their project mould. Tanzanian newspaper, *The Citizen*, reported at the time that 'KPL's fiasco follows a long list of failed big agriculture projects in Africa in recent years, including Agrisol and Sun Biofuels in Tanzania; Karuturi in Kenya and Ethiopia; Nile Trading in South Sudan; Senhuile in Senegal, and Bukanga Lonzo in the Democratic Republic of Congo.'[41] The role of these large-scale

---

[37] See, for example, Chambi Chachage, *Land Acquisition and Accumulation in Tanzania* (Dar es Salaam, 2010); Jennifer J. West and Ruth Haug, 'The vulnerability and resilience of smallholder-inclusive agricultural investments in Tanzania', *Journal of Eastern African Studies* 11:4 (2017), 670–91; John P. Connors, 'Agricultural Development, Land Change and Livelihoods in Tanzania's Kilombero Valley' (PhD thesis, Arizona State University, 2015); Catherine Wilson, *Norfund's Kilombero Plantation in Tanzania – Meagre Results from a Large Investment* (Oslo, 2016); Emma L. Johansson and Ellinor Isgren, 'Local perceptions of land-use change: Using participatory art to reveal direct and indirect socioenvironmental effects of land acquisitions in Kilombero Valley, Tanzania', *Ecology and Society* 22:1 (2017), Article 3; Emmanuel Tumusiime, 'Suitable for whom? The case of system of rice intensification in Tanzania', *The Journal of Agricultural Education and Extension* 23:4 (2017), 335–50; Bergius et al., 'Green economy', 1–13; Ernest Nkansah-Dwamena and Aireona Bonnie Raschke, 'Justice and fairness for Mkangawalo People: The case of the Kilombero Large-scale Land Acquisition (Lasla) Project in Tanzania', *Ethics, Policy & Environment* (Published online: 25 November 2020).

[38] 'Crop firm wilts under cash crunch', *The Citizen*, 5 November 2019.

[39] Sophia Lüttringhaus, 'Farming in Africa is like farming on Mars', *Climate Analytics* 20 November 2015, https://climateanalytics.org/blog/2015/farming-in-africa-is-like-farming-on-mars.

[40] Danny Fortson, 'World grabs at Africa's land', *The Sunday Times*, 8 September 2013.

[41] Ibid.

projects in rural transformation, their controversial nature, and risk of failure resonates with recent studies of larger-scale 'megaproject development' in Africa and its position as a form of future making, 'driven by the mobilizing power of the "politics of aspiration"'.[42] The scale of investment in KPL was unprecedented in the valley, and its demise emerged as a coda to a long history of failed attempts to develop the natural resources of Kilombero.[43] But while this can be shown as a typical example in a long history of such outcomes, the sorry tale has parallels to stymied ambitions far beyond the valley, which may have proved unsuccessful for a myriad of divergent reasons. This characteristic of local specificity with broader relevance is emblematic of the examples of development visions and efforts forwarded in this study, and which serve to reveal experiences within this one locale, but may also serve as the basis for comparative studies. At the time of writing, the farm that was KPL had returned to government ownership and was parcelled out to local farmers for continued rice production.

One highly significant and truly positive development in recent years speaks to the last major theme to address: infrastructure. Tanzania's presidents and its bridges enjoy a close association. Nyerere Bridge has liberated commuters in Dar es Salaam through its linking the city centre to the southern neighbourhood of Kigamboni. Mkapa Bridge spans the Rufiji River and is Tanzania's longest bridge, at 970 metres. Kikwete Bridge spans the Malagarasi River, and Selander Bridge continues Dar es Salaam's Ali Hassan Mwinyi Road – named for Tanzania's second President – but the bridge itself was built in 1929 and named after Tanganyika's first Director of Public Works. Now, the modern Tanzanite Bridge runs superiorly parallel as the 'new' Selander.

So, too, did John Magufuli – the nation's fifth President – grant his name to a crossing, and in 2018 inaugurated 'his' bridge over the Kilombero River. This bridge bears not only his name, but also far greater significance than most Tanzanians realise. It reportedly cost $27m and stretches for 384 metres as an all-weather and all-year connection across a river that has divided this region for as long as it has been settled. Magufuli Bridge was built as part of an ambitious infrastructure development programme under the Government's

---

[42] For example, see Detlef Müller-Mahn, Kennedy Mkutu, and Eric Kioko, 'Megaprojects – mega failures? The politics of aspiration and the transformation of rural Kenya', *The European Journal of Development Research* 33 (2021), 1069–90.

[43] According to Agrica's website, declared investment in KPL included: a 6,200m² warehouse, and two industrial rice mills; a 3,000-ton automated cleaning and drying facility; a fleet of John Deere and Claas tractors, planters, and combine harvesters; a 500KW biomass gasification plant; the refurbishment of a 320KW mini-hydro station; 3,000 hectares of overhead centre-pivot irrigation circles fed by a river pump station, 4km of underground pipes, and two canals of 4.5km and 6km length.

Five-Year Development Plan, 2016/17–2020/21.[44] It is both remarkable and unsurprising that this investment has only so very recently been made. The question of whether to bridge the Kilombero River is an old one. In 1964, the FAO did not 'recommend that present improvements should include the bridging of the Kilombero at Ifakara or elsewhere. A bridge would be exceedingly costly. The money could be better spent in other ways.'[45] Construction of a bridge over the Kilombero at Swero was, however, under consideration by the FRG in late 1964, yet unfunded.[46] This was, the FAO decreed, a 'more distant project'.[47] But the frequency of accidents and deaths during ferry crossings into the twenty-first century became too tragic to ignore. At least 100 people were initially feared drowned after the MV Kiu ferry capsized in heavy rains on 11 April 2002.[48] This figure was later reduced to thirty-eight people feared drowned.[49] In January 2016, the MV Kilombero II ferry capsized during a rainstorm with fifty people on board, including passengers inside three vehicles ferried over the river.[50] Its sister ferry – the MV Kilombero – had been replaced as new in March 2007 as part of a World Bank loan that enabled a new ferry costing €830,500 to be supplied by the Dutch firm of Dutchmed International B.V.[51] It was also in 2007 that a feasibility study was carried out with a view to construct a bridge over the Kilombero. Construction was 'justified because the current dependence on ferry transport across the Kilombero River is not reliable and poses a great risk to human life and their properties' and would 'reduce if not eliminate risk of accidents'.[52] Conversely, one concern raised

[44] 'President Magufuli Inaugurates Bridge Named after Him', *TanzaniaInvest*, 8 May 2018, https://www.tanzaniainvest.com/transport/president-magufuli-inaugurates-bridge-named.
[45] FAO, *Possibilities for Agricultural and Related Development*, 21.
[46] TNA 601/CW.44194/67, Junior Minister to Regional Commissioner, Morogoro, 31 December 1964.
[47] FAO, *Possibilities for Agricultural and Related Development*, 21.
[48] 'Tanzania ferry sinking kills "at least 100"', *The Irish Times*, 12 April 2002, https://www.irishtimes.com/news/tanzania-ferry-sinking-kills-at-least-100-1.419843.
[49] 'Tanzania ferry tragedy "kills 38"', *BBC News*, 12 April 2002, http://news.bbc.co.uk/1/hi/world/africa/1924578.stm.
[50] United Republic of Tanzania, 'Sinking of ferry at Kilombero River', *Crime and Traffic Incidents: Statistics Report, January to December 2016* (Dar es Salaam, 2017), 71.
[51] World Bank, 'Implementation completion and results report (IDA-38880) on a credit in the amount of SDR81.6 million (US$122 million equivalent) to the United Republic of Tanzania for the Central Transport Corridor Project', Report No. ICR1299, 19 June 2010 (Washington, D.C., 2010).
[52] United Republic of Tanzania, 'Detailed Engineering Design of Kilombero Bridge and its Approach Roads: Environmental Scoping Report', Scoping Report, 17 April 2009 (Dar es Salaam, 2009), 1.

through public consultation was that there would be an increase in road traffic accidents. Another concern was that improved transportation could lead to 'family breakup' due to an 'outmigration of men looking for business opportunities'.[53] But the bridge was clearly a long-overdue infrastructural fulcrum which sadly did not materialise rapidly enough to avert the tragic accident in 2016, after which regular passengers and local residents recounted how 'every year around this time people using the pontoon had been losing lives' during the heavy rains that continued to cut off the Kilombero and Ulanga Districts from one another.[54] Construction of the Magufuli Bridge thus closed an excruciatingly long chapter in the history of the Kilombero valley region. This significance was expressed in a speech given at the formal opening of the bridge, as Professor Makame Mbarawa – then Minister for Works, Transport, and Communication – declared: 'We are writing history.'[55]

We are writing history. It seems a hackneyed phrase, but such is the strength of the sentiment that it may never be cliché. This book has connected the concept of 'futures' to the past, through its examination of 'past futures' and processes of 'future making' through a history of development in Kilombero. Could the writing of history, then – and in the sense conveyed by Professor Mbarawa – be seen as a counterpart to the making of futures? The fulfilment of the second by the first? To some extent, yes – as they are both contingent parts of a broader metaphysical process.

Nearly two decades have passed since David Anderson noted that 'history is increasingly seen as relevant by those involved in the implementation of development' and in the intervening years this attitude has both broadened and strengthened. The pursuit of further understanding into the past continues to prove fundamentally important when addressing present ecological change, together with future development planning. Moreover, Anderson warned that the 'structures of colonial rule – ideologies, systems, and practices – cannot be ignored in a reconstruction of the history of colonial development'.[56] This is fitting, for it is these very structures that so profoundly shaped the development history of Kilombero.

This study has revealed Kilombero as one of the starkest examples of how colonial development programmes, in particular, were 'doomed to failure because of errors, ignorance, misjudgements and simple misunderstandings on

---

[53] Ibid., 9.

[54] 'Ferry accident foreseen', *The Citizen*, 29 January 2016, https://www.thecitizen.co.tz/tanzania/news/ferry-accident-foreseen-users--2545904.

[55] Press Statehouse, 'Kipindi cha Uzinduzi wa Daraja la Magufuli na Barabara ya Kidatu-Ifakara', 11 June 2018, https://www.youtube.com/watch?v=uoVTWRQWozA. Author's transcription and translation.

[56] Anderson, *Eroding the Commons*, 8.

Plate 8 'Magufuli Bridge' adjacent to the old Kilombero ferry site at Kivukoni, 2019 [Photograph by author].

the part of developers'.[57] What makes Kilombero so exceptional, however, is the sheer number of schemes envisaged for the valley that never materialised. It has been shown that an inordinate number of programmes were never given the chance to fail. They met their doom *before* materialising. Moreover, the examples presented in this conclusion – from the present and recent past in Kilombero – show that 'errors, ignorance, misjudgements and simple misunderstandings' were not confined to colonial development programmes. But this is not the whole picture. Complexities remain, and it remains clear that no-one can truly lay claim to Kilombero's future. This is still a valley flanked by the two highest capacity hydropower dams in Tanzania at Kihansi and Kidatu, but also home to a National Development Corporation rubber plantation at Mang'ula that rudimentarily taps trees planted by German colonists.[58] This is indeed a complex place.

[57] Ibid., 6.
[58] Both will be surpassed by the Julius Nyerere Hydropower Station (formerly 'Stiegler's Gorge Dam') on the Rufiji when completed.

By reviewing 'past futures' through former visions for this valley, this book has shown how these have taken many forms and are textured by degrees of contestation, subjective legitimacy, and community inclusion. These futures might have been visionary, rhetorical, or ideological; but if one thing is clear, it is that the state wields the greatest power in effecting the future of a locale, and of course, a nation and its people. Despite levied accusations, criticisms, and failings, the state continues – and it must – to express the intent to create a better future for its citizens, to progress, and to develop. To this point, one slogan popularised under President Kikwete was, *'Maisha bora kwa kila Mtanzania'* or, 'a better life for every Tanzanian'.[59] This is itself a form of 'future making' – and it is just as important to make futures as it is to make history. It is important to maintain a 'capacity to aspire' but also to recognise that there are uncertainties, that expectations may not be met, and visions may not materialise.[60] This was well understood by Julius Nyerere, who at the dawn of Tanzania's independence – its most puissant 'future-making' moment – wrote:

> *Unless I can meet at least some of these aspirations, my head will roll just as surely as the tickbird follows the rhino.*[61]

---

[59] INT/01/SK, Simon Kinyaga, Sonjo, 6 July 2019. Author's translation.
[60] Appadurai, *Future as Cultural Fact*, 179–198.
[61] 'Tanganyika's President Nyerere', *Time Magazine* 83:11, 13 March 1964.

Bibliography

Archival Sources

National Library of France – Bibliothèque nationale de France (BnF). Paris, France.

IFN-53029138. 'Karte der Nyasa-Expedition des Gouverneurs Obersten Freiherrn von Schele', (Berlin: E. Miller, 1894).

Chartwell Papers, University of Cambridge (CHAR). Cambridge, UK.

10/27/66-69 Winston Churchill to King Edward VII, 27 November 1907.

Collections of the Royal Geographical Society (RGS). London, UK.

CB6/2290 Gerald Waller: Correspondence.
LMS/P22 'Account of travel in East Africa: journeys through Kutu and exploration of the Ulanga, 1888', by Joachim Graf von Pfeil.
SSC/136 Joseph Thomson: Observations, Africa. Tanzania S.83, Preliminary Survey of the Proposed Railway Line from Ulanga Plain.

German Federal Archives – Bundesarchiv (BArch). Koblenz, Germany.

B 213/33060, Technische hilfe für Tansania: Zuschuss zum Kilombero-Projekt Kenaf.
R 1001/278/66–84, Heinrich Fonck, 'Bericht uber die wirtschaftliche Verhältnisse in der Ulangaebene und ihre Nachbargebieten', Dar es Salaam, 15 January 1908.

The National Archives of the UK (TNAUK). London, UK.

- CO   Colonial Office
- DO   Dominion Office
- FCO Foreign and Commonwealth Office
- FD   Medical Research Council
- OD   Overseas Development
- WO   War Office

Tanzania National Archives (TNA). Dar es Salaam, Tanzania.

Accession 61   Eastern Province
Accession 213   Ministry for Agriculture and Co-operative Development
Accession 460   Labour Department
Accession 461   Ulanga District
Accession 601   Ministry of Communications and Construction

MF.17 Mahenge District Book. 2 vols. 1922–1949. Secretariat Files

University of Oxford, Bodleian Libraries (OBL). Oxford, UK.

Mss.Afr.s.1175, Clement Gillman papers.
MSS.Afr.s.1295, M. J. W. English papers.
MSS.Afr.s.2228, Photographs of Kiberege taken by Arthur Theodore Culwick, 1931–37.

Wellcome Collection for Contemporary Archives (WCCA). London, UK.

WTI/TRY, Wellcome Museum of Medical Science Trypanosomiasis Collection

Oral Histories and Interviews

Thomas Likalagala, Sonjo, 3–5 July 2019.
Ally Mtemangani, Sonjo, 4 July 2019.
Rashidi Kinyaga, Sonjo, 5 July 2019.
Simon Kinyaga, Sonjo, 6 July 2019.
Juma Juma Kiswanya, Mgudeni, 7 July 2019.
Hamisi Simba Mkuti, Mkula, 8 July 2019.
Yayaha Kassimu, Ifakara, 9 July 2019.
Mzee Liseki, Lumemo, 10 July 2019.
Bibi Madenge, Kitongoji cha Magoa, 11 July 2019.
Binti Mwanahanji, Kitongoji cha Magoa, 11 July 2019.
Mzee J. Kiwenji, Kitongoji cha Igombati, 11 July 2019.
Mzee Mhomela, Kitongoji cha Magoa, 11 July 2019.
Steven Kivurenge, Ifakara, 12 July 2019.
Alfons Muonga, Kivukoni, 14 July 2019.
Mashaka Kipye, Mahenge, 15 July 2019.
Father Aristides Luwanda, Mahenge, 16 July 2019 and via call, 28 October 2020.
Father Nikas Kiuko, Mahenge, 16 July 2019.
Father Abdon Mkope, Kwiro, 17 July 2019.
Joseph Mkude, Mahenge, 18 July 2019.
Juma Kapilima, Mahenge, 18 July 2019.
Abraham Mwaikwila, Mahenge, 20 July 2019.
Hamisi Saidi Salum, Mang'ula, 14 October 2019.
Graham Anderson, Dar es Salaam, 22 October 2019.
Alfons Muonga, Kivukoni, 29 June 2020 *
Bibi Kutabika, Namwawala, 30 June 2020 *
Beda Goah, Mofu, 5 July 2020 *
Alvenus Ngwila, Mofu, 5–6July 2020 *
Raphael Mbaruka, Mofu, 6 July 2020 *
Nyota Adam, Kivukoni, 7 July 2020 *
Mama Njoka Mahenge, Lumemo, 8 July 2020 *
Mzee Macha, Lumemo, 8 July 2020 *
Mwalimu Ngwega, Lumemo, 8 July 2020 *
Father Paschal Luhengo, Itete, 12 December 2020.

Simran Bindra, Mbingu, 15 December 2020.
Mama Luwanda, Sonjo, 18 December 2020.
Joseph Rugai Mukamu, Mikumi, 18 December 2020.
Tarquin Olivier, London, 10 March 2021.
Ryan Skaife, via call, 12 September 2021.
*Interviews marked * were conducted by Francis Ching'ota.*

Government Publications

I. Government of Tanganyika/Tanzania

Tanganyika. *Report of the Tanganyika Railway Commission* (London: Crown Agents, 1930).

Tanganyika. *Tsetse Reclamation Annual Report for the year ended 31st March, 1929* (Dar es Salaam: Government Printer, 1930).

Tanganyika. *Tanganyika Railway Division. Appendices to the Report of the Tanganyika Railway Commission containing Oral Evidence and Memoranda.* (London: Crown Agents for the Colonies, 1930).

Tanganyika. Medical Department. *Sleeping Sickness Problem in the Western and Lake Provinces, and in relation to Uganda.* Sessional Paper No. 7 (Dar es Salaam: Government Printer, 1933).

Tanganyika. *Blue Book for the year ending 1938* (Dar es Salaam: Government Printer, 1939).

Tanganyika. *Report of the Central Development Committee* (Dar es Salaam: Government Printer, 1940).

Tanganyika. *An Outline of Post-War Development Proposals* (Dar es Salaam: Government Printer, 1944).

Tanganyika. Clement Gillman. Water Consultant's Report, No. 6 (1940): *A Reconnaissance Survey of the Hydrology of Tanganyika Territory in its Geographical Settings* (Dar es Salaam: Government Printer, 1944).

Tanganyika. Development Commission. *A Ten-Year Development and Welfare Plan for Tanganyika Territory* (Dar es Salaam: Government Printer, 1946).

Tanganyika. *Proposed Branch Railway from Kilosa to Mikumi* (Dar es Salaam: Government Printer, 1958).

Tanganyika. Lupiro Farm: *Accounts, Reports of the Director of Audit and Report of the Director of Agriculture for period of operation as a commercial enterprise 1st July, 1955 to 31st December, 1957 together with Final Realisation Account and Summary* (Dar es Salaam: Government Printer, 1959).

Tanganyika. *Tanganyika Agricultural Corporation: Report and Accounts, 1958–59* (Dar es Salaam: Government Printer, 1960).

Tanganyika. *Tanganyika Agricultural Corporation: Report and Accounts 1960–61* (Dar es Salaam: Government Printer, 1961).

Tanganyika. *Tanganyika Agricultural Corporation: Report and Accounts 1961–62* (Dar es Salaam: Government Printer, 1963).

Tanganyika. *Tanganyika Agricultural Corporation: Report and Accounts, 1962–1963* (Dar es Salaam: Government Printer, 1964).

Tanganyika. *Development Plan for Tanganyika, 1961–64* (Dar es Salaam: Government Printer, 1961).
Tanganyika. *Souvenir Catalogue: Tanganyika 1961 Independence Exhibition* (Arusha: Tanganyika Publications, 1961).
Tanganyika. *Proposals of the Tanganyika Government for a Republic* (Dar es Salaam: Government Printer, 1962).
Tanganyika. Tanganyika Information Services, Press Release: 'Mr Bryceson Returns from Europe with Promises of Aid', 11 May 1962.
United Republic of Tanganyika and Zanzibar. *Tanganyika Five-Year Plan for Economic and Social Development: 1st July, 1964 – 30th June, 1969*. 3 vols. (Dar es Salaam: Government Printer, 1964).
United Republic of Tanzania. Ministry of Lands, Settlement and Water Development. *The Rural Settlement Commission: A Report on the Village Settlement Programme from the Inception of the Rural Settlement Commission to 31st December, 1965* (Dar es Salaam: Rural Settlement Commission, 1966).
United Republic of Tanzania. *Second Five-Year Plan for Economic and Social Development, 1st July, 1969 – 30th June, 1974. Volume I: General Analysis* (Dar es Salaam: Government Printer, 1969).
United Republic of Tanzania. *Second Five-Year Plan for Economic and Social Development, 1st July, 1969 – 30th June, 1974. Volume III: Regional Perspectives* (Dar es Salaam: Government Printer, 1970).
United Republic of Tanzania, 'Detailed Engineering Design of Kilombero Bridge and its Approach Roads: Environmental Scoping Report', Scoping Report, 17 April 2009 (Dar es Salaam: Ministry of Infrastructure Development, 2009).
United Republic of Tanzania. *Halmashauri ya Wilaya ya Kilombero, Rasimu ya Mpango wa Matumizi Bora ya Ardhi wa Kijiji cha Sonjo, 2012–2022* (Dar es Salaam: NLUPC, 2012).
United Republic of Tanzania. 'Sinking of ferry at Kilombero River', Crime and Traffic Incidents: Statistics Report, January to December 2016 (Dar es Salaam: Tanzania Police Force Headquarters, 2017).

II. Government of the UK

Great Britain and W.G.A. Ormsby-Gore. *Report of the East Africa Commission* (London: HMSO, 1925).
Great Britain. Colonial Office. *First Interim Report of the Colonial Development Advisory Committee Covering the Period 1st August 1929 – 28th February 1930* (London: HMSO, 1930).
Great Britain. Colonial Office. Gerald Lacey and Robert Watson. *East Africa Rice Mission Report, 1948* (London: HMSO, 1949).
Great Britain. Colonial Office. *Notes on Some Agricultural Development Schemes in the British Colonial Territories*. 3rd ed., 2nd rev. (London: Colonial Office, 1955).
Great Britain. *East Africa Royal Commission 1953–1955 Report* (London: HMSO, 1956).
Great Britain. Colonial Office. *Despatches from the Governors of Kenya, Uganda,*

and Tanganyika and the Administrator, East Africa High Commission, commenting on the East Africa Royal Commission 1953–1955 Report (London: HMSO, 1956).
Great Britain. Colonial Office. *Tanganyika under United Kingdom Administration: Report to the United Nations for 1956* (London: HMSO, 1957).

Non-Governmental Actors' Publications and Reports

Arthur D. Little, Inc. *Tanganyika Industrial Development: A Preliminary Study of Bases for the Expansion of Industrial Processing Activities* (Dar es Salaam: Govt. Printer, 1961).
Chamber of Commerce and Agriculture, Dar es Salaam. *Memorandum on the Report of the Central Development Committee, Tanganyika* (Dar es Salaam: s.n., 1940).
East African Railways and Harbours. *Report on the Kilombero Railway Project* (Nairobi: EARH, 1961).
FAO. *Possibilities for Agriculture and Related Development in the Kilombero Valley: Report to the Government of Tanganyika* (Rome: FAO, 1964).
FAO. *The Rufiji Basin, Tanganyika: FAO Report to the Government of Tanganyika on the Preliminary Reconnaissance Survey of the Rufiji Basin*. 7 vols. (Rome: FAO, 1960).
FAO. *The Rufiji Basin, Tanganyika: Report on Agriculture and Trial Farms* (FAO: Rome, 1960).
ILACO. *Interim Report Concerning the Results of the Field Study (1965) in the Kilombero Valley – Tanzania. Volumes I and II* (The Hague: ILACO N.V./ NEDECO, 1966).
International Bank for Reconstruction and Development. *The Economic Development of Tanganyika* (Baltimore: John Hopkins Press, 1961).
International Bank for Reconstruction and Development and International Development Association (World Bank). *Report and Recommendation of the President to the Executive Directors on a Proposed Loan and Credit to the United Republic of Tanzania for a Sugar Development Project*. Report No. P-1468-TA (Washington, D.C.: The Bank Group, 1974).
League of Nations. 'British Mandate for East Africa'. C. 449 (1) a. M. 345 (a). 1922. VI., 1 October 1922 (Geneva: Society of the League of Nations, 1922).
League of Nations. Permanent Mandates Commission. *Minutes of the Thirty-Seventh Session held at Geneva from December 12th to 21st, 1939* (Geneva: League of Nations, 1940).
Sir Alexander Gibb & Partners and Overseas Consultants, Inc. *Report on Central African Rail Link Development Survey*, vol. 1 (London: Government Printer, 1952).
UNESCO. *A Study on Strategies for Tackling the Problems of Rural Development with Particular Reference to the Role of the Education System* (Paris: UNESCO, 1982).
World Bank. 'Implementation completion and results report (IDA-38880) on a credit in the amount of SDR81.6 million (US$122 million equivalent) to the United Republic of Tanzania for the Central Transport Corridor Project', Report No. ICR1299, 19 June 2010 (Washington, D.C.: World Bank Group, 2010).

Secondary Sources

Adams, Vincanne, Michelle Murphy, and Adele E. Clarke. 'Anticipation: Technoscience, life, affect, temporality', *Subjectivity* 28 (2009), 246–265.

Adams, W.M. *Wasting the Rain: Rivers, People and Planning in Africa* (London: Earthscan, 1992).

Ahearne, Robert M. 'Development and progress as historical phenomena in Tanzania: "Maendeleo? We had that in the past"', *African Studies Review* 59:1 (2016), 77–96.

Allan, William. *The African Husbandman* (London: Oliver and Boyd, 1965).

Amery, L.S. *My Political Life. Volume One: War and Peace, 1914–1929* (London: Hutchinson, 1955).

Anderson, Benedict. *Imagined Communities: Reflections on the Origin and Spread of Nationalism* (London: Verso, 1985).

Anderson, David M. 'Depression, dust bowl, demography, and drought: The colonial state and soil conservation in East Africa during the 1930s', *African Affairs* 83:332 (1984), 321–43.

Anderson, David M. *Eroding the Commons: The Politics of Ecology in Baringo, Kenya 1890–1963* (Oxford: James Currey, 2002).

Appadurai, Arjun. *The Future as a Cultural Fact: Essays on the Global Condition* (London: Verso, 2013).

Apted, F. 'Sleeping sickness in Tanganyika: past, present, and future', *Transactions of The Royal Society of Tropical Medicine and Hygiene* 56:1 (1962), 15–29.

Armitage-Smith, Sydney. *Report on a Financial Mission to Tanganyika* (London: HMSO, 1932).

Arnold, David. '"Illusory riches": Representations of the tropical word, 1840–1950', *Singapore Journal of Tropical Geography* 21:2 (2002), 6–18.

Austin, Gareth. 'African economic development and colonial legacies', *International Development Policy* 1 (2010), 11–32.

Bamford, Andrew J., Daniella Ferrol-Schulte, and Hillary Smith. *The Status of the Ruipa Corridor Between the Selous Game Reserve and the Udzungwa Mountains* (London: Frontier, 2011).

Bates, Margaret L. 'Tanganyika: The development of a trust territory', *International Organization* 9:1 (1955), 32–51.

Battye, R.K.M. 'Kilombero,' *Tanganyika Notes and Records* 30 (1951), 1–5.

Beardall, William. 'Exploration of the Rufiji River under the Orders of the Sultan of Zanzibar', *Proceedings of the Royal Geographical Society and the Monthly Record* 3:11 (1881), 641–56.

Beck, A. *A History of the British Medical Administration of East Africa, 1900–1950* (Cambridge, 1970).

Beinart, William. 'Soil erosion, conservationism and ideas about development: A Southern African exploration, 1900–1960', *Journal of Southern African Studies* 11:1 (1984), 52–83.

Beinart, William. *The Rise of Conservation in Southern Africa: Settlers, Livestock and the Environment, 1770–1950* (Oxford: Oxford University Press, 2008).

Bennett, George. 'An outline history of TANU', *Makerere Journal* 7 (1963), 15–32.

Berger, John. *Ways of Seeing* (London: BBC and Penguin, 1972).

Bergius, Mikael, Tor A. Benjaminsen, and Mats Widgren, 'Green economy, Scandinavian investments and agricultural modernization in Tanzania', *Journal of Peasant Studies* 45:4 (2018), 1–28.

Bergius, Mikael, Tor A. Benjaminsen, Faustin Maganga, and Halvard Buhaug. 'Green economy, degradation narratives, and land-use conflicts in Tanzania', *World Development* 129 (2020), 1–13.

Berry, Sara. 'Hegemony on a shoestring: Indirect rule and access to agricultural land', *Africa: Journal of the International African Institute* 62:3 (1992), 327–55.

Berry, V. (ed.). *The Culwick Papers, 1934–1944: Population, Food and Health in Colonial Tanganyika* (London: Academy Books, 1994).

Biermann, Werner. *Tanganyika Railways, Carrier of Colonialism: An Account of Economic Indicators and Social Fragments* (Münster: LIT Verlag, 1995).

Biermann, Werner. 'Introduction: Contextualising poverty in Africa', in Werner Biermann and Humphrey P.B. Moshi (eds), *Contextualising Poverty in Tanzania: Historical Origins, Policy Failures and Recent Threads* (Dar es Salaam: Dar es Salaam University Press, 1997), 1–18.

Biswas, Asit K. 'Irrigation in India: Past and Present', *Journal of the Irrigation and Drainage Division* 91:1 (1965), 179–89.

Bohlen, Eberhard. *Crop Pests in Tanzania and their Control* (Hamburg: Verlag Paul Parey, 1973).

Boswell, Alexandra and Andrew Marshall. *Saving Our Forests: 1. Kilombero and the Udzungwa Lowlands* (Dar es Salaam: CIRCLE Books, 2011).

Bowles, Brian D. 'Export crops and underdevelopment in Tanganyika, 1929–61', *UTAFITI* 1:1 (1976), 71–85.

Braun, K. 'Der Reis in Deutsch-Ostafrika', *Berichte über land- und forstwirtschaft in Deutsch-Ostafrika* 3:4 (1908), 204–6.

Brennan, James R. 'Youth, the TANU Youth League, and managed vigilantism in Dar es Salaam, 1925–73' in Andrew Burton and Hélène Charton-Bigot (eds), *Generations Past: Youth in East African History* (Athens: Ohio University Press, 2010), 196–220.

Brennan, James R. *Taifa: Making Nation and Race in Urban Tanzania* (Athens: Ohio University Press, 2012).

Burgess, G. Thomas. 'Introduction to youth and citizenship in East Africa', *Africa Today* 51:3 (2005), vii–xxiv.

Burton, Andrew. 'Raw youth, school-leavers and the emergence of structural unemployment in late-colonial urban Tanganyika', *The Journal of African History* 47:3 (2006), 363–87.

Buxton, P.A. *Trypanosomiasis in Eastern Africa, 1947* (London: Colonial Office by His Majesty's Stationery Office, 1948).

Bryceson, D. 'Household, hoe and nation: Development policies of the Nyerere era' in Michael Hodd (ed.), *Tanzania after Nyerere* (London: Pinter, 1988), 36–48.

Callahan, M.D. 'NOMANSLAND: The British Colonial Office and the League of Nations Mandate for German East Africa, 1916–1920', *Albion* 25:3 (1993), 443–64.

Calvert, Alfred F. *German East Africa* (London: T. Werner Laurie, 1917).

Cameron, Donald. 'Native Administration in Tanganyika and Nigeria', *Journal of the Royal African Society* 36:145 (1937), 3–29.

Cameron, Donald. *My Tanganyika Service and Some Nigeria* (London: Allen and Unwin, 1939).

Chachage, Chambi. *Land Acquisition and Accumulation in Tanzania* (Dar es Salaam: PELUM, 2010).

Carroll, Toby. *Delusions of Development: The World Bank and the Post-Washington Consensus in Southeast Asia* (New York: Palgrave Macmillan)

Chambers, Robert. *Settlement Schemes in Tropical Africa: A Study of Organization and Development* (London: Routledge, 1969).

Cliffe, L. 'Nationalism and the reaction to enforced agricultural change in Tanganyika during the Colonial Period', in L. Cliffe and J. Saul (eds), *Socialism in Tanzania: Volume 1* (Dar es Salaam: East African Publishing House, 1972), 17–24.

Cliffe, L. and G.L. Cunningham. 'Ideology, organization and the settlement experience in Tanzania', in L. Cliffe and J. Saul (eds), *Socialism in Tanzania: Volume 2* (Dar es Salaam: East African Publishing House, 1973), 131–40.

Coghe, S. 'Sleeping sickness control and the transnational politics of mass chemo-prophylaxis in Portuguese colonial Africa', *Portuguese Studies Review* 25:1 (2017), 57–89.

Conte, Christopher A. 'Imperial Science, tropical ecology, and indigenous history: Tropical research stations in northeastern German East Africa, 1896 to the present', in Gregory Blue, Martin Bunton, and Ralph Croizier (eds), *Colonialism and the Modern World: Selected Studies* (Armonk, NY: M.E. Sharpe, 2002), 246–61.

Conte, Christopher A. *Highland Sanctuary: Environmental History in Tanzania's Usambara Mountains* (Athens: Ohio University Press, 2004).

Cooper, Frederick and Ann Laura Stoler (eds), *Tensions of Empire: Colonial Cultures in a Bourgeois World* (Berkeley: University of California Press, 1997).

Cooper, Frederick and Randall Packard, 'Introduction', in Frederick Cooper and Randall Packard (eds), *International Development and the Social Sciences: Essays on the History and Politics of Knowledge* (Berkeley: University of California Press, 1997), 1–41.

Cooper, Frederick. 'Writing the History of Development', *Journal of Modern European History* 8:1 (2010), 5–23.

Coulson, Andrew. *Tanzania: A Political Economy* (Oxford: Clarendon Press, 1982).

Cowen, Michael and Robert Shenton. *Doctrines of Development* (London: Routledge, 1996).

Culwick, A.T. 'The hoe in Ulanga,' *Man* 34 (1934), 9.

Culwick, A.T. 'Ngindo honey-hunters', *Man* 36 (1936), 73–4.

Culwick, A.T. 'The population trend', *Tanganyika Notes and Records* 11 (1941), 13–17.

Culwick, A.T. 'New beginnings', *Tanganyika Notes and Records* 15 (1943), 1–6.

Culwick, A.T. *Britannia Waives the Rules* (Cape Town: Nasionale Boekhandel, 1963).

Culwick, A.T. *Don't Feed the Tiger* (Cape Town: Nasionale Boekhandel, 1968).

Culwick, A.T. and G.M. Culwick. *Ubena of the Rivers* (London: George Allen & Unwin, 1935).

Culwick, A.T. and G.M. Culwick. 'Ulanga: The Valley of the Kilombero River', *East African Annual, 1935–36* (Nairobi: East African Standard, 1936), 65–70.

Culwick, A.T. and G.M. Culwick. 'What the Wabena think of indirect rule', *Journal of the Royal African Society* 36:143 (1937), 176–93.

Bibliography

Culwick, A.T. and G.M. Culwick. 'A study of population in Ulanga, Tanganyika Territory', *The Sociological Review* 30:4 (1938), 365–379.
Culwick, A.T. and G.M. Culwick. 'A study of factors governing the food supply in Ulanga, Tanganyika Territory', *The East African Medical Journal* 16 (1939), 43–61.
Dahl, Roald. *Going Solo* (London: Jonathan Cape, 1986).
Deckard, Sharae. *Paradise Discourse, Imperialism, and Globalization: Exploiting Eden* (London: Routledge, 2010).
Decker, Corrie and Elisabeth McMahon. *The Idea of Development in Africa* (Cambridge: Cambridge University Press, 2020).
Dinesen, L., Thomas Lehmberg, Marcel C. Rahner, and J. Fjeldså. 'Conservation priorities for the forests of the Udzungwa Mountains, Tanzania, based on primates, duikers and birds', *Biological Conservation* 99 (2001), 223–236.
Doyle, Shane. 'Social disease and social science: The intellectual influence of non-medical research on policy and practice in the Colonial Medical Service in Tanganyika and Uganda', in A. Greenwood (ed.), *Beyond the State: The Colonial Medical Service in British Africa* (Manchester: Manchester University Press, 2015), 126–52.
Eberlie, Richard F. *The Winds and Wounds of Change* (Bristol: Bluemoon, 2016).
'Editorial note', *Tanganyika Notes and Records* 15 (1943), n.p.
'Editorial notes', *Journal of the Royal African Society* 32:126 (1933), 94–107.
Ehrlich, Cyril. 'Some aspects of economic policy in Tanganyika, 1945–60', *The Journal of Modern African Studies* 2:2 (1964), 265–77.
Elton, J.F. *Travels and Researches among the Lakes and Mountains of Eastern and Central Africa, from the journals of the late J.F. Elton, edited and completed by H.B. Cotterill* (London: John Murray, 1879).
Engelhardt, Philipp. 'Meine reise durch Uhehe, die Ulanganiederung und Ubena über das Livingstone-Gebirge zum Nyassa,' *Beiträge zur Kolonialpolitik und Kolonialwirtschaft, Dritter Jahrgang, 1901–1902* (Berlin: Deutschen Kolonialgesellschaft, 1903), 69–98.
Ferguson, James. *The Anti-Politics Machine: "Development," Depoliticization, and Bureaucratic Power in Lesotho* (Minneapolis: University of Minnesota Press, 1994).
Ford, John. *The Role of Trypanosomiasis in African History* (Oxford: Oxford University Press, 1971).
Fisher, E. 'Forced resettlement, rural livelihoods and wildlife conservation along the Ugalla River in Tanzania', in D. Chatty and M. Colchester (eds), *Conservation and Mobile Indigenous Peoples: Displacement Forced Settlement, and Sustainable Development* (Oxford: Oxford University Press, 2002), 119–41.
Freyhold, Michaela von. *Ujamaa Villages in Tanzania: Analysis of a Social Experiment* (New York: Monthly Review Press, 1979).
Furedi, F. 'The demobilized African soldier and the blow to white prestige', in D. Killingray and D. Omissi (eds), *Guardians of Empire* (Manchester: Manchester University Press, 2017), 179–97.
Gailey, Harry. *Sir Donald Cameron: Colonial Governor* (Stanford: Hoover Institution Press, 1974).
Geiger, Susan. *TANU Women: Gender and Culture in the Making of Tanganyikan Nationalism, 1955–1965* (Oxford: James Currey, 1997).

'Geographical notes', *Proceedings of the Royal Geographical Society and Monthly Record of Geography* 3:5 (1881), 305–15.
'Geographical notes', *Proceedings of the Royal Geographical Society and Monthly Record of Geography* 9:1 (1887), 47–53.
Ghai, Dharam P. (ed.). *Portrait of a Minority: Asians in East Africa* (Nairobi: Oxford University Press, 1965).
Giblin, James L. 'Trypanosomiasis control in African history: an evaded issue?' *The Journal of African History*, 31:1 (1990), 59–80.
Giblin, James L. *The Politics of Environmental Control in Northeastern Tanzania, 1840–1940* (Philadelphia: University of Pennsylvania Press, 1992).
Giblin, James L. and Jamie Monson. 'Introduction', in James L. Giblin and Jamie Monson (eds), *Maji Maji: Lifting the Fog of War* (Leiden: Brill, 2010), 1–30.
Gillman, Clement. 'South-West Tanganyika Territory', *The Geographical Journal* 69:2 (1927), 97–126.
Gillman, Clement. *Report on the Preliminary Surveys for a Railway Line to Open Up the South-West of Tanganyika Territory, 1929* (London: Crown Agents for the Colonies, 1929).
Gillman, Clement. 'A short history of the Tanganyika Railways', *Tanganyika Notes and Records* 13 June, 1942), 14–56.
Gissibl, Bernhard. *The Nature of German Imperialism: Conservation and the Politics of Wildlife in Colonial East Africa* (New York: Berghahn, 2019).
Götzen, Gustav Graf von. *Deutsch-Ostafrika im Aufstand, 1905–06* (Berlin: Dietrich Reimer, 1909).
Graham, James D. 'The Tanzam Railway: Consolidating the people's development and building the internal economy', *Africa Today* 21:3 (1974), 27–42.
Green, Maia. *The Development State: Aid, Culture and Civil Society in Tanzania* (Woodbridge: James Currey, 2014).
Gregory, R.G. *India and East Africa: A History of Race Relations within the British Empire, 1890–1939* (Oxford: Clarendon Press, 1971).
Gunderson, Frank. *Sukuma Songs from Western Tanzania* (Leiden: Brill, 2010).
Gwassa, G.C.K. and John Iliffe (eds). 'Records of the Maji Maji Rising: Part One', *Historical Association of Tanzania*, Paper No. 4 (Nairobi: East African Publishing House, 1967).
Hall, R. and H. Peyman, *The Great Uhuru Railway* (London: Gollanz, 1976).
Hambidge, Gove. *Story of FAO* (New York: Van Nostrand, 1955).
Hatchell, G.W. 'An early "sleeping-sickness settlement" in south-western Tanganyika', *Tanganyika Notes and Records* 27 (1949), 60–4.
Havinden, M.A. and D. Meredith. *Colonialism and Development: Britain and its Tropical Colonies, 1850–1960* (London: Routledge, 1995).
Havnevik, Kjell J. *Tanzania: the Limits to Development from Above* (Uppsala: Nordiska Afrikainstituet, 1993).
Haynes, Jane Banfield. 'The British East Africa High Commission: An imperial experiment' in Harvey Dyck and H. Peter Krosby (eds), *Empire and Nations: Essays in Honour of Frederic H. Soward* (Toronto: University of Toronto Press, 2017), 180–94.
Headrick, D.R. 'Sleeping sickness epidemics and colonial responses in East and Central Africa, 1900–1940', *PLoS Neglected Tropical Diseases*, 8:4 (2014), 1–8.

Hide, G. 'History of sleeping sickness in East Africa', *Clinical Microbiology Review*, 12:1 (1999), 112–125.
Hinds, Allister. 'Sterling and decolonization in the British Empire, 1945–1958', *Social and Economic Studies* 48:4 (1999), 97–116.
Hoag, Heather J. and May-Britt Öhman. 'Turning water into power: Debates over the development of Tanzania's Rufiji River Basin', *Technology and Culture* 49:3 (2008), 624–51.
Hill, J.F.R. and J.P. Moffett. *Tanganyika: A Review of its Resources and their Development* (Dar es Salaam: Government Printer, 1955).
Hill, M.F. *Permanent Way: The Story of the Tanganyika Railways, Volume II* (Nairobi: EARH, 1950).
Hodge, Joseph M. *Triumph of the Expert: Agrarian Doctrines of Development and the Legacies of British Colonialism* (Athens: Ohio University Press, 2007).
Hodge, Joseph M. 'Epilogue: Taking stock, looking ahead', in Joseph M. Hodge, Gerald Hödl, and Martina Kopf (eds), *Developing Africa: Concepts and Practices in Twentieth-Century Colonialism* (Manchester: Manchester University Press, 2014), 367–76.
Honey, Martha. 'Asian Industrial Activities in Tanganyika', *Tanzania Notes and Records* 75 (1974), 55–70.
Hoppe, K.A. *Lords of the Fly: Sleeping Sickness Control in British East Africa, 1900–1960* (Westport, CT: Praeger, 2003).
Hoyle, Brian. *Gillman of Tanganyika, 1882–1946: The Life and Work of a Pioneer Geographer* (Aldershot: Gower, 1987).
Hu, Zhichao. 'The Past, Present and Future of the Tanzania-Zambia Railroad', *Economic Research of the Railroads* (2000), 46–7.
Huxley, Elspeth. *White Man's Country: Lord Delamere and the Making of Kenya* (London: Macmillan, 1935).
Hydén, Göran. *No Shortcuts to Progress: African Development Management in Perspective* (Nairobi: Heinemann, 1983).
Iliffe, John. 'The effects of the Maji Maji Rebellion of 1905–06 on German occupation policy in East Africa', in Prosser Gifford and Wm. Roger Louis (eds), *Britain and Germany in Africa: Imperial Rivalry and Colonial Rule* (New Haven, CT: Yale University Press, 1967), 557–76.
Iliffe, John. *Tanganyika under German Rule, 1905–1912* (Cambridge: Cambridge University Press, 1969).
Iliffe, John. *Agricultural Change in Modern Tanganyika* (Nairobi: East African Publishing House, 1971).
Iliffe, John. *A Modern History of Tanganyika* (Cambridge: Cambridge University Press, 1979).
Isaacman, Allen and Barbara. *Dams, Displacement and the Delusion of Development: Cahora Bassa and its Legacies in Mozambique, 1965–2007* (Athens: Ohio University Press, 2013).
Jack, E.M. 'Railway development in Tanganyika Territory', *The Geographical Journal* 79:2 (1932), 117–24.
Jätzold, Ralph, and Eckhard Baum. *The Kilombero Valley* (Munich: Welftorum Verlag, 1968).

Jennings, Michael. '"A very real war": Popular participation in development in Tanzania during the 1950s and 1960s', *The International Journal of African Historical Studies* 40:1 (2007), 71–95.
Jennings, Michael. *Surrogates of the State: NGOs, Development and Ujamaa in Tanzania* (Bloomfield: Kumarian Press, 2008).
Joelson, F.S. *The Tanganyika Territory (formerly German East Africa): Characteristics and Potentialities* (London: T. Fisher Unwin, 1920).
Johansson, Emma L. and Ellinor Isgren. 'Local perceptions of land-use change: using participatory art to reveal direct and indirect socio-environmental effects of land acquisitions in Kilombero Valley, Tanzania', *Ecology and Society* 22:1 (2017), Article 3.
Johnston, Keith. 'Native Routes in East Africa, from Dar-es-Salaam towards Lake Nyassa', *Proceedings of the Royal Geographical Society and the Monthly Record* 1:7 (1879), 417–22.
Jones, G.I. 'Social anthropology in Nigeria during the colonial period', *Africa: Journal of the International African Institute*, 44: 3 (1974), 280–89.
Jones, Trevor, Andrew J. Bamford, and Daniella Ferrol-Schulte. 'Vanishing wildlife corridors and options for restoration: A case study from Tanzania', *Tropical Conservation* 5:4 (2012), 463–74.
Kaplan, Benyamin. *New Settlement and Agricultural Development in Tanganyika: Report and Recommendations to the Government of Tanganyika resulting from a study mission sponsored by the Government of Israel* (Be'er Sheva: State of Israel, 1961).
Karioki, James N. *Tanzania's Human Revolution* (University Park: Pennsylvania State University Press, 1979).
Kiepert, Richard. 'Begleitworte zur Karte der Nyasa-Expedition', *Mittheilungen von Forschungsreisenden und Gelehrten aus den Deutschen Schutzgebieten: VII* (Berlin: Ernst Siegfried Mittler, 1894), 296–305.
Kimambo, Isaria K., Gregory H. Maddox, and Salvatory S. Nyanto. *A New History of Tanzania* (Dar es Salaam: Mkuki na Nyota, 2017).
Kirk-Green, Anthony. *Symbol of Authority: The British District Officer in Africa* (London: Bloomsbury, 2006).
Kjekshus, Helge. *Ecology Control and Economic Development in East African History: The Case of Tanganyika, 1850–1950*, 2nd ed. (London: Heinemann, 1997).
Knight, C.G. 'The ecology of sleeping sickness', *Annals of the Association of American Geographers* 61:1 (1971), 23–44.
Koponen, Juhani. *People and Production in Late Precolonial Tanzania: History and Structures* (Helsinki: Finnish Historical Society, 1995).
Künhe, Winrich and Bernard von Plate. 'Two Germanys in Africa', *Africa Report* 25:4 (1980), 11–16.
Lacey, Gerald, Claude Inglis, and A.M.R. Montague. 'Irrigation in India: Past and Present', *Journal of the Irrigation and Drainage Division* 91:1 (1965).
Lacey, Gerald, Claude Inglis, and A.M.R. Montague. 'Discussion of "Irrigation in India: Past and Present"', *Journal of the Irrigation and Drainage Division* 91:4 (1965), 123–30.
Lachenal, G. *The Lomidine Files: The Untold Story of a Medical Disaster*, trans. Noémi Tousignant (Baltimore: Johns Hopkins University Press, 2014).

Lal, Priya. 'Self-reliance and the state: The multiple meanings of development in early post-colonial Tanzania', *Africa* 82:2 (2012), 212–34.
Lal, Priya. *African Socialism in Postcolonial Tanzania: Between the Village and the World* (Cambridge: Cambridge University Press, 2015).
Lameck, Dudley. *My Autobiography: A Personal Journey in the Life of a Poor African Boy* (Bloomington, IN: Xlibris, 2012).
Lawi, Y. 'Tanzania's Operation *Vijiji* and local ecological consciousness: The case of eastern Iraqwland, 1974–1976', *The Journal of African History* 48 (2007), 69–93.
Leemhuis, Constanze, Frank Thonfeld, Kristian Näschen, Stefanie Steinbach, Javier Muro, Adrian Strauch, Ander López, Giuseppe Daconto, Ian Games, and Bernd Diekkrüger. 'Sustainability in the food-water-ecosystem nexus: The role of land use and land cover change for water resources and ecoytems in the Kilombero Wetland, Tanzania', *Sustainability* 9:9 (2017), 1–18.
Leubuscher, Charlotte. *Tanganyika Territory: A Study of Economic Policy under Mandate* (London: Oxford University Press, 1944).
Lieder, Georg. 'Beobachtungen auf der Ubena-Nyasa Expedition vom 11 November 1893 bis 30 Marz 1894', *Mittheilungen von Forschungsreisenden und Gelehrten aus den Deutschen Schutzgebieten: VII* (Berlin: Ernst Siegfried Mittler, 1894), 271–77.
Lingelbach, Jochen. 'Refugee Camps as Forgotten Portals of Globalization: Polish World War II Refugees in British Colonial East Africa', *Comparativ* 27: 3–4 (2017), 78–93.
Listowel, Judith. *The Making of Tanganyika* (London: Chatto & Windus, 1965).
Longford, Michael. *The Flags Changed at Midnight* (Leominster: Gracewing, 2001).
Lonsdale, John. 'African pasts in Africa's future', *Canadian Journal of African Studies* 23:1 (1989), 126–46.
Low, D.A. and John M. Lonsdale. 'Introduction: Towards the new order 1945–63', in D.A. Low and Alison Smith (eds), *Oxford History of East Africa: Vol. III* (Oxford: Clarendon Press, 1977), 1–64.
Lumley, E.K. *Forgotten Mandate: A British District Officer in Tanganyika* (London: C. Hurst, 1976).
Lyons, M. 'From "death camps" to *cordon sanitaire*: the development of sleeping sickness policy in the Uele district of the Belgian Congo, 1903–14', *The Journal of African History*, 26 (1985), 69–91.
Lyons, M. *The Colonial Disease: A Social History of Sleeping Sickness in Northern Zaire, 1900–1940* (Cambridge: Cambridge University Press, 1992).
Maclean, G. 'Sleeping sickness measures in Tanganyika Territory', *Kenya and East African Medical Journal* 7 (1930), 120–6.
Maddox, Gregory, James Giblin, and Isaria N. Kimambo (eds). *Custodians of the Land: Ecology and Culture in the History of Tanzania* (Dar es Salaam: Mkuki na Nyota, 1996).
Marsh, Zoë. *East Africa through Contemporary Records* (London: Cambridge University Press, 1961).
Martin, Ged. *Past Futures: The Impossible Necessity of History* (Toronto: University of Toronto Press, 2004).
Maxwell, Sean L., R. Fuller, and T. Brooks. 'Biodiversity: The ravages of guns, nets and bulldozers', *Nature* 536 (2016), 143–5.

McCann, James C. *People of the Plow: An Agricultural History of Ethiopia, 1800–1990* (Madison: University of Wisconsin Press, 1995).
McCann, James C. *Green Land, Brown Land, Black Land: An Environmental History of Africa, 1800–1990* (Oxford: James Currey, 1999).
McHenry, Dean. *Tanzania's Ujamaa Villages: The Implementation of a Rural Development Strategy* (Berkeley: University of California, 1979).
Moffett, J.P. 'A strategic retreat from tsetse fly: Uyowa and Bugomba concentrations, 1937', *Tanganyika Notes and Records* 7 (1939), 35–7.
Monson, Jamie. 'From commerce to colonization: A history of the rubber trade in the Kilombero Valley of Tanzania, 1890–1914', *African Economic History* 21 (1993), 113–30.
Monson, Jamie. 'Canoe-building under colonialism: Forestry & food policies in the Inner Kilombero Valley, 1920–40' in Gregory Maddox, James Giblin, and Isaria N. Kimambo (eds), *Custodians of the Land: Ecology and Culture in the History of Tanzania* (Oxford: James Currey, 1996), 200–12.
Monson, Jamie. 'Memory, migration and the authority of history in Southern Tanzania, 1860–1960', *The Journal of African History* 41:3 (2000), 347–72.
Monson, Jamie. *Africa's Freedom Railway: How a Chinese Development Project Changed Lives and Livelihoods in Tanzania* (Bloomington: Indiana University Press, 2009).
'The Monthly Record', *The Geographical Journal* 14:6 (1899), 660–1.
Morgan, B.H. 'Power alcohol', *Royal United Services Institution Journal* 71:482 (1926), 373–6.
Muehlenbeck, Philip E. *Betting on the Africans: John F. Kennedy's Courting of African Nationalist Leaders* (Oxford: Oxford University Press, 2012).
Müller-Mahn, Detlef, Kennedy Mkutu, and Eric Kioko. 'Megaprojects – mega failures? The politics of aspiration and the transformation of rural Kenya', *The European Journal of Development Research* 33 (2021), 1069–90.
Munishi, Subira Eva and Graham Hewitt. 'Degradation of Kilombero Valley Ramsar Wetlands in Tanzania', *Physics and Chemistry of the Earth* 112 (2019), 216–27.
Mutukwa, Kasuka Simwinji. 'Tanzania-Zambia Railway: Imperial dream becomes pan-African reality', *Africa Report* 17:1 (1972), 10–15.
Mwakikagile, Godfrey. *Nyerere and Africa: The End of an Era* (Dar es Salaam: New Africa Press, 2010).
Mwase, Ngila. 'The Tanzania-Zambia Railway: The Chinese loan and the pre-investment analysis revisited', *The Journal of Modern African Studies* 21:3 (1983), 535–43.
'Nachrichten aus den deutschen Schutzgebieten: Deutsch-Ostafrika', *Deutsches Kolonialblatt: Amtsblatt für die Schutzgebiete des Deutschen Reichs* 8:21 (25 October 1897).
Nellis, John R. *A Theory of Ideology: The Tanzanian Example* (Nairobi: Oxford University Press, 1972).
Neumann, R. 'Africa's "last wilderness": Reordering space for political and economic control in colonial Tanzania', *Africa: Journal of the International African Institute* 71:4 (2001), 641–65.
Novack, George. *Understanding History* (New York: Pathfinder Press, 1995).

Nyerere, Julius K. *The Second Scramble* (Dar es Salaam: Printed by the Tanganyika Standard, 1962).
Nyerere, Julius K. *Freedom and Unity: A Selection from Writings and Speeches, 1952–65* (Dar es Salaam: Oxford University Press, 1966).
Nyerere, Julius K. *Ujamaa: Essays on Socialism* (Dar es Salaam: Oxford University Press, 1968).
Nyerere, Julius K. *Man and Development* (Dar es Salaam: Oxford University Press, 1974).
Nyerere, Julius K. 'Non-alignment and its future prospects', *India Quarterly* 39:1 (1983), 1–5.
Nzomo, Maria. 'The Foreign Policy of Tanzania: From Cold War to Post-Cold War', in Stephen Wright (ed.), *African Foreign Policies* (New York: Routledge, 1999), 182–198.
'Obituary: Alexander McMenegal Telford, 1895–1963', *Proceedings of the Institution of Civil Engineers* 32:4 (1965), 697–98.
Oswald, F. *Alone in the Sleeping-Sickness Country* (London: Kegan Paul, Trench, Tübner & Co., 1923).
Paice, Edward. *Tip and Run: The Untold Tragedy of the Great War in Africa* (London: Weidenfeld and Nicolson, 2007).
Paice, Edward. *Lost Lion of Empire* (London: Harper Collins, 2011).
Pels, P. 'The pidginization of Uluguru politics: Administrative ethnography and the paradoxes of indirect rule', *American Ethnologist*, 23:4 (1996), 738–61.
Pels, P. 'Global "experts" and "African" minds: Tanganyikan anthropology as public and secret service, 1925–61', *The Journal of the Royal Anthropological Institute* 17:4 (2011), 788–810.
Perham, Margery. 'Some Problems of Indirect Rule in Africa', *Journal of the Royal Society of Arts* 82:4252 (1934), 689–710.
Perrenoud, Marc. 'Switzerland's relationship with Africa during decolonisation and the beginnings of development cooperation', *International Development Policy* 1 (2010), 77–93.
Peters, P.E. 'Land appropriation, surplus people and a battle over visions of agrarian futures in Africa', *Journal of Peasant Studies* 40:3 (2013), 537–62.
Pfeil, Joachim Graf von. 'Die Erforschung des Ulanga-Gebietes', *Petermanns geographische Mitteilungen* 12 (1886), 353–63.
Phillips, John. 'Ecology in the service of man in British territories in Africa: Selected aspects and examples', *Vegetatio* 5/6:1 (1954), 72–82.
Pratt, Cranford. 'Foreign-policy issues and the emergence of socialism in Tanzania, 1961–8', *International Journal* 30:3 (1975), 445–70.
Pratt, Cranford. *The Critical Phase in Tanzania, 1945–68: Nyerere and the Emergence of a Socialist Strategy* (Cambridge: Cambridge University Press, 1976).
Prittwitz und Gaffron, Georg von. 'Untersuchung der Schiffbarkeit des Kihansi und eines Theiles des Ulangaflusses', *Mittheilungen von Forschungsreisenden und Gelehrten aus den Deutschen Schutzgebieten*, 11 (Berlin: Ernst Siegfried Mittler, 1898), 255–83.
Prothero, G.W. (ed.). *Tanganyika (German East Africa)* (London: HMSO, 1920).
Puxley, F.L. *In African Game Tracks: Wanderings with A Rifle through Eastern Africa* (London: H.F. & G. Witherby, 1929).

Rakove, Robert B. *Kennedy, Johnson, and the Nonaligned World* (New York: Cambridge University Press, 2013).
'Recent Changes in the Map of East Africa', *Proceedings of the Royal Geographical Society and Monthly Record of Geography*, 9:8 (1887), 490–6.
Redmayne, Alison. 'Mkwawa and the Hehe Wars', *The Journal of African History* 9:3 (1968), 409–36.
Reid, Richard. 'Africa's revolutionary nineteenth century and the idea of the "Scramble"', *The American Historical Review* 126:4 (2021), 1424–47.
Ricciardi, Lorenzo and Mirella Ricciardi. *African Rainbow: Across Africa by Boat* (London: Ebury Press, 1989).
Roberts, George. *Revolutionary State-Making in Dar es Salaam: African Liberation and the Global Cold War, 1961–1974* (Cambridge: Cambridge University Press, 2021).
Rodney, Walter. *How Europe Underdeveloped Africa* (Cape Town: Pambazuka Press, 2012).
Ruthenberg, Hans. *Agricultural Development in Tanganyika* (Berlin: Springer-Verlag, 1964).
Sathyamurthy, T. V. 'Tanzania's non-aligned role in international relations', *India Quarterly* 37:1 (1981), 1–23.
Sayers, Gerald (ed.). *The Handbook of Tanganyika* (London: Macmillan, 1930).
Schilling, Britta. *Postcolonial Germany: Memories of Empire in a Decolonized Nation* (Oxford: Oxford University Press, 2014).
Schneider, Leander. *Government of Development: Peasants and Politicians in Postcolonial Tanzania* (Bloomington: Indiana University Press, 2014).
Scott, James. *Seeing like a State: How Certain Schemes to Improve the Human Condition Have Failed* (New Haven, CT: Yale University Press, 1998).
Seki, Hamidu A., Deo D. Shirima, and Colin J. Courtney Mustaphi. 'The impact of land use and land cover change on biodiversity within and adjacent to Kibasira Swamp in Kilombero Valley, Tanzania', *African Journal of Ecology* 56:3 (2018), 518–27.
Sircar, Parbati K. 'The Great Uhuru (Freedom) Railway: China's Link to Africa', *China Report* 14:2 (1978), 15–24.
'Sleeping sickness in Tanganyika Territory', *The Lancet* (3 July 1926), 29–30.
Stanford Research Institute. *Tanzania-Zambia Highway Study* (Menlo Park: Stanford Research Institute, 1966).
Steel, R.W. 'The future of East Africa: Review of the report by the East Africa Royal Commission, 1953–1955' *The Geographical Journal* 122:3 (1956), 366–9.
Stengers, Jean. 'British and German imperial rivalry: A conclusion', in Prosser Gifford and Wm. Roger Louis (eds), *Britain and Germany in Africa: Imperial Rivalry and Colonial Rule* (New Haven, CT: Yale University Press, 1967), 337–350.
Strachan, Hew. *The First World War. Volume 1: To Arms* (Oxford: Oxford University Press, 2001).
Strandmann, Harmut Pogge von and Alison Smith. 'The German Empire in Africa and British perspectives: A historiographical essay', in Prosser Gifford and Wm. Roger Louis (eds), *Britain and Germany in Africa; Imperial Rivalry and Colonial Rule* (New Haven, CT: Yale University Press, 1967), 709–96.

Sulle, Emmanuel. 'Social differentiation and the politics of land: Sugar cane outgrowing in Kilombero, Tanzania', *Journal of Southern African Studies* 43:3 (2017), 517–33.
Sunderland, David (ed.). *Communications in Africa, 1880–1939: Volume I* (London: Pickering & Chatto, 2012).
Sunseri, Thaddeus. 'The *Baumwollfrage*: Cotton Colonialism in German East Africa' *Central European History* 34:1 (2001), 31–51.
Symes, Stewart. *Tour of Duty* (London: Collins, 1946).
'Tanganyika: A Nation Is Born', *Africa Today* 8:10 (1961): 6–9, 20.
Tanganyika (Southern Highlands) Estates, Ltd. *Farming in the Southern Highlands* (Amersham: S.G. Mason, 1936).
Tanner, Marcel, Andrew Kitua, and Antoine A. Degrémont. 'Developing health research capability in Tanzania: From a Swiss Tropical Institute field laboratory to the Ifakara Centre of the Tanzanian National Institute of Medical Research', *Acta Tropica* 57:2/3 (1994), 153–73.
Telford, Alexander M. *Report on the Development of the Rufiji and Kilombero Valleys* (London: Crown Agents, 1929).
Thomson, Joseph. *To the Central African Lakes and Back; The Narrative of the Royal Geographical Society's East Central African Expedition, 1878–80, Vol. I* (London: Sampson Low, Marston, Searle & Rivington, 1881).
Tilley H. and R. Gordon (eds). *Ordering Africa: Anthropology, European Imperialism and the Politics of Knowledge* (Manchester, 2010).
Tribe, Keith. 'Introduction', in Reinhart Koselleck, *Futures Past: On the Semantics of Historical Time*, trans. Keith Tribe (New York: Columbia University Press, 2004), vii–xx.
Tumusiime, Emmanuel. 'Suitable for whom? The case of system of rice intensification in Tanzania', *The Journal of Agricultural Education and Extension* 23:4 (2017), 335–50.
Twining, E.F. 'The last nine years in Tanganyika', *African Affairs* 58:230 (1959), 15–24.
Unangst, Matthew. 'Changes in German travel writing about East Africa, 1884–1891', *Colloquia Germanica* 46:3 (2013), 266–71.
Webel, M.K. 'Medical auxiliaries and the negotiation of public health in colonial north-western Tanzania', *The Journal of African History* 54 (2013), 393–416.
Webel, M.K. 'Ziba politics and the German sleeping sickness camp at Kigarama, Tanzania, 1907–14', *The International Journal of African Historical Studies* 47:3 (2014), 399–423.
Webel, M.K. *The Politics of Disease Control: Sleeping Sickness in Eastern Africa, 1890–1920* (Athens: Ohio University Press, 2019).
West, Jennifer J. and Ruth Haug. 'The vulnerability and resilience of smallholder-inclusive agricultural investments in Tanzania', *Journal of Eastern African Studies* 11:4 (2017), 670–91.
Westcott, Nicholas. *Imperialism and Development: The East African Groundnut Scheme and its Legacy* (Woodbridge: James Currey, 2020).
Wicker, E.R. 'Colonial Development and Welfare, 1929–57: The Evolution of a Policy', *Social and Economic Studies* 7:4 (1958), 170–92.
Willet, K.C. 'Trypanosomiasis research at Tinde', *Tanganyika Notes and Records* 34 (1953), 33.

Willis, Justin. 'The administration of Bonde, 1920–60: A study of the implementation of indirect rule in Tanganyika', *African Affairs* 92:366 (1993), 53–67.
Wilson, Catherine. *Norfund's Kilombero Plantation in Tanzania – Meagre Results from a Large Investment* (Oslo: FIVAS, 2016).
Wood, A. *The Groundnut Affair* (London: Bodley Head, 1950).
Žumer, Majda. 'Natural resources research in East Africa', *Bulletins from the Ecological Research Committee/NFR* 12 (1971), 1–87.

Newspapers, Magazines, and Gazettes

East Africa

Official Gazette of the Occupied Territory of German East Africa
SPEAR (East African Railways & Harbours)
Sunday News
Tanganyika Gazette
Tanganyika Standard
Ngurumo

United Kingdom

Daily Mirror
The Birmingham Post
The Guardian
The Manchester Guardian
The Sphere
The Times / The Sunday Times

Rest of World

The Chicago Defender USA
The Royal Gazette and Colonist Daily Bermuda
Der Spiegel Germany
Time Magazine USA

Unpublished Theses, Papers, and Reports

Bolstad, Paul. 'Recollections and Observations: Kilombero Settlement Scheme, October 1966 – October 1968' (Manuscript in author's possession).
Bourbonniere, Michelle Elise. 'Using the Past to Imagine the Future: The TAZARA Railway, 1925–1976' (PhD thesis, Stanford University, 2013).
Chitukuro, Jacob K. 'Impact of the Uhuru Railway on Agricultural Development in the Kilombero District' (MA thesis, University of Dar es Salaam, 1976).
Connors, John P. 'Agricultural Development, Land Change and Livelihoods in Tanzania's Kilombero Valley' (PhD thesis, Arizona State University, 2015).
Dreier, Marcel. 'Health, Welfare and Development in Rural Africa: Catholic Medical Mission and the Configuration of Development in Ulanga/Tanzania, 1920–1970' (PhD thesis, University of Basel, 2019).

Haule, Kennedy Sabas. 'Wildlife Prospects in Kilombero Game Controlled Area' (MSc thesis, Centre for International Environment and Development Studies, Agricultural University of Norway, 1997).

Kazimoto, A.A. 'Political Development of Mahenge' (Manuscript, University College, Dar es Salaam, 1967).

Larson, Lorne. 'Witchcraft Eradication Sequences among the People of the Ulanga (Mahenge) District, Tanzania' (unpublished working paper, 1975).

Larson, Lorne. 'A History of the Mahenge (Ulanga) District, c. 1860–1957' (PhD thesis, University of Dar es Salaam, 1976).

Makombe, Wilfred and Jaclyn Kropp. 'The Effects of Tanzanian Maize Export Bans on Producers' Welfare and Food Security', Paper presented at the Agricultural and Applied Economics Association's 2016 AAEA Annual Meeting, Boston, MA, 31 July–2 August 2016.

Mbosa, Mkeli. 'Colonial Production and Underdevelopment in Ulanga District, 1894–1950' (MA thesis, University of Dar es Salaam, 1988).

Meier, Lukas. 'Striving for Excellence at the Margins: Science, Decolonization, and the History of the Swiss Tropical and Public Health Institute (Swiss TPH) in (post-) colonial Africa, 1943–2000' (PhD thesis, University of Basel, 2012).

Monson, Jamie. 'Agricultural Transformation in the Inner Kilombero Valley of Tanzania, 1840–1940' (PhD thesis, University of California, Los Angeles, 1991).

Rizzo, Matteo. 'The Groundnut Scheme Revisited: Colonial Disaster and African Accumulation in Nachingwea District, South-Eastern Tanzania, 1946–67' (PhD thesis, SOAS, 2005).

Rockel, Stephen. 'Porters and Imperialists: A Study of African Labour in Tanzania, 1850–1917' (PhD thesis, University of Toronto, 1990).

Starkey, M., N. Birnie, A. Cameron. R.A. Daffa, L. Haddelsey, L. Hood, N. Johnson, L. Kapapa, J. Makoti, E. Mwangomo, H. Rainey, and W. Robinson. 'Kilombero Valley Wildlife Project: An Ecological and Social Survey in the Kilombero Valley, Tanzania', Final Report, Kilombero Valley Wildlife Project, Edinburgh (2002).

Weiskopf, Julie M. 'Resettling Buha: A Social History of Resettled Communities in Kigoma Region, Tanzania, 1933–1975' (PhD thesis, University of Minnesota, 2011).

Westcott, Nicholas. 'The Impact of the Second World War on Tanganyika, 1939–1949' (PhD thesis, University of Cambridge, 1982).

Wilson, Ed, Robert McInnes, Damas Patrick Mbaga, and Paul Ouedraogo. 'Kilombero Valley, United Republic of Tanzania. Ramsar Site No. 1173', Ramsar Advisory Mission Report, April 2017.

Online Sources

Arthur D. Little Global, 'Our History', https://www.adlittle.com/en/about-us/history.

Associated British Foods, plc. 'Our History', https://www.abf.co.uk/about_us/our_history.

'Ferry accident foreseen: users', *The Citizen*, 29 January 2016, https://www.thecitizen.co.tz/tanzania/news/ferry-accident-foreseen-users--2545904.

Illovo Sugar Africa, 'Kilombero Announces Significant Sugar Expansion Project', 20 May 2021, https://www.illovosugarafrica.com/announcements/kilombero-announces-significant-sugar-expansion-project.

Lüttringhaus, Sophia. 'Farming in Africa is like farming on Mars', *Climate Analytics*, 20 November 2015, https://climateanalytics.org/blog/2015/farming-in-africa-is-like-farming-on-mars.

Nkansah-Dwamena, Ernest and Aireona Bonnie Raschke, 'Justice and Fairness for Mkangawalo People: The Case of the Kilombero Large-scale Land Acquisition (Lasla) Project in Tanzania', *Ethics, Policy & Environment*. Published online, 25 November 2020: https://doi.org/10.1080/21550085.2020.1848187.

The Oakland Institute, 'Getting the Facts Right on Agrica/KPL Agricultural Investment in Tanzania', 2 July 2015, https://www.oaklandinstitute.org/getting-facts-right-agrica.

'President Magufuli Inaugurates Bridge Named after Him', *TanzaniaInvest*, 8 May 2018, https://www.tanzaniainvest.com/transport/president-magufuli-inaugurates-bridge-named.

Press Statehouse, 'Kipindi cha Uzinduzi wa Daraja la Magufuli na Barabara ya Kidatu-Ifakara', 11 June 2018, https://www.youtube.com/watch?v=uoVTWRQWozA.

'Prospects for Mankind with Eleanor Roosevelt – Africa: Revolution in Haste', 6 March 1960. Great Blue Hill (GBH) Archives. https://youtu.be/MSmYoNmN40s?t=475.

Ramsar Convention, 'Information Sheet on Ramsar Wetlands: The Kilombero Valley Floodplain', Internal Ramsar document, 19 June 2002, https://rsis.ramsar.org/RISapp/files/RISrep/TZ1173RIS.pdf.

Smallteacher, Richard. 'Agrica's Tanzania Rice Scheme Has Devastated Local Farmers, say NGOs', *CorpWatch*, 7 July 2015, https://www.corpwatch.org/article/agricas-tanzania-rice-scheme-has-devastated-local-farmers-say-ngos.

'Tanzania ferry sinking kills "at least 100"', *The Irish Times*, 12 April 2002, https://www.irishtimes.com/news/tanzania-ferry-sinking-kills-at-least-100-1.419843.

'Tanzania ferry tragedy "kills 38"', *BBC News*, 12 April 2002, http://news.bbc.co.uk/1/hi/world/africa/1924578.stm.

Tongaat Hulett. 'History Timeline', https://www.tongaat.com/overview/history.

Zee, Bibi van der, and Sophie Tremblay, 'Tanzania's ghost safari: How Western aid contributed to the decline of a wildlife haven', *The Guardian* [UK], published online 13 August 2017, https://www.theguardian.com/environment/2017/aug/13/tanzanias-ghost-safari-how-western-aid-contributed-to-the-decline-of-a-wildlife-haven.

Index

agricultural intensification   4, 13, 20–1, 24, 25, 211, 216, 218
alluvium   18, 20, 28, 38, 55–6, 62–3, 67, 88, 110, 136, 140
annular arguments *see* petitio principii
anti-colonial sentiment *see* resistance to colonialism *under* colonialism
Arusha Declaration   16, 18, 161, 167, 186–7, 203, 205, 208
Associated British Foods plc   167 n.72

baboons   198
Beardall, William   5, 29–30, 33
bees   212
   wax   94
Behobeho   28
birds   40, 213–14
Bismarck, Otto von   31–2
boats   42, 87, 98, 100–1, 210
   attacks by hippopotami   39, 41, 144
   steamboats   38
   Uhuru boats   155
   see also canoes; ferries
Bolstad, Paul   202–3
Bomani, Paul   167, 167 n.68, 192, 195
bridges   22, 24, 74–5, 83, 90–1, 134, 145, 151, 220–2
Bryceson, Derek   173–4
Burton, Richard   37
buying posts   88–9, 99
Byatt, Horace   52–3

Cameron, Donald   52–3, 64–8, 76, 79–80
canalisation   66–7, 83, 97, 129–31, 136, 150–1, 158, 220 n.43
canoes   29, 33, 41, 73–4, 82, 90–2, 99–101, 101 n.125, 210
   building of   159–60

canoe-men   28, 101, 210
   precarity of   41, 74–6
capitalism   29, 31, 79, 80, 92, 173
cartography *see* mapping
cashew   95
cassava   176
castor oil   28
cattle   75, 96
   see also livestock
Central Development Committee   96–7, 125, 185
cereals   28
   global shortage of   129
Chamberlain, Neville   184
Chesham, Lord   54
Cheyne, James   116
China   170–1, 181–2
Churchill, Winston   106
cocoa   63, 157 n.16, 176
coercion   18, 45, 103–24
coffee   14, 63, 175
Cold War, the   157–8
Coleman, Carter   219
Colonial Development Act of 1929   78
Colonial Development Corporation   129, 132–3, 154, 163, 165–6, 197
   see also Commonwealth Development Corporation
Colonial Development Fund   85
Colonial Office, the (London)   64, 79, 85, 125, 135, 137, 140–1
colonial thinking   37, 82, 99, 106, 108
colonialism   12, 27–48, 105
   and anthropologists   105, 110, 112
   and authority   78, 103, 116, 120, 124
   European mania for   31
   prestige of   25, 88, 118, 204

resistance to 16, 25, 36, 40, 42, 105, 115–16, 124, 150
Commonwealth Development Corporation 160
  see also Colonial Development Corporation
cotton 14, 28, 45, 47, 48, 56, 60, 62, 66, 68, 70, 72, 74, 75, 85–9, 92–100, 136, 151, 199
  Ulanga Cotton & Rice Co. 196
Culwick, Arthur Theodore (A.T.) 25, 87, 91, 94, 105, 109–23, 126, 128
Culwick, Geraldine Mary (G.M.) 110
Culwick, A.T. and G.M. 110, 112

Dahl, Roald 87
dams 143–4, 146 n.115, 147, 223
Dar es Salaam 7, 29, 38, 40, 48, 57, 91, 125, 158, 163, 164, 171, 179, 190–2, 194, 196, 199, 202, 220
  unemployment in 186–8, 190
  University of 14
Delamere, Lord 52–3
Deutsch-Ostafrikanische Gesellschaft
  see German East Africa Company
development 9–18
  aid 172, 177–8, 200–1, 215, 218
  as hydra's head 96–7
  déjà vu 135
  impact of First World War on 43–4
  palimpsestic nature of 26, 187, 203–4, 209
  plans and planning 1–3, 99, 127, 128, 135, 141, 222
  schemes in aspic 83–6, 126
  surveys and reports 133–48
    East Africa Rice Mission 129–31
    East Africa Royal Commission 133, 137–41
    Gibb 133, 135–7, 169
    Loxton 133–6, 146
    Rufiji Basin Survey (FAO) 133, 142–8, 151, 170, 174, 188, 198

Telford 65–71
  see also Alexander Telford
syndicates 64–8, 75–6, 79–81, 147, 168
territorialisation 173–5
Western notions of 1, 5, 10
  see also underdevelopment
District Officers 20, 52, 70, 80, 73, 86–7
  as dictators 123
  as symbols of authority 86
  Roald Dahl on 87
  see also A.T. Culwick; Michael Longford; Edward Lumley
Dodd, Norris E. 16, 142

East Africa Rice Mission 129–31
East Africa Royal Commission 133, 137–41
East African Railways and Harbours 169–70, 172
ecology control 4, 7, 21–2, 24–5, 211
elephants 45, 113, 144, 149–51, 175 n.109, 198, 210, 215
  fear of bees 212
Engelhardt, Philipp 38–41
epidemiological crisis 25, 103, 105–7, 109, 115, 122
eugenics 123

Fairbairn, Harold 122–3
famine 43, 46, 49, 81, 116, 183, 198
  of margarine 198
FAO 16, 21, 142–7, 150, 160, 170, 174, 188, 190, 221
ferries 24, 42, 90–3, 221–3
fertiliser 165 n.55, 173
First World War 6, 15, 43, 46, 191 n.30, 210
fish 28, 72, 213
flooding 19–22, 29, 35, 43, 74, 90, 129, 134, 136, 138–9, 140, 145, 147–51, 199, 217
  flood control 134, 136, 143–8, 150, 162
floodplain *see* plain *under* Kilombero
Fonck, Henrich 5, 20, 46–8

forests   127, 159–60, 211–12
  clearance   191, 195, 199, 201
  conservation   214
  deforestation   214
  policy   159
  product industries   159
  see also Kilombero Forest
    Reserve; timber
Frederic, J. Elton   27–8, 37
future-making   2, 26, 126, 154, 182, 224

game (wild) *see* wild game
Geigy, Rudolf   174–5
German Democratic Republic   180
German Development
    Corporation   175–6
German East Africa Company   32, 36, 42, 176
Germany, Federal Republic *see* West Germany
Germany, West   162, 169–70, 172–81, 200–1, 221
Geuting, Horst   179–80, 199–200
Gezira Irrigation Scheme
    (Sudan)   66, 68, 74
Gillman, Clement   6, 54, 57–61, 64, 68, 71–2, 75, 81–4, 96, 145–6, 171
ginneries   70, 74 n.122, 88, 92, 101
giraffes   211, 213
Götzen, Gustav von   5, 45–6
Governors of German East Africa
    see Gustav von Götzen;
    Eduard von Liebert; Albrecht
    von Rechenberg; Freiherr von
    Schele
Governors of Tanganyika *see* Horace
    Byatt; Donald Cameron; Harold
    MacMichael; Stewart Symes;
    Richard Turnbull; Edward
    Twining
Great Depression, the   76, 78
Great Ruaha River   27–8, 36, 56, 129, 143, 169
Groundnut Scheme, the   137, 197–8
groundnuts   150, 199

Hallstein Doctrine   180
Hassel, Kai-Uwe von   175–6
Hassel, Theodor von   175, 175 n.109
hemp   63, 162, 176
  see also kenaf
Henn Railway Commission   73, 80
Henn, Sydney   73, 79
hibiscus   150–1
  fibre   156
  see also kenaf
high modernism   137, 137 n.64
Hitler, Adolf   54
Hulett & Sons (sugar firm)   163–6, 184, 189, 198
hydro-electric power   79, 143–4, 223

Ichonde   187–90, 192–201, 204
Ifakara   42, 44, 47–8, 58, 70, 75, 91, 94–5, 99, 169, 174, 179
  Kilosa-Ifakara road   85, 90, 97–8
  Lumemo-Ifakara bridge   151
  Msolwa-Ifakara road   169
  plan to expand   113
  railway to   72–6, 79, 84, 130, 140, 168
  river transport to   82, 86, 100–1
Illovo Sugar, Ltd.   167–8
imagined futures   1, 25, 57, 211
immigration   54, 61, 66, 131, 214–15
Independence   173
  of Tanganyika   154–7, 182, 192–3, 224
  of Zambia   170
India   46–7, 53, 129–30, 143
Indian merchants   47, 70, 73–4, 92, 95
indirect rule   52, 86
infrastructure   4, 7, 22–5, 35, 44, 46, 57, 64, 70, 74, 78, 86, 89–90, 163, 211, 214, 216–17, 219–20
International Bank for Reconstruction
    and Development   156 n.14, 167
International Finance
    Corporation   165
International Land Development
    Consultants   201
International Monetary Fund   15

internationalism 26, 135, 143, 154–82
Iragua 99, 121 n.108
Ireland 200
Iringa 19, 41, 49, 52, 71–5, 91, 95, 190
irrigation 21, 25, 57, 61, 63, 66–8, 74, 130, 134, 136, 140, 143–7, 150–1, 162, 170, 220 n.43
   futility of schemes for 81, 136, 139, 162
Itete 99
   river 82
ivory 29–30, 45

jaggery 162
Japan 170
Jardine, Douglas 80
Jardine Matheson & Co. 79, 79 n.6
Johnston, Keith 27–8, 38
Jühlke, Karl Ludwig 32
Julius Nyerere Hydropower Station 223 n.58
jute 162, 176
   see also kenaf

Kahama, C. George 159
KATRIN 161–2, 172–3, 178–81, 200
Kaunda, Kenneth 170
Kawawa, Rashidi 200
kenaf 162, 172, 175–81
Kennedy, John F. 158
Kenya 51–2, 56, 94, 137, 139–41, 181, 184, 219
Kenya United Party 123
Kibasira (swamp) 34
Kiberege 37, 59, 87–93, 95, 109, 113
Kichangani 187, 199–201, 204
Kidatu 33, 56, 169, 192, 200, 223
Kiepert, Richard 37–8, 40
Kikwete, Jakaya 224
Kilimanjaro 14, 36, 44
Kilombero 18–20
   as breadbasket 21, 41, 47, 81
   as ghost safari 214–15
   as prism 5, 10
   as Ramsar site 24, 213
   caravan trade through 30

morphological zones 60
   paradox of 164
   plain 5, 9, 18, 24, 110, 213
   remoteness of 4, 7, 19–20, 44, 46, 94, 139, 163–4
   unhealthiness of 20, 37, 41, 48, 58, 75
Kilombero Agricultural Training and Research Institute *see* KATRIN
Kilombero Forest Reserve 160
   see also forests; timber
Kilombero Game Control Area 22, 215
Kilombero Plantations Limited (KPL) 24, 216–20, 220 n.43
Kilombero, River 19, 24, 27–8, 32, 42, 59, 61, 69, 72, 86, 90, 149, 220–1
   as fairy godmother 19, 211
   as ogre 19, 211
   comparisons to world rivers 61 n.65
   drowning 101, 145, 221
   experimental transport service on 96–101
   mapping and navigation of 38–41, 46–8, 55, 76–7, 81–3
Kilombero Settlement Scheme 26, 183–209
   palimpsestic nature of 203–5
Kilombero Sugar Company 6, 26, 162–8, 175, 181, 188–9, 215
   sugar estate 6, 23, 165–6, 169, 175–6, 178, 189, 195, 197
Kilombero Valley Teak Company 160–1, 216
Kilosa 41, 49, 63, 74, 91, 169
   railhead 46–7, 71, 98, 192
Kilosa kwa Mpepo 89 n.56, 98
Kilwa 29–30, 38
Kinyuku (river) 95
Kirby, A.H. 61–4, 66–7, 69–70
Kivukoni 148–9
   ferry crossing 223
Kiwanga (Sultan) 41, 123
Korea, North 218, 218 n.32
Kotakota 82, 86, 98–9

Kuhnert, William   210–13

labour   49, 51–2, 61, 66–7, 69, 90 n.64, 133, 136, 165, 189, 191, 194, 197–8
  conditions   145, 148, 152, 166–7
  migration   45, 61, 114
  policies   66
  supply   23, 46, 63–4, 66, 150, 164, 184
Lacey, Gerald   129–31
land alienation   51–2, 152
land clearance   107, 165, 189–91, 194–6
League of Nations   50, 56, 76, 80, 125
  Mandate   6, 8, 11, 15, 50–1, 120
    confusions over   50, 114
    divergent views on   25, 50, 114
Legislative Council   192–3, 204
Lennox-Boyd, Alan   163
Lettow-Vorbeck, Paul von   50
Liebert, Eduard von   38–9
Lieder, Georg   38
Lindi   30, 44
Lindt, August   175
lions   144, 215
  as metaphor for LegiCo candidates   192–3
livestock   96, 103, 106–7, 136, 214
logical fallacy *see* annular arguments
Longford, Michael   20
Lucan, Lord   59
Lufthansa   177
Luhombero   114, 116–17, 119–20
Lumemo (farm)   148, 150–2, 174–5, 198
Lumemo (river)   133–4
Lumley, Edward   112–13
Lupiro (farm)   148–50
Luwegu River   29, 39

MacMichael, Harold   85
Madabadaba   99
Madhvani Group   94 n.79
Magufuli, John   193, 220–3

Mahenge   19, 33, 38, 47, 55, 74, 81, 175
  and the Maji Maji Rebellion   41–3
  and military action   36, 49–50
  isolation of   90–1
  Militarbezirk   36, 41, 44, 49
  mountains   18, 37, 58
mahogany *see under* timber
maize   24, 28, 41, 47, 63, 68, 70, 72, 75, 85, 100, 150–1, 195, 198–9, 216–17
Maji Maji Rebellion   25, 41–3, 45–6, 48–9, 61, 183
Majiji   99
Makwaia, David Kidaha   138
malaria   37, 41, 139, 174, 176
Malawi, Lake *see* Lake Nyasa
Malinyi   89 n.56, 98, 101
mango trees   152
mapping   30, 38, 55, 129–30, 144–5, 195
  inaccuracy of   130
  lure of the map   81–3
margarine famine   198
markets   67, 81, 88, 98–9, 159
  access to   46, 57, 63
  development of   30, 88–9
  global   11, 31
  lack of   92
  trading posts   88–9, 99
Mbarawa, Makame   222
Mbingu   89 n.56, 99, 115–16, 120, 121 n.108
Mbulu (District)   128
Mbunga   36, 42, 92
medicine   87
melons   28
Meru   36, 44
Mgeta   89 n.56, 99, 116, 120, 121 n.108
  river   19, 82
  see also Mngeta
missionaries   31, 41, 80
  Baldegg Sisters   174
  Benedictines   41
  Capuchin Roman Catholic   98, 100, 174

education provision 125
missions *see under* missionaries
Mkwawa (Chief) 36, 40
mica 55
Mikumi 169, 192, 200
millet 28
mineral wealth 29–30, 72, 140
mining 31
   Nigerian Consolidated Mines 70
Mitchell, Phillip 66, 74–5, 112
Mkasu (reservoir) 146
Mngeta 217
Mnyera (river/river system) 19, 61, 82, 91, 144, 146 n.115
Mofu 89 n.56, 98–9, 120, 121 n.108
Morogoro
   plans for a railway from 140
   price of cotton in 93
   Region 1, 169, 173 n.98, 204
   rural resettlement from 186, 188, 190, 192
   town 70, 196
   unemployment in 186, 188, 190
mosquitos 41
Msolwa 169, 181
Msolwa (river) 33
Mtera 144
Mtimbira 99, 121 n.108
Mufindi 160
Mwanjisi, Roland 195
Mwanza 107, 191 n.32

nationalisation 161, 167
nationalism 16, 150–1, 156, 161, 188, 198
   nation-building 156, 187–8, 193–4, 204–5, 207
Ngombo 87 n.48, 89 n.56, 98–101
Njelima, Frederick 191, 191 n.30
Njombe 19, 110
Norfund 217
Nyasa, Lake 27, 29, 30, 37, 48, 56–7, 71, 139 n.74, 171
Nyerere, Julius 12, 17–18, 23, 124, 142, 153–5, 157–8, 166–7, 169–70, 173, 179–80, 182, 186–9, 191, 193, 197–9, 204–9, 215, 224

   in conversation with Eleanor Roosevelt 207
Nyerere, Maria 206
Nyerere National Park 22, 28, 117 n.77, 212

Oakland Institute, the 218
oil palm 63, 150
onions 150
optimism 72, 83, 154, 199, 202, 206
   misleading 58
   roseate 82
   tempered 61, 79, 128, 136
Overseas Food Corporation 129, 132, 197–8
OXFAM 205

palimpsest 26, 187, 203–4, 209
pastoralists 24, 96, 215
paternalism 25, 51, 78, 105, 112
Pawaga Plain 143
Peace Corps (US) 202
pestilence 4, 25, 34, 48, 55, 75
Peters, Carl 32
petitio principii *see* logical fallacy
Pfeil, Joachim Graf von 32–5, 39, 46
pigs (domestic) 96
pigs (wild) 151
Pitu (river) 61
Pitu (valley) 56, 71
plantation industry 15, 31, 44, 47, 52, 55, 62, 132, 176
   kenaf 175, 177
     see also hemp; jute
   rice 24, 216
     see also rice
   rubber 46, 160, 223
     see also rubber
   sisal 44, 46
     see also sisal
   softwood 160
     see also timber
   sugar 215
     see also Kilombero Sugar Company; sugar estate

under Kilombero Sugar
    Company; sugar
teak 215
    see also Kilombero Valley Teak
    Company
Pogoro 42, 117–18
Presidents of Tanzania *see* Jakaya
    Kikwete; John Magufuli; Julius
    Nyerere
Prittwitz und Gaffron, Georg von
    38–40, 44, 214
public works 87, 158
Public Works Department 92, 129
Puku (antelope) 213

racial segregation 123
racism 37, 123
railways 6, 46, 56, 71–7, 135, 169–70
    Central African Link 135, 139,
    146
    Central Line 47, 51, 56–8, 61, 71,
    170 n.82
    Kilosa-Ifakara 72, 130
    TAZARA 171–2, 182, 217
    see also East African Railways
    and Harbours; Tanganyika
    Railway Commission
rainfall 4, 6, 19, 20, 43, 60, 63,
    67–8, 72, 74, 134, 141, 150–1,
    160, 217
Ramsar Convention 24, 213
Ramsay, Hans von 37–8
Rechenberg, Albert von 45–6
refugees (Polish) 184
reports *see* surveys and reports *under*
    development
retrenchment 85
rice 6, 19–20, 28, 30, 37–8, 40–1,
    45–8, 56, 60, 62–3, 65, 68, 70,
    72–5, 85–9, 91, 94–9, 129–32,
    134, 136, 161, 173, 181, 190, 195,
    198–9, 214–15, 217–20
    as both food crop and cash
        crop 88
    buying rights 93
    East Africa Rice Mission 129–31
    import from India 46–7

mechanised production of 24,
    148–53
mills 92, 94–5, 101
paddy 94, 100–1, 130, 134, 149–50
research 173
source of tax revenue 87
Ulanga Cotton & Rice Co. 196
river vessels *see* boats
Rodney, Walter 13–14
Royal Geographical Society 27, 39,
    61
rubber 29–30, 38, 45–6, 48, 63, 160,
    170, 176, 199, 223
Rufiji Basin Survey 133, 142–8, 151,
    170, 174, 188, 198
Rufiji (river) 27, 29, 39, 47, 129,
    220
Ruhuji (river/river system) 19, 82,
    91, 98, 144, 146
Ruipa (corridor) 212
Ruipa (river) 19, 39–40, 42, 82,
    98–9, 133–4, 146 n.115
Rural Settlement Commission 188,
    204, 206
Ruvuma (river) 107

Sakamaganga 62, 102
Scheel, Walter 179
Schele, Freiherr von 37
Second World War 11, 15, 78, 97,
    142, 178, 184, 198
self-reliance 17, 161
Selous Game Reserve
    see Nyerere National Park
Sen, Binay Ranjan 142
sesame 47, 63, 199
settlement 4, 22–4, 96, 122
    density 107–8
    European 37, 39, 47–8, 53, 55,
        75, 136, 185
    Israeli 'moshav' model of 206
    Italian 185–6
    of Jewish refugees 184
    schemes 17, 26, 96, 127, 173,
        183–209
    spontaneous 198–9, 207
    white 51–4

Shinyanga 107
Shughuli Falls 29, 39
Simansky, Nicholas 143, 145
Singh, Hazara 95
  see also Indian merchants
sisal 14, 44, 46, 75, 95, 114, 165, 196
sleeping sickness 23–5, 103–24
  historiography of 103–5
  history of (in East Africa) 106–9
Smuts, Jan 49, 55
social engineering disguised as disease control 23, 122
socialism (African) 12, 16–17, 157, 161, 186, 203–5
  see also Ujamaa
Society for German Colonisation 32
Sofi-Majiji 121 n.108
soil erosion 108, 216
Songea 19, 40–1, 110, 117, 119–20
sorghum 37, 47
Southern Highlands 36, 44, 57, 71–2, 184
  Club 138
  European settlement of 36, 52–5
  routes to 38, 83
  see also Mkwawa; Uhehe
Southern Tanzania Elephant Program 212
sovereignty 50, 52, 137
Soviet influence 158
soya 150–1
Speke, John Hanning 37
steam plough 47
Stiegler's Gorge 144
  see also Julius Nyerere Hydropower Station
Sudan Plantations Syndicate 64, 66, 68
sugar 23, 62, 65, 69–70, 93, 95, 132, 136, 161–70, 175–6, 178, 180, 183–209, 215
  roads paved with 202
  sucrose content of cane 199, 202
  sugarcane 28, 37, 47, 56, 62, 72, 152, 162–70, 183–209
sunflowers 150

surveys see surveys and reports under development
swamps 28, 34–5, 58, 82, 210
sweet potato 28, 37, 47
Swero (river) 144, 221
Swiss Tropical Institute Field Laboratory 174–5
Symes, Stewart 53, 76, 80

Tabora 30, 44, 58
Tanganyika Agricultural Corporation 143, 197–200, 205
Tanganyika Electric Supply Company (TANESCO) 154
Tanganyika Engineering and Contracting Co. 154
Tanganyika, Lake 27, 30
Tanganyika Railway Commission 79, 135, 172
Tanganyika Sugar Company, Ltd. 164
TANU 23, 23 n.87, 154, 166–7, 187, 190, 190 n.29, 191–2, 193–7, 198, 204, 206–8
  Youth League 191
tapioca 176
taxation 44 n.77, 44–5, 80, 86–90, 116, 120
TAZARA see under railways
tea 157 n.16
Telford, Alexander 65–9, 73–4, 80–1, 130–4, 143, 147, 184
Temu, Felix 202
Thomson, Joseph 5, 27–30, 33, 37
timber 98, 134, 137, 159–61, 170
  antiaris 159, 159 n.27
  hardwood 136, 160
  mahogany 98, 159–60, 159 n.28
  plantations 160, 215
  plywood 159–61
  scarcity 90 n.62
  teak 160, 215
  see also forests; Kilombero Forest Reserve; Kilombero Valley Teak Company
tobacco 28, 63, 157 n.16
Tossamaganga 73

trading posts   89
    see also buying posts
trypanosomiasis *see* sleeping sickness
tsetse fly   24, 96, 106–8, 111, 121–2, 139, 145
    see also sleeping sickness
Turnbull, Richard   142, 153–4, 161
Twining, Edward   128, 138, 140–2, 153, 163–4, 185–6

Ubena   27, 110
Udzungwa   18, 99, 160 n.28, 212
Uhehe   36–40
Uhuru *see* Independence
Uhuru Railway *see* TAZARA *under* railways
Ujamaa   12, 17–18, 124, 186–7, 195, 203–5, 208–9
    see also socialism (African)
Ujiji   30
underdevelopment   13–14, 57, 71, 90, 132, 151
    see also development
underpopulation   22–3, 131, 147, 183
United Nations   3, 11, 15
    and Julius Nyerere   166
    Food and Agricultural Organisation (FAO)   16, 142
    Tanganyika as Trusteeship   8, 11, 157
University of Dar es Salaam   14
Usangu (plain)   143
USSR   157–8, 200
    Soviet influence   158
Utengule   87 n.48, 89 n.56, 98, 113
Uzaramo   27

vessels *see* boats
Victoria, Lake   104, 158

Vithaldas Haridas and Company   92–5, 101
    see also Indian merchants

Wandamba paddlers   210
    see also canoe-men *under* canoes
Watson, Robert   129
wild game   37, 45, 113, 144–5, 149, 211, 214–15
    conservation of   24, 212
    depredation of crops by   21–2, 211, 215
    destruction of   24, 107–8, 150, 214
    marauding   112–13, 149–50
    shooting of   89, 112
    see also baboons; buck; buffalo; crocodiles; elephants; giraffes; hippopotami; lions; pigs (wild)
wildfowl *see* birds
witchcraft   118
World Bank   15, 156, 156 n.14, 157, 198, 216, 221
World Food Programme   205
World War One *see* First World War
World War Two *see* Second World War

yams   28
yellow wilt   167

Zambezi (river)   98
Zanzibar   27, 29–30, 32, 132, 179–80
    union with Tanganyika   180, 182
    Sultan of   29
zebra   37
Zhou Enlai   170

Future Rural Africa

Previously published titles

Pokot Pastoralism: Environmental Change and Socio-Economic Transformation in North-West Kenya
Hauke-Peter Vehrs

The Kenyan Cut Flower Industry & Global Market Dynamics
Andreas Gemählich

Conservation, Markets & the Environment in Southern and Eastern Africa: Commodifying the 'Wild'
Edited by Michael Bollig, Selma Lendelvo, Alfons Mosimane and Romie Nghitevelekwa

Forest Politics in Kenya's Tugen Hills: Conservation Beyond Natural Resources in the Katimok Forest
Léa Lacan

Printed and bound by CPI Group (UK) Ltd, Croydon, CR0 4YY
31/07/2025
14712019-0004